THE COST OF LIBEL

Columbia Studies in Business, Government, and Society
Eli M. Noam, General Editor

Columbia Studies in Business, Government, and Society
ELI M. NOAM, GENERAL EDITOR

THE COST OF LIBEL

Economic and Policy Implications

Everette E. Dennis
Eli M. Noam
EDITORS

Columbia University Press
New York

Columbia University Press
New York   Oxford
Copyright © 1989 Columbia University Press
All rights reserved

Library of Congress Cataloging-in-Publication Data

The Cost of Libel : economic and policy implications /
Everette E. Dennis, Eli M. Noam, editors.
p. cm.——(Columbia studies in business, government, and society)
Includes bibliographies and index.
ISBN 0-231-06692-9 (alk. paper)
1. Libel and slander—United States.
2. Libel and slander—Economic aspects—United States.
3. Press law—United States.
4. Actions and defenses—United States.
I. Dennis, Everette E.   II. Noam, Eli M.   III. Series.
KF1266.A75C67   1989
346.73034—dc19
[347.30634]   88-25734
                                                        CIP

Printed in the United States of America

Casebound editions of Columbia University Press books are Smyth-sewn
and printed on permanent and durable acid-free paper

CONTENTS

INTRODUCTION

Libel law deals with a clash of two important societal values—freedom of speech and freedom from defamation. The proper balance between these goals has been vigorously debated over the years. Libel cases make for interesting news copy, since their casts of characters tend to involve the powerful and the famous, often marking the political battles of the day—Civil Rights, Vietnam, Lebanon, Chile. It is therefore not surprising that battles over libel law often have an intensity that far transcends the dispute over the actual damaging words, and this, in turn, leads to a certain loss of perspective. Members of the press sometimes find a fundamental threat to the vigor of political debate when a sloppy article gets a publication into trouble. The objects of press coverage, in turn, complain of an "open season" on anyone in the public eye, with journalists and publishers motivated by Pulitzer Prizes and increased circulations.

In the words of the classic commentator of tort law, Dean Prosser, "It must be confessed at the beginning that there is a great deal of the law of defamation which makes no sense" (Prosser and Keaton, *The Law of Torts,* 5th ed. [St. Paul: West Publishing Co. 1984], p. 771). One way to establish analytical order is to recognize that libel is part of the broad class of legal wrongs or torts. Torts generally involve questions of liability for a harm inflicted by one party on another, intentionally or unintentionally.

It can be generally observed that any given class of potential tort-feasors will attempt to reduce its exposure to legal liability. Because the group's financial well-being typically has no priority for the rest of society, it must frame arguments for liability restriction in terms of greater societal values. Journalists and publishers are no different; as a profession and industry, their primary exposure to litigation is the libel suit, and they do not like it any more than doctors like malpractice cases. And, just as one may not want to insulate a surgeon from the consequences of outrageous behavior, even if it raises the cost of surgery or deters new procedures, it is not obvious why a total absence of liability would be the optimal policy for a society that balances multiple values and rights.

Until the mid-1960s there was little reason for citizens not intimately involved in libel disputes to care much about them. They were typically played out in state courts and involved modest awards of little public consequence. The law of libel, while always perplexing and complex even to authorities on tort law, changed glacially and attracted relatively little public or scholarly attention.

The terms of the debate over libel law changed with a landmark case, *New York Times v. Sullivan,* decided by the Supreme Court of the United States in 1964. The case involved a dispute between a public official in Alabama and the *New York Times,* which had run a paid advertisement that criticized, rather indirectly, his public performance. All this occurred in the heat of the civil rights movement of the 1960s and involved, again indirectly, Dr. Martin Luther King.

The case, which extended constitutional protections to the press in its coverage of public officials and public policy, was seen by the media as a great victory—both real and symbolic. Some critic even declared that the law of libel involving public officials had been all but abolished. There followed, in the late 1960s and early 1970s, a number of important progeny cases, most of which continued to expand the concept of the public official and public figure, thus extending press protections. These protections were tied to the concept of actual malice, which was defined by the Court as "reckless disregard of the truth" or "knowing falsehood." The media were given great latitude in gathering news and information, and could even be forgiven some inaccuracies, as long as their journalistic efforts had been made in good faith and they did not breach the malice standard.

When Chief Justice Earl Warren retired in 1969, leaders of the American news media and the legal-judicial community began to speculate about what changes would be in store. Would the Court overturn what seemed to be an increasingly permissive standard for public criticism and assessment of public people? Would it, in Mr. Dooley's phrase, "follow the election returns," and redefine the role of the press, whose public approval and credibility seemed on the downslide at a time when the President of the United States could appeal to a moral majority? Would increasingly conservative justices adhering to a doctrine of judicial restraint curtail or at least slow the rapidly expanding definition of freedom of the press?

The dire predictions and nervous speculation of media leaders and their critics never materialized. While there was some softening in the public figure definition and a tendency to be more rigid in what kind of political speech could be punished after the fact of publication with attending proof of harm, courts did not dismantle the doctrine of *New York Times v. Sullivan.*

But something else did happen. Those on the receiving end of press revelations and criticism began to fight back, using their full resources and pressing their battles in the legal system. They demanded and were given the right to examine the process of news gathering and editing to determine whether the malice standard had been breached. This allowed them to learn more about how reporters, editors, and other media personnel did their work, what precautions they exercised, and whether the eventual publication or broadcast was the result of appropriate procedures and practices. And while it was considered somewhat out-of-bounds to raise the question of "fairness," something not required by the Constitution, it was nonetheless often discussed.

All this occurred at a time when serious questions were being raised about media credibility. One national survey conducted by the nation's newspaper editors even declared that "three-fourths of the American people have some problem with media credibility."

In the midst of this upheaval, there were a number of dramatic libel cases involving major public figures—military leaders like General William Westmoreland and former Israeli defense minister Ariel Sharon; business leaders like William Tavoulareas and entertainers like Carol Burnett. Juries began to return multi-million dollar verdicts against the news media. From major media like CBS and the *Washington Post* to smaller midwestern and western publications, libel judgments seemed to be large and growing; public attention to libel issues grew.

New York Times v. Sullivan had affected libel law in two significant ways. First, it brought state libel law under the purview of the First Amendment and thus constitutionalized it. And second, it changed the legal rules affecting libel from those of a "strict" liability for falsity to those of behavior—the standards of actual malice and reckless disregard. While this was first viewed as helpful to defendants, in time—particularly after the 1979 decision in *Herbert v. Lando*—plaintiffs turned the tables and began to investigate the investigators. This should not necessarily be viewed as negative. Openness of institutions, after all, is what the press seeks, so why should it itself be an exception? But there were also practical burdens associated with the change in liability rules: focusing on the *process* of reporting and editing makes for more complex and costly litigation. And while this may scare away some plaintiffs, others may be encouraged by the possibility that their media adversaries would settle or retract in order to avoid a protracted law suit. All this led to an escalation of the stakes. Plaintiffs raised the damages they sought to more than half a billion dollars. Juries, in turn, awarded ever-increasing damages, reflecting a pro-plaintiff attitude in tort cases generally as well as their willingness to ignore the reckless disregard standard if a sympathetic plaintiff had been harmed by what was perceived as an arrogant press. The number of libel suits grew, and created their own momentum: as libel actions became common, some people felt compelled to sue only to negate the impression that they had acquiesced in the story.

This led to proposals for reform of the libel law by academics such as Marc Franklin, David Anderson, and David Barrett and to legislation, such as the Schumer and Lockyer bills, all of which aimed at affecting damages, legal expenses, and incentives to sue, as well as the framing of the issues. In assessing their potential impact it is important to remember that many of the effects of *New York Times v. Sullivan* had not been anticipated at the time. How then should the new and more complex proposals be analyzed? The conventional approaches are those of legal constitutional discussion, or of an investigation of practical ramifications for newsrooms and publishers. But there is also another way to proceed. Defamation is, after all, a subcategory of tort law, and tort law has been in the past twenty years the subject of an increasingly sophisticated analysis by academic economists and lawyers. They have focused primarily on the impact of liability and damage rules, primarily for product liability and safety issues, but their methodology applies to libel, too. One illustration: When a newspaper invests in a story, it normally gains only a relatively small benefit, since the new information is rapidly used by other publications, too. This has to do with the peculiar economic properties of information. On the other hand, if the story turns out to be false and defamatory, the initial publisher may be held liable for the entire damages, even though it enjoyed only part of the benefits. Such asymmetry is further enhanced by juries' building into their awards a deterrent element for other publications' sins. In such a situation, the economically efficient—let alone socially optimal—investment into news stories would not take place.

Thus, liability rules require careful analysis as to their treatment of gains and risks. For example, the absence of an economic or legal corrective force, in the face of vigorous competition and profit motivation, can lead to a deterioration of the news product, i.e. to less fact and more fiction or errors. Ideally, of course, readers would honor quality, but the circulation figures of various journals suggest that audiences like to be entertained as well as informed, and fiction is cheaper to produce than facts. Hence, bad journalistic practices could abound, and could also affect the credibility of those segments of the press that do not succumb to them. Like a common meadow that becomes overgrazed as each participant strives to maximize its own benefit, respect for the media's role erodes.

Similar negative "externalities" occur when a publication is overzealous in defense of a weak case. In the case of *Sharon v. Time,* a magazine's reporting, editing, and promotion practices led the jury to find defamation and falsehood in the story, and negligence and carelessness among certain of its employees; only the reckless disregard standard saved the publication from a legal defeat. Millions of dollars in litigation fees could have been avoided if *Time* had been willing to admit imperfection. Renata Adler (*Reckless Disregard* [New York: Knopf, 1986]), Steven Brill ("Say it Ain't So, Henry," *The American Lawyer,* Feb. 1985, p. 1), Rodney A. Smolla (*Suing the Press* [New York: Oxford University Press,], 1986). In the words of the distinguished trial judge Abraham Sofaer "[I]t would be pure fantasy to treat *Time* in this case like some struggling champion of free expression, defending at great risk to itself the right to publish its view of the truth."

These examples show that the "market place of ideas" does not necessarily lead to a flawless product, i.e. truth, anymore than an unfettered market leads necessarily to optimal quality of clean environment, safe products, or technical innovation. And while the outcome may still be far preferable to regulated alternatives, one should understand the tradeoff.

To discuss libel issues, theoretical analysis must be accompanied by empirical research. For example, if it can be shown that juries will strongly decide on the grounds of falsity rather than on behavior, regardless of instructions, either the behaviorist liability rules must be changed, or the role of juries must be limited in this field. The media and many civil libertarians warn about the high and growing costs of libel, and their chilling effect on the freedom of expression. In scores of articles and public forums, it has been argued that the role of the press to engage in reporting on activities affecting the public is being restrained by onerous threats of libel suits that could result in multi-million dollar judgments. This is partly an empirical question. Were there, in fact, more libel suits with bigger judgments? Did the press do less well in the courts than other institutions? Were there excessive costs not only in jury verdicts, but also in legal fees? Were the costs simply the natural outgrowth of an increasingly litigious society, or were the libel verdicts more costly and thus cause for real concern? Did the economics of libel, including all costs—direct and indirect—involving judicial awards, legal fees, lost time, productivity, and information, really pose a threat to freedom of expression and to the proper functioning of the mass media? Were these major economic changes simply typical of legally determined damages and costs generally, or was there something different about the economics of defamation? Finally, has the libel regime gone out of control? Does it need new understandings and assumptions, possibly involving legislation or court-directed reform?

Clearly, many of these questions cannot be addressed by economic analysis as the only discipline. Libel is a peculiar tort insofar as damages are highly subjective and often relate to an individual's standing in society. The Bible admonishes "[A] good name is rather to be chosen than great riches" (Proverbs 22:1). Or in Shakespeare's words, "Take honour from me and my life is done" (Richard II, I, i, l. 182).

But these questions do have consequences for the public. The public has a stake in the system of freedom of expression, including the news media, which increasingly act as a central nervous system for our social, political, and economic communication. The public might also be concerned about an efficient system of accountability in which the mass media, as with other social institutions and entities, must allow for feedback. But before citizens or their surrogates can make sense of the current debate over the economics of libel and its effects, they need more information and analysis, gathered systematically and presented cogently enough to be useful.

That is what this book attempts to do. In the chapters that follow, the editors have commissioned leading legal scholars, communication researchers, and economists to pursue many of the questions mentioned above. Happily, we have tuned in to a considerable amount of ongoing research that probes questions about the costs of litigation involving torts and other areas of the law. This book also provides background information, some derived empirically, some through documentary study and qualitative analysis. The studies commissioned here help to define the problem of libel in an economic sense, offer data and scholarly evidence, speculate knowledgeably about the impact of particular court rulings, provide a close-up look at *New York Times v. Sullivan* and the nearly quarter-century experience with its rules, and lay out some alternative approaches to our complex libel regime.

While the free speech discussions of libel are useful and help derive a proper theory for the adjudication of disputes, they are less than fully pertinent without consideration of other costs, especially economic ones. This book tries therefore to synthesize research on law and economics as it can be applied to libel, and to suggest public policy solutions to a problem that once may have seemed distant from citizen concern, but which now threatens to have impact on the quality of public discussion and debate in America.

This book was developed concurrent with work on a national conference on the economics of libel cosponsored by the Gannett Center for

Media Studies and the Center for Telecommunication and Information Studies, both at Columbia University. The conference, held in New York in June 1986, featured some of the nation's leading communication lawyers, media and legal economists, media decision-makers representing communication companies, broadcasters, newsmagazines, and newspapers. Also in attendance were media scholars and practitioners of communication law, especially those who work for media companies and who are therefore quite directly concerned with libel issues. Libel plaintiffs, who take quite a different view, also attended and took part in the proceedings. The leading scholars of the economics of libel, some represented in this volume, as well as those who have proposed solutions —law professors, legislators, and judges—were also participants in this unique event.

(A record of the conference does exist in the form of a Gannett Center report, *The Cost of Libel: Economic and Policy Implications.*)

In planning and completing this volume, the editors benefited from the help of many. A special acknowledgment for their invaluable help goes to Mark Nadel, Sandy Hausler, and Douglas Conn.

The chapters that follow either (a) assemble new data and help define the libel-economics problem, (b) provide analysis of the present legal regime, or (c) propose revision or reform.

In chapter 1, Henry R. Kaufman, general counsel of the Libel Defense Resource Center, sets the stage for analysis and discussion of the economics of current libel litigation by providing new data tracing trends in damage awards by juries, as well as insurance premiums and litigation itself. (It should be noted, however, that a majority of these awards is subsequently scaled down by the judge or the appellate process.) Mr. Kaufman finds the trends toward increased libel litigation troubling, especially in light of accelerating insurance premiums. Costs, he concludes, must be brought into line with the constitutional mandate for protection of First Amendment freedoms.

In chapter 2, legal scholar Randall P. Bezanson and two journalism professors, Gilbert Cranberg and John Soloski, provide a glimpse of the nonconventional costs of libel litigation that involve ideology. Money, they argue with the support of solid evidence, is not the chief motivating factor for the parties in a libel suit; in fact, the economic issues involved in negotiation and dispute resolution have little to do with the rules of liability. Their study involved detailed and systematic interviews with plaintiffs and defendants in libel suits between 1974 and 1984 and is probably the most complete portrait of the views of those important sources ever assembled.

Three economists, Stephen M. Renas, Charles J. Hartmann, and

James L. Walker, offer an empirical analysis of "the chilling effect" in chapter 3. To what extent, if at all, they ask, is the behavior of newspapers affected by the liability standards they face in defamation actions? In their survey of newspapers, the economists conclude that the greater the prospect of public persons prevailing in libel suits, the less the likelihood that the press will publish articles and opinion pieces of a highly controversial and potentially litigious nature.

Chapters 4, 5 and 6 all address the role, dimensions, impact, and probable future of the *New York Times* standard. Ronald A. Cass, a law professor at Boston University on leave as a member of the International Trade Commission, offers what he calls "an incentive analysis," sorting out the relationship between the *Sullivan* case's impact both on First Amendment principles and on economic interests. He argues that when the *New York Times* case introduced the concept of "actual malice" into the law of libel and raised it to a constitutional level, it altered the incentives of some press defendants to resist libel suits. All this, Cass says, may even have an impact on the press's credibility.

Richard A. Epstein, professor of law at the University of Chicago, gets right to the point, asking bluntly whether the *New York Times* doctrine that led to a more explicit definition of actual malice was, in fact, wrong, and whether the initial media enthusiasm over the case was shortsighted. While agreeing that the decision was decided correctly on its facts, Mr. Epstein believes that the common law rules of libel, as administered by state courts, were thrown out prematurely. He suggests a pathway toward reform and toward correcting what he regards as the public policy mistakes of the *New York Times v. Sullivan* decision and its subsequent interpretations.

Mark S. Nadel, of the U.S. Congress Office of Technology Assessment, tries to redefine the doctrine of *New York Times v. Sullivan*. He suggests two major changes: one that would require the press to admit either error or some degree of uncertainty when responding to a libel complaint where there is not a situation of incontrovertible fact and, secondly, allowing the press to recover attorneys' fees when a libel plaintiff fails to prove that an uncorrected defamation was false.

In chapter 7, Marc A. Franklin, professor of law at Stanford University, looks at the costs incurred by defendants in the current libel system and then examines them speculatively in terms of three different proposals for reform of the libel system: (1) the Lockyer Bill introduced in the California legislature that would allow public officials to seek a declaratory judgment in instances where statements are defamatory and false; (2) the Schumer bill in the U.S. Congress, which is similar to the Lockyer bill but would bar a plaintiff who seeks declaratory relief from also seeking damages; and (3) the Plaintiff's Option Libel Reform Act

(POLRA), which would require all plaintiffs to show falsity and actual malice with convincing clarity and would eliminate punitive damages. Mr. Franklin's impact analysis predicts that none of the proposals would cost more than the present system and all could produce lower costs for the media, especially smaller publications. In any event, he says, the economic concerns of the media in carrying out their public function would not likely be harmed by proposed alternatives to the current libel regime.

In chapter 8, Alain Sheer, an attorney for the Federal Trade Commission, and management professor Asghar Zardkoohi ask whether the current law of defamation as it relates to public officials is economically efficient. They are especially concerned with the efficiency of the old strict liability rule, which was replaced by the public law of libel. Neither old rules nor new rules seem fully appropriate or especially efficient, they argue. One, the strict liability rule, includes too much self-censorship, while the other, the actual malice rule, induces too little self-censorship and concern for accuracy.

Judith Lachman, professor at MIT's Sloan School, examines the relationship between reputation and risk-taking in chapter 9. Using a framework familiar in the analysis of tort law, she considers both the costs of injury and the costs of avoiding injury, suggesting that these tradeoffs ought to be central concerns in any proposal for libel law reform.

Finally, in chapter 10 David Hollander, an attorney, provides an analysis of the economics of libel litigation, focusing on constitutional protection for false and defamatory statements. Hollander discusses how much protection is needed, and what the proper form of that protection should be. His model focuses on the professional media in order to determine the effect of various tort liability rules on the production of information and to demonstrate how constitutional privilege increases the quantity of speech. He also explores the effects of protective rules on the accuracy of speech. Litigation costs have a far greater impact on both the quantity and accuracy of the media's output than do damage awards. His conclusions lead him to a discussion of possible reforms of libel law.

These essays taken as a whole document quite dramatically show the inhibiting effect of the present libel regime on freedom of expression in America. They provide a cogent analysis of the conceptual thicket and suggest that there may be pathways out that will benefit all parties, especially the public, which has the greatest stake of all in the economics of libel.

Everette E. Dennis
Eli Noam

New York City, Autumn 1987

ABOUT THE EDITORS

EVERETTE E. DENNIS is the executive director of the Gannett Center for Media Studies at Columbia University. Previously, he was dean of the School of Journalism at the University of Oregon and was for nine years a member of the faculty of the University of Minnesota School of Journalism and Mass Communication. He also was director of Minnesota's graduate studies program in mass communication. Dennis also has taught at Kansas State University and Northwestern University. Among his 11 books are the popular text *Understanding Mass Communication*, coauthored with Melvin L. DeFleur (Houghton-Mifflin), *The Media Society* and *Justice Black and the First Amendment*. He has also written more than 60 magazine and journal articles. His honors include three fellowships at Harvard University: the Liberal Arts Fellowship at Harvard Law School, a research fellowship at the J. F. Kennedy School of Government, and a special Nieman Foundation fellowship.

ELI M. NOAM is currently serving as Commissioner of the New York State Public Service Commission. He is on leave as Professor at the Columbia Business School, where he has taught since 1976, and as Director of The Center for Telecommunications and Information Studies, which he founded in 1983. He has also taught at the Columbia Law School and has been a Visiting Professor at the Economics Department of Princeton University's Woodrow Wilson School. He has published extensively in economic journals, law reviews, and interdisciplinary journals on issues of telecommunications and regulation. His books include volumes on telecommunications in Europe and the Pacific; television diversity; international media flows; and U.S. regulation. He received an A.B. from Harvard College in 1970, and a Ph.D. in Economics and a J.D. in Law from the same University in 1975.

ABOUT THE CONTRIBUTORS

RANDALL P. BEZANSON is Dean and Professor of Law at the Washington and Lee University School of Law in Lexington, Virginia. He was a professor of law at the University of Iowa from 1973 to 1988, and Vice President of the University from 1979 to 1985. Bezanson served as a law clerk to Judge Roger Robb of the U.S. Court of Appeals for the D.C. Circuit, and Justice Harry A. Blackmun of the U.S. Supreme Court. He has written widely on a variety of legal subjects, including freedom of the press, and is a co-author of the 1977 book *Libel Law and the Press*. Professor Bezanson received his undergraduate degree from Northwestern University, and his J.D. from the University of Iowa College of Law.

RONALD A. CASS is Commissioner, U.S. International Trade Commission, on leave from his position as professor of law at Boston University, where he has taught since 1981. Cass has recently been Legal Advisor to the FCC Office of Plans and Policy; and consultant to the Administrative Conference of the United States and the American Trial Lawyers' Association. He received his B.A. from the University of Virginia in 1970, and his J.D. from the University of Chicago in 1973.

GILBERT CRANBERG is George H. Gallup Professor at the University of Iowa's School of Journalism and Mass Communication. Before his teaching career, Cranberg worked as a journalist for 33 years, and was editorial page editor for the *Des Moines Register and Tribune* from 1975 until his early retirement in 1982. He founded the Iowa Libel Research Project that same year, with help from the Markel Foundation, to study the feasibility of resolving libel disputes without resorting to litigation. Cranberg has a B.A. from Syracuse University and a Master's degree in social work from Drake University in Des Moines.

RICHARD A. EPSTEIN is the James Parker Hall Distinguished Service Professor of Law at the University of Chicago, where he has taught since 1972. He has been the editor of the *Journal of Legal Studies* since 1981, and a member of the American Academy of Arts and Sciences since 1985. He has taught and written extensively in the areas of civil procedure, contract, land development, property, torts (including defamation and privacy), jurisprudence, legal history, and constitutional and labor law. He is a graduate of Columbia College, Oxford University (Juris.) and the Yale Law School.

MARC A. FRANKLIN is the Frederick I. Richman Professor of Law at Stanford University, where he has taught since 1962. He was a Fellow at the Center for Advanced Study in Behavioural Sciences in 1968–69, and a Fulbright Research Scholar at the Victoria University of Wellington, New Zealand in 1973. Mr. Franklin teaches communication law and torts, and is the author of several books concerning First Amendment issues. He received his A.B. in 1953, and his LL.B. in 1956, both from Cornell University.

CHARLES J. HARTMANN is a professor of law at Wright State University in Dayton, Ohio. His articles on the economic analysis of law have appeared in *The International Review of Law and Economics* (London), *The Journal of Media Law and Practice* (London), and *The American Business Law Journal.* Hartmann received his A.B. in economics from Washington University, and his J.D. from the University of Missouri at Columbia, Missouri.

DAVID A. HOLLANDER is an associate with the law firm of O'Melveny & Myers in Los Angeles. He received his Bachelor of Science in Economics from the Wharton School, University of Pennsylvania in 1982, and his J.D. from Stanford University Law School in 1985.

HENRY R. KAUFMAN is an attorney in New York City specializing in media litigation, publishing, First Amendment, and copyright law. He is also General Counsel to the Libel Defense Resource Center, a position he has held since 1980. Previously, he had been Vice President and General Counsel to the Association of American Publishers, the book publishers' trade group. He received his bachelor's degree from Hamilton College in 1967 and his law degree from Harvard Law School in 1971.

JUDITH A. LACHMAN is Associate Professor of Law and Management at the Sloan School of Management at MIT. She has previously taught at the University of Wisconsin. She received her J.D. from Yale, and her Ph.D. from Michigan State University.

MARK S. NADEL is a policy analyst in the Communications and Information Technologies Program of the U.S. Congress Office of Technology Assessment. His research has focused on the First Amendment and economic regulation of the communications media, particularly cable television; he has also written and consulted widely on these issues. He has taught at the Benjamin Cardozo and New York Law Schools. Nadel earned a B.A. from Amherst College in 1978, and a J.D. from Harvard Law School in 1981.

STEPHEN M. RENAS is a professor of economics at Wright State University in Dayton, Ohio and has been on the faculty at Wright State since September 1971. He has published extensively in a wide range of journals, and is sought after as an expert economic witness in personal injury, wrongful death, malpractice, discrimination, and divorce cases by both plaintiff and defense counsel. He holds a Ph.D. (1971), and M.A. (1969), and a B.A. (1968) in economics from George State University in Atlanta.

ALAIN SHEER is currently an attorney in the Office of Policy Development of the Federal Trade Commission. Previously, he taught law, economics, and public policy in the Graduate School of Business at Texas A&M University. He earned a B.A. degree in economics at Muhlenberg College and was awarded M.A. and Ph.D. degrees, in economics, and a J.D. by Duke University. His fields of specialization include international economics, industrial organization and regulation, antitrust law, tort law, international law, and law and economics. He has published articles in the *Southern Economic Journal, Weltwirtschaftliches Archiv, Law & Contemporary Problems,* and *Northwestern Law Review.*

JOHN SOLOSKI is associate professor and head of graduate studies in the School of Journalism and Mass Communication at the University of Iowa. He is co-author of the book *Libel Law and the Press,* and has published numerous scholarly articles. Soloski is one of the principal members of the Iowa Libel Research Project, and has worked professionally as a copy editor and reporter. He received his Ph.D. in mass communications and his M.A. in journalism from the University of Iowa, and his undergraduate degree from Boston College.

JAMES L. WALKER is associate professor in the Department of Political Science at Wright State University in Dayton, Ohio. He received his Ph.D. from the University of California, Berkeley.

ASGHAR ZARDKOOHI is an associate professor of business in the Business and Public Policy Group in the Department of Management at Texas A&M University. He received his B.A. in Business Administration from Abadan Institute of Technology, M.S. in Economics from Auburn University, and Ph.D. in Economics from Virginia Polytechnic Institute and State University.

THE COST OF LIBEL

1

TRENDS IN DAMAGE AWARDS, INSURANCE PREMIUMS AND THE COST OF MEDIA LIBEL LITIGATION

Henry R. Kaufman

One of the driving forces behind the "constitutionalization" of American libel law effected by *New York Times v. Sullivan* and its progeny was an economic concern that the imposition of large civil damage awards could have an undue "inhibiting" effect on the exercise of first amendment freedoms. This paper presents trend data on damage awards, insurance premiums, and the cost of libel litigation suggesting that, despite *Sullivan*, these potentially "chilling" economic effects remain perhaps the pre-eminent feature of media libel litigation in the United States today. A comparison of pre-*Sullivan* damage awards with current damage awards clearly demonstrates the drastic increase in potential liability which is outpacing even increases in key areas of nonconstitutional tort litigation. An analysis of insurance premiums for libel coverage shows that premiums have also risen dramatically over the past few years. Even more precipitous increases loom on the horizon accompanied by a severe shrinkage of the libel insurance market that could make coverage unavailable for large and small media enterprises. Finally, an assessment of the onerous and increasing costs of defending libel actions, the vast majority of which involve legally meritless claims, reflects the failure of *Sullivan* to make good on its promise to impede the adverse economic effects of civil libel litigation. Indeed, because of the unusual liability

The observations in this paper reflect the author's personal views and should not be understood as necessarily reflecting the views of the Libel Defense Resource Center or any of its supporting organizations. The assistance of Linda S. Friedner, Peter Gladstone, William A. Rome, and Barbara Raab in the development of certain of the data herein and in the preparation of this paper is gratefully acknowledged.

This paper was originally presented in June of 1986 and was thereafter reduced to final written form in July and August, 1986. Accordingly, the data it includes and assesses in great detail are limited to those available at that time. No effort has been made to include more recent data for purposes of publication. While developments since that time have generally not changed the fundamental patterns and basic conclusions reflected in the paper, the succeeding period has seen many new developments also pertinent to the economics of libel litigation. For example, on the negative side, in March, 1988 the U.S. Supreme Court let stand a $3 million damage reward, the first million dollar media libel award ever finally affirmed on appeal. On the positive side, the predicted libel insurance "crunch" has apparently now eased, riding yet another general cycle in the market for liability insurance. Although libel insurance costs remain high today, those high rates have apparently leveled off to some extent and the feared crisis in overall availability of libel insurance has not materialized.

standards and procedures applied in constitutional libel actions, media libel litigation has become substantially more, rather than less, expensive to defend than run-of-the-mill, non-libel tort actions.

My purpose here is to set the stage for analysis and discussion of the economics of current libel litigation. As the media's central clearinghouse for information on libel trends and developments, the Libel Defense Resource Center's (LDRC) previous studies have, over the past few years, helped to define the empirical terms of debate in the libel field. It is to be hoped that LDRC's often gloomy data have had at least some salutary effect in sharpening the debate over libel law and its operation —for good or ill—within our delicate but critically important American "system," as Tom Emerson put it, "of freedom of expression."[1]

In connection with the ongoing debate over the functioning of our current system of libel, lawyers for libel plaintiffs and those representing media libel defendants seem to be able to agree on only one thing: the costs are too high! And for every multi-million dollar pot of gold emanating from the libel jury room, there seems to be (or at least until now there has always been) a judgment of reversal or substantial modification looming at the end of the appellate rainbow.

This article presents data that should flesh out our understanding of the current operation of the libel system. It is eminently appropriate that, in assessing the state of American libel law, we address the *economics* of libel and that we begin with a focus on empirical data regarding libel litigation. Indeed, as noted, the "constitutionalization" of American libel law effected by *New York Times v. Sullivan* and its progeny was largely motivated by a distinctly economic concern, that the fear of large civil damage awards, even more than possible criminal sanctions, could have an undue "inhibiting," or "chilling" effect on the exercise of our constitutionally-guaranteed freedoms of speech and of the press.[2] Justice Brennan's historic opinion in *Sullivan* characterized the ultimate economic impact in these terms:

> Whether or not a newspaper can survive a succession of such judgments, the pall of fear and timidity imposed upon those who would give voice to public criticism is an atmosphere in which the First Amendment freedoms cannot survive.[3]

I. TRENDS IN DAMAGE AWARDS

A. Historical Perspective

In terms of dollars and cents *New York Times v. Sullivan* is also an apt starting point for an empirical tour of the libel landscape. The jury verdict in *Sullivan* was $500,000—the full amount of the *ad damnum* clause in that action. Today, a libel plaintiff's *ad damnum* more often reads like a substantial chunk of the national debt. The "succession" of judgments over which Justice Brennan expressed such constitutional trepidation was, in addition to the $500,000 in *Sullivan,* an award of $500,000 in a second action and the pendency of three more actions seeking a total of $2 million in damages. In other words, just twenty-two years ago the spectre of damages totalling $3 million in five separate libel actions was perceived as possibly threatening the very survival of one of our great newspapers and certainly as foreboding the demise of freedom of expression.[4]

B. Current and Past Damage Awards Compared

The contrast between Justice Brennan's concerns of a generation ago and current experience could not be more stark. Today's *average* damage award in just a *single* media libel case, where a plaintiff's verdict is entered, comes very close to equalling the maximum total of *all* awards feared by Justice Brennan in the *five* related cases of *New York Times v. Sullivan.* I would not even venture to speculate on what the average total of *ad damnum* damages sought would be for five cases against a major media company in today's Alice-in-Wonderland litigation climate.

To put this contrast into perspective, in media libel actions since 1980 there have been approximately thirty damage awards in excess of a million dollars. Three of these have been in excess of $25 million.[5] The average for 81 initial damage awards between 1980 and 1984 was $2,043,702.[6] The experience with punitive damages is still worse. In 46 of the 81 cases, punitive damages were granted as a part of the award. In those cases, the average damage award was even higher than the $2 million figure just mentioned, with the punitive component alone averaging $2,680,620.[7] Of course, inflation has a lot to do with these high figures, but even adjusting for inflation, the data strongly suggest that Sullivan and subsequent cases, including *Gertz,*[8] have completely failed in their mission to put a brake on runaway damage awards that would threaten to chill freedom of expression.

C. Damages 1954–1964

Reported cases involving damage awards against medial libel defendants were divided into two periods: (1) the decade before *New York Times v. Sullivan,* 1954–1964; and (2) a somewhat longer period after *Sullivan,* 1964–1977.[9] Before *Sullivan,* there were 55 media libel cases that went

to trial (34 state cases, 21 federal). Of course, those 55 plaintiffs prevailed with an award of damages in 40 of the cases tried (26 state; 14
federal), or a defense loss rate of 73 percent.[10] (It is noteworthy that,
despite *Sullivan,* the libel trial loss rate in the 1980s has actually been
worse than the 73% pre-Sullivan rate, with three out of four trials lost
by media defendants.)

The damage awards in those pre-*Sullivan* cases were averaged
$128,933, including one multi-million-dollar award—$3 million-plus—in
Butts,[11] a case well-known as a post-*Sullivan* precedent, but one whose
initial damage award was actually entered prior to *Sullivan.* (The *Faulk*
case, the only other million-dollar libel judgment during the period, is
actually best viewed as a "non-media" action and was excluded from the
sample.)[12] If *Butts* were excluded, the average initial damage award in
the decade before *Sullivan* was less than $50,000 ($49,715).[13] Indeed,
the *total* of the awards in the thirty-seven cases for which damage figures
were available (again excluding *Butts*) was $1,839,468, or less for thirty-
seven cases than a single average case in today's world of libel litigation.
One can manipulate these figures in one final way by adjusting for
inflation, which obviously explains some portion of the huge disparity
from pre-*Sullivan* cases to cases in the 1980s. Using a rough U.S.
Department of Labor CPI factor of 3.69 the pre-*Sullivan* decade damage
figures can be converted into current dollar levels.[14] Even so adjusted,
the average damage award in the decade prior to *Sullivan,* was $475,764,
and the average excluding *Butts* was $183,448. Thus, the current expe-
rience, even corrected for inflation, is still somewhere between 400 and
500 percent greater than the decade before *Sullivan.*

D. Damages 1964–1977

The same analysis was performed for the post-*Sullivan* period, 1964–
1977. The disparities are not quite as dramatic, but they are nonetheless
of interest. In the 104 trials identified, plaintiffs secured 73 damage
awards (48 state, 25 federal—defense loss rate of 70%).[15] During this
period, there were two awards of $1 million or more. The average
award, including the million-dollar judgments, was $180,597. Adjusting
for inflation using a factor of 2.66,[16] the figure is $480,388, up only
slightly from the pre-*Sullivan* decade. Adjusting for the pair of million-
dollar awards has less of an impact, leaving a current-dollar adjusted
average (net of mega-awards) of $356,449—but still between 200 and
400% lower than the current experience.

E. Libel Damages Contrasted with Medical Malpractice and Product Liability

The figures for malpractice and products liability damage awards, however, show that libel defendants are in fact worse off than defendants in those other two categories, themselves said to be experiencing a wild pattern of inflation and million-dollar awards.[17] It is also well to remember that the media's worst experience is in a category of actions where there are rarely if ever the kinds of "special" or out-of-pocket damages —often reflecting huge medical bills and lifelong impairment of physical health, earning capacity, and quality of life—that are characteristic of these other torts. Thus, 1980–82 data for medical malpractice cases showed an average award of $665,764,[18] compared to the libel average of $2 million-plus for the same period. Excluding million-dollar awards the medical malpractice average dropped to $238,032. In contrast, the adjusted libel average, excluding only mega-awards, was in excess of three-quarters of a million dollars. The story was the same regarding product liability cases for the same period. The product liability average was $785,651; the average, adjusted to exclude million-dollar awards, was $278,266—well below the media's libel experience.[19]

Unfortunately, systematic medical malpractice and product liability award averages do not appear to be available for twenty or thirty years ago. However, there are data for the last ten or a dozen years. As might be expected they confirm a dramatic increase in damage awards for these non-libel torts in the past decade.[20] Significantly for our purposes, however, the increase has not been nearly so dramatic as the media's experience in libel actions during that same period.

Thus, for the period of 1974–76, and using Jury Verdict Research data, the average medical malpractice award was $192,208; excluding million-dollar awards (there were only *eleven* during that early period), the average dropped to $147,078.[21] The average product liability award during the same period was $369,297; $171,373, when twenty-eight million-dollar verdicts are excluded. Averages for media libel during the same period, working with the cases referred to above, were $239,527 and, excluding the one million-dollar case during that period, $186,895. Thus, about a dozen years ago, media libel awards were comparable with or only marginally higher than the awards for these non-libel torts. Six years later, libel damages were approximately three times greater than damages for those other two torts.

To update these figures as much as possible, medical malpractice and product liability awards for 1983 and 1984, the two most recent complete

years available, were reviewed.[22] Again, not unexpectedly, non-libel
damages showed a significant increase. In fact, overall the damage gap
between these torts and libel seems to have shrunk somewhat. This
shrinkage appears to be due largely to the stabilization of libel damages
in the period 1980–84, at a heady $2 million average per verdict through
1984.[23] Medical malpractice damages increased from an average of
$665,674 to $771,805 during the period from 1980–82 to 1983–84.[24]
The medical malpractice numbers, excluding million-dollar verdicts, actually decreased slightly, from $238,032 to $235,900. Product liability
experienced a much more dramatic increase, with the average going
from $785,651 to $1,139,997. As with medical malpractice, product
liability awards decreased somewhat when million-dollar awards were
excluded (there were a whopping 176 million-dollar verdicts out of 710
cases reported), from $278,266 to $263,761.[25] But even with these
increases in overall damage averages, the two non-libel torts still fall far
short of the averages being experienced by media libel defendants both
through 1984 and in the most recent cases as well.

   In sum, it is well worth reflecting upon the remarkable disparities
between the large awards being granted to libel plaintiffs for allegedly
injured reputations and those awards being granted to plaintiffs in medical malpractice and product liability cases for concrete economic injury
and severe physical debilitation. The damages being awarded in non-libel
cases are being cited around the nation, with some success, in support
of wide-ranging tort law reforms.[26] It would certainly seem, at least from
these data, that media libel defendants have an equal, if not a superior,
claim for law reform relief.

II. COST OF MEDIA LIBEL LITIGATION

One could argue that there is a remedy to this parade of horribles.
According to available data, the great majority of libel cases never get to
the stage of plenary trial, much less to the moment of potential imposition of any damage award at all. Even putting aside for the moment
abandoned and settled cases, all the available data indicate that more
than 90 percent of seriously litigated media libel cases never go to trial.[27]
Pretrial dismissals on the merits are granted with notable frequency in
libel cases. A study of motions to dismiss and demurrers made from
1981 to 1983 found that, when made, two out of three such motions
resulted in the complete dismissal of the action (including appeals) in
favor of the libel defendant.[28] A more recent study of motions to dismiss
in libel actions brought by public official plaintiffs from 1976 to 1984

showed similar results: more than 60 percent were granted.[29] More-over, approximately 75 percent of motions for summary judgment are granted in favor of the libel defendant.[30] This high rate has persisted despite negative comments on the availability of summary judgment by the Supreme Court in dictum in two cases after 1979,[31] and the Supreme Court's most recent ruling on summary judgment in libel actions in *Anderson v. Liberty Lobby.*[32]

Even when libel cases do manage to slip through the pretrial net (and, despite the foregoing, this does appear to be occurring today with somewhat greater frequency) those cases that are lost at trial are, as previously suggested, still subject to an arduous appellate process that very much favors the libel defendant, both substantively and statistically. There is a 60 to 70 percent reversal rate on appeals from adverse judgments, with an additional 10% modification rate in cases that uphold the finding of liability but substantially reduce the initial damages awarded in the trial court.[33] Thus far, for example, no million-dollar media libel damage award has been upheld after all appeals have been exhausted. Indeed, in contrast to the average $2 million-plus initial damage award, the average of those few awards that are finally affirmed after all appeals has been below $100,000 over the past four or five years.[34]

So, if this is an accurate picture, what is the problem? Today, the greatest problem is probably the cost of litigation. The cost of success-fully defending media libel claims is high and getting worse. It has been estimated that defense costs amount to an astonishing 80 percent or more of the dollars spent by insurers of the media in libel cases.[35] In contrast, general data on the civil justice system indicate that plaintiffs' attorneys fees range in cost between approximately forty and seventy cents for every dollar awarded in a final judgment, depending on the type of case.[36] Workers compensation cases generally yield lower liability costs, while cases involving automobile accidents, medical malpractice, and product liability generate higher costs.[37] These kinds of figures have been widely cited as demonstrating the tort system's gross inefficiency in compensating injured claimants. Yet if this is woeful inefficiency, then what is the 80%-plus figure for defense costs experienced in the libel field? Obviously, that figure represents a system that has almost nothing to do with compensation and almost everything to do with funding litigation—litigation that in almost all cases compensates only the attor-neys involved.

Within a system of this kind an obvious goal should be to reduce the time and expense of disposing of cases that will not result in the imposi-tion of liability. But here, too, although the statistics appear to show the outlook is promising that the lion's share of cases can be disposed of prior to trial, even pretrial motion practice is expensive in libel actions and is getting more costly all the time. For example, while the media defense bar has managed to hold the line on summary judgment as a statistical matter, the tradeoff has been that more, and more costly, discovery is now generally required before a serious summary judgment motion can be made. Ironically, onerous and expensive discovery also appears to be a corollary of the special constitutional rules that apply in the libel field, at least as they have been interpreted by the Supreme Court. In particular, the court in *Herbert v. Lando* held that extensive discovery into the editorial process was a reasonable—indeed necessary —aspect of the development of a libel plaintiff's case on the issue of constitutional malice.[38] While it is difficult to quantify or generalize, there is little question that inquiry into the subjective state of mind of the journalist or publisher has substantially increased the extent, duration, and cost of libel litigation—not to mention its intrusiveness—even when that litigation can be disposed of on pretrial motion.[39]

Thus, paradoxically, while far more libel cases are disposed of "earlier" in the litigation process than other nonconstitutional torts, it appears that getting the average libel litigation dismissed prior to trial may well be more expensive, on average, than the trial (where necessary) and disposition of the average nonconstitutional tort action. The breadth of the inquiry required, the complexity of the legal standards and fact patterns, as well as the duality of the constitutional inquiry both into the truth or falsity of the underlying publication and into the fault or lack of fault in the manner of the publication have all lead to an explosion of litigation costs for both libel plaintiffs and defendants. And these costs are incurred whether the case is won or lost.

The threat of mega-damage awards surely has a significant impact on the costs of libel litigation. No evaluation of the downside risks of litigating even what may appear to be an obviously nonmeritorious claim can ignore the open-ended liability that could be imposed in almost any libel action should a libel claim get to a jury—particularly where non-economic and punitive damages are sought. This, in theory at least, differentiates libel from other torts where concrete damages are measurable and predictable, at least within some meaningful parameters. The awareness of potentially huge risk—however unlikely the final affirmance of a huge award may be—surely filters down through all stages of libel litigation, affecting "nuisance" value, settlement value, and all aspects of litigation strategy.[40]

In terms of specific dollar costs of libel litigation, it is impossible to come up with meaningful "averages" when the nature, extent, and duration of such litigation can vary so widely from one case to the next.

The cost to defend two claims, each based on the identical legal standards and each theoretically involving the same potential for concrete damages—great, small, or nonexistent—can vary as widely as the minimal costs of reviewing a summons or complaint, thereupon abandoned, to the costs of retrying aspects of the Vietnam war and the practices and procedures of a major news network in a months-long libel trial—from almost nothing to millions of dollars.[41]

Reports place defense costs in the *Westmoreland v. CBS* action at $6 million; *Sharon v. Time, Inc.* at $5 million; and *Tavoulareas v. Washington Post* at $1.5 million, presumably with more yet to come.[42] But these are clearly extremes. In terms of averages, one representative from a leading insurance carrier has estimated that defense costs in the average litigated case (at least in larger cities) have perhaps doubled in the last four years from an estimated $75,000 to $150,000 or more—and these are cases that are most often favorably disposed of on the merits prior to trial.[43] This means that in the average case more is spent to win the case before trial than would be paid over in damages, after appeal, if the case were lost and the average affirmed award of less than $100,000 were collected.[44] Needless to say, the cost of litigating that case through a full plenary trial and necessary appeals will presumably far exceed the $150,000 average for pretrial disposition.

These huge average cost figures stand in stark contrast to the cost of litigating the average civil tort action. A Rand Corporation Institute for Civil Justice study estimated that the average expenditure per tort case filed in the federal court system was only $1740.[45] The average cost for a federal jury trial in all cases ranged from $8,000 to $15,000! Obviously, these numbers are minuscule compared to the average libel action.[46]

But is there any feasible method, short of abolishing the libel cause of action, for reducing libel defense costs? Certainly it is clear, whatever the rise in costs of pretrial disposition, that dismissals and summary judgments will remain a vital factor in keeping costs to a minimum. Earlier and more frequent dismissals would appear to be called for— even if only because experience has shown that extensive trials and appeals simply build up litigation costs without yielding the libel plaintiff any meaningful prospect of success on the merits. If so many cases are won by the media—either because of the lack of factual merit or because of the substantial legal burdens that must be overcome by the libel plaintiff—it seems ridiculous not to devise methods to assure that the money, time, and energy of all parties is not wasted on fruitless litigation.

The importance of efficiency is, of course, enhanced when constitutional considerations are taken into account. The Supreme Court's recent ruling in *Anderson v. Liberty Lobby, Inc.*,[47] recognizing the need to enforce the heightened constitutional standards at early stages of a libel litigation, would appear to have sustained, if not strengthened, the present levels of availability of summary judgment in media libel actions. While the *Anderson* decision clearly represents a significant victory for the media, whether that decision will sufficiently avoid unnecessary litigation and attendant costs in the future remains to be seen.

Another proposal to reduce the costs of libel litigation has focused on a so-called "declaratory judgment" action, potentially obviating the need for an examination of state of mind issues and eliminating the threat of large damage awards.[48] I am not myself convinced that the creation of such an action is a wise approach in general, particularly to the extent that declaratory judgments would require courts to become deeply involved in the purported adjudication of the "truth" or "falsity" of varying perspectives on public, political, or historical events.[49] But even if courts were the proper forums for such inquiries, it is not clear to me that declaratory judgments would effect net cost savings as compared to the current system. Although litigating state of mind is hardly inexpensive, in many cases—perhaps most—adjudication of the underlying truth or falsity of events would be even more costly.[50] Currently such expense can in many cases be avoided altogether by focusing on state of mind, for unless the plaintiff meets its burden of proving fault there is no need to tackle the potentially more expensive issue of truth or falsity. An even greater potential danger of the declaratory judgment approach is the real possibility that many more claims would then be pursued— claims that would otherwise not have been filed, or that would have been quickly dismissed prior to trial for want of proof on the state of mind issue.

Apart from the substantive nature of the legal issues and the unique procedures that were intended to save time and money but now appear to be costing more, there are other aspects to the escalation of libel litigation costs that may be among the factors that distinguish the media defendant's situation from that of other litigants—for presumably, the general economics of legal practice and attendant rising costs are not simply limited to libel litigation. First, libel law is a rather arcane field. Often leading specialists are the most appropriate, if not the only appropriate, counsel. While specialization is often necessary, it is also costly. Top lawyers cost more—they are generally more senior in status, more in demand, and their hourly fees are higher.

In addition, for better or worse, the rigorous defense of libel claims— particularly those without any merit—has most often been seen by the media as being a matter of principle. Many media companies have felt that libel cases should not be settled. To some extent this may represent an economically prudent step to avoid attracting claims filed solely for nuisance settlements. To a greater extent, however, it reflects the perception that libel defense involves more important principles than mere economics. Inevitably, it is more costly to litigate from principle than from practicality. I suppose product manufacturers are also unhappy to settle what they view as unmeritorious claims. But manufacturers *do* pay plaintiffs and one justification, at least, is that the plaintiff's broken finger is real and undeniable even if the manufacturer believes that the injury was not its responsibility, or believes that the plaintiff used its product recklessly.[51] Indeed, it will almost always be more economical to litigate with a view to securing the most propitious and low-cost result or settlement than to litigate solely with an eye toward vindicating the defendant organization as a matter of principle.

This pressure to defend principle becomes even greater—and even more costly—when the plaintiff's libel action is consciously structured so as to attack the defendant. Indeed, the Iowa Libel Study teaches that plaintiffs are most often seeking "vindication."[52] The other side of the vindication coin is proof of the *mal fides* of the media defendant. And, of course, *New York Times v. Sullivan* in a sense always requires precisely this proof of morally significant "fault." Few media companies are so thick skinned that they can ignore such a challenge and direct their energies solely to the minimization of litigation costs rather than to the defense of its journalistic honor. In the end, the kind of lawyer one wishes to engage to defend the integrity of the organization—and the cost of that lawyer and the litigation strategy he is likely to pursue—will certainly far exceed the cost of engaging another kind of lawyer hired solely to extricate the defendant for the least possible monetary award or settlement. With libel defense costs wildly escalating and libel insurers vigorously complaining, whether the media will continue to be able to afford—or be allowed to indulge in—the arguable luxury of litigating libel claims from principle remains to be seen.[53]

IV. TRENDS IN INSURANCE PREMIUMS

Whatever the risk of the imposition of huge damage awards, or the incurring of onerous defense costs, insurance has for many years acted as a safety valve. But this protection is now under very serious pressure; there are at present adverse trends in the general insurance market, for some of the very same reasons already discussed regarding special problems in the libel field.

There is little question that relatively low cost libel insurance has for many years represented an asset of great value to the media community in helping to provide a financial safety net for fearless and robust journalism. Insurance coverage of relatively modest cost has not always been universally available, but generally, up until the past few years, relatively low cost insurance has been widely available.[54] This, in turn, has served to soften somewhat the impact of the increasingly adverse trends outlined above.

Moreover, although the insurance industry has previously experienced cyclical crises, the crisis in libel insurance is a new phenomenon. The last major insurance downturn, in the mid-1970s, is reported to have had no significant impact on the libel insurance market. That was an era when the number of libel claims was still relatively small; when the era of mega-damage awards had not yet arrived; and, perhaps most importantly, when American libel law was still perceived as quite favorable to the media defendant. In the 1970s libel litigation was not yet viewed as a serious risk by those writing and reinsuring media coverage.

No more. The crunch is upon us, and we are now in danger of careening to the other extreme. A significant erosion in the availability and affordability of libel insurance is currently threatened. And unfortunately those hardest hit by these new insurance trends are likely to be the smaller organizations, the offbeat, and the anti-establishment media, as well as outspoken individuals and nonmedia, nonprofit organizations —precisely the targets whose existence is the most tenuous, whose ability to survive is the most fragile, and who are most likely to be the lightning rods for libel litigation with either the intent, or at least the effect, of chilling freedom of expression.[55]

An informal review of current trends in insurance premiums shows, not unexpectedly, substantially increasing costs, substantially diminishing coverage, and other adverse changes in the way libel insurance is being written. More frighteningly, the spectre of unaffordability or even total unavailability for an increasing number of media entities—may be close at hand.

What is perhaps the most economical libel insurance currently on the market has been available over the past few years. It is obtained through certain group programs available under the auspices of media trade associations to their members. Two of the leading programs offer such insurance coverage to small and weekly newspapers and to small television and radio broadcasters.[56] Similar coverage is also available to public broadcasters and their independent producers. Since 1984 these inexpensive association policies have experienced increases in excess of 100 percent. New treaties are currently being negotiated for these policies. Predictions are that this new round of negotiations will lead to increases of at least 50 percent, and it is even possible that such group programs may be cancelled.

If the situation is tenuous for those lucky enough to qualify for group coverage, it is far worse for those who must deal individually in the current insurance market where the cost of insurance coverage is generally far greater. Although it is difficult to generalize, it is fair to say that on average most individual media companies have experienced a 200 to 300 percent increase in their insurance premiums during the same period.[57] In many instances, the premium increases have been far more substantial.

Despite higher premiums, libel insurance coverage has actually contracted while premium rates have been rising. This is the result of a number of factors, including a reduction in the number of companies writing libel insurance and in what apparently is a radical contraction of the reinsurance market for libel. As a result of the current crisis, the leading libel insurance carriers are reported to have made or to be contemplating dramatic alterations in policy. Lloyd's of London is said to have begun rejecting new business altogether and to be renewing only certain preferred clients. In the United States, the number of companies writing libel insurance has also dwindled over the past several years. A recent development was CNA Insurance's complete withdrawal from the media-related market, which briefly left Employers Reinsurance Corporation the sole surviving predominant insurer for publishers and broadcasters. The Safeco Insurance Company has now come in to replace CNA in underwriting media-type risks through Media Professional Insurance, but Safeco is currently reported to be imposing conservative risk limits. Chubb, once among the leaders writing insurance for publishers and broadcasters, is reported to now restrict its business to producers, distributors, and cable television operators. The Seaboard Surety Company, once a major source of advertising insurance, is reportedly providing only moderate coverage to publishers and broadcasters. The Fireman's Fund is reported to be continuing to provide coverage to producers and broadcasters, but is said also to be affected by reinsurance difficulties. American International Group (AIG) is reported to have implemented significantly more demanding approval criteria. Finally, Mutual Insurance Ltd. of Bermuda, one of the leading players in the field, which writes much of the coverage for the nation's leading newspapers, is also reported to be adopting modified underwriting criteria, utilizing experience-rated renewal and 20 percent participation (co-insurance) clauses, while declining to renew certain policies where an adverse loss record anticipates too great a risk.[58]

As mentioned, one fundamental element of the present insurance crisis is the inability of underwriters to reinsure the risks they cover. The higher cost of reinsurance necessarily forces premiums upward. Absent reinsurance capacity, primary coverage may also be substantially restricted. The U.S. General Counsel for Bermuda's Mutual Insurance Company, for example, has been quoted as acknowledging a severe shrinkage in the libel reinsurance market, thus restricting the amount and type of coverage that the libel insurers can offer.[59] Ann Heavner, a specialist in media coverage at Johnson & Higgins, a leading insurance brokerage firm in New York, recently even suggested the dire possibility that as of January 1, 1987, reinsurance for libel policies might become almost entirely unavailable, sending insurance companies' maximum capacities drastically downward and potentially forcing several to stop doing business altogether.[60] Whether or not such a total catastrophe ultimately occurs, it is certainly clear that the libel insurance market is, at the present time, experiencing its greatest crisis and it is difficult to envision precisely how these fundamental problems will be resolved.

As a result of these troubling market trends, other aspects of libel insurance have also been severely affected. Deductibles for libel coverage have sharply increased at the same time that limits have sharply decreased. Where once $10 or $20 million in excess could readily be obtained for relatively low marginal cost, now it is said to be difficult to obtain more than $1 million in coverage, and it is a real struggle to obtain levels of $5 or $10 million; the additional premiums for such excess can be staggering.[61] In this era of potential multi-million-dollar litigation costs, and threatened multi-million-dollar damage awards, the availability of such excess may no longer be a luxury but a pressing necessity for full protection. Where once deductibles might have fallen in the $10,000 to $20,000 range for larger media entities, today those same companies may be required to accept deductibles of at least $75,000 or $100,000 per claim.[62] With defense costs continuing to rise, deductibles of this size have serious implications. Although the average defense cost has been estimated to be $150,000, the somewhat lower American Society of Newspaper Editors estimates would mean virtual self-insurance as the majority of companies are required to accept $100,000 deductibles.[63] While a number of the specialized carriers still insure 100 percent of defense costs, as noted above at least one major carrier has already introduced a 20 percent co-insurance feature and other carriers are aggressively seeking ways to reduce defense costs—an effort that may well be economically justified, but that in the long run could have a greater impact on how libel cases are defended than any substantive ruling by the Supreme Court.

The rising costs of libel insurance could perhaps be dismissed or at least discounted if this issue were simply a matter of increased but still affordable costs for insurance coverage. However, the issue may be rapidly becoming one of outright unavailability of coverage, either because carriers are refusing to write policies for certain kinds of media entities and risks, or because cost increases have become so dramatic that they are simply not affordable, particularly to smaller or economically marginal operations, but also to some of the largest entities as well. Right now the data are incomplete, with scattered but troubling reports of unavailability. It is unclear whether this suggests continued general availability, or a failure of reporting more widespread instances of unavailability.

CONCLUSION

The major conclusion that must be drawn from all of the hard economic realities outlined above can be briefly stated: The more than twenty-year-old promise of constitutionally guaranteed protection from the unduly chilling *economic* effects of libel claims remains today decidedly unfulfilled. It remains to be seen whether—and if so, how—the economics of libel litigation can be brought more closely into line with that constitutional mandate for the protection of First Amendment rights, now or in the future.

NOTES

1. T. Emerson, The System of Freedom of Expression (1970).

2. 376 U.S. 254 (1964). Justice Brennan put it this way in *Sullivan:* "The fear of damage awards . . . may be markedly more inhibiting than the fear of prosecution under a criminal statute." *Id.* at 277. In subsequent opinions, the potentially chilling effect of the cost of libel on publishers was specifically articulated. *See* e.g., Time, Inc v. Hill, 385 U.S. 374, 389 (1967) (citing Speiser v. Randall, 375 U.S. 256 at 526): "Fear of large verdicts in damage suits . . . even fear of the expense involved in their defense, must inevitably cause publishers to 'steer . . . wider of the unlawful zone' . . . and thus 'create the danger that the legitimate utterance will be penalized.' " The Court echoed this economically based concern four years later in *Rosenbloom* v. *Metromedia,* 403 U.S. 29, 52–53 (1971): "The very possibility of having to engage in litigation, an expensive and protracted process, is threat enough to cause discussion and debate to 'steer far wider of the unlawful zone' thereby keeping protected discussion from public cognizance." Even in the ultimately unfavorable decision of the Court in Gertz v. Robert Welch, Inc., 418 U.S. 323 (1974), its concern over the chilling effect of excessive damage awards was reiterated: "The largely uncontrolled discretion of juries to award damages where there is no loss unnecessarily

compounds the potential of any system of liability for defamatory falsehood to inhibit the vigorous exercise of First Amendment freedoms." *Id.* at 349.

3. 376 U.S. at 278 n.18.

4. See *id.*

5. LDRC Bulletin no. 4, part I, August 15, 1982 [hereinafter LDRC Damages Study no. 1] at 11, 16; LDRC Bulletin no. 11, August 15, 1982 [hereinafter LDRC Damages Study no. 2] at 29.

6. LDRC Damages Study no. 2 at 14, 18. All averages computed for LDRC Studies, including this paper, are "mean" averages. A "median" average would not, in our view, meaningfully present the data. However, all of LDRC's published damages studies included detailed cases and damages lists which would make possible the development of median and other alternative methods of analyzing these data.

7. *Id.* at 18.

8. Gertz v. Robert Welch, Inc., 418 U.S. 323 (1974). While the *Gertz* case cut back on the number of claims that would be subject to the constitutional limitations imposed by *Sullivan*, it did purport to define certain limits on damages applicable even to non-*Sullivan* libel actions, including the requirement that *Sullivan* standards be met before punitive damages could be imposed.

9. Lists identifying each of these cases, including initial and final award, can be found in LDRC Bulletin no 17, July 31, 1986 at 6–16.

10. LDRC Damages Study no. 2 at 6, 10. For one period, in the early 1980s, the media's libel loss rate at trial was approaching 90%. See LDRC Damages Study no. 1 at 5.

11. Curtis Publishing Company v. Butts, 388 U.S. 130 (1967).

12. Faulk v. Aware, Inc., 35 Misc 2d 302, 231 N.Y.S.2d 270 (Sup. Ct. N.Y. County 1962), rev'd 19 A.D. 2d 464, 244. N.Y.S. 2d 259 (1st Dep't 1963), (*aff'd* 14 N.Y. 2d 899, 252 N.Y.S. 2d 95 (1964). According to the New York Court of Appeals, the chief publication found to have defamed the plaintiff was a "News Supplement" to Aware, Inc.'s own Membership Bulletin. Aware served as a consultant to various organizations for the stated purpose of identifying the "political backgrounds" of radio and television performers. This type of internal publication of information, developed under contract to various clients, is hardly a typical "news media" type of publication.

13. The average final award for 1954–1964 after appeal was $29,153.89. Adjusted for inflation, that figure becomes $107,577.85. See *infra* note 14.

14. The factor was obtained by dividing the CPI number for April 1986 by the average CPI number for the years 1954–1964, as listed in the Historical Table of U.S. City Average CPI Numbers for All Items.

15. The average final award for 1964–77 was $18,613.14. Adjusted for inflation, the amount becomes $49,510.95. See *infra* note 16."

16. This factor was obtained by the method described *supra*, note 17, using the average CPI number for the years 1964–1977.

17. LDRC Bulletin No. 9, January 31, 1984. The data used for these comparisons were developed by Jury Verdict Research, Inc. (JVR) and published in JVR's *Injury Valuation Reports, Current Award Trends*, No. 270 (1983).

18. *Id.* at 26.

19. *Id.*

20. A more detailed report of this comparison data will also be published in a forthcoming LDRC Bulletin.

21. Jury Verdict Research, No. 270, *supra* note 17, at 18-19.

22. More details on this updated data will also be published in a future LDRC Bulletin.

23. Incomplete but more recent libel data, covering 1985 and part of 1986, actually

shows a modest *decrease* in the average libel damage award based upon interim LDRC reports covering news trials in the period 1984–85. *See* LDRC Bulletin no. 13 at 45–46 and No. 16 at 46–48. For the 13 verdicts therein reported, the overall average was "only" $1,480,192. Excluding one award of only $10,001 against a student newspaper, the overall average was $1,602,708. Although the overall average was down, this should not be read as suggesting a significant amelioration in the media's libel experience. The reason for the downturn is that during this recent period there were no distorting eight-figure verdicts. Excluding such "mega-verdicts," the average figures are actually up again very significantly, from three-quarters of a million to the figures just mentioned. In sum, these interim figures for new libel cases show a marked and troubling trend toward damages consistently above a million dollars (7 of the 13 recent awards exceeded $1 million), albeit without the small number of grotesquely huge awards experienced in the earlier years of this decade.

24. When LDRC had initially reported these data, only partial figures were available for 1982. Now completed data for the 1980–82 period indicate that the medical malpractice average verdict was a slightly higher $783,652; $240,346, excluding million-dollar verdicts, while the updated products liability average for the same period was actually a lower $772,444 average award; $271,164, excluding million-dollar verdicts. Jury Verdict Research, *Injury Valuation: Current Award Trends,* No. 304, at 18–19 (1986).

25. *Id.* Interestingly, however, million-dollar awards, as a percentage of current libel awards, are significantly more frequent than in these other two categories. The most recent figures indicate that between 1982 and 1984, million-dollar verdicts accounted for 21% and 23% of medical malpractice and products liability awards respectively, whereas 32% of libel damage awards reported for the same period were in excess of a million dollars. The percentage has been even higher for the most recent libel cases where 7 of 13 surpassed a million dollars. *Id.* at 18–19.

26. *See, e.g.,* Tort Policy Working Group, U.S. Department of Justice, U.S. Department of Commerce, and the Small Business Administration, *Report of the Tort Policy Working Group on the Causes, Extent and Policy Implications of the Current Crisis in Insurance Availability and Affordability* (hereinafter *Working Group Report*), Feb. 1986, at 35–42 (analysis of growth of civil tort damage awards from 1975–1985) and at 66–69 (proposal, *inter alia,* to limit "non-economic" damages in such actions); Sidley & Austin, *The Need for Legislative Reform of the Tort System* (hereinafter *Sidley & Austin Report*), May 1986 at 32–40 (description of growth of economic, noneconomic and punitive damages; proposal to limit jury discretion in awarding damages and to institute legislative limitations on awards for pain and suffering).

27. *See, e.g.,* Bezanson, "Libel Law and the Press: Setting the Record Straight," 71 *Iowa L. Rev.* 217, 218 (1985) a comprehensive report of the findings and supporting data of the "Iowa Libel Project" will be published in a forthcoming book); Franklin, "Suing Media for Libel: A Litigation Study," 1981 *Am. Bar. Found. Research Journal* 795 (1981).

28. LDRC Bulletin No. 8, September 30, 1983, at 2.

29. LDRC Bulletin No. 16, March 15, 1986, at 15.

30. LDRC Bulletin No. 4, Part II, October 15, 1982, at 2; LDRC Bulletin No. 12, December 31, 1984, at 1–37.

31. *Hutchinson v. Proxmire,* 443 U.S. 111, 120 n. 9 (1979), elevated to the text in Calder v. Jones, 465 U.S. 783, 791 (1984).

32. See Anderson v. Liberty Lobby, Inc., 471 U.S. 477 U.S. 242 (1986). 54 U.S.L.W. 4755 (June 25, 1986). The media's concerns over the previous negative intimations by the Supreme Court regarding the availability of summary judgment have now been at least diminished by the Court's most recent statement on the issue. Justice White, writing for the 6–3 majority in *Anderson,* rather blithely dismissed the notorious footnote 9 of

Hutchinson, stating that footnote 9 was "simply an acknowledgement of our general reluctance 'to grant special procedural protections to defendants in libel and defamation actions in addition to the constitutional protections embodied in the substantive laws.' " *Id.* at 256 n. 7.

33. LDRC Damages Study No. 1 at 7; LDRC Damages Study No. 2, at 19–21. A recent study of appellate review in all civil actions indicates that the reversal rate of plaintiff's awards is relatively high in all cases—over 50% according to the Study—although not nearly so high as in libel actions. The highest reversal rates, according to that Study, are found in actions raising constitutional issues. This data would appear to be consistent with the LDRC findings concerning libel appeals. Schnapper, *Appellate Review of Civil Jury Verdicts,* Yale Law School (unpublished study) (October 1985). Indeed, regarding libel, when the special constitutional standard of "independent" appellate review is found to govern, the reversal rate is even higher than in other libel actions. LDRC Bulletin No. 11, November 15, 1984, at 2.

34. LDRC Damages Study No. 2, at 23.

35. Lankenau, "Living With the Risk of Libel," *Folio Magazine,* November 1985, at 171; Greenwald, "Libel Cover Crisis Puts the Press on the U.S. Media," *Business Insurance,* March 10, 1986, at 19; Newsom, "Insurance," *Presstime,* March 1985, at 19.

36. *See, Sidley & Austin Report, supra* note 26.

37. *Sidley & Austin Report* at 40 n. 69.

38. 441 U.S. 153 (1979). One remand from the Supreme Court, after several additional years of litigation the district court in *Herbert* granted defendant's motion for summary judgment in part, 596 F.Supp. 1178 (S.D.N.Y. 1984), *reh'g denied,* 603 F. Supp. 983 (S.D.N.Y. 1985). On appeal the Second Circuit ruled that summary judgment should have been granted as to all claims and dismissed the action, 781 F.2d 298 (2d Cir. 1986). The Supreme Court then denied *certiorari,* 54 U.S.L.W. 3823 (U.S. June 16, 1986) (No. 85–1685).

39. *See* Cendali, "Of Things to Come—The Actual Impact of Herbert v. Lando and a Proposed National Correction Statute," 22 *Harv. J. on Legis.* 441, 465–72 (1985) (delineating the "rising costs" of discovery resulting from *Herbert* and the attendant chilling effect on investigative journalism).

40. The onerous costs associated with libel litigation may also be affecting settlements, for "nuisance value" or otherwise. Systematic information regarding the size of libel settlements has never been available. Many settlements in all civil actions are specifically denominated as confidential and even settlements that could be revealed are not widely or regularly reported. Nonetheless, there is some evidence to suggest that the size of settlements has increased over the past few years in response to these economic factors. *Compare* Franklin Study I [Marc A. Franklin, *"Winners and Losers and Why: A Study of Defamation Litigation,"* 1980 A.B.F.RES.J. 455] (noting the relative infrequency of settlement in libel suits) *with* Franklin Study II [Franklin, Suing Media for Libel: A Litigation Study, 1981 *Am. Bar Found. Research Journal* 795, 798 (1981)] (acknowledging a higher settlement rate among suits brought involving smaller dollar amounts). Since Franklin's studies there have been at least a few publicized settlements for substantially higher figures. *See, e.g.,* "Dow Jones Settles Libel Suit for $800,000," *Editor & Publisher,* June 16, 1984 at 20; *The New York Times,* Sept. 26, 1984, C22, (ABC's $238,000 settlement of libel suit against the "20/20" news magazine program); *The Washington Post,* June 5, 1982, at A8, ($1.25 million settlement paid by ABC to Synanon just before submission of case to jury after four-month trial, despite reports that defense was winning the trial).

41. The difficulties in estimating average costs, or specifically predicting costs in any single action, are greatly compounded by the varying and uncertain motivation of libel

plaintiffs in pursuing their claims. *See generally,* DeLanson, *supra* note 27. It is reasonably safe to predict that an injured patient in a medical malpractice action, although she may also wish a measure of revenge for injury, is generally seeking measurable damages and, at least assuming the predictable recovery is sufficient, will have an attorney willing to stay the course through to a settlement or judgment on the merits. A libel plaintiff may often be seeking "vindication" or revenge, or simply positive publicity, wholly unrelated to any real injury and uncertainly related to the likelihood of sustained litigation through to a final judgment.

42. Lankenau, *supra* note 35, at 171. In addition to these estimated defense costs, it is known that William Tavoulareas, as a libel plaintiff, had spent as much as $2 million as of the entry of the jury verdict in his action against the *Washington Post. The New York Times,* June 2, 1983, at A20. Mr. Tavoulareas recently indicated, at the conference at which this paper was first presented, that his expenses have now risen to $3 million, with additional court proceedings still likely.

43. A recent study by the American Society of Newspaper Editors estimated that the average costs for all newspapers engaged in libel and privacy litigation over a three-year period was $95,852. The average three-year defense costs for large newspapers, with a circulation above 400,000, was $541,967. Weber, *Editors Surveyed Describe Half of All Libel Cases as 'Nuisance' Suits, ASNE Bulletin,* Jan. 1986, at 38. Although the ASNE study represents an ambitious effort to estimate costs and the frequency of litigation among a broad sample of newspapers, unfortunately its figures are difficult to use in assessing per-case defense costs. The data obtained involved costs per newspaper over a three-year time span rather than on a case-by-case basis. Moreover, an unknown number of editors indicated that they had not included in their estimates defense costs that had been paid by their insurance companies, the inclusion of which would presumably dramatically increase the cost figures in those cases where insurance was available.

44. *See supra* notes 33–34 and accompanying text.

45. Kakalick, *Costs of the Civil Justice System Court Expenditures for Processing Tort Cases,* Rand Corporation Institute for Civil Justice at 56–57 (1982).

46. *Id.* at 65–66.

47. See *supra* note 32.

48. *See, e.g.,* H.R. 2846, 99th Cong., 1st Sess. (1985); Franklin, *The Plaintiff's Option Libel Reform Act;* Lockyer, Senate Bill 1979 (California).

49. The argument that courts often are called upon to consider difficult, or controverted, issues regarding "truth" and "falsity" is correct, but misses the point. In libel declaratory judgment actions, of the kind proposed, the issue of truth or falsity would represent not simply one subsidiary finding leading toward a judgment based, *inter alia,* on that finding and others; rather it would be the ultimate finding in the action. I am aware of no other circumstance where the courts are engaged in making findings respecting truth or falsity for their own sake, particularly where such findings involve complex public, political, or historical events where "truth" is a relative and potentially changing concept, yet where a court judgment, with its *res judicata* effect, is expected to be a singular and binding event.

50. *See, e.g.,* comments of George Vradenburg, General Counsel of CBS, Inc., at "The Cost of Libel: Economic and Policy Implications" conference sponsored by the Gannett Center for Media Studies and the Center for Telecommunications and Information Studies, Columbia University Graduate School of Business, June 13, 1986: "The bulk of the cost of litigation, the high-price[d] suits, are truth/falsity suits. The actual malice suits tend to be low-cost suits." Transcript of Proceedings, Part II, at 43.

51. Even in statutory litigation, such as workers compensation—where the central

factor is proving physical injury—actual damage suffered is basically ascertainable and thus a dollar value might more easily be affixed to the injury sustained. While it is true that pain and suffering related to physical injury has a certain open-ended potential, the value of a reputation in libel actions has generally proven to be even more nebulous and open-ended.

52. Bezanson, *supra* note 27, at 217, 221, 226.

53. Potential insurance-related constraints on principled libel litigation, some of which have already been adopted, are noted in the section below. These include insurance-carrier control over the selection of counsel, the imposition of shared defense costs and/or the imposition of strict litigation budgets. *See also* note 56, *infra*.

54. Heavner, "Developments in Obtaining Insurance, Changing Terms, and Market Restrictions," *P.L.I.: Media Insurance and Risk Management* at 113–115 (1985); Worrall, "Libel Policy Deductibles and Limits," *P.L.I.: Media Insurance and Risk Management* at 149–156, 158 (1985).

55. Although the plight of publishers with regard to libel insurance has been briefly noted in at least one insurance and tort reform study (*see, e.g., Working Group Report, supra* note 26 at 9) the problems facing the media have not generally received as much attention as those confronting other professions and industries. Nevertheless, the need for reform affecting the media is acute. One example of the practical plight of one segment of the media was recently cited in *The New York Times,* June 23, 1986, at C11 (discussing the rising costs of liability insurance for book publishers, and the inability of at least one maverick publishing house to acquire libel insurance coverage).

56. Such group programs are currently being written for the National Newspaper Association (covering smaller and weekly newspapers) and the National Association of Broadcasters (radio and television stations).

57. Greenwald, *supra* note 35, at 1; Newsom, *supra* note 35, at 16.

58. *See* Greenwald, *supra* note 38 at 19; Heavner, *supra* note 54 at 117–19; and Heavner, "Libel Insurance: Notes for the Practitioner," *P.L.I. Libel Litigation,* at 42, 43 (1986). The information in this and the following paragraph is based solely on the secondary sources cited here and *infra,* notes 59 and 60.

59. Radolf, "Libel Rates Are Expected to Increase," *Editor and Publisher,* April 26, 1986 at 19 (quoting Paul O'Brien, U.S. Counsel for Mutual Insurance Company of Hamilton, Bermuda, Ltd.).

60. Address by Ann. L. Heavner, P.L.I.: *Libel Litigation* (June 20, 1986).

61. Greenwald, *supra* note 35 at 19.

62. For other sources expressing concerns over the dramatic increase in libel insurance deductibles, *see* Greenwald, *supra,* note 35 at 1, and Garbus, "The Cost of Libel Actions—Pressure Not To Publish," *New York Law Journal* 12 (July 17, 1986) at 1, col. 3.

63. See *supra* note 43.

2

THE ECONOMICS OF LIBEL
An Empirical Assessment

Randall P. Bezanson
Gilbert Cranberg
John Soloski

Economic analysis is being applied to an ever-widening range of legal problems these days, and often with results that significantly advance our understanding of the law and the legal process. The contribution that economics can make is not surprising, for many of the economist's analytical tools are closely akin to those traditionally employed by the lawyer and legal scholar, and they reflect a more or less coherent analytical perspective. Like legal forms of analysis, however, their advantage is also a defect, for economic analysis often rests on certain underlying premises that give it coherence but may not reflect reality.

The subject of today's conference is the economics of libel—more specifically the "cost" of libel. Implicit in this title is a central focus on cost—cost measured largely in financial terms. Implicit also is the assumption that cost is an important, if not the determinative, ingredient of and explanation for libel suits. We suggest, however, that cost—at least in its conventional sense—is not determinative, and that nonfinancial considerations of an individual and ideological character may dominate the libel suit.

Our conclusions can most clearly be summarized by their contrast with more conventional approaches to economic analysis of law. Generally speaking, economic analysis of legal problems rests on three related assumptions: first, that parties to a dispute are motivated chiefly by money; second, that the parties' actions are based on economically rational decisions about financial risks, costs, and benefits of recovery in litigation; and third, that negotiation and litigation are governed by an economic calculus shaped by the doctrines and rules of liability within the formal legal system. These economic assumptions and the approach they reflect are a function not so much of the economist's preconceptions as of the legal system itself, for the law in most instances (including libel) translates disputes into financial terms for purposes of recovery in litigation.

We undertook an empirical analysis of libel suits in order to understand the actions of the parties in the libel suit, and their motivations and objectives. We did so because, on the face of it, much that we knew about libel litigation seemed to defy the conventional patterns of litigation. We wanted to find out whether this was true and, if so, why. What we found was a dispute that defied the conventional expectations of economic rationality, and defied the conventional rules of the legal system itself. Specifically, we found:

- that the parties are often *not* motivated chiefly by money;
- that the parties' actions are *not* based on economically rational decisions about the prospects of financial recovery in litigation;
- and that the economic calculus that governs negotiation and litigation *has surprisingly little relation* to the rules of liability in the legal system.

Most libel plaintiffs lose; most media defendants win. For plaintiffs, the prospect of judicial victory is extraordinarily small, but the cost of suing is also small, as most lawyers work on contingency. For media defendants, the prospect of judicial victory is very high, but the price in terms of costs and fees is dear.

The strictly financial odds of victory or loss in the former legal system seem to play a distinctly secondary role in libel suits; the parties' stakes seem largely nonfinancial. Settlement and negotiation are infrequent when compared with other forms of civil litigation; the incidence of financial settlement is even less frequent. Plaintiffs believe that they win by suing, for the act of suing achieves an important measure of vindication. Media believe that they win by defending, and the high price is borne in order to avoid losing credibility.

In the following pages we will discuss selected findings of the Iowa Libel Research Project in some detail. Our analysis in this paper will principally rely on three data sets: 1) analysis of virtually all defamation cases with a reported decision or order in which the defamation claim is treated as colorable, and which were decided between 1974 and mid-1984; 2) interviews conducted with 164 plaintiffs who sued the media for libel; and 3) interviews conducted with 67 news organizations. Our objective is to outline the fabric of the libel dispute—who sues and who defends, and why. The actions and motivations of libel plaintiffs and defendants are, we believe, rational; but they do not follow patterns that either economics or law deem conventional. After reviewing our findings, we will return to the question of economics, and outline some of the implications of our analysis for the way in which the economics of the libel dispute should be approached.

I. THE PLAINTIFFS AND THEIR OBJECTIVES

Libel suits are generally inexpensive for plaintiffs. But low litigation costs cannot fully explain why plaintiffs sue, for the hazards of suing, and the odds against prevailing in court, are immense. With the filing of a libel suit, especially one against the media, there is a strong likelihood that the alleged libel will be repeated in the media's coverage of the suit. Indeed, nearly 70 percent of the responding plaintiffs said that their lawyer warned them that the alleged libel would be repeated if the plaintiffs sued. In addition, 70 percent of the plaintiffs reported that their lawyer discussed the possibility that the libel suit would result in publicity about their past. With libel suits taking an average of four years to complete, any vindication of reputation from suit will occur long past the time when the offending statements can be recalled. The plaintiffs were aware of the likely delay. More than 45 percent of the plaintiffs reported having been told that the suit would take between two and five years to complete.

Nevertheless, plaintiffs have brought suit, and continue to do so. Why? They will almost certainly lose. Is it simply, as some people in the media have suggested, that plaintiffs see their libel suit as an opportunity to profit by winning large damage awards at the expense of the media? We think not. We have concluded that money is a surprisingly small element in a complex of factors contributing to the libel plaintiffs' decision to sue.

Let us begin by examining the types of people who do sue. The libel plaintiffs we interviewed shared a number of characteristics. As a rule, they tended to be well-educated; many held graduate or professional degrees. Most plaintiffs were well-off financially, and they were long-time and highly visible residents in their communities. Most held jobs that brought them into contact with the public.

Many plaintiffs were community leaders. It was common for them to have held public office or to have been a public employee. Even those plaintiffs who worked in business or in a profession often had held public office either before or during the time the alleged libel appeared. In fact, about 45 percent of the plaintiffs we interviewed had held public office or had been a candidate for office before or during the time the alleged libel occurred. Most plaintiffs, in short, were community leaders, active in community affairs, who had a long-standing relationship with other members of their communities and who were associated publicly with the issues related to the subject of the alleged libel. As a rule, libel plaintiffs are not fly-by-night operators.

It was not a surprise, then, for us to find that when we analyzed the universe of reported cases in the decade following *Gertz v. Welch,* upwards of 60 percent of libel suits brought against the media involved public plaintiffs. Public plaintiffs almost always sued over stories that dealt with their public or political activities. Private plaintiffs, on the other hand, tended to sue over stories that dealt with business or professional activities or with their allegedly criminal activities. The public plaintiffs we interviewed had a very high degree of community visibility, and the content of the alleged libel focused on their public activities.

The strong correlations among plaintiffs' legal status, degree of community visibility, and content of the alleged libel indicate that the courts have been consistent in applying the constitutional standards. The most important and obvious conclusion reached from these comparisons is that most libel suits involving the media result from stories that deal with a plaintiff's public activities. This suggests that, for most plaintiffs, the alleged libel is likely to be seen as damaging their public or political reputation.

To find out how the alleged libel affected the plaintiffs, we asked them a series of open-ended questions about what upset them about the alleged libel. Nearly all of the plaintiffs said that what upset them most about the alleged libel was that it was false. Some plaintiffs provided additional responses; almost all of these concerned reputational harm.

Plaintiffs were then asked open-ended questions about how they believed the alleged libel had harmed them. Plaintiffs offered a number of responses, but most related to reputational or emotional harm. In general, damage to their reputation, emotional harm, and damage to their political status were most often mentioned by the plaintiffs. While a minority of plaintiffs expressed their harm in financial terms (often in combination with another, more principal harm), and while some who expressed reputational harm may have considered financial damage to fall within that category, it appears that a minority of the plaintiffs surveyed expressed the harm in terms of money, whether separately or in combination with other factors.

Plaintiffs who were most likely to cite financial harm were those in business, especially plaintiffs who owned or managed a business. Plaintiffs who held public office or who were public employees were more likely to say that the alleged libel had damaged their political status or had caused them emotional harm.

It does not necessarily follow that plaintiffs who said that they suffered financial harm were bent on obtaining money from the media. To further gauge what it would have taken to rectify the situation, we asked the plaintiffs what the media could have done immediately after the alleged libel appeared that would have satisfied them. Nearly three-quarters of the plaintiffs said that they would have been satisfied with a retraction, correction, or public or private apology. Less than 4 percent said that they would have been satisfied only if the media paid them money damages. Nearly all of the plaintiffs who said the alleged libel caused them some financial harm said that they would have been satisfied with a retraction, correction, or apology.

This finding is supported when the plaintiffs' actions following publication of the alleged libel are examined. About half of the plaintiffs interviewed said that they contacted the media after the alleged libel appeared, and about half contacted a lawyer. But nearly three-quarters of the plaintiffs—on their own, through their lawyer, or with their lawyer—contacted the media prior to filing their libel suit.

Nearly all of the contacts with the media occurred within two days of publication or broadcast of the alleged libel. And nearly all of the plaintiffs said that the media were asked to run a retraction, correction, or apology. Even those plaintiffs who said that they were financially harmed by the alleged libel said they were more interested in obtaining a retraction, correction, or apology than they were in obtaining money. The media turned down most of the plaintiffs' requests. Retractions, corrections, or apologies were forthcoming in roughly 20 percent of the cases. The plaintiffs who sued despite receiving a retraction, correction, or apology said they did so because they viewed the response as insufficient, often compounding the libel.

Once the plaintiffs have decided to sue, they appear to shift their objectives. When asked why they sued the media, plaintiffs predominantly said they sued in order to restore their reputation or to punish the media. Roughly 20 percent of the plaintiffs said that they sued to win money damages as compensation for actual economic harm. This is much higher than the 4 percent who said that money would have been necessary to satisfy them shortly after the alleged libel appeared. Of equal note, about half of the plaintiffs said that one of the reasons they were suing was to deter similar incidents and to punish the media.

Those plaintiffs who claimed money as the reason for suing usually were those most likely to have experienced financial harm because of the alleged libel. Money and punishment represent the predominant motives for suit when the alleged libel focused on private activities. In contrast, reputation is the chief reason for suit when the alleged libel dealt with plaintiffs' public or political activities. Plaintiffs who sued over stories that dealt with their public or political activities quite consistently gave reputation-related reasons for bringing suit.

One conclusion that emerges from our study is that plaintiffs' motivations are related predominantly to reputation. Those plaintiffs who gave money as a reason for suit tend to have experienced financial harm. In these circumstances, only money will fully compensate for the harm. The low frequency with which money figured into the thinking of plaintiffs immediately following the publication or broadcast of the alleged libel may be related to the fact that an immediate correction or retraction can often avoid financial harm. As time passes and litigation costs increase, plaintiffs are more apt to think of, or need, money. Even then, however, money damages as compensation for economic harm appear to play a role only in a distinct minority of the cases.

What, then, led most plaintiffs to sue? No single factor can adequately explain the reasons for suit. Rather, we found that there are a number of interrelated factors that pushed the plaintiffs into court. One is that plaintiffs were disturbed chiefly by what they saw as the falsity of the alleged libel and its damage to their reputation. The impact of the alleged libel on plaintiffs' reputation is magnified for many plaintiffs because of their active involvement in their communities. For a large number of plaintiffs, the successful pursuit of their careers is dependent on their public reputation. Their concern with restoring their reputation underlies their contact with the media.

The plaintiffs' post-publication contact with the media reveals another key reason for suit. Nearly all of the plaintiffs said that they were angered or dissatisfied by their contact with the media. Especially noteworthy is the vehemence with which the plaintiffs described their reaction to their post-publication contact with the media. Plaintiffs regularly used such terms as "extremely angry," "incensed," "seething," and "very mad" to describe their reaction to their dealings with the media, which in turn were described as "arrogant," "rude," "indifferent," and "callous." Most of the plaintiffs told us that it was more than the rejection of their requests for a retraction, correction, or apology that angered them; it was the *way* they were treated by the media. In the words of one plaintiff, "I never confronted such arrogance in my life." In the words of another, "I was insulted. They did not treat me decently."

Plaintiffs who contacted the media prior to contacting a lawyer reported overwhelmingly that their post-publication experience was a factor in their decision to sue. These plaintiffs were likely to commit to suing before they contacted a lawyer. Moreover, they contacted a lawyer with the specific intention of filing suit.

II. THE MEDIA'S ROLE IN THE LIBEL SUIT

Most plaintiffs reported that the response of the media to their pre-suit contact played a significant role in their decision to sue. To assess this response from the defendant's point of view, we collected information from editors and other news people as well as from libel plaintiffs. We anticipated when we went from interviewing plaintiffs to interviewing members of the press that we would encounter conflict. Instead, we found far more agreement than disagreement. Basically, the news people reinforced what the plaintiffs told us.

Yes, editors told us, there's a lot of rudeness and arrogance, and the press by and large does not do well in responding to complaints. As one newsman told us, "You get a quart of sour milk at your local grocery store, put it in a paper bag and take it back to the check-out counter and say the milk is sour and the guy will say to you either, 'Get a new quart' or 'Here's your money back.' The equivalent of taking a quart of sour milk back to a newspaper is you're lucky if they don't pour it on your head."

We found a newspaper environment unconducive to creating satisfied customers. As Paul Neely of the Chattanooga *Times* wrote in 1984, "There seems to be a newspaper curse that at least every other complaining caller will be referred to at least one wrong place, and when the responsible person is finally identified, he or she is invariably at lunch." The brushoff at some places has become an art form. "Call your city desk sometime," publishers were advised by Kurt Luedtke, former executive editor of the Detroit Free Press, "and see if you like the feeling."

In a sense, newspapers are extremely efficient institutions. They could not gather and process the vast amount of information they handle daily, under deadline pressure, unless they were tightly organized. But all the attention focused on producing tomorrow's and next Sunday's paper exacts a price. These institutions, so highly organized and systematic in producing their product, too often are disorganized and unsystematic in dealing with the hurt that is sometimes caused by the product.

You can bet that editors are fully aware of how their papers are put together. However, time after time during our interviews we had editors describe procedures for dealing with complaints that were news to the subeditors, desk people, reporters, telephone operators, and receptionists we interviewed who were actually fielding the complaints in newsrooms. Practices that editors assumed were being followed simply weren't. In the absence of clearly articulated and communicated procedures, staff members haphazardly improvised their own.

And when you add to this disorganization the defensiveness that makes "I was wrong" the least used statement in the English language, the failure to isolate from the complaint process the staff members who wrote or edited the disputed story, and a mind-set that equates demands for retraction or apology with pressure, you have a recipe for trouble—which starts with t, and rhymes with d, and stands for defamation suits.

Of the obstacles in the way of doing a better job of dealing with complaints, the mind-set against pressure may be the most difficult to overcome. As one newspaper's lawyer told us:

"There's tremendous pressure exerted on the paper all the time—financial pressure, political pressure to tone down its stories, not to do certain stories. It's a constant fight against all those pressures that are brought to bear. And so the editors just in their day-to-day business have to have this kind of defensive attitude in some respects. They've got to resist all this pressure and their reflex is to resist. . . . And when that special pressure of legal threat is brought to bear the reflex action is to resist all that much more. That's the posture that they're in and it takes a lot of confidence to overcome that reflex and to really allow yourself to hear that person who has a complaint and to admit that you're wrong and to run that correction, so you're fighting that kind of built-in attitude that is required by the job in some ways."

The determination not to knuckle under to pressure, or not to be seen as knuckling under, perhaps helps explain why settlement is so much more common in other civil litigation than in suits for libel.

Contributing to the problem is the almost total absence of written procedures for dealing with complaints. At some papers this is attributed to legal advice that the less put in writing the better. One editor has described his lawyer's advice this way:

He explains [to staffers] that internal memos can present difficulties. . . . This goes not just for 'cute comments' or wisecracks, but also for explicit, dead-sober critiques of stories written, say, from a copy editor to a desk or a reporter. If memos are necessary at all, they should be routinely destroyed when no longer timely. In addition, reporters should, at least, consider discarding their own notes and story drafts when no longer needed—all their notes, not just those for sensitive stories."

Organizations ordinarily instruct and learn from their institutional experience by communicating to employees in writing. One of the oft-cited advantages of the print press, in fact, is that you can clip stories and save them. While much has been said about the chilling effect of libel on news coverage, not enough has been said about the way libel has made institutions whose reason for being is the written word afraid to communicate internally in writing.

The legal advice to shun permanent written records may be sound in light of the way the law has evolved, but the ironical consequence is that advice intended to protect the press against libel suits may make the press less able to prevent them.

The plaintiffs told us that the thing that bothered them most about the allegedly libelous story was its falsity. Most of the press strives for accuracy, but given the way newspapers are produced, error is bound to occur. While error cannot be eliminated, it can be corrected.

Clearly, the press must improve its response to complaints. That means developing systematic procedures for receiving, checking, and responding to requests for correction, retraction, or apology. It means dealing in a considerate manner with people whose complaints are un-warranted and making adequate amends when they are justified.

Plaintiffs sometimes sue after they receive a correction or retraction. Many in this category told us that the paper's response was so grudging and unsatisfactory that the correction or retraction made matters worse. Examination of the paper's response in these instances suggests that the plaintiffs had reason for the dissatisfaction in possibly as many as half the cases.

The dissatisfaction may be due in some degree to the excessive involvement in the corrections process of the persons responsible for the disputed story. We found it to be common for those who wrote or edited the story either to do the follow-up checking or to write the correction. The experience of James Squires, editor of the Chicago *Tribune,* suggests that this is a mistake. "I do not make the people who made the error write a retraction and deal with the response," Squires told us. "That's where I got into trouble years ago. I learned that they cannot bring themselves far enough along to admit the error with enough flourish to appease the aggrieved party. And by this time they're usually mad, everybody's mad."

Improved systems for dealing with complaints must include whatever investment in time and personnel is necessary to have a disinterested person, preferably one with good human-relations skills, respond to complaints. At many papers this could be an added responsibility of a person already on the payroll. At papers receiving large numbers of complaints, it may be advisable to employ the equivalent of an ombuds-man, with or without that title. The ombudsman should deal solely with complaints and not, as most of the same 30 ombudsmen now do, also write critical columns or in-house memos assessing the paper's perfor-mance. The latter duties, we found, antagonize news personnel and lead them to divert complaints from the ombudsman.

The point is that at minimal or modest expense, newspapers can do much to buy protection against the disorganization and defensiveness that afflict too many of their newsrooms and expose them unnecessarily to libel suits.

Newspapers nowadays have rid themselves of the notion that to admit a mistake is to undermine their credibility. Almost all papers periodically run corrections. But almost always it is about a factual error. As former *Wall Street Journal* editor Vermont Royster has pointed out, while newspapers are willing to "confess they misstated the date of the public school board meeting," most are reluctant to admit publishing stories that are "basically wrong or misleading or unfair." The *New York Times* now does this in its "Editor's Notes." A newspaper's or broadcaster's complaint procedure needs to include similar means to confess to short-comings in the tone and balance of stories.

In other words, far better—and far less costly—than the courtroom for resolving libel disputes in the newsroom. As James Squires told us:

"I have over the years become a firm believer that even a serious post-publication complaint could best be handled by the newspaper, through its policy, before it gets to the lawyers and the libel people. I think, in other words, that the best defense against libel in newspapers is the newspaper's response after it's done something wrong. . . . The people who sue us either are jerks looking for a deep pocket and never getting anywhere, so they're not that big of a problem—they're a nuisance—or people who are forced to sue us because we ignore them and kick them and refuse to deal with them."

Money may be the root of all evil, but it is not the root of all libel cases. The combination of plaintiff responses and their actions lead us to conclude that the underlying motivation for the libel suit in many cases is something other than avarice. For many plaintiffs, the objective is some type of reputational repair or vindication. As William Tavoulareas (who incidentally, was not one of the plaintiffs we interviewed) has said, "Monetary compensation in cases of libel is not, I think, the real issue. Of far greater consequence to a 'public figure' than the prospect of collecting damages is the right to clear the record when he has been falsely maligned."

On this issue, too, we found editors inclined to agree. While the editors we interviewed were more apt than the plaintiffs to attribute a money motive, we found more agreement than not on the importance to plaintiffs of some form of non-monetary exoneration.

We undertook our study to see if it were possible to develop alterna-tives to litigation. If plaintiffs' chief goals were to obtain money, it's highly doubtful that the idea of alternatives would appeal to the press. As unsatisfactory as the libel system is for the media, it does produce victory for them nearly all the time. Very few members of the press are likely to be attracted to an alternative that would create a greater risk of having to pay damage awards.

Eliminating money from the picture would not necessarily make a non-litigation alternative, whatever its form, attractive to the press. News people cherish their independence. Many of them were hostile to the National News Council because they objected to the idea of being held accountable to an outside agency. The adverse reaction to the National News Council by important segments of the press is a sign that moves to develop substitutes for the legal process would face rough sledding.

But the experience with the National News Council is not conclusive. For one thing, the News Council's jurisdiction extended far beyond libel-type complaints. The Council was neither touted as an alternative to the courts for libel disputes nor was it perceived that way by the press. Moreover, the News Council process was bound to create resentment. Complainants who used the process were expected to first seek redress from the party who published the disputed story. When that attempt failed, the News Council entered the picture. Thus, the complainant chose the forum and the press was placed in the position of being summoned to answer for its misdeeds. It's not surprising that editors were put off and were disinclined to cooperate.

A more attractive alternative to litigation, with its high costs and its intrusiveness into the newsroom, would be a forum in which both parties would have a voice in establishing the ground rules and in choosing a neutral party or parties to arbitrate.

A consensus seems to be emerging that a key missing ingredient in the legal system for dealing with libel suits is an assured way to resolve the issue of truth. The plaintiffs, we have seen, are upset most by the alleged falsity of the story. The press, which is, of course, not in the misinformation business, has an equal interest in the truth. The public's interest, too, is served whenever the record is set straight. Seldom, however, does libel litigation produce a clear-cut verdict on the issue of truth.

Various proposals have been advanced to reshape the legal system to make such verdicts common. The Schumer bill would do it by giving media defendants the option of converting defamation actions by public officials and public figures into proceedings concerned solely with the question of truth.

You don't need a law, however, to convert a libel dispute from a traditional civil suit for damages into a proceeding on the issue of the truth of the alleged libel. Media defendants could offer *now* to participate in such proceedings. If the plaintiffs we interviewed were telling us the truth about their interest in vindication rather than money, and about their willingness to participate in alternatives to litigation, there should be no shortage of takers. The shortage is in the availability of such non-litigation remedies. The people who bring libel actions do so at least in part because they have no other recourse.

There seems to be growing awareness, however, that not every problem calls for a legal solution. In New York, the Center for Public Resources has proposed one such alternative for libel disputes, and in Minneapolis, Otto Silha, former publisher of the Minneapolis *Star and Tribune,* who recently contributed $25,000 to the Minnesota News Council, has suggested that the Minnesota state council broaden its mandate and serve as a resource for resolving libel-type disputes that originate outside the state.

For our part, the Iowa Libel Research Project has begun an inquiry into the establishment of alternative forums, and the testing of voluntary nonlitigation processes for libel disputes. These processes will be evaluated to determine their strengths and weaknesses and to determine whether they offer a realistic alternative to litigation or create more problems than they solve.

No system, whether established by statute or court rulings or by voluntary action, will be without drawbacks. The question, though, is not whether a proposal meets some abstract standard of perfection, but whether it represents an involvement over the existing system. The present system is seriously flawed. Our study has made us acutely aware of how defective the system is in such proceedings.

III. SUING FOR LIBEL: WHAT PLAINTIFFS WANT AND WHAT PLAINTIFFS GET

The decision of plaintiffs to bring suit is an outgrowth of their perceived harm and of their interaction with the media. The media's decision to defend rather than to negotiate and settle is a byproduct of their organizational arrangements and the fear of buckling under to pressure and losing credibility. The decision to sue is made in the environment of these general objectives and perceptions.

That decision, of course, is much more complex than this statement of general objectives might suggest, and it is to these complexities that we will now turn. We know, for example, that lawyers play a role in the decision to bring and defend a libel suit. We also know that negotiation and settlement are infrequent in libel litigation. Finally, we know that, in retrospect at least, the *act* of suing, without anything more, achieves substantial vindication for many plaintiffs. In the following pages we will discuss selected data that bear on these and related issues, and will outline the principal conclusions that tell us something about the dynamics of the libel dispute. We will also touch on suggestions for reform in libel law, including the libel dispute's susceptibility to nonjudicial resolution. Our analysis will focus on six conclusions drawn from the Iowa Libel Research Project.

Our first conclusion is that the remedial focus of the legal system is frequently inconsistent with, or irrelevant to, the remedial interests of the plaintiffs. The legal system's response to libel is built upon money damages, and this is particularly so today because of the constitutional privileges. Indeed, one occasionally reads of cases in which an otherwise successful libel suit is dismissed notwithstanding its merits because no money damages were sought or awarded, but we have, of course, found that a majority of plaintiffs say they are interested in curing alleged falsity, not in receiving money; and that a surprisingly large proportion of the plaintiffs report that their injury is truly reputational in character, but not necessarily financial or economic.

Even more ironically, the plaintiffs seeking correction or reputational repair are *in fact* employing the legal system to achieve that objective, notwithstanding the law's formal refusal to respond to their perceived harm. For instance, the plaintiffs who are most frustrated with the legal system are those who explain their harm in economic terms, and express a need for economic relief in the form of money damages. In contrast, the plaintiffs who seek correction of reputational repair express the least frustration with the legal system, the greatest satisfaction with the results of their litigation, and an extraordinary intention to sue again if faced with the same situation. Is this because such plaintiffs win? Certainly not, as the plaintiffs seeking nonfinancial remedies through suit lose more often than any other group. Yet they do often win, even though they lost in court; for commencing suit achieves their nonfinancial objectives remarkably well (and they have no other effective alternative).

Our second conclusion relates to the role of lawyers. By any measure and anyone's statistics, the likelihood of recovery of money through judicial victory or settlement in libel litigation is low. For seriously litigated libel claims, the incidence of success is less than 10 percent; for plaintiffs who are public figures, success is even more fleeting. Our analysis indicates that no more than 25 percent of libel suits are settled; in only 10 to 15 percent does money change hands. Moreover, with but very few exceptions, the recoveries and settlements that are obtained are pretty small, averaging around $20,000 in judicial recoveries, and

$7000 per settlement. Yet more than two-thirds of the plaintiffs whose claims were seriously pursued engaged counsel on some form of contingency arrangement, and average lawyer fees and total litigation costs to plaintiffs were quite low—less than $10,000, with the vast majority below $5000. Indeed, 16 percent of the plaintiffs reported that they bore no litigation costs at all, and 30 percent reported costs under $1000. Finally, most of the lawyers appear to have been optimistic in their predictions of success, and while many of the lawyers appear to have been inexperienced, this tendency was not unique to that lawyer group.

These observations about fees, costs, and recoveries raise perplexing questions about the role of lawyers in libel litigation. Why are the plaintiffs' lawyers so optimistic in the face of such odds (roughly three-quarters tell their clients that the odds of winning are 50 percent or better)? Why do they work on contingency in such a large proportion of the cases? Why do they usually recommend suit?

While we do not have conclusive answers to these questions, our data provide us some insight with which to suggest possible answers. The plaintiffs who are most often represented on a contingency basis are the public plaintiffs—especially the public officials. Private plaintiffs most often pay the legal bill. The influence of the lawyer on the decision to sue is greatest with the private plaintiffs, where lawyers are somewhat more pessimistic in their advice. Public plaintiffs, in contrast, tend to have decided to sue before seeing the lawyer, and consider the lawyer's advice least influential. Roughly half of the plaintiff lawyers seem to be relatively inexperienced in litigation and more than two-thirds had no experience with libel litigation.

These and other observations lead us to some tentative conclusions about lawyers' optimism and the apparently low fees born by plaintiffs. Because of experience, many lawyers may not fully understand the odds faced in a libel suit or the intricacies of the litigation. In any event, the "equitable" appeal of a plaintiff's claim is often great. Perhaps most important, for relatively inexperienced lawyers—and even for experienced ones—the prospect of representing a well-known public figure or official has appeal beyond the fee, for libel suits often attract publicity which may inure to the lawyer's benefit. Finally, the cost of filing a libel suit is often not great, and frequently little more is involved than filing a complaint and briefing points of law, as 75 percent of the cases are resolved in advance of trial. Once a case passes through the pretrial privilege phase, the odds of success for plaintiffs increase markedly, with plaintiffs winning at trial in roughly two-thirds of the cases. Costs of litigation, it appears, are generally much greater for the defendant than for the plaintiffs. A recent study indicated that average media libel defense costs may range as high as $95,000.

More basically, the information about costs of litigation points to ironies in the operation of the rules and assumptions of the legal system itself. The plaintiffs who were more frequently represented on contingency, and whose lawyers were remarkably optimistic about success, tended to be the public plaintiffs whose rate of success in court was lowest, and there is no reason to expect that this low success rate does not apply as well to the incidence of settlement. Interestingly—if not ironically—it is the public plaintiffs, and particularly the public official plaintiffs, whose suits should be most deterred by the onerous privilege requirements. Yet with the public plaintiff group, and particularly with the public officials who sue, contingency arrangements are most frequent, predictions of success are optimistic, and the lawyer's advice is deemed least influential (but most satisfying, as most of these plaintiffs —unlike the private plaintiffs—would employ the same lawyer again). The public plaintiffs are predetermined to sue, their lawyers seem to help them by reinforcing their decision to sue and by bearing most of the costs, and—not surprisingly—the public plaintiffs are most satisfied with the litigation experience, notwithstanding ultimate loss. The public plaintiffs, in particular, seem to win by suing. The rules of the legal system are in a real sense irrelevant to *their* dispute.

Our third conclusion relates to the definition of the dispute itself. As we have indicated, the basic dispute from the plaintiffs' perspective is clear-cut: falsity. In contrast, the legal system defines the dispute in fundamentally different terms: fault. Largely, although not exclusively, because of the constitutional privileges and their practical operation, the litigation process is geared to resolving a dispute about whether the publisher was at fault: whether the offending statement, independent of its truth or reputationally damaging character, was published negligently or recklessly in light of what was or should have been believed by the publisher at the time of publication. This issue frequently has little relation to falsity and reputational harm, and often it has no relationship whatsoever.

The plaintiffs are largely interested in falsity, not in fault. Interestingly, the media defendants understand this. Indeed, in terms of their institutional mission, the media defendants are also interested in truth or falsity. They pursue the denial of fault not because they view that as the relevant professional question, but because fault represents an inviting opportunity to escape liability in the legal system. Whatever the reasons accounting for this situation, the important observation is that the dispute over fault is fundamentally different from the dispute over falsity. The legal system is simply *not* adjudicating the same dispute that lies at the core of the real conflict between the plaintiffs and the defendants. Ironically, what the legal system *is* doing—under the banner of first amendment fault privileges—is crafting a legal action to enforce press responsibility.

Our fourth conclusion concerns the way in which the legal system is operating for those plaintiffs who do need and seek money damages. We have found that not all plaintiffs sue only because of falsity; and that not all plaintiffs would be satisfied with correction rather than money damages. Actually, roughly one-fifth of the plaintiffs do sue to obtain money damages, and most of these (largely private) plaintiffs feel that they have suffered real economic consequences because of the libel. We have also found that up to 30 percent of the plaintiffs are—often understandably —motivated by a desire to get even. These findings do not detract from the fundamental insight that most plaintiffs are interested in correcting falsity rather than in money damages, but they do suggest that other motivations are at work for a significant proportion of the plaintiffs.

We have drawn some limited, but important, conclusions from this mixture of motives. Roughly one-fifth of the plaintiffs seek and appear to need some form of financial remedy coupled with correction of factual error, as real and material economic loss ensues from the alleged libel. For these plaintiffs, alternatives to litigation might appear more difficult to structure, at least in the absence of financial remedy. Our study of these plaintiffs, however, has led us to a less certain conclusion, as virtually all of these plaintiffs expressed an interest in a nonjudicial process involving a prompt, fair, and public determination of truth— without money damages. We should not automatically assume, therefore, that alternatives to suit do not exist for these plaintiffs.

A significant proportion of the plaintiffs mentioned "punishment" as a motive for litigation. While we found that the majority of such plaintiffs are nevertheless principally concerned with falsity, some may not be. There is reason to suspect that, in a *limited* group of cases, vengeance and punishment may be paramount, irrespective of the merits of the claim. Because the fault issue rests upon the question of subjective state of mind in light of what was known at the time of publication, it is more than theoretically possible to recover in such a libel action even though the published statement was true. While this is not a quantitatively substantial problem, it is a qualitatively troubling one.

Our fifth and related conclusion is that fault, combined with the disjunction between the plaintiffs' interests and the legal system's focus, may encourage litigation—or at least may leave undeterred libel suits that should not be encouraged. On the basis of our review of the limited material available in the published record of virtually all reported media libel cases between 1974 and 1984, we have concluded that a majority of such suits are insubstantial when judged by the underlying interests in material falsity and material reputational damage. I should note that such cases may involve falsity or inaccuracy, and surely may involve emotional distress. In many such cases, however, the falsity may be technical only, or the falsity and reputation claimed may pale in the face of other known facts.

Even a 50 percent rate of insubstantial claims, so defined, seems high, especially since we were dealing almost exclusively with seriously litigated cases that involved at least one instance of formal reported judicial actions. How can we account for the phenomenon? While we can provide no conclusive explanation, we believe that two factors contribute to it. First, as mentioned earlier, prior to the recent *Hepps* decision, and even after it, the law does not technically foreclose the prospect of recovering significant damages in the absence of falsity being shown, as long as the plaintiff can show calculated indifference to the known facts by the publisher at the time of publication. This seems a small crack in an otherwise largely closed door, but perhaps it is not an irrelevant factor, for a showing of actual malice can go a long way in substituting for a showing of material falsity and material reputational harm. Second, and we believe more importantly, the high incidence of apparently nonsubstantial claims is a direct function of the plaintiffs' chief interest, and the law's indifference to it. Plaintiffs are interested in falsity and the emotional manifestations of perceived reputational harm. Bringing a lawsuit is an apparently inexpensive and virtually risk-free means of achieving vindication of those interests. Put differently, if, as we believe, plaintiffs often and largely win by suing, the legal system provides an invitingly open and effective means of accomplishing this objective, with but a minimal risk that the issue of truth will be substantially explored or be decisive in the outcome.

Our sixth and final conclusion concerns the reputational interests served through the libel suit. If we judge reputational relief to the plaintiffs in terms of the effect of bringing suit, without more (and many plaintiffs seem to do just that), the libel action seems to provide a most effective remedy for plaintiffs, although the legal system plays no part in this, and attempts no distinction among cases in terms of this interest. If, on the other hand, we judge reputational relief in terms of the formal legal response in finally decided cases, we find that the results bear only the most idiosyncratic relationship, if any, to the interest in reputation, although the law purports at this stage to have distinguished among cases in terms of this interest. The results of the formal legal system, in short, bear no apparent systematic relationship to reputation. On this question Robert Sack made the point both effectively and, as we have discovered, quite accurately when he said:

> The few plaintiffs who succeed resemble the remnants of an army platoon caught in an enemy crossfire. Their awards stand witness to their good luck, not to their virtue, their skill or the justice of their cause. It is difficult to perceive the law of defamation, in this light, as a real "system" for protection of reputation at all.

CONCLUSION

What, in light of our findings, can we say about the "economics" of libel litigation? We would venture a few general conclusions.

- When we analyze the economics of the libel suit, we should not focus too heavily on the incidence of judicial victory, the likelihood and amount of money damages, or the strict rules of liability within the legal system. The "economics" of libel suits seem to be largely nonfinancial, and to exist outside the confines of the rules governing liability in the legal system.
- Libel plaintiffs and media defendants act in consistent, predictable patterns. Their actions appear to be rational, but they are responsive to objectives that are not strictly economic (in the financial sense of the term). Both plaintiffs and defendants are resistant to negotiation and settlement unless their reputational and ideological concerns (vindication through admission of falsity for plaintiffs; resistance to pressure and maintenance of credibility for the media) are satisfied more effectively than they would be in litigation. This is a tall order, if as we conclude, plaintiffs win by suing, while media always in court.
- Major participants in the libel dispute may serve, for reasons extrinsic to the dispute, to encourage litigation. The media tend to foster suit by organizational practices that anger plaintiffs. Human relations skills, more careful attention to the complaint process, and willingness to admit error and apologize for it when it occurs, might go a long way toward avoiding litigation. Plaintiff lawyers, too, may distort the calculus of risk in litigation by underwriting litigation costs which they recover indirectly through representation of prominent clients.
- Finally, the legal system seems to have contributed to the pres-

ent mix of factors at work in libel suits. From a dispute whose essence seems straightforward—truth or falsity and reputational harm—the legal system has evolved an intricate, complex, and expensive set of rules and procedures having little relationship to the underlying dispute, but which may be providing an ironic safe harbor in which plaintiffs and defendants can act out their separate drama. The direct social costs in terms of judicial time and energy are immense, and appear to us to be of little value.

The libel dispute could, in our view, be efficiently adjudicated, either within the judicial system or outside of it. But the sad fact is that there are no alternatives to either party. In reality, for many plaintiffs and defendants alike, libel litigation is the only available choice today. It is toward development of efficient and effective alternatives that we hope economic analysis will turn.

3

AN EMPIRICAL ANALYSIS OF THE CHILLING EFFECT
Are Newspapers Affected by Liability Standards in Defamation Actions?

Stephen M. Renas
Charles J. Hartmann
James L. Walker

Libel law in the United States has generally been a matter of state concern and part of the general body of civil law known as torts. But since 1964, libel law in the United States has come under the influence of federal constitutional law. In that year, in the landmark case of *New York Times v. Sullivan,*[1] the United States Supreme Court ruled that state laws making newspapers strictly liable for false defamatory statements were generally inconsistent with First Amendment rights of freedom of the press.

The reasoning in that case is very straightforward. The central purpose of the First Amendment is to ensure and even to promote vigorous and robust debate and comment on matters of public importance. If public officials are allowed to recover damages for any false and defamatory statement, regardless of the level of care taken, then newspapers will be discouraged, or "chilled," from printing stories on matters of public interest. The notion of the chilling effect is firmly rooted in American Constitutional Law and was expressed by Justice Brennan in *Sullivan:*

> . . . critics of official conduct may be deterred from voicing their criticism, even though it is believed to be true and even though it is in fact true, because of doubt whether it can be proved in court or fear of the expense of having to do so. They tend to make statements which steer far wider of the unlawful zone.[2]

In order to moderate the chilling effect, the Supreme Court imposed a standard of proof in libel cases involving public official plaintiffs which was much higher than that used in most state courts at the time. Public officials could recover damages only if they could prove that the false and defamatory statement was made with actual malice, that is, with "knowledge that it was false or with reckless disregard of whether it was false or not."[3]

Later cases extended the *Sullivan* role to public figures,[4] and in 1974 the Court even raised the standards for most private litigants from strict liability to at least negligence.[5] Although the principles in the *Sullivan* case were generally received with praise,[6] significant doubt about the actual existence of the chilling effect has always been present. Justice White, in his dissent in *Gertz v. Robert Welch,* argued:

> The press today is vigorous and robust. To me, it is quite incredible to suggest that threats of libel suits from private citizens are causing the press to refrain from publishing the truth. I know of no hard facts to support that proposition, and the Court furnishes none.[7]

The *Sullivan* case and its progeny have not entirely eased the media's fear of being sued. Many newspapers, even the smallest, have prepublication review by experts on defamation law, a practice known as "vetting."[8] In a recent article in the *Columbia Journalism Review,*[9] based on over 150 interviews with media editors and lawyers, Michael Massing cites numerous examples in which the fear of a defamation action was given as the reason for a no-publication decision. Editors of papers which have been sued and have paid damages in the past were reported to be particularly sensitive to the threat of a defamation action. Also, it seems clear that current high standards of proof do not necessarily discourage litigants who are more interested in "clearing the air" than in being awarded money damages. Most plaintiffs have been found to be more interested in restoring their reputation or punishing the media than in winning money damages.[10] The plaintiffs sue to set the record straight and this objective is accomplished independent of the judicial result. Suits are seen as a means of vindicating the plaintiff's claim of falsehood so that while few public party plaintiffs win, the vast majority would sue again knowing what the outcome would be. Plaintiffs who lose because of the difficulty of overcoming the Constitutional privileges can claim a moral victory arguing that they were defeated because of a technicality of the system.[11] Recent cases which illustrate these points are General Westmoreland's suit against CBS and Ariel Sharon's suit against *Time* magazine.[12] Estimates of the cost of defending against these suits have ranged in the millions of dollars.

The fears expressed by the media notwithstanding, some commentators maintain that current libel laws are necessary to restrain press abuse. Others take the position that the press has been afforded too much protection in libel actions, and that a lower standard of proof is required. Lester Bernstein, writing in the op-ed page of the *New York Times,* argues that fear of libel does not deter the press from providing the information that the public needs to govern itself, and that libel laws chill only the "feverish pursuit of sensation." James Cain, writing in the "At Issue" page of the *American Bar Association Journal,* argues that "rash procedures, reckless allegations and subjective viewpoints" have become matters of policy with the news media and can be traced directly to the *Sullivan* decision.[13] Cain opts for a negligence standard.

If the *Sullivan* standard were abandoned, the effects on the media and on society at large could be profound and far-reaching. Not the least of these is the effect on the media's willingness to cover and to print stories on matters of public concern. The purpose of this research is to determine the existence and magnitude of the presumed chilling effect on newspapers and the type of newspaper that would be most affected if the actual malice standard for public person plaintiffs were replaced by a negligence or a strict liability standard. As a means of answering these questions, we have surveyed newspaper editors to determine their willingness to publish potentially defamatory material under various standards of liability.

Obviously, any decision to reduce the liability standard for libel actions must be based on a number of competing factors. Society is concerned not only with encouraging public discourse but also in protecting reputation. But freedom of the press has been considered to be a transcendent value, and since *Sullivan,* the courts have attempted to tip the balance in favor of public discourse. From an economic perspective, the Constitution was interpreted in *Sullivan* and its progeny as requiring a subsidy for public discourse at the expense of reputation.[14]

We begin with a brief description of the evolution of libel law in the United States, and then describe the methodology of the study and present and analyze the findings. Finally, we offer our conclusions. Legal standards in libel actions do in fact affect editorial behavior; here the effect is not uniform: it depends on the manner in which the paper is marketed, its competitive environment, and the paper's experience with libel suits and payment of damages.

I. EVOLUTION OF LIBEL LAW IN THE U.S.

In the thirty-year period between the publication of the first and fourth editions of Prosser's monumental *Handbook of the Law of Torts,*[15] the author observed, apparently with approval, that a shift had occurred in favor of plaintiffs in *almost* every area of tort law.[16] The exception was the field of defamation law. Prosser found, as a result of the constitutional expansion of the area of privilege, "unquestionably the greatest victory won by the defendants in the modern history of the law of torts."[17] This bold proclamation, though omitted in the recent fifth edition, revised by Professor Keeton,[18] still stands as an accurate assessment of the decreasing scope of the liability of the press for defamation actions in the past two decades.

The early standard of liability for defamation by the press in the United States was said to rest on a theory of "strict accountability for the substance of a defamatory statement."[19] Traditional arguments in support of strict liability in other fields of tort law were advanced to hold the press strictly liable for defamation. Publishers became, in effect, insurers of the reputations of those affected partly because the press was viewed as a powerful force with considerable ability to harm innocent persons. Further, it was argued that through insurance and risk spreading, the media was able to mitigate the harmful effects of the strict liability rule. As late as 1956, it appears that there existed little evidence that a strict liability standard unduly inhibited press activities.[20]

It is clear that certain common law defenses to defamation liability aided the press, and some states provided relief in the form of retraction statutes.[21] The defense of "fair comment" extended to the press with regard to defamatory remarks concerning matters of public concern. And even this limited protection was mitigated in a majority of states by the rule that only matters of comment, opinion, and criticism were covered, leaving the press vulnerable to suit for false statements of fact. The courts appeared to fear the effect on the public should candidates for office be discouraged by false statements of fact which they could not redress. In a minority of states the press was afforded a defense under the common law fair comment rule for statements of fact made for the public benefit, with an honest belief in their truth, because of the *public interest* in having a press free of fear of having to prove in court the truth of a statement made about a matter of public concern.[22]

It is the rationale underlying this minority view which prevailed as a constitutional right of the American press, providing a profound victory for defendants in an era of expanding tort plaintiffs' rights. This view led eventually to the landmark Supreme Court case of *New York Times v. Sullivan*[23] which held that the First Amendment afforded the press a limitation on liability in defamation cases. Although *Sullivan* dealt only with the public activities of an elected public official, the Court has since expanded the policies underlying the decision to govern all defamation by media defendants—in effect, constitutionalizing the common law of defamation. While *Sullivan* and its progeny have afforded considerable protection to the press, at least two former members of the Supreme Court have expressed the view that all defamation actions are incompatible with the First Amendment. Justices Black[24] and Douglas[25] would have held that neither Congress nor the states may establish legal sanctions on free speech through the imposition of defamation laws. It is clear that, to date, the majority of the Court has rejected this view of press freedom in the area of defamation.

II. METHODOLOGY

The population of interest in this study is the general-readership, daily newspaper in the United States. A "National Libel Survey" was constructed and pretested. Based on the results of the pretest, the instrument was revised and was mailed, during January and February of 1986, to the managing editors of the 1688 U.S. daily newspapers listed in the Editor and Publisher Company's 1985 *International Year Book* (New York, 1985). The editors were first reminded of the definitions of the three standards of proof under consideration: actual malice, negligence, and strict liability. They were then presented with four scenarios, each of which described hypothetical editorial decision-making situations. All four involve public officials:

1. A political advertisement names a member of the city planning board as the "kingpin" of the local pornography business.

2. A news story describes a local City Council meeting at which the Mayor is accused of being a slumlord.

3. An editorial accuses the Chief of Police of being deceptive and of lying to the City Council.

4. A humor columnist claims that the County Administrator is such a skinflint that he is "building his own casket and digging his own grave to save on funeral expenses."

The survey instrument used in the study is reproduced in Appendix A.

Each of the editors was asked to evaluate each scenario and to indicate a relative willingness to publish on a scale from 0 (absolutely unwilling) to 10 (absolutely willing) under each of the three standards of proof. Our hypothesis was that editors would be relatively less willing to publish the same material as the standard of proof required for the plaintiff to prevail became more relaxed or less demanding. Thus, we expected that an editor would be less willing to publish the same material under negligence than under the actual malice rule, and even less willing to publish under strict liability. The editor was then asked to complete a section of the paper's circulation characteristics, market size, competitive environment, history with libel litigation, and libel insurance status.

The scenarios, except for the first, were designed to lean in the direction of being publishable. The scenarios were reviewed by a team of attorneys who specialize in defamation litigation. The evaluations below are based in part on the responses from this panel. Scenario 1 involves the use of a highly charged word (kingpin) and a possibly gratuitous attack on a marginally public figure. It represents the use of the paper by private parties or groups for the purpose of criticism or exposure when the paper itself might not have had the desire to raise the issues on its own. There is a question as to whether the statements in the ad would be construed as opinion or fact. It is not clear that constitutional privileges or common law privileges apply.

A competitive factor may be involved in Scenario 2, since many City Council meetings are covered either by cable or local television stations, which may find a raucous meeting irresistible. Failure by print media to include a complete account of such a meeting could be damaging to the paper. Both constitutional and common law privilege are involved, since the Mayor is a public figure and the story would be a truthful and accurate reporting of a newsworthy event. In order to prevail in a libel suit, the Mayor would probably have to prove actual malice. Some states have statutes that would grant an absolute privilege in the publication of this story.

Scenario 3 involves a commentary—in this case an editorial about the police chief. Once again, both constitutional and common law privileges apply and the only question would be whether the statement that "he blatantly lies" would be considered a statement of fact or opinion. The weight of opinion of the attorneys was that Scenario 3 can safely be published, especially if the word "lies" is omitted.

Scenario 4 asks how far may humor or ridicule go in entertaining the audience of the print medium. The case law on humor has been exceedingly generous to the defendants, especially when the statement cannot reasonably be understood to be factual. The almost unanimous opinion of the legal authorities consulted was that Scenario 4 can be printed, since the likelihood of suit is low and the chance of a summary judgment for defendant is high.

Of the 1688 surveys that were mailed, 220 were returned, of which 14 could not be used because of incomplete or conflicting responses. The remaining sample of 206 represented 12.2 percent of the population.

When the survey instrument was being constructed, pretested, and modified, it was obvious that a tradeoff existed between avoidance of ambiguity in the wording of the material and avoidance of excessive complexity and length. We struck a balance between these two competing needs that we believed would provide a high degree of clarity without undue complexity, recognizing at the same time that a few respondents might still misinterpret some of the material.

The sample thus obtained was compared with the population on the basis of circulation size and regional distribution. The sample was found to be representative of the population based on these two factors using standard statistical criteria.[26] A description of the characteristics of the sample is found in Appendix B.

A question that invariably arises in this type of research is whether editors would respond to an actual change in the standard of proof in the same way that they responded to the hypothetical questions in the survey. Can editors be expected to know in advance how they would respond in the event the standard of proof were actually to change? Also, the sample was self-selected—editors chose whether they wished to respond and be included as part of the sample. Does the self-selection process itself introduce bias? Are respondents more or less likely to be chilled than nonrespondents? A related question is whether respondents would have any incentive not to accurately reveal their preferences. Editors who are particularly fearful of a libel suit may be inclined to respond and to exaggerate the chilling effect. Other editors may wish to minimize it. Several editors whom we contacted during the pretest were adamant that editorial decisions at their paper are made on the basis of newsworthiness and fairness to the subject of a news inquiry. They argued that when editors do their jobs, it is not necessary to consider the statement of proof for libel. These editors are proud that they are not chilled and may be inclined to respond. Thus, to the extent that the editors may not accurately reveal their preferences, two biases may be present. These biases are, at least to some extent, mutually offsetting.

The approach we have used to measure the chilling effect is superior to one that attempts to compare newspapers' willingness to publish over time—i.e., before and after the *Sullivan* decision was handed down. Even if the problem of obtaining data over a 22-year period could somehow be overcome, it would be virtually impossible to control for all of the other factors that influence a newspaper's decision to publish. The approach used in this study evaluates the change in willingness to publish resulting from a change in the standard of proof, holding all other factors constant.

III. FINDINGS

A summary of the responses to the four scenarios under the three standards of proof is presented in table 3.1. Willingness-to-publish responses spanned the spectrum from 0, absolutely unwilling to publish, to 10, absolutely willing to publish. A large number of the responses were clustered at or near the extremes: many newspapers were either very willing or very unwilling to publish. The editors expressed somewhat more reluctance to publish, even under the actual malice rule, then the authors had anticipated. The scenarios, with the exception of the first, were designed to lean in the direction of being publishable.

As anticipated, editors were far more reluctant to publish the antipornography advertisement in Scenario 1 than any of the other pieces. In written comments, some of them expressed an aversion to the use of the word "kingpin," indicating this term would invite a lawsuit. For the same reason, several of the attorneys who reviewed the scenarios at our request advised against publication of Scenario 1 as written. Moreover, the attorneys' relative ranking of the four scenarios on the basis of libel risk was close to our own ranking.

A chilling effect resulting from a reduction in the standard of proof can be observed in table 3.1. The percentage of editors absolutely willing to publish declines as the standard of proof is reduced, while the percentage absolutely unwilling to publish increases as the standard of proof declines. The magnitude of the chilling effect is not insubstantial. A change in the standard from malice to negligence reduces the percentage of editors who are absolutely willing to publish by between 9.7 percent and 16.5 percent. A change from malice to strict liability reduces the percentage by between 13.6 percent and 28.7 percent.

Data on mean changes (reductions) in willingness to publish as the standard is reduced are found in table 3.2. In Scenario 1, the mean change is greatest when willingness to publish under the higher standard of proof is equal to 10. As willingness to publish under the higher standard declines, the mean change in willingness to publish declines as well.

In Scenarios 2 through 4, the pattern is somewhat different. The mean change is relatively small when willingness to publish under the higher standard of proof is equal to 10. As willingness to publish under the higher standard declines, the mean change at first increases, but then decreases. This is the pattern predicted by several editors we contacted during the survey. They indicated that the chilling effect resulting from a reduction in the standard would be small if an editor were strongly in favor of or strongly opposed to publication under

TABLE 3.1: Willingness to Publish Under Different Scenarios and Different Liability Rules

Scenario	Liability Rule	Percentage of Papers Indicating Willingness to Publish										
		0	1	2	3	4	5	6	7	8	9	10
1	Malice	46.6	3.4	4.9	3.9	3.9	3.4	1.9	2.4	8.7	4.9	16.0
	Negligence	51.5	5.8	4.9	3.9	2.9	10.2	3.9	3.4	4.4	2.9	6.3
	Strict Liability	63.6	9.2	6.3	6.8	2.4	4.4	1.5	1.5	1.9	—	2.4
2	Malice	1.9	1.5	1.0	1.0	1.5	1.9	2.4	3.9	10.7	9.7	54.6
	Negligence	2.9	1.0	1.9	1.5	4.4	6.3	7.3	8.3	9.7	8.7	48.1
	Strict Liability	10.2	4.9	6.3	4.9	5.8	6.8	3.4	7.8	7.8	6.3	35.9
3	Malice	13.6	3.9	2.9	1.0	1.5	3.9	2.9	3.4	6.3	8.7	51.9
	Negligence	14.0	4.9	2.9	2.9	1.0	9.2	5.8	6.3	7.8	8.7	36.4
	Strict Liability	22.3	4.9	6.3	6.3	3.9	7.3	5.3	1.0	5.3	5.8	31.6
4	Malice	16.0	1.5	1.9	1.5	1.9	3.4	3.4	6.3	3.9	5.8	54.4
	Negligence	17.0	1.9	5.3	1.5	1.9	7.8	2.9	4.9	6.8	6.8	43.2
	Strict Liability	24.3	3.9	3.9	2.4	3.4	6.3	3.9	4.4	4.9	6.8	35.9

malice, while it would be much greater if the editor were initially uncertain whether to publish. The anomalous results in Scenario 1 may be related to the fact that the vast majority of editors were not in favor of publication. The relatively few who indicated they were absolutely willing to publish under the higher standard of proof may have harbored reservations, and therefore may have experienced a significant change of heart when the liability standard changed.

Data on the proportion of editors who were chilled in specific scenarios by a change in the standard appear in table 3.3 Chilling is defined as a non-zero change in willingness to publish brought about by a reduction in the standard of proof. A reduction in willingness to publish of six units along the 0 to 10 scale is equivalent to a reduction of only one unit using this definition. This proportion of editors who were chilled as a result of a change in the standard from actual malice to negligence ranges in value from 23.3 percent to 34.0 percent. The proportion chilled as a result of a change in the standard from actual malice to strict liability ranges in value from 35.9 percent to 49.5 percent. Roughly seventy percent of the papers that were chilled as a result of a change in the standard from actual malice to strict liability were also chilled when the standard changed from actual malice to negligence.[27]

What types of papers are particularly sensitive to a change in the

TABLE 3.2: Mean Change in Willingness to Publish

Scenario	Change in Liability Rule		Mean Change When Response Under i Equals				
	From (i)	To (j)	0	1–3	4–6	7–9	10
1	Malice	Negligence	0	.80	.33	2.18	2.33
	Malice	Strict Liability	0	1.28	3.37	5.55	5.73
	Negligence	Strict Liability	0	.97	3.03	3.64	3.85
2	Malice	Negligence	0	.71	.75	1.38	.70
	Malice	Strict Liability	0	1.14	2.83	3.22	2.19
	Negligence	Strict Liability	0	1.33	2.87	1.64	1.11
3	Malice	Negligence	0	.25	.71	1.42	.78
	Malice	Strict Liability	0	.63	2.06	3.55	1.97
	Negligence	Strict Liability	0	.86	2.24	2.34	.47
4	Malice	Negligence	0	.60	.72	1.15	.66
	Malice	Strict Liability	0	1.30	1.61	2.76	1.55
	Negligence	Strict Liability	0	1.06	1.88	1.76	.46

liability standard? A smaller chilling effect is expected to result from a change in the standard when a large percentage of a paper's circulation is accounted for by street and machine sales rather than carrier delivery and mail subscription. Within the sample, the percent of circulation accounted for by street and machine sales ranges in value from a low of 0 percent to a high of 85 percent. Unlike newspapers that rely on home delivery, newspapers sold principally on the street must have attention-getting front-page headlines that will capture the attention of passers-by. The content of the stories accompanying those headlines may be controversial. If the standard proof were reduced, newspapers that sell a large percentage of papers through street and machine sales would have a financial incentive to attempt to maintain this marketing strategy. The chilling effect would therefore be smaller for this type of paper.

It is possible, of course, that a paper sold primarily through home delivery may be less willing to publish controversial material, under the existing standard of malice, than one sold principally in stores, at news-stands, and by machines. If so, a reduction in the standard of proof may have a greater chilling effect in the latter case, simply because more potential exists to modify editorial policy. Home-delivered papers are already more conservative in their willingness to assume risk.

The relationship between circulation size and the chilling effect is

TABLE 3.3: Proportion of Papers Chilled by Change in Liability Rule

Scenario	Change in Liability Rule		Proportion of Papers Chilled
	From	To	
1	Malice	Negligence	34.0
	Malice	Strict Liability	44.2
	Negligence	Strict Liability	35.9
2	Malice	Negligence	33.5
	Malice	Strict Liability	49.5
	Negligence	Strict Liability	44.2
3	Malice	Negligence	29.6
	Malice	Strict Liability	42.2
	Negligence	Strict Liability	37.9
4	Malice	Negligence	23.3
	Malice	Strict Liability	35.9
	Negligence	Strict Liability	32.0

indeterminate, *a priori*. A large newspaper has greater financial resources necessary to defend a libel action, and, hence, may be chilled to
a lesser extent than a small paper if the liability standard were changed.
However, it may well recognize that potential plaintiffs view it as a more
prominent target—and one with "deeper pockets" than a small newspaper; consequently, the chilling effect may actually be greater for large
papers. The impact of population of market area and market penetration,
defined as the ratio of circulation to population of market area, is similarly
ambiguous.

A newspaper's competitive environment is expected to affect its response to a change in the standard. If the standard of proof is reduced,
a newspaper that competes against other papers for market share is less
likely to be deterred from publishing a controversial and high reader
interest piece than a paper with no competition, especially if the paper
believes its competitors will react similarly. The number of competitors
is typically small, and each paper will consider the possible reaction of
its rivals in formulating its own strategy.[28]

The effects of having been sued in the past and of having paid damages
are difficult to assess *a priori*. The chilling effect resulting from a reduction in the standard may be greater for a paper that has been sued within
the last fifteen years than for a newspaper which has not been sued.
Even if a paper carries libel insurance (and 189 of the 206 papers did)
the deductibles can exact a heavy burden on the paper in defending the
suit.[29] A paper that has incurred such a cost (out-of-pocket expenses
and the opportunity cost of time spent in meetings with attorneys, in
preparing a defense, in discovery, depositions, and trial) may be especially sensitive to the threat of a future libel suit and may be chilled to a
greater extent by a decrease in the standard than a paper that has not
been sued. Another possibility exists, however. A paper that has de-
fended a libel action may already have modified its editorial policy and
become more cautious. If such is the case, a change in the standard may
have little further effect.

A paper that has paid damages in the past may be acutely aware of
the hazards of libel litigation and may be chilled to a greater extent by a
change in the standard than a paper that has not paid damages. However, as before, a paper that has paid damages may already have become
very cautious, in which case further caution would not be expected by a
change in the standard. Still another possibility is that of a newspaper
which has paid damages in the past because it had (and continues to
have) a propensity toward highly controversial and potentially defamatory articles and may be willing to accept risk. Such a paper would not
be expected to be deterred a great deal if the standard of proof were
reduced.

We used least-squares regression and logistic regression analysis to see which factors will in fact influence the chilling effect. Logistic regression treats the chilling effect as categorical: A reduction in the standard of proof either will create a chilling effect or it will not. Least-squares regression analysis treats the chilling effect as continuous: it attempts to explain the *magnitude* of that effect. Both techniques assess the relationship between the chilling effect and all of the factors that are hypothesized to influence it simultaneously. Such an approach is superior to one that evaluates the impact of each factor separately on a paper's reaction to a change in the standard. Let us say, for example, that we had measured the impact of a paper's competitive environment on the chilling effect, without considering the influence of all the other factors that may be involved. We might have obtained spurious results, which we would have attributed to competitive environment—an explanation that rightfully belongs to one of the other variables. An explanation of the results of the statistical analysis is provided here. Those who wish technical documentation of the analysis are referred to Appendix C and to the endnotes.

An examination of the statistical results demonstrates that the percent of circulation accounted for by street and machine sales exerts a significant influence on a paper's reaction to a change in the standard of proof in several of the regressions. As hypothesized, those papers with large street sales are least likely to be chilled by a reduction in the standard of proof. An economic factor is clearly at work here. Papers sold primarily on the street must, out of necessity, be greater risk takers.

A newspaper's competitive environment is also of importance. Our statistical analysis confirms our hypothesis that a paper is less likely to be chilled when it competes against other papers for market share. This finding is especially significant in view of the trend toward one-newspaper markets.

We found no statistical evidence whatsoever that small newspapers are more adversely affected than large papers by a change in the standard. Moreover, evidence from two of the least-squares regressions and from several of the logistic regressions, indicates that large newspapers would be chilled to a greater extent than small papers by such a change. The evidence concerning market penetration, defined as the ratio of circulation size to population of market area, is mixed. Some of the results point to a larger chilling effect among papers having greater market penetration; whereas others point to a smaller chilling effect among this type of paper.

The effect of a newspaper's experience in defining libel actions and in paying damages is quite interesting. The statistical results show that a newspaper which has been sued in the last fifteen years but has not paid damages would be chilled to a greater extent by a reduction in the standard than a paper that has not been sued. Yet the *marginal* effect of payment of damages, once the paper has been sued, is to reduce the chilling effect resulting from a change in the standard. In fact, there is some evidence that the chilling effect resulting from a reduction in the standard is *smaller* for newspapers that have been sued and have paid damages in the past than for newspapers that have never been sued.[30] Either payment of damages in the past has already caused the paper to exercise more caution, so that a change in the liability standard will have little further effect, or it may have a natural propensity toward controversial stories and will not react a great deal to a reduction in the standard of proof. Further statistical analysis[31] was performed which indicates that a newspaper that has paid damages in the past is less likely to publish, under the existing standard of malice, than a paper that has not paid damages in the past. Therefore, the more likely explanation is that a paper that has paid damages in the past has already become more cautious.

The statistical results concerning the influence of the newspaper's initial willingness to publish are consistent with our earlier findings. In scenarios 2 through 4, the chilling effect resulting from a reduction in the standard of proof is relatively small when the paper is either strongly in favor of or strongly opposed to publication under the higher liability standard, but is greater when the paper is initially uncertain concerning the advisability of publication. When the standard proof in Scenario 2 is reduced from actual malice to negligence, for example, the peak chilling effect occurs when willingness to publish under malice is equal to 5.99.[32] As before, the pattern in Scenario 1 is somewhat different. When the standard proof in Scenario 1 is changed from actual malice to strict liability, or from negligence to strict liability, the chilling effect is greatest when willingness to publish under the higher standard is equal to 10, and declines as willingness to publish falls. When the standard in Scenario 1 is changed from malice to negligence, the maximum chilling effect occurs when willingness to publish under the higher standard (malice) is equal to 9.30.

Libel insurance would be expected to reduce the chilling effect, yet no such pattern was detected. What may be occurring is that newspapers that obtain coverage (as the vast majority of papers have done) may be more averse to risk and hence more sensitive to the threat of a libel action than those papers that choose to publish without insurance. The presence of libel insurance may simply compensate for the additional aversion to risk among those papers that obtain coverage.[33] The statistical results also show no variation in the chilling effect based on region of the country in which the newspaper is located.[34] There may be variation from city to city within the same region, but there is no evidence of variation across regions.

CONCLUSION

The results of the survey show that a deviation from the *Sullivan* rule increases the likelihood that public persons will prevail in libel actions, while newspapers will be less likely to publish articles and opinion pieces on matters of public concern. The chilling effect is not uniform: it is most pronounced among papers that do not face competition, for which street and machine sales constitute a small percentage of circulation, and that have been sued but have not paid damages in the past.

The findings appear to argue against a reduction in the standard of proof in libel actions since such a change would discourage the media from gathering and disseminating information necessary for rational and informed judgment. By extension, the findings appear to argue against any change that would increase the likelihood that the media would be sued, would have to defend against a libel action, or would be required to pay damages. Yet society has an interest not only in encouraging public discourse but also in protecting reputation. Decisions concerning the optional liability rule must take into account both of these factors. Two of the authors have investigated the issue of the optimal liability rule elsewhere. [35]

The question of whether the protection afforded to the press in libel actions will be reduced and what the effects will be may not be merely academic. Even in some recent U.S. Supreme Court decisions favorable to the press, sharply worded dissents indicate great dissatisfaction with the current level of protection afforded the media. [36] The Supreme Court has refused to broaden the concept of libel to include the intentional infliction of emotional distress due to satirical comment. It was urged to do so by the Reverend Jerry Falwell in his suit against *Hustler* Magazine. [37] In contrast, shortly thereafter, that same court upheld the largest libel award ever brought before it, over $3 million, against CBS, for commentary severely critical of the tobacco industry. [38] It is not at all clear, given the changing composition of the Court, that the media will enjoy the same protection in the future.

APPENDIX A: NATIONAL LIBEL SURVEY

INSTRUCTIONS: The purpose of this survey is to discover the effect that standards of legal liability in libel actions have on the decision to publish or not to publish an item. In answering the questions, simply react as you would in your capacity as an editor of a newspaper. We realize that actual decisions are made in a much more complex environment than that which is presented here. But, we are interested in the relative weight of the factors discussed rather than an absolute judgment.

The standards of legal liability under study and their definitions are as follows:

1. *Strict Liability:* Any false, defamatory statement published can result in an award of damages *no matter how much care* was taken to avoid the false statement. It is easiest to win damages under this standard.

2. *Negligence:* A false, defamatory statement can result in an award of damages *only if the newspaper did not use reasonable care* in checking on the truth or falsity of the statement. It is more difficult to win damages under this standard than under strict liability.

3. *Actual Malice: Only knowledge of the falsity* of a statement or *reckless disregard of whether the statement was true or false* can result in an award of damages. Sometimes referred to as the Sullivan Rule, it is most difficult to win an award of damages under this standard.

As you read each of the following brief situations, we would like to know whether your decision to publish would be influenced by the legal standard that applied in the case. Simply circle the number that you feel best indicates your willingness to publish the relevant item having followed normal editorial procedures under each of the standards.

Please Proceed to Situation One—

Situation One

A citizens group has formed to combat pornography. It wishes to purchase a half page ad in your paper. The ad supports the closing of pornography outlets in your city. The ad also names a particular individual as the "kingpin of the pornography business" in your city. The ad further details the harm that pornography does, especially to women, and then details the connections between organized crime and the pornography business nationally. It does not name a specific individual as associated with organized crime. The alleged "kingpin" is a person well known in the community and sits on the city plan board. It is verified by a staff member that he owns several "adult bookstores."

WILLINGNESS TO PRINT

	ABSOLUTELY UNWILLING								ABSOLUTELY WILLING	
STRICT LIABILITY	0	1	2	3	4	5	6	7	8	9	10
NEGLIGENCE	0	1	2	3	4	5	6	7	8	9	10
ACTUAL MALICE (Sullivan Rule)	0	1	2	3	4	5	6	7	8	9	10

Situation Two

During the "open forum" segment of a local city council meeting, a citizen complains vehemently about the new, more stringent housing inspection plan. When he is chastised by the mayor for his intemperate remarks, the citizen replies, "Why you are the biggest slumlord in the city," and then proceeds to produce what he claims is evidence of the fact that the mayor owns numerous properties that were cited even under the old, more lenient code. It is established that the mayor owns numerous rental properties. The reporter on the scene, an experienced staff writer, is certain of the correctness of the quotes and includes them in a story she files. It is established, through further investigation, that some of the mayor's properties were indeed cited, but for relatively minor violations.

WILLINGNESS TO PRINT

	ABSOLUTELY UNWILLING								ABSOLUTELY WILLING	
STRICT LIABILITY	0	1	2	3	4	5	6	7	8	9	10
NEGLIGENCE	0	1	2	3	4	5	6	7	8	9	10
ACTUAL MALICE (Sullivan Rule)	0	1	2	3	4	5	6	7	8	9	10

Situation Three

An editorial critical of the Chief of Police refers to him as "deceptive." The writer states that "he often misleads the City Council, sometimes blatantly lies to them." The basis of the editorial is a series of news stories by three reporters over a six-month period in which various officials are quoted as saying that the Police Chief had furnished the Council with inaccurate, misleading, and self-serving information about steps he was taking to reduce the crime rate. The editorial concludes that "we can't have honest law enforcement if we don't have honesty at the top."

	WILLINGNESS TO PRINT										
	ABSOLUTELY UNWILLING								ABSOLUTELY WILLING		
STRICT LIABILITY	0	1	2	3	4	5	6	7	8	9	10
NEGLIGENCE	0	1	2	3	4	5	6	7	8	9	10
ACTUAL MALICE (Sullivan Rule)	0	1	2	3	4	5	6	7	8	9	10

Situation Four

Your humor columnist, who is compared by many local people to Art Buchwald, makes the claim in a column that the country administrator is such a skinflint that he is "building his own casket and digging his own grave to save on funeral expenses." In an interview in your paper somewhat earlier, the administrator had spoken with pride of his frugal nature. No specific criticism is made of the performance of the administrator's public duties in the column.

	WILLINGNESS TO PRINT										
	ABSOLUTELY UNWILLING								ABSOLUTELY WILLING		
STRICT LIABILITY	0	1	2	3	4	5	6	7	8	9	10
NEGLIGENCE	0	1	2	3	4	5	6	7	8	9	10
ACTUAL MALICE (Sullivan Rule)	0	1	2	3	4	5	6	7	8	9	10

Finally, in order to classify your opinions, would you please give us the following information about your paper.

1. Approximately what percentage of circulation is accounted for by:

  ___% Carrier Delivery
  ___% Street and Machine Sales
  ___% Mail Subscriptions
  100% TOTAL

2. Average Daily (Mon.–Fri.) Circulation _____

3. Approximate Population of Market Area _____

4. How many papers do you directly compete with in your market area? _____

5. How many of your competitors, if any, are owned by the same company that owns or controls your paper? _____

6. Approximately how many times has your paper been sued for libel in the last fifteen years?

      Never   1 to 3   4 to 6   7 to 9   10 or more

7. Have you ever had to pay an award for damages in a libel case?

8. Does your newspaper carry insurance in the event you are sued for libel?

             YES   NO

Thank you for your help.

APPENDIX B: SAMPLE

Characteristics—Distribution of Respondents by Circulation Size, Population of Market Area, Number of Competitors, Percent of Circulation through Street and Machine Sales, Number of Times Sued, Damages Paid, Insurance Status, Region ($N = 206$).

TABLE 3.B.1

Circulation	Percent
5,000 or less	9.2
5,001–10,000	24.3
10,001–25,000	26.7
25,001–50,000	22.8
50,001–100,000	9.7
100,001–250,000	4.9
250,000–500,000	1.5
More than 500,000	1.0

TABLE 3.B.2

Population of Market Area	Percent
25,000 or less	16.0
25,001–50,000	21.8
50,001–100,000	20.4
100,001–500,000	33.0
500,001–1,000,000	5.3
More than 1,000,000	3.4

TABLE 3.B.3

Number of Competitors	Percent
0	18.4
1	23.8
2–3	33.0
4–5	17.0
6 or more	7.8

TABLE 3.B.4

Percent of Circulation Through Street/Machine Sales	Percent
5 or less	24.3
6–10	32.0
11–15	12.6
16–20	17.0
More than 20	14.1

TABLE 3.B.5

Number of Times Sued	Percent
0	36.9
1–3	39.3
4–6	13.6
7–9	4.9
10 or more	5.3

TABLE 3.B.6

Paid Damages	Percent
No	84.0
Yes	16.0

TABLE 3.B.7

Insured	Percent
Yes	91.7
No	8.3

TABLE 3.B.8

Region*	Percent
North	14.2
Midwest	33.8
South	31.9
West	19.1
Pacific	1.0

*Standard Bureau of the Census Classification

APPENDIX C: ECONOMETRIC RESULTS

The results of least-squares estimation of the regressions are found in table 3.1. Variables are defined as follows:

TABLE 3.C.1: Regression Results

EQ.	DEPENDENT VARIABLE	INTERCEPT	CIRSMS	AVGDIR	POPMKT	PCTMKT
1	DIFAMNI	−0.21163 (0.371)	0.00456 (0.010)	0.63721* (0.193)	−0.05916* (0.019)	0.68177 (0.933)
2	DIFAMSL1	0.59699 (0.475)	−0.00433 (0.013)	0.38515 (0.247)	−0.06011* (0.024)	−1.79004* (1.195)
3	DIFNSL1	0.74708 (0.400)	−0.01028 (0.011)	0.02658 (0.207)	−0.02505 (0.020)	−2.04500* (1.002)
4	DIFAMN2	−0.07478 (0.642)	−0.02271* (0.010)	0.33080* (0.196)	−0.02272 (0.019)	0.58339 (0.953)
5	DIFAMS2	−0.33910 (1.352)	−0.04072* (0.021)	0.26723 (0.413)	−0.01985 (0.041)	1.35783 (2.007)
6	DIFNSL2	−0.14334 (0.872)	−0.01668 (0.015)	−0.03371 (0.296)	0.00077 (0.029)	0.10210 (1.449)
7	DIFAMN3	0.21837 (0.420)	0.00397 (0.0097)	−0.05795 (0.190)	−0.00643 (0.019)	−0.30347 (0.908)
8	DIFAMSL3	1.15422 (0.825)	0.00810 (0.019)	−0.16486 (0.374)	−0.01391 (0.037)	−2.01870 (1.785)
9	DIFNSL3	0.88829 (0.500)	−0.00518 (0.012)	0.05359 (0.228)	−0.01618 (0.022)	−2.14449* (1.091)
10	DIFAMN4	−0.96105 (0.423)	−0.00459 (0.011)	0.19482 (0.204)	−0.01714 (0.020)	2.69375* (0.977)
11	DIFAMSL4	−0.64223 (0.710)	−0.00963 (0.018)	0.17577 (0.342)	−0.02281 (0.033)	2.11581* (1.641)
12	DIFNSL4	0.46199 (0.431)	−0.01564* (0.011)	0.06307 (0.206)	−0.00324 (0.020)	−0.71335 (0.991)

*Indicates significance at the .10 level. Standard errors appear below each coefficient.

DEP. VARIABLE = Change in willingness to publish resulting from a specified reduction in the standard of proof, e.g., DIFAMN1 = difference (DIF) in willingness to publish when standard of proof is reduced from actual malice (AM) to negligence (N) in Scenario 1.

CIRSMS = Percent of circulation accounted for by street and machine sales.

AVGDIR = Average daily (Monday–Friday) circulation.

COMPETS	SUED	PAYDAM	SITXXX	SITXXX2	R^2	$\bar{R}^2$	F
0.05196 (0.251)	−0.13716 (0.213)	−0.34317 (0.280)	0.47835* (0.107)	−0.02571* (0.011)	0.40	0.37	14.371*
−0.16315 (0.322)	−0.28334 (0.273)	−0.62632* (0.359)	0.79139* (0.137)	−0.01816* (0.014)	0.69	0.68	49.14*
0.11099 (0.271)	−0.18919 (0.230)	−0.42574 (0.302)	0.68954* (0.107)	−0.02611* (0.012)	0.56	0.54	27.99*
−0.34062* (0.256)	0.44265* (0.219)	−0.53711* (0.286)	0.58927* (0.197)	−0.04919* (0.016)	0.11	0.06	2.57*
−0.50007 (0.540)	0.68784* (0.462)	−0.81391 (0.603)	1.29782* (0.415)	−0.10138* (0.033)	0.09	0.05	2.14*
−0.29899 (0.388)	0.28163 (0.329)	−0.19495 (0.434)	0.96950* (0.247)	−0.08507* (0.019)	0.12	0.08	2.91*
−0.30075 (0.247)	0.17642 (0.210)	−0.55123* (0.274)	0.33187* (0.125)	−0.02392* (0.012)	0.10	0.06	2.48*
−0.87749* (0.485)	0.03168 (0.413)	−1.05142* (0.539)	0.92547* (0.245)	−0.06920* (0.023)	0.16	0.12	4.12*
−0.42735* (0.297)	−0.15024 (0.252)	−0.34607 (0.329)	1.03655* (0.127)	−0.09561* (0.012)	0.29	0.26	8.86*
−0.33866* (0.265)	0.49950* (0.225)	−0.71607* (0.297)	0.32292* (0.128)	−0.02717* (0.012)	0.13	0.09	3.37*
0.04033 (0.445)	0.88557* (0.379)	−1.33760* (0.499)	0.80195* (0.216)	−0.06597* (0.020)	0.15	0.11	3.84*
−0.43173* (0.269)	0.39687* (0.228)	−0.52423* (0.300)	0.86631* (0.122)	−0.08103* (0.011)	0.24	0.20	6.83*

POPMKT = Population of market area.
PCTMKT = Market penetration (ratio of circulation size to population of market area).
COMPETS = 1 if paper faces competition; 0 otherwise.
SUED = 1 if paper was sued for libel in last fifteen years; 0 otherwise.
PAYDAM = 1 if paper paid award for damages; 0 otherwise.
SITXXX = Willingness to publish under higher standard of proof.
SITXXX2 = SITXXX squared.

SITXXX and SITXXX2 were included as regressors to test for an inverted-U response based on willingness to publish under the higher standard. The expected signs of the coefficients on SITXXX and SITXXX2 are positive and negative respectively. Measurement of the chilling effect when the paper has been sued and has paid damages in the past, relative to the omitted class (not sued), is made via the coefficient sum on SUED and PAYDAM in table C.2.

Logistic regressions were used to identify variables that can distinguish between chilled and non-chilled categorical states. The dependent variable CHILL is defined as 0 when a reduction in the standard of proof does not result in a change in willingness to publish and 1 when it does.

TABLE 3.C.2: Significance of Coefficient Sum (SUED and PAYDAM)

Eq.	Sum	Standard Error[a]
1	−0.48034	0.302
2	−0.90966*	0.387
3	−0.61492*	0.327
4	−0.09445	0.310
5	−0.12607	0.653
6	+0.08667	0.470
7	−0.37481	0.295
8	−1.01974*	0.580
9	−0.49631	0.355
10	−0.21657	0.318
11	−0.45203	0.534
12	−0.12736	0.323

[a] Calculated from the $\hat{\sigma}^2 (X'X)^{-1}$ matrix.
* Indicates significance at the .10 level.

Application of least-squares regression in this situation may yield predicted values of the dependent variable which are greater than 1 or less
than 0. Also, with a binary dependent variable, the assumption of hom-
oskedastic disturbances in least-squares regression is untenable. As a
result, logistic regression, which constrains the response to the unit
interval, is used. Logistic regression is preferred to the linear discriminant model in our application since several of the explanatory variables

TABLE 3.C.3: Logistic Analysis—*Actual Malice to Strict Liability
in Scenario 2*

Variable	Coefficient	Stand. Error	χ^2	Probability
INTERCEPT	−0.33612	0.428	0.62	0.432
PCTMKT	2.99701	1.450	4.27	0.039
CIRSMS	−0.02001	0.014	2.18	0.140
PAYDAM	−0.42768	0.410	1.09	0.297

Model Chi-Square 9.81
(−2Log Likelihood Ratio)

Probability 0.020

TABLE 3.C.4: Logistic Analysis—*Actual Malice to Negligence
in Scenario 4*

Variable	Coefficient	Stand. Error	χ^2	Probability
INTERCEPT	−2.06086	0.624	10.92	0.001
PCTMKT	3.13639	1.505	4.34	0.037
PAYDAM	−1.19176	0.643	3.43	0.064
COMPETS	0.56414	0.505	1.25	0.264

Model Chi-Square 10.11
(−2Log Likelihood Ratio)

Probability 0.018

are qualitative, violating the multivariate normality assumption of discriminant analysis. Since the logistic model is highly nonlinear in the parameters, problems of convergence to the final solution, using the maximum likelihood approach, can become very serious as the model size and model complexity increase. The results of two logistic regressions are found in tables 3.C.3 and 3.C.4.

ACKNOWLEDGMENTS

The authors acknowledge the research assistance of Elinor G. Sorkin and the constructive comments of Eli Noam, Mark Nadel, Frederick Whatley, Esq., and John Treacy. Grants from the College of Business and Administration and the College of Liberal Arts of Wright State University made possible a portion of this research.

NOTES

1. 376 U.S. 254 (1964).
2. *Id.* at 279.
3. *Id.* at 279–80.
4. Associated Press v. Walker, 388 U.S. 130 (1967).
5. Gertz v. Robert Welch, Inc., 418 U.S. 323 (1974).
6. See Kalven, "The New York Times Case: A Note on The Central Meaning of the First Amendment" *1964 Sup. Ct. Rev.* 191.
7. 418 U.S. at 390.
8. See Riley, "Lawyers Who Look for Libel" 7 *National Law Journal* 1 (May 27, 1985).
9. Massing, "The Libel Chill: How Cold Is It Out There?" *Columbia Journalism Review* 31 (May–June 1985).
10. See Soloski, "The Study and the Libel Plaintiff: Who Sues for Libel?" 71 *Iowa L. R.* 217, 220 (1985) in which the results of a survey of libel plaintiffs between 1974 and 1984 reveal that seven out of ten cases were against the news media and that among media defendants, newspapers were the medium most often sued. Only one-fifth of the plaintiffs said they sued for money. Most said they sued to restore their reputation or punish the media.
11. Bezanson, "Libel Law and the Realities of Litigation: Setting the Record Straight" 71 *Iowa L. R.* 226–230 (1985).
12. *Westmoreland v. CBS, Inc.,* 82 CIV. 7913, S.D.N.Y.; *Sharon v. Time, Inc.,* 83 CIV. 4460, S.D.N.Y.
13. Bernstein, "Chilling Effect" or Fresh Air?, *N.Y. Times,* December 23, 1984, at E 13; Cain, "Protect Us From A Reckless Press," *ABA Journal,* July 1985, at 38.
14. Two of the authors have shown elsewhere that the *Sullivan* rule affords the press too much protection and that a new standard, known as "relaxed liability," is required based on the economic theory of the second best. See Renas, Hartmann *et al.*, "Toward

an Economic Theory of Defamation, Liability, and the Press" 50 *Southern Economic Journal* 451 (Oct. 1983) and Hartmann, Renas *et al.,* "Relaxed Liability: A Proposed New Standard for Defamation by the Press" 22 *Am. Bus. L. J.* 93 (1984). The authors have elsewhere compared defamation laws in the United States and the United Kingdom. See Hartmann and Renas, "Anglo-American Defamation Law: A Comparative Economic Analysis" 5 *Journal of Media Law and Practice* 3, London (April 1984).

15. Prosser, *Handbook of the Law of Torts* (1941) (1971).

16. *Id.* 4th edition (1971) at xi.

17. *Id.* at 819.

18. *Prosser and Keeton on the Law of Torts* (1984).

19. "Developments in the Law—Defamation" 69 *Harv. L. R.* 875, 904-5 (1956).

20. *Id.* at 906 (citing as *contra* Swindler, *Problems of Law in Journalism* 99 [1955]).

21. Concerning defenses of privilege and truth and retraction, *see generally* Developments, *supra* note 19 and Prosser and Keeton, *supra* note 18, Sections 114–116A.

22. Prosser, *supra* note 15 at 819–20 (1971).

23. 376 U.S. 254 (1964).

24. "Justice Black and the First Amendment, 'Absolutes': A Public Interview" 37 *N.Y.U. L. Rev.* 549, 557–58 (1962).

25. *Supra* note 5 at 356 (Douglas J., dissenting).

26. Chi-square goodness-of-fit tests were conducted. Pacific and Western regions were combined to ensure that expected cell frequencies were sufficiently large.

27. The proportion of papers that were chilled in none, one, two, three, and all four of the scenarios was also calculated. When the standard is changed from malice to negligence, 41.3% of the papers were not chilled in any of the scenarios. The proportion chilled in only one of the scenarios was 21.4%; the proportion chilled in two of the scenarios was 17.5%; and the proportion chilled in three of the scenarios was 15.5%. Approximately 4% of the papers were chilled in all four of the scenarios. When the standard changes from malice to strict liability, 29.1% of the papers were not chilled in any of the scenarios. The proportion chilled in one, two, three, and all four of the scenarios is 14.6%, 23.8%, 20.4%, and 12.1%, respectively.

28. Papers will behave as non-collusive oligopolists. The argument regarding carrier delivery vs. street sales may also apply to the impact of competitive environment and circulation size on the chilling effect.

29. Deductibles in libel insurance policies have been increasing. See Greenwald, "Libel Cover Crisis Puts the Press on U.S. Media," *Business Insurance* (March 10, 1986) at 19.

30. Tests of significance of the coefficient sum on SUED and PAYDAM, which deal with this issue, are found in Table 3.C.2.

31. Regressions were estimated in which willingness to publish under malice was the dependent variable.

32. The peak chilling effect is determined by setting the first partial derivative of DIFXXX with respect to SITXXX equal to zero and solving. The second partial derivative is negative, ensuring a maximum.

33. This point came out in a conversation with Henry Kaufman, General Counsel, Libel Defense Resource Center. Since virtually all of the papers sampled carried such insurance, and since this factor was found to be statistically insignificant, the insurance variable was dropped from the least-squares and logistic regressions.

34. Regional dummy variables were included as regressors in the least-squares and logistic regressions. Also, chi-square contingency tests were performed.

35. See *supra* note 14.

36. See, e.g., Bose Corp. v. Consumers Union of U.S., Inc., 80 L Ed 2d 502 (1984)

and Philadelphia Newspapers, Inc. v. Hepps, 89 L Ed 2d 783 (1986) (dissenting opinions). The Burger Court was sometimes regarded as anti-defendant in libel actions. See Garbus, "New Challenges to Press Freedom," *New York Times Magazine,* (Jan. 29, 1984) at 34.

37. Hustler Magazine v. Falwell, —US—107 Sct 3259, 97 LEd 24 788.

38. Jacobson v. Brown & Williamson, NDI 11, 644 FSup 1240, 1988.

PRINCIPLE AND INTEREST IN LIBEL LAW AFTER *NEW YORK TIMES:*
An Incentive Analysis

Ronald A. Cass

I. TWO FACES OF LIBEL

The law of libel has two very different faces. The first is derived from
tort law. The issues there are the appropriate restraints on defamatory
speech and the efficient mechanisms for imposing those restraints. The
argot of efficiency analysis, if still not entirely common, provides an
accepted vocabulary for this discussion. The other face of libel law is
turned toward the First Amendment. The discussion of First Amendment concerns rarely includes explicit reference to dollar-valued costs
and benefits. Rather, the high ground of principle provides the terms for
this discussion, arguing the requisites of free speech or the virtues of
vindication. Some commentators acknowledge that competing principles
must be "balanced," and all commentators in fact engage in this practice,
but many find the concern with economic costs and benefits misguided.
The two different faces of libel, thus, produce two divergent conversations: one about economic interests among economists and economically
oriented law professors, the other about First Amendment principles
among other law professors, representatives of the news media, and
plaintiffs' lawyers.

It should come as no surprise that the conversations are not so
radically different in substance as in the lexicons they employ. The
disparate focal points, however, draw the attention of torts discussants
more quickly to some issues, of First Amendment discussants more
readily to others. Discussion of *New York Times v. Sullivan*[1] illustrates
the manner in which the conversations diverge. At the same time,
examination of the decision's impact reveals how First Amendment
principle and economic interest interact. Specifically, analysis of the
incentive effects of *New York Times* reveals the economic basis for
various parties' reactions, including parties that speak in terms of principle.

II. CHANGE OF *TIMES:* COMPETING EXPLANATIONS

A. Libel Litigation: Old and New

Before *New York Times,* libel law was a subject of tort law, but not a subject of serious constitutional concern.[2] The Supreme Court's dicta on the subject for some time had suggested that defamatory speech did not trigger First Amendment scrutiny.[3] Unlike its treatment of obscenity, the Court had not followed these dicta with efforts to define the excluded speech.[4] The law of libel thus was left to state control. The prevailing rule was strict liability with various privileges to defame.[5]

The Supreme Court's *New York Times* decision changed the law of libel in several ways. First, the decision explicitly brought defamatory speech within the ambit of First Amendment protection.[6] Second, it mandated proof of falsity as a constitutional prerequisite to a public figure's recovery for defamation.[7] Third, the decision forbade recovery by defamed public officials without clear and convincing proof that the defamatory statement had been made with "actual malice."[8]

Two decades later, the intensifying debate over libel law has begun to focus on the effects of this last change of *Times,* especially its effects on suits against news media.[9] So far as one can tell from available data (admittedly a qualification of no small significance), the post-*New York Times* world is characterized by suits against media defendants that have risen quite steeply in amounts claimed, in mean jury awards (when damages are awarded), and in the costs of litigation (at least to defendants), although the proportion of these suits won by plaintiffs is extraordinarily low.[10] The explanations for these changes vary with the author's perspective.

B. View from the First Amendment

Commentators writing from the First Amendment tradition suggest that non-economic factors provide the key.[11] One such author blames increased juror distrust of news media for the increase in awards.[12] This explanation of high awards may identify one factor behind initial jury awards, which are more likely than ultimate judgments following appeal to favor plaintiffs. It is not, however, a complete explanation of the current state of libel, as it does not address the relative infrequency of trials or of ultimate recoveries against media defendants.

Other commentators writing from the First Amendment vantage opine that the low incidence of pro-plaintiff judgments reflects libel plaintiffs' general uninterest in the financial stakes of litigation: these plaintiffs seek to establish not the fault of press defendants (the legal requisite of recovery) but the falsity of the critical press statement.[13] The plaintiffs also sue out of irritation with the institutional press' unresponsiveness to informal complaints.[14] These plaintiffs assertedly are represented by attorneys who are unfamiliar with libel law and over-optimistic about the success of these cases.[15] Plaintiffs are said to succeed simply by getting their case to court and are able to do so at a cost only a fraction of that spent on average by libel defendants.[16]

There is much to this explanation, but it leaves many questions unanswered. Why, for instance, do libel defendants settle cases only one-half to one-sixth as often as all tort defendants,[17] given the high costs of defense and the plaintiffs' lack of interest in financial recompense? Why do plaintiffs pursue litigation through trial if they cannot get a favorable judgment? Why would plaintiffs' attorneys systematically misperceive the chance of success? And why are jury libel awards rising rapidly, if plaintiffs are generally uninterested in recovering money judgments?

C. Views from the Economics of Tort

Commentators more familiar with economic tort analysis offer a different view of the developments in libel law, focusing first on the effect of the *New York Times* actual malice rule on the probability of recovery.[18] Raising the threshold of recovery, as *New York Times* did, naturally reduces the incidence of recovery. This change would not provide anything approaching an efficient deterrent to harmful speech unless the size of adverse judgments increased.[19] For various reasons, however, juries and judges have increased damage awards, raising the noncompensatory component of damage awards either expressly through punitive damages or implicitly through inflated compensatory awards.[20]

Whether these changes on balance reduce or enhance efficiency depends on the degree to which the changes in probability of recovery and in award level are correlated and on the extent to which the rule change increases or decreases litigation costs. Presently available data do not suggest a clear answer. The increase in damage awards might be too great or too small to provide optimal deterrence of false statements. So, too, the economic implications of *New York Times* for litigation costs are not entirely clear. As damage awards rise, costs per case should be expected to increase (as these are in part determined, under standard assumptions of rational expectations models, by the award at issue), but the total level of process costs might rise or fall.[21]

This economic explanation, thus, does not produce strong conclusions about the change in libel law, and it also leaves subsidiary questions

unanswered. If expected damage awards drive litigation, why are so
many unsuccessful claims not only brought but also litigated to judgment?[22] Why are defense costs so much greater than plaintiffs' costs?[23]
Why do press defendants lose much less often than other defendants?[24]
If economic factors such as the level of libel damage awards and the
probability of recovery explain the structure and costs of libel litigation,
how do they account for the very different reactions of judges and juries?
Notably, judges, who see many more libel cases than any juror, generally have played the role of reducing large jury libel verdicts, and post-
New York Times libel law has restricted plaintiffs' ability to secure
noncompensatory damages.[25]

At the heart of the tort-economic argument is the relationship between the probability of recovery and the expected award if damages
are obtained. Economic analysis suggests that these are not wholly
independent variables. The governing legal rule, of course, affects the
probability of recovery in any class of cases, but litigation outcomes are
not entirely a function of the governing legal rule. As others have
argued, it seems likely that the success rate of litigation is also a partial
variable of litigation expenditures, which in turn are partially determined
by the litigation stakes and partially by the expected probability of
recovery.[26] Lowering the chance of recovery will decrease the overall
expected return from plaintiffs' litigation expenditures, but it also will
increase the marginal return from some litigation expenditures.[27] Given
that expenditures help determine outcomes, the magnitude of the decline in libel plaintiffs' recovery rate cannot be thought to follow simply
and directly from the rule change without explanation of parties' incentives to invest in litigation. The coincidence of a decline in the proportion
of plaintiffs recovering damages and an increase in defendants' litigation
costs calls for further explanation.

D. Integrating Analysis: Litigation Stakes and Litigation Incentives

What is at issue in libel suits, money or principle? The starting point for
inquiry into the effect of *New York Times'* impact should be the stakes
of the litigation, the point where First Amendment and economic tort
analysis part company. The tort discussion equates litigation stakes to
potential recovery, a common simplifying assumption of economic analysis.[28] First Amendment analysis finds the assumption misplaced:[29] plaintiffs declare that they seek vindication, not dollars;[30] spokesmen for the
media assert that the media fight for freedom, not money.[31] Resolution
of this argument is critical to understanding the nature of libel litigation,

to assessing the effect of the *New York Times* actual malice standard, and to evaluating proposals to change the law of libel.

Examination of the arguments from tort and First Amendment analysis reveals that each has insights to contribute. Surely, as tort analysis assumes, the prospect of gaining or losing money has a great deal to do with how much is invested in prosecuting and defending libel actions.[32] But the parties' claims to act in large measure without respect to the expected award of money damages have considerable substance as well.[33] Both analytic strands must be integrated to obtain a complete picture of the dynamics of libel. The following sections are a preliminary effort to incorporate into an economic analysis the First Amendment claims that much more is at stake in libel litigation than the possible transfer of damage payments from defendant to plaintiff. Part III offers an incentive-based explanation of these claims, focusing on the special interest of news media defendants.

III. THE MEDIA'S INTEREST IN PRINCIPLE: NON-AWARD STAKES

A. Plaintiffs and Defendants: Award and Non-Award Stakes

For centuries it has been a staple of libel law that information reflecting adversely on someone's performance in his chosen profession harms the subject's reputation, causing tangible, if not always provable, harm.[34] The law reflected an assumption that the information would be credited by some listeners, that some would act on the basis of the information, and that efforts to rebut the information would not be fully successful at dispelling its effect. (Imagine a lawyer running a series of full page advertisements under the bold-face heading "John Jones is not an incompetent attorney.")[35] The information thus is expected to have a negative effect on the subject's earnings from his profession.[36]

Although not traditionally a matter of concern for libel law, the same supposition should hold true for libel defendants: information reflecting adversely on a libel defendant's professional performance should reduce that defendant's earnings as well. This is one determinant of the stakes in libel litigation; judgment for the plaintiff may (partially) reinflate his reputation, but in many instances it will damage the defendant's. Interest in the reputation effect of litigation is a "non-award" stake, separate from the stake each party has in the damage payment explicitly at issue. Another source of non-award stakes, which can be found in any litigation involving a "repeat-play" party,[37] is the expected effect of this litigation on future suits involving that party. For non-media defendants, there is no reason to believe any greater non-award stake is present in libel suits than in litigation generally.[38] For these defendants, expected transfer payments from them to plaintiffs are a suitable proxy for litigation stakes.

For news media defendants, however, the libel case entails significant non-award stakes. Understanding how losing a libel case can impose additional costs on a media defendant is critical to evaluation of the effect of *New York Times* on libel litigation.

B. Pre-*Times* Libel Stakes

Before examining the peculiar effects of *New York Times* on the non-award stakes of news media defendants, the non-award costs to media defendants from a pre-*New York Times* libel judgment are identified. One source of additional costs to media defendants from loss of a libel suit is the encouragement of additional litigation against the defendant.[39] In addition, loss of a libel case can impose three sorts of reputation-related costs on media defendants beyond those explicitly captured by the damage award.

1. Media Consumers' Demand

The first reputation-related non-award cost derives from reduced consumer demand for the defendant's product. News media are in the business of selling information in packages differentiated by various features: quality and quantity of information, the particular types of information presented (political news, sports, business news, advertising, and so on), the accessibility and attractiveness of its presentation, and price.[40] Consumers do not, of course, all place the same value on every feature. Their varied tastes will lead to their varied choices among news media products, according to the value they place on particular features. And within the group of consumers for any given news product, differences in the importance attached to particular features will cause different sensitivities to changes in that product. Some newspaper readers, for example, may value sports coverages especially; others may prize a comic strip. Changes will affect these groups in very different ways.

Of particular concern here are those consumers who are especially concerned with one aspect of news quality—its veracity. Most news consumers, even within this group, undoubtedly have poor information on the news they buy. But in a competitive market, some well-informed news consumers probably "comparison shop" for news in the same way especially price-conscious or quality-conscious shoppers do for other goods.[41] These news consumers, whose demand is sensitive to the veracity, or more commonly the *perceived* veracity, of news products, police the quality (and price) of information even if the average consumer is relatively insensitive to, or uninformed about, news veracity.[42]

An adverse libel judgment provides such truth-sensitive consumers with additional information about the truth of the media defendant's product. The information can be useful even when it is ambiguous.

An adverse judgment under pre-*New York Times* law indicated simply that the defendant published a false and defamatory statement. In a world of imperfect information, truth-sensitive consumers would have been uncertain exactly how to evaluate this fact. After all, some errors are expected even from the most accurate sources. News reporting, like other businesses, has an optimal error rate above zero errors.[43] A publication that never prints a falsehood must compromise on some other desirable feature of a news publication: its information will not be so new, its topics not so interesting or important; or it may not be written so well, presented so attractively, or available so inexpensively as it otherwise might have been. For each publication, there is some ideal (profit-maximizing) compromise among these features.[44]

When a news media defendant is found to have published a false statement, consumers who are sensitive to truth may not find that fact very informative. They might conclude that the defendant's truthfulness is within the range they expected or, on the same evidence, they might conclude that the defendant is less truthful than they previously thought.[45] Even if adverse libel judgments are less frequent than the number of errors a given truth-sensitive consumer thinks acceptable, the consumer may believe that only a relatively small number of errors produce libel suits. Hence, when there is any adverse judgment, such consumers may conclude—perhaps unfairly—that the defendant publishes false information more frequently than they previously had thought.[46]

Although the number of truth-sensitive consumers who draw one or the other of these conclusions cannot be known, some consumers should conclude after an adverse libel judgment that the defendant is less trustworthy.[47] It seems probable that these consumers will not be willing to pay so much for the defendant's publication as before, and some may stop buying it altogether. When that happens, of course, the publication's earnings will decline. The potential magnitude of this effect is discussed further below.[48]

2. Media Labor Costs

Libel judgments also affect news media employees. Those who work for news enterprises—at whatever level—are concerned about their professional reputations, which inevitably are tied to the reputation of the enterprise for which they work.[49] Future employers and peers will, like truth-sensitive consumers, probably infer—again, fairly or unfairly— some greater incidence of falsity after an adjudication of falsity.[50]

Critical to the inference drawn from the adverse judgment is the relative frequency of adverse judgments among comparable news enterprises. The reaction of peers is likely to be based on better information than that of consumers. This has two contradictory effects, increasing the proportion of the group that is aware of the judgment but, given greater confidence in *ex ante* assessments, reducing the likely impact of new information.[51] As with the consumer reaction, the direction, but not the magnitude, of the reaction among journalists to an adverse media libel litigation can be predicted: reputation of the defendant and its employees for truthful reporting will decline. The adverse reputation effect on employees raises labor costs to the enterprise: to get or hold the same caliber employee, the enterprise now must, at the margin, pay more.

3. Media Information Costs

Finally, the reputation of a news enterprise for veracity will affect the cost of acquiring accurate information.[52] Some news sources—those who most value faithful transmission of their information—will discriminate in favor of news enterprises with higher expected fidelity to the truth. At least some of these news sources—most probably those who are frequent sources of significant information—may be both aware of and responsive to judgments of false publication. These sources will therefore also perform a role in monitoring media accuracy.

C. Post-Times Libel Stakes

For all three groups—consumers, employees, and sources—the *New York Times* case should change the effect of an adverse media libel judgment. A finding of false publication will increase doubts about a publication's performance on one important aspect of its job and reduce its value.[53] But the fact of false publication in and of itself does not necessarily suggest serious professional deficiencies; after all, some false statements should be expected.[54]

The natural inference from a finding of publication with actual malice is different. The statement about a losing libel defendant sued by a public official (later public figure) that became implicit in the judgment after *New York Times* is: "defendant is the sort of person (company) who not only prints false information; he does so *knowingly* or *recklessly*." Publication with actual malice suggests that the defendant has little respect for the truth, which allows the further inference that the veracity of its stories will generally be subject to much more serious question than that of one who merely made a false statement in good faith.[55]

All three monitor groups should react more strongly to this signal. Even if members of the monitor groups do not know or do not fully understand the exact meaning of the actual malice test, the *New York Times* rule indicates that a much more serious delict is necessary for adverse libel judgments and that such judgments implicate not just the veracity of the statement but the process of producing it.[56] Thus, for readers interested in veracity, there will be a greater decline in the expected value of the defendant's product.

No effort has been made to test this hypothesis through rigorous empirical research, but rudimentary data on changes in circulation for recent press libel defendants suggest that, temporarily at least, adverse judgment indeed is followed by a decline in sales.[57] The effect of the more serious adverse finding in libel cases after *New York Times* should also lead to greater downward adjustment in defendant's expected veracity for media employees and sources. This change then will make it that much more difficult to attract and retain qualified employees and to secure information from reliable sources at any given level of investment.

Additional, although similarly inconclusive, evidence of the increase in non-damage stakes wrought by *New York Times* can be found in the difference between the news media's response to accusations of falsity and their reaction to post-*New York Times* libel suits. Outside the context of a threatened suit, most media enterprises are willing, although obviously not eager, to publish corrections or retractions (acknowledging prior publication of false or misleading statements).[58] In contrast, media enterprises' response to the threat of post-*New York Times* libel liability frequently shows no room for compromise. Some media representatives have declared that they never settle a libel suit, at least not a public figure suit.[59] And a greater number of media enterprises have loudly proclaimed the important constitutional principles involved in libel suits against press defendants.[60]

These declarations could simply be strategic ploys by repeat-play defendants who intend to deter similar suits from being brought. After all, the no-settlement strategy at times is observed in other contexts where a large number of nuisance suits—suits for injuries too insubstantial or claims too unlikely to prevail to be worth the full cost of suit—are expected. Both the no-settlement announcement and the invocation of principle can serve this strategic function by raising the expected cost of the suit. Following such pronouncements, compromise is especially embarrassing to defendants, thus committing them, and consequently the plaintiff, to see the litigation through.[61]

The very fact that gives impact to such statements—these statements burn one of the few bridges affording a defendant inexpensive escape from the cost of suit, and especially of meritorious suits[62]—however, suggests the possibility that something beyond the possible future damage payments is at issue. Settlement often is a useful money-saving device, especially where large sums are at issue.[63] But if the admission of possible liability itself is costly, the normal economic advantages of settlement will be outweighed in many cases. Indeed, settlement, while undoubtedly saving defendants some of the expected costs of trial, may impose higher non-award costs than court-decreed liability, since settlement does seem to carry an implicit admission of fault.[64]

A related reason for the resistance to settlement in the libel context and for the public assertion that any libel damage payment threatens the very existence of a free press also suggest the role of the press' interest outside the award in this case, its *non-award* interest. These press moves signal not just potential plaintiffs but also other potential monitors —consumers, journalists, and news sources—that the press enterprise does not expect ever to be liable and that it attaches great importance to avoiding liability. The enterprise conveys the message of such confidence it will not commit the sort of error at issue as to be willing to lock itself into a position from which there is no easy escape if a meritorious suit is brought. This signal itself may be valuable enough to overcome the cost of the pronouncements' limitation on litigation strategy. The benefit of such announcement effects depends on the value of the enterprise's veracity to its monitors and the extent to which that value would decline if there were a finding of liability.

D. Effect of *Times*: Efficient Markets and Agency Costs

This analysis posits two principal assumptions as the basis for analysis of *New York Times'* impact on non-award stakes. First, it supposes the existence of groups at the margin of the larger categories of consumers, employees, and sources, who have information respecting, and are sensitive to, media enterprises' veracity. Second, it assumes that there is a response by these groups to media libel judgments, increasing substantially after *New York Times*.

The analysis need not suppose strong equation of the non-award costs actually represented by these effects with a news enterprise's evaluation of its non-award stakes. In a standard equilibrium model of competitive markets, the economic costs of reduced demand and increasingly costly factors of production (inputs) would define the non-award stakes in any case.[65] The media defendant would behave as though the amount at issue in a libel suit exactly equaled the predicted dollar costs to the news enterprise from the potential damage award and the reactions of monitor groups. Agency-cost analysis[66] suggests that if the response to libel suits lies in the hands of employees-managers who are imperfectly monitored *within* the enterprise and whose individual interests (personal standing and marketability within their profession) are implicated in such suits, the enterprise might overreact to libel suits and overinvest in avoiding adverse judgment.[67]

The choice between these divergent assumptions—efficient, profit-maximizing reaction or inefficient overreaction to post-*New York Times* libel suits—is not critical to the analysis here. It will, however, affect the magnitude of the effects discussed below and, thus, will affect ultimate evaluation of the *New York Times* rule, matters I do not reach in this chapter.

In sum, as First Amendment discussion stresses, to understand libel, one must begin with appreciation of the non-award stakes in libel litigation. First Amendment discussion errs, however, in suggesting that the presence of important non-award interests makes the economic-tort analysis of libel irrelevant. Economic-tort analysis provides useful insight into both the effect of non-award interests on libel litigation and the probable distribution of non-award stakes. Even if non-award stakes derive in part from unknown forces that induce belief in moral principles, the non-award interests represented by invocation of constitutional principle in arguments over media liability for libel also have roots in economic forces. And, regardless of their source, these interests usefully may be incorporated in an economic-tort model. The general implications of non-award interests are explored in part IV below, while effects on various plaintiff and defendant classes are explored in parts V and VI, respectively.

IV. ECONOMICS OF LITIGATION: THE EFFECT OF NON-AWARD STAKES

A. General Effects: Rational Expectations, Media Investment, and Libel Plaintiffs

1. Basic Effects and Litigation Models

Several characteristics of post-*New York Times* libel litigation flow from the increase in non-award liability stakes to press defendants. First, treating investment in litigation as a positive function of stakes, the investment in defense of libel suits will increase dramatically for some press defendants even if the damage award at issue remains small. Second, the added investment by these defendants decreases the chance of recovery against them for any given investment by plaintiffs, with a consequent reduction in the number of judgments against such defendants.[68] Third, reducing the chance of recovering money damages promotes a shift toward increased use of libel litigation for other purposes. If some press defendants are motivated largely by non-award stakes, one would expect less litigation against them by plaintiffs who are motivated solely by the prospect of obtaining money damages and relatively more litigation by those plaintiffs who, like the media, have substantial non-award interests at stake.[69]

The last effect is premised on the assumption that asymmetric stakes incline litigation outcomes in favor of the party with the greater interest. The model of litigation that supports this prediction posits rational decisions regarding expenditures, designed to secure returns the expected value of which equals or exceeds the sums invested in litigation.[70] The last dollar spent should just equal the expected value of its contribution.[71] The model also posits that litigation expenditures influence outcomes positively—the more a party invests relative to the opposing party, the greater his chance of success.[72]

Under one variant of this model, litigation outcomes are directly determined by expenditures which in turn are directly determined by stakes.[73] Were that so, suit should almost never be against the press by a public figure libel plaintiff interested only in the damage award.

The more likely variants of this model assume that litigation expenditures are only a partial determinant of outcomes.[74] Further, litigation expenditures are assumed to exhibit declining marginal utility past some point.[75] The party with the larger stake—by definition, the party with the greater non-award stake—remains the more likely victor even under this less extreme set of assumptions, but some lower-stakes parties prevail.

2. Plaintiffs: High Stakes and High Awards

Under this model of litigation, plaintiffs generally will be expected to lose libel suits against press defendants. The few plaintiffs who win should, for two reasons, be among those with larger damage award stakes. First, other things being constant, the larger the damage award at issue, the greater the probability that the plaintiff's stake will approach the defendant's.[76] Also, as the stakes, and derivatively the investment in litigation, increase, it is increasingly probable that the defendant's expenditures on litigation will pass the point at which the returns from litigation investment begin to decline.[77] Thus, given the relatively large non-award stakes for legitimate press defendants under the actual malice rule, plaintiffs interested solely in the award will sue such defendants only if a very large damage award is a realistic possibility.

Under the same assumptions about litigation, plaintiffs with non-award stakes will find libel litigation relatively attractive (compared to parties with purely financial stakes).[78] Two different effects explain the advantage of non-award interests. First, the non-award stakes will justify increased litigation expenditures which will raise the probability of success. Only plaintiffs with very high non-award stakes are likely to invest amounts comparable to the press-defendant's litigation expenditures. This may translate into a substantial proportion of whatever libel recoveries there are against the legitimate press seeming to be uneconomical —the plaintiff may spend on the litigation sums well in excess of the damage award even where the award far exceeds the norm for tort litigation.[79]

At the same time, there should be a relative increase in suit by those for whom the damage award is not a necessary part of litigation success. For some plaintiffs, non-award success may come from developments related to the course of the litigation. These are discussed more fully below in part V. For other plaintiffs, the filing of suit itself confers a benefit. Just as the press' invocation of principle or declaration of strategy may have important announcement effects for monitor groups, so, too, plaintiffs may secure announcement effects from the filing of suit:[80] the more expensive a suit becomes and the lower the success rate for a class of plaintiffs, the greater the effect. The announcement implicit in the filing is that the plaintiff has so strong a case that he is willing to pursue his suit despite the obvious obstacles. This is not to say that the demand curve for litigation is positively sloped; litigation rates should fall, not rise, as the price of litigation increases. For certain plaintiffs, however, the benefit from filing suit is positively related to the cost (or at least the perceived cost) of the litigation.[81]

The benefit to plaintiffs from filing or from prosecuting a low-probability libel suit flows largely from the press' non-award stake in the litigation. Once the basis for liability is narrowed to exclude reasonable publication of falsehoods, a finding of liability against a member of the legitimate press is itself newsworthy.[82] By extension, the mere prospect of liability—the challenge to press credibility—becomes a matter worthy of news coverage. The extent to which the filing or trial of the case itself is publicized will differ with certain fairly obvious variables: the circulation and prestige (reputation for veracity) of the press defendant, the notoriety of the plaintiff, and the notoriety of the asserted libel.[83] In at least a subset of libel cases against the legitimate press, the press' stake in avoiding non-award costs of libel assures sufficient publicity to alter both parties' course of action.

B. Paying for Suit: Attorneys' Incentives

The publicity attendant to press libel cases also has an effect on plaintiffs' counsel opposite to the general impact of *New York Times*. Given the role of legal counsel as the necessary intermediaries for suit, their incentives as well as the parties' incentives merit examination.

1. Before *Times:* Fees for All

Counsel may agree to represent clients on a straight-fee, contingency fee, or *pro bono* basis. In a pre-*New York Times* world, the contingency fee would have been the most likely arrangement for financing litigation. Parties were expected to be motivated in the main by direct financial gain from the suit.[84] The parties generally would not pursue a case without the expectation of a probability of recovery that justified the necessary expenditures. Budget constraints and limitations on sale of legal claims would have prevented some parties from committing to finance the litigation directly.[85] Attorneys, who enjoy a comparative advantage in evaluation of claims and in pooling claims to reduce the risks associated with suit, however, generally would underwrite suit through acceptance of contingency fees in cases for which suit seemed justified on the basis of the expected value of the award and the costs of suit.[86]

In contigency-fee litigation, the expected recovery by the attorney, not the client, must equal or exceed the expected costs of suit.[87] Therefore, not all suits that are fair bets will be taken by attorneys on a contingency fee basis. Nonetheless, in a competitive market for lawyers' services, most suits for which expected costs are marginally less than the expected recovery should be pursued on a contingency fee basis. Clients should be willing to trade away increasing shares of the recovery as the probability of recovery falls and the cost of suit rises, and attorneys should, at varied contingency rates, be willing to take nearly every cost-justified action.

There are, however, two impediments to a perfect market in lawyers' services that preclude this result in some cases: competitive constraints[88] and the substantial transactions costs involved in securing representation (including the costs to attorneys of eliciting and evaluating information concerning the facts of the plaintiffs' case as well as the costs to plaintiffs of obtaining information concerning attorneys' fees and quality of ser-

vice). Still, the contingency fee works sufficiently well to be the dominant payment arrangement for most ordinary tort litigation, including
pre-*New York Times* libel suits.[89]

2. After *Times:* Representation Without Taxation?

The actual malice standard, by changing the expected value of libel
claims, alters the attractiveness of contingency fee arrangements. The
lower probability of recovery and higher cost of litigation under an actual
malice rule reduce the expected value of many claims, thus making
economically motivated (award-based) litigation unattractive for many
cases. As this is the pool of cases suitable to contingency-fee financing,
the actual malice rule decreases the number of cases that will be brought
on a contingency fee arrangement. The existence of substantial non-
award stakes for press defendants further reduces expected value of
claims and further increases costs, leaving few cases for which a contingency fee would seem to provide reasonable compensation for the attorney. At the same time, the increased riskiness of contingency fee
litigation should cause attorneys to decline more cases that might be fair
bets to be remunerative.

The immediate effect of the *New York Times* decision, thus, is to shift
away from contingency fee to other bases of representation. Plaintiffs
who accrue substantial non-award benefits from litigation and who are
substantially free from budget constraints may pay attorneys on a direct,
fee-for-time basis to undertake libel litigation that is not justified by the
expected value of the award.[90] One would expect that most other puta-
tive plaintiffs would not be able to secure representation.[91]

A by-product of the press' non-award stake in libel litigation does,
however, facilitate contingency-fee or even *pro bono* representation of
plaintiffs in some circumstances.[92] The press considers press libel litigation newsworthy, some cases especially so—this assures counsel that if
the case goes to trial the plaintiff's attorney will be in the news. The
legal profession, even when competing aggressively for business, traditionally has eschewed formal advertising. This tradition is changing, but
the change is mainly affecting the "fast-food" end of the law business.
The opportunity for effective, public advertising of high-quality legal
services has been and remains restricted.[93] The availability of highly-
visible news coverage, mentioning counsel by name, should present a
significant inducement to representation of some clients whose cases of
themselves do not promise a fair chance of financial reward.[94]

After *New York Times,* then, libel litigation should exhibit a characteristic that has largely been confined to criminal law: increased willingness
of attorneys to undertake uneconomical representation in hopes of sub-

stantial future gains from a case's public notoriety.[95] *Pro bono* representation and contingency fee arrangements in cases in which the plaintiff is almost certain not to gain a damage award should therefore increase significantly following adoption of the actual malice rule.[96] The press' characterization of its interest in terms of principle further facilitates uneconomical litigation by providing a ready explanation for the attorney's promoting the set of opposed principles: assuring press responsibility, protecting the objects of press scrutiny from unfair, untrue, and unsupported accusations, and safeguarding the public from the misinformation that an unaccountable press might too readily provide.[97]

At the same time, the press spotlight on libel litigation offers the potential to create a few highly visible stars in the libel defense bar.[98] These attorneys even more than their opposite numbers are likely to become closely associated with the principles advocated by the press. The small number of libel cases, their high stakes, and the cost of information about lawyers' views and talents should assure that a select group of defense lawyers is able to earn rents from their libel practice.[99] This should be especially true so far as the litigation enterprise becomes theater rather than law.

C. Summary

The importance of a reputation for veracity to the income of press defendants transforms the public figure libel case after *New York Times* from a relatively routine contest between legal adversaries into a battle of competing principles and high stakes players where gains and losses cannot be measured solely in terms of the court-ordered transfer of dollars among the parties. The predictable responses of lawyers, plaintiffs, and defendants to incentives shaped by the actual malice rule reinforce the notion that reputation can command substantial economic value. The initial press reaction to a threat to reputation and income begins a series of responsive moves each of which increases the stakes and alters the rules of the libel game. The game, now defined largely by non-award stakes, plainly is not the same for all plaintiffs nor for all defendants. Distinctions among the potential parties are explored below.

V. PLAINTIFFS' STAKES: POLITICIANS AND OTHER FIGURES

A. Sorting Out the Effects: the Central Case

The facts of *New York Times* reveal the particular set of plaintiffs, defendants, and circumstances that informed the Court's analysis. The plaintiff in *New York Times* was an elected official associated with locally popular policies.[100] The defendant was the quintessential representative of the legitimate press, a paper foreign to the locality of suit and associated with locally unpopular views.[101] The *New York Times* court assumed that in these circumstances the local legal system would err frequently in favor of the plaintiff, that the class represented by the defendant would substantially alter its behavior in response to these errors, and that this response would generate significant social costs.[102]

The actual malice rule was fashioned to guard against the predicted errors and press reaction to them in these particular circumstances.[103] That standard was soon extended to other public figures, on assumptions similar to those relied on in *New York Times,*[104] but the contest between a popular, elected public official and an unpopular though widely respected press defendant has remained the central image sustaining the rule.[105]

The standard formulated with special reference to elected officials and press defendants does indeed have special application to these groups. This section focuses on the distinction among plaintiffs, and the succeeding section elaborates the rule's different effects on defendants.

B. Politicians: Plaintiffs' Corps, *Times'* Core

1. Wealth, Power, and Non-Award Stakes
The requirement that public figure plaintiffs prove actual malice with convincing clarity reduces the chance of recovery and increases the cost of suit against the press by all public figures, including elected officials.[106] The elevation of non-award stakes' importance, however, makes it peculiarly likely that certain public figures, disproportionately including elected public officials, will continue to pursue libel litigation against the press. Although the *New York Times* standard should reduce the number of suits filed by elected public officials, it should have less effect on this class of suits than on litigation by other public figures.

The intuition here can be presented in the following syllogism. After *New York Times,* press libel suits will be motivated largely by non-award interests.[107] For plaintiffs, this interest will be a subset of reputation interests: the idiosyncratic interest in reputation, which is not reflected in lost income and, thus, often is not a basis for damage awards, defines plaintiffs' non-award stakes.[108] As a class, elected public officials are likely more often than other plaintiffs to place a high value on this interest. Therefore, elected public officials will be less deterred from suit.

The systematic bias toward higher idiosyncratic value on reputation for elected officials is inherent in the difference between elective office and other high-visibility employment. Elective office generally entitles the officeholder to a relatively modest salary compared with those of public figures as a class. The emoluments of office consist instead principally of power over important decisions now being made and of greatly enhanced prospects for the exercise of power over future decisions.[109] The power exercised by elected officials—their ability to influence important decisions—generally seems disproportionate to the pay they receive. For many private sector employees, the value of the decisions they make appears congruent with their pay: if a large sum of money, for instance, is at stake, the employer will pay a significant fraction of it to the employee whose decisions help determine its gain or loss. For elected officials, this is not the case. Officials overseeing multi-billion dollar public enterprises may receive far less than mid-level managers of much smaller private firms.

The importance of officials' decisionmaking authority is reflected in the fact that private parties will pay a great deal to influence the decisions of quite modestly paid officials.[110] The expenditure of large sums on election contests is but one aspect of this private investment in influencing official decisionmaking.[111]

The combination of modest salary and high dollar value to others of the work done by elected officials creates substantial nonmonetary rewards for officeholding and attracts office-seekers who place a high value on those non-monetary rewards. It is common to hear of office-seekers willingly exchanging greater salaries elsewhere for lower salaries as elected officials. Outside of this context, the exchange of more money for less is exceptional—how often have you read of one company luring a key executive from another firm with a substantial pay cut? The point is not that elected officials are indifferent to money; it is by no means clear that the choice to seek elected office reduces the candidate's expected lifetime earnings and less clear that successful pursuit of elected office does so.[112] Yet, unlike other publicly notable occupations, little of the personal value of officeholding is captured in direct payments during the term of office.

If a principal component of libel damages is lost income resulting from the libel,[113] elected officials are in a peculiar position. A serious libel that adversely affects a plaintiff's electability may force an official from office but leave him with a higher income than before. The provable money damages from injury to an elected officeholder's reputation, therefore, often will be smaller and the non-money damage to the official often will be larger than for other public figures. Of course, elected officials need not place a high value on non-monetizable injury to reputation. Some elected officials possess relatively little power and probably derive slight idiosyncratic reward from office.[114] Just as plainly, some non-officials do place a high idiosynacratic value on their reputation.[115] As a class, however, elected officials seem most likely to value injury to reputation well above the harm to income.

2. Notoriety and Electoral Advantage

The non-award stakes to elected officials are further increased by the linkage of officeholding and notoriety. Holding an elected office plainly increases the officeholder's notoriety—and notoriety seemingly increases an individual's chance of holding elected office. The coverage given by the press to libel suits against them thus should act as a magnet for suit by elected officials, other things being equal. The opportunity for increased media coverage should encourage elected officials, relative to other public figures, not only to file libel suits more often but also to pursue the suits more vigorously, assuring continued coverage of their claims.[116]

Of course, the "other things being equal" assumption slips a rabbit into the magician's hat. Other things seldom are equal. For instance, the notoriety derived from libel litigation need not be beneficial; even if notoriety generally aids candidates, certainly some sorts of media coverage must hurt. Spiro Agnew was more notorious after he was accused of bribe-taking and bid-rigging than before. Richard Nixon received considerable notoriety from the Watergate episode, Gerald Ford from his pardon of Nixon, and Jimmy Carter for his handling of the Iranian hostage crisis. It is difficult to believe that any of this publicity helped enhance these officals' reputations or their electoral prospects (Nixon, already in his second term as President, may be excused on this score).

The non-award inducement for elected officials to sue press defendants for libel, hence, must take account of three considerations, beyond probability of press coverage, that help define the costs and benefits of suit. These considerations can be framed as practical prerequisites to suit by elected officials. First, the press coverage accorded the suit must not be expected to contain new damaging information or to increase substantially the audience for the initial critical statement. Second, the suit must provide the official the opportunity to make at least a semi-plausible claim of vindication. And, third, the suit must provide better opportunities for useful publicity than alternative courses of action.

The first of these additional requirements—damage minimization—limits probable libel suits to challenge of critical press statements that received considerable notice. Such notice may be due to the seriousness of the charge, such as allegations of criminal behavior by officials.[117] Or it may be due to the visibility of the event that spurred the critical statement, for instance, the killings at the Sabra and Shatila refugee camps in Lebanon.[118] The damage minimization requirement prevents suit where the initial libel merely scratched the surface of a more serious problem. Politicians' concern with damage minimization also gives an incentive to the press to let officials know that any libel suit will elicit a vigorous press effort to uncover new critical information.

The second added requirement—recoupment of reputation—has more ambiguous implications. If an election is imminent, the mere filing of suit may provide an opportunity for enhancement of the official's reputation sufficient to justify suit. The official-politician reaps the benefit of the suit's announcement effect on constituents and, if he is successful or his case is factually weak, he can quietly let the suit languish afterward.[119]

More generally, however, the ability to recoup one's reputation will rest on the opportunity to publicize information that casts doubt on the initial critical speech. In this regard, no elected official worthy of his peers' respect would be limited to a requirement that he prevail in the courtroom or even that he prove falsity, much less fault. The legal requirement of *New York Times* that the official prove with convincing clarity the defendant's knowing or reckless publication of information that is false and defamatory diverges sharply from the far more modest political imperative that the politician be able to use the suit to his advantage. Officials who can with a straight face claim, for example, that they took bribes as a secret ploy to catch the briber[120] certainly can make use of litigation that merely reduces the clarity and credibility of a critical statement without anything approaching *New York Times* proof of falsity and fault.

The third added requirement—relative advantage—merely restates the standard inquiry of economic analysis, "compared to what?" Some officials enjoy myriad opportunities for low-cost, high-yield publicity. For high-ranking incumbent officials such as the President, suit offers very little that cannot be attained at less cost (in his own time, in risk of further reputational damage, and so on) in other ways. Officials with enough superior publicity-generating alternatives may choose simply to stand above the libel, to answer it in a press conference and not pursue it in court, or to follow other alternative strategies. The value of publicity from the suit is far greater to less publicly visible elected officials.

Consideration of relative advantage suggests that libel suits may be most valuable to would-be elected officials who are not now in office. The interests and behavior of nonincumbent candidates for elected office generally resemble those of elected officials, but these other candidates generally enjoy fewer alternatives for repairing damage to their reputations than do incumbent officials. The greatest difference is between those incumbent officials in very high office (such as Governors or U.S. Senators) who have considerable opportunity to manipulate the levers of power in ways that generate favorable publicity and nonincumbent aspirants to such office (including former officeholders whose taste for office is not yet sated).[121] Non-incumbents, thus, should value even more than incumbent elected officials the opportunities for useful publicity that press libel litigation affords and should be relatively more inclined to file suit, to press for trial, and to pursue appeals.[122]

3. Suits and Slack: General Effects and Criticism of Official Performance

These three additional, practical prerequisites to suit by political office-holders or aspirants indicate that, although the *New York Times* rule will be less effective at preventing suit by current or prospective elected officials than by other classes of public, it clearly will prevent many suits by officials. For reasons given earlier, the rule generally will preclude suit where only financial and not political gain is to be had.[123]

The additional requirements, which define political gain, suggest that once prospects for financial gain are removed an important class of cases is quite unlikely to be brought. Press statements critical of an elected official's performance in office, even to the point of intimating incompetence, are apt to be poor candidates for post-*New York Times* suit. This sort of criticism is not likely to leave readers or auditors with so clear an impression as, say, a charge of criminal misconduct.[124] Litigation to correct misstatements about official performance probably will generate publicity that supports a broader perception that there are serious questions concerning the official's competence than existed as a result of the asserted libel. Even if no new, damaging, specific information emerges, the opportunity to enhance one's reputation through litigation over such libels is slim. Apart from the *New York Times* actual malice standard, the law excludes statements of opinion on public issues from the ambit of potentially libelous statements, which makes recovery for such criticism difficult.[125] The pragmatic non-award considerations that largely inform officials' decisions here work hand-in-glove with the law in discouraging suit.

The cases in which the non-award stakes of elected officials and candidates continue to support suit, then, are those involving relatively well-known charges of specific, significant delicts. These are also the cases in which subsidized representation is likely. To some extent, nonparties may be expected to underwrite the cost of suit in these cases. The substantial investment private parties make in influencing the election of official decisionmakers suggests an interest that could be tapped to subsidize litigation efforts. Insofar as libel litigation is able to boost reelection prospects for an official or increase his influence on government decisions, the suit may be an attractive investment to parties who do not have a direct stake in the damage award. In addition, litigation over charges of serious official misconduct may be especially attractive for representation on a contingency fee arrangement.[126] These cases combine high stakes for both the official-plaintiff and the press-defendant and involve matters already of public note. In sum, these cases are tailor made for publicity and, therefore, are ideal vehicles for counsel interested in such exposure. Counsel's interest in these cases as well as the plaintiff's often will militate against settlement and in favor of continued litigation, even where the decision to press on seems, strictly in terms of expected recovery in the case, economically unsound.[127]

C. Other Public Figures

The other groups of plaintiffs who may be classified as public figures probably will have high non-award stakes less often than elected officials and non-incumbent aspirants. Other public figures, hence, should be more discouraged by the cost of post-*New York Times* libel litigation against the press. Nonelected public officials generally (although certainly not invariably) may be expected to have low public visibility, greater congruence between job value and pay, and less to gain from increased public notoriety (as opposed to notoriety within a specialized audience of potential government or nongovernment employers) than elected officials.

The principal exception here will be those nonelected officials who aspire to higher, elected office.[128] Performers, like candidates for elective office, seem to benefit greatly from general notoriety, but the benefit is reflected in their earnings and, derivatively, should be reflected in damage award stakes.[129] Corporations and corporate managers probably benefit less from general notoriety; certainly they capture more of their interest in income and reflect the interest in damage award stakes. Particular corporate managers may place high idiosyncratic value on their reputation and may find an expensive, unremunerative libel suit a good investment both for its initial announcement effect with a particular group of associates or peers and for its subsequent exposure of factual errors or editorial doubts.[130] As a class, however, managers seem to gain less apart from the damage award than elected officeholders or candidates. The actual malice rule, hence, discourages litigation least by the very group with which it was directly concerned.

VI. PAYING FOR PRINCIPLES: DEFENDANTS' INTERESTS

A. Differential Effects: The Bipolar Media Model

As with plaintiffs, defendants also are affected differently by the actual malice rule. Also, as with the differential effect on plaintiffs, the distribution among media enterprises of benefits and burdens consequent to adoption of the actual malice standard may not be those anticipated by the Supreme Court.

The simple explanation of *New York Times'* expected impact begins with a division of media enterprises into two polar groups: (1) those that occasionally and unknowingly publish false statements but, for non-liability reasons, never do so with actual malice, and (2) those that, but for liability, would publish principally statements they know to be false. If judicial processes are error-free and plaintiffs are interested solely in financial gains from suit (damage recoveries less expenses), the *New York Times* rule clearly benefits the high-care media. There would be no judgments against those enterprises; potential plaintiffs would not sue, and these enterprises would incur no costs from the actual malice rule. Low-care media enterprises, in contrast, would lose all suits for which they exercise less than *New York Times'* mandated level of care. These enterprises would be forced to internalize the costs of their harmful, false speech unless or until they increase their level of care.

The reality, of course, diverges significantly from the assumptions on which this explanation is based. Media enterprises do not divide neatly into the invariably careful and the irretrievably sleazy. Plaintiffs sue for reasons other than immediate financial gain.[131] And judicial processes sometimes err.[132] There is, thus, some possibility that even the most careful media enterprises will bear some cost from libel litigation under the actual malice rule.

When the costs and benefits of the change to an actual malice standard are sorted out, it may be that all media enterprises gain. I do not here pass judgment on the social value of *New York Times,* an undertaking that requires more information on the magnitudes of the various effects discussed here than current data provide.[133] My endeavor instead is to provide the framework for analysis and to assess some of the probable distinctions among plaintiffs and defendants. The effects analysis used here suggests that, unlike the stark bipolar analysis, the greatest gains

from *New York Times* probably do not accrue to the media enterprises
that use the highest level of care in their discussion of public figures.

B. Effects Analysis and Defendant Classes

1. Variables and General Effects

The impact on any given media enterprise of the *New York Times* shift
to an actual malice rule will depend on the relative values attached to six
variables under each alternative legal regime: the cost of damage awards,
non-award costs, defense costs, risk costs, costs of investment in care,
and gains or losses from altering the amount of speech produced.[134] The
more readily observed effects of *New York Times* that may benefit the
press are not directly relevant to this analysis. These observable benefits, decreased incidence of damage awards against media defendants
and decreased incidence of suit,[135] do not correlate exactly with the
factors that determine the rule change's effect. It is possible, for instance, that even with fewer suits and fewer adverse judgments, total
defense costs and total money damages paid by a particular class of
media defendants increase.[136] Available data are not sufficiently complete to resolve argument over the exact dimensions or, in some cases,
the direction, of less readily observed effects.

Nonetheless, certain general conclusions seem plausible. The *New
York Times* rule, of itself, undoubtedly reduces, first, the number of
adverse judgments and, second, the number of suits against all media
defendants. Third, the rule probably reduces total award costs. The
most significant effects question, however, cannot be answered from
this information alone. One also needs to know the level of non-award
costs, actual and potential, and then the level of defense costs before
one can assess the other effects of *New York Times*. The total amount
of damages and non-award losses realistically at issue in suits against the
press largely will determine defense costs[137] and also will substantially
affect both risk costs and behavioral responses (alteration in the standard
of care or level of speech activity).[138] Total (actual) non-award costs
may increase for some defendants and decrease for others. Certainly,
as discussed in part III above,[139] the potential non-award cost of a
liability finding rises substantially for some press enterprises. Distinguishing those enterprises that face substantially higher actual potential
non-award costs from those that do not largely explains *New York Times'*
disparate impact on media enterprises.

2. Media Defendants: Separating the Classes

In analyzing *New York Times*, the media will be segregated into three
rough groups: high care, low care, and hybrid. The first group on

average employs a high level of care respecting the truth of reported statements.[140]

The second group is relatively unconcerned with the truth of its reports, functioning principally as an entertainment medium, albeit through stories that intrigue because they involve real people and because there is at least some basis for believing the stories true. The low-care media probably are not unaffected by proof that they published false information, but the demand for their product, and, derivatively, the cost of employee and source inputs, are not closely tied to credibility.

The third group is composed of media that on average use a high level of care but that also compete in an entertainment market. For these hybrid enterprises, the liveliness of presentation and the "shock value" of the news are more substantial influences on demand than for the first category, while veracity is a far more important demand determinant than for the second category. Concomitantly, the other monitors of this hybrid group's behavior—managers, employees, and sources—will be more sensitive to variations in the level of the enterprises's veracity than will monitors of low-care media performance and, perhaps, more sensitive to variations in income (for other reasons) than high-care media.[141] The foremost example of such a hybrid enterprise is CBS's *60 Minutes*, a news program competing against entertainment programs for a mass audience, well in excess of the normal audience for successful news media. Local television investigative news reports are similar, though on a much smaller scale. Some newspaper columns also may fit in this category. To a great extent, of course, all news media exhibit some mixture of entertainment and informational functions; the hybrid category is intended to separate those enterprises that, while subject to substantial monitoring for veracity, are unusually affected by the constraints of competition in the entertainment market.

3. Veracity Variability: Reputation and Reality

This categorization recognizes that media differ in levels of care and in incentives to use care. Both the high care and hybrid categories can be classified as belonging to the "Legitimate Press," defined as the class of press enterprises for which credibility substantially influences consumer demand and, immediately or indirectly, the enterprise's income and influence. Among these press enterprises however, the mixed news-entertainment media may be particularly susceptible to pressures that can produce publication with *New York Times* actual malice.

Apart from the variation between categories, this division, framed in nonpolar terms, recognizes that some variation in the level of care is likely within any one press enterprise. This inhouse variation occurs in large part because the enterprise is not an integrated whole but rather a collection of individuals with different interests, information, pressures, and responsibility; it is costly for organizations, and especially for large organizations, to ensure that information is routed to the appropriate actors, to constrain the authority of subordinate employees, or to identify in advance those who on occasion will act with less than the optimal level of care.[142] Thus, while the least careful enterprise often will exercise care well above what *New York Times* requires, decisionmakers at the most careful enterprise at times may act with actual malice.

Overall, the assumption here is that, at least down to some level of tolerance, an enterprise's reputation for veracity will be related to its average level of care. Variance from the average is discussed but is not treated here as a distinct variable, although for any enterprise and any given average level of care variance from the average may have significant consequences for reputation and, independently, for suit. Analogously, a reputation for ill health may be tied to the number of severe illnesses or injuries an individual suffers, rather than to his average level of health. The number of pathological cases bears no necessary relation to the general level of health. The common supposition, however, is that good health and few pathologies more often than not go hand-in-hand That simplifying assumption is indulged here.

C. High-Care Enterprises

The defendants on which the *New York Times* Court focused were these: traditional, respected, credible news media, especially those with national audiences that might be subject to local antipathy. These are the media that, as a group, probably have not only the highest average level of care but also the lowest variance.

1. Defense and Discontinuity: The Change to Actual Malice

The high-care media almost never lose under the actual malice standard.[143] But, as that high level of care is employed for reasons divorced from liability, they probably are insulated from relatively few adverse judgments by the change in standard. The dollar value of judgments precluded for most enterprises in this category is uncertain, but for the largest high-care press enterprises the dollar value of even a modest reduction in adverse damage awards might be considerable.[144] Because there are almost never adverse judgments against these enterprises, the actual malice rule may generate non-award savings for them as well. Whatever costs—in decreased readership, revenues, influence, employee satisfaction, and the confidence placed in them by sources—

formerly attended adverse libel judgments disappear along with the decline in judgments.

The critical difference, however, is the actual malice rule's introduction of a sharp discontinuity in the yield from investment in avoiding liability. Prior to *New York Times,* damage awards were more frequent and smaller, and the non-award costs of loss also were smaller. By raising the award and non-award costs of liability, *New York Times* increased the marginal return from defense expenditures for suits of any given (exogenous) probability of success; with more at stake, a slight increase in the chance of winning is worth more.[145] The increase in marginal return must be set off against the decrease in the probability of success effected by *New York Times.* The data on settlements and defense expenditures suggest, however, that the increase in potential non-award costs to press defendants dominates the decrease in probability of plaintiffs' success attributable to the actual malice rule, apart from changes in the parties' litigation expenditures.[146]

It follows that high-care defendants will spend more on defense of each suit after *New York Times,* perhaps in excess of the dollar value of awards prevented. A rational defendant would not pay more than $50,000 to avoid a one-in-four chance of a $200,000 liability judgment, but the defendant will spend up to $300,000 if the adverse judgment is predicted also to cause a $1 million loss in advertising and subscription revenues or in costs of retaining (in their current level and quantity) employees and sources.[147]

The increase in marginal return of defense expenditures aimed at preventing an adverse judgment in a given case, thus, may explain burgeoning defense costs. But, given an offset for the reduced probability of loss, this is not apt to be a complete explanation.

2. Non-Award Costs and Non-Judgment Goals

The rest of the explanation for rising defense costs may be that the press defendant's expenditures are in part directed at ends other than preventing an adverse judgment in the immediate suit. One goal of defense expenditures may be to prevent trial, rather than loss. If non-award costs of *liability* have increased since *New York Times,* so should non-award costs of *trial* insofar as trial now raises questions over the care a defendant uses as well as the truth of the statement at issue. It appears in fact that sales of high-care press defendants' products decline during libel trials,[148] and monitor groups other than consumers also seem likely to react to disclosures during trial. The negative effects of trial should be especially pronounced if the reputation of the defendant is strong and if scrutiny focuses on defendant actions in a pathological case, one in which normal, healthy defenses against faulty publication fail.

Beyond its immediate value in preventing trial or liability, a defense investment also has value insofar as it raises the possibility of success in future litigation—as by the creation of favorable precedent—or otherwise decreases the likelihood of future litigation. The effort to influence the incidence of litigation is particularly important if the filing of suit conveys announcement effects.[149] The other side of the benefit a plaintiff receives from filing suit is a cost to the defendant: the filing, of itself, raises some question as to defendant's veracity.

Of course, expenditures that help a defendant win the instant suit also pay future dividends: future litigation will probably decrease following a decrease in the likelihood of plaintiffs' success. Expenditures on litigation defense, however, can reduce filings another way. Some defense investments not only influence a litigation's outcome but also directly raise plaintiffs' litigation costs. A variety of defense strategies—refusal to answer interrogatories, delayed responses to discovery requests, aggressive pursuit of discovery requests directed at the plaintiff, frequent filing of motions respecting either process issues or ultimate judgment —should be useful to this end.[150] High-care press defendants, having the greater stakes in libel litigation, should invest more heavily than others in such strategic behavior as well as in announcements indicating the level of the press enterprise's resistance to suit, which signal the probable level of defense investment if suit is filed.

These cost-raising defense expenditures are especially attractive for high-care press enterprises in light of the likely incidence of suit motivated by plaintiffs' non-award stakes. A subset of these suits—those tied to the publicity given the libel suit—should be brought principally against legitimate press defendants (those in the high-care and hybrid categories). These defendants' greater non-award stakes cause them to take such suits more seriously and, therefore, to publicize them more. The *New York Times, Time* magazine, or CBS is likely to give far more coverage to a libel suit against it or a fraternal member of the legitimate press than will *The National Enquirer, The Star,* or *Penthouse* to a similar libel suit against one of those publications.[151]

Further, apart from the *amount* of publicity the suit draws, press enterprises are especially good targets for suit by elected officials because of the *type* of publicity. Legitimate press enterprises often are associated with particular political ideologies.[152] The focus on "hard news," and the inevitable choices of coverage and tone inherent in that focus, make perceptions of ideological bias common. Put the label liberal or conservative in one column and the names *New York Times, Boston*

Globe, Washington Post, Newsweek, Chicago Tribune, Los Angeles Times, Time, Commentary, and *The National Review* in another column; few consumers of news will have difficulty matching the two columns. Suit against a press enterprise associated with an ideology that is unpopular with a politician's constituency not only gains extra publicity at home; it also sends the message that the official has been libeled for illegitimate, ideological reasons and is willing, for the sake of principle, to incur the cost of fighting back. The *New York Times* case itself is illustrative. Sullivan was not engaged simply in litigation over a personal injury; he was vindicating the honor of the South against the hostile, liberal, northern press that carried anti-South statements.[153]

The incidence of suit, thus, will not decline so much for high-care press enterprises as the incidence of damage awards. Consequently, even if both award and non-award costs have declined for these enterprises since *New York Times,* aggregate defense costs, as well as costs per suit, may rise. Whether high-care enterprises in fact face an overall increase in expected costs for libel defense is difficult to say without better data. Certainly, the demonstrable increase in defense expenditures per suit does not conclusively demonstrate this effect. The most that can be said at this point is that an increase in total libel defense costs for high-care press enterprises is possible.[154]

3. Insurance

More clearly, the press' non-award incentives to contest libel litigation in combination with the non-award incentives of some plaintiffs to pursue libel suits alters the insurance picture for press enterprises. Normally, assuming risk aversion, the risk of a large loss would be reduced by purchasing insurance, thereby pooling risks and increasing certainty respecting loss.[155] Given their likely defense expenditures, high-care press enterprises will find insurance of libel defense costs quite expensive.[156] The resistance of these press defendants to settlements deprives the insurer of an important means of controlling cost.[157]

This same factor will increase, albeit less dramatically, the liability component of insurance cost. The insurance company will want to retain flexibility to buy out of a suit when the price seems right.[158] Nonetheless, when other factors are considered, the price of liability-only insurance for high-care press enterprises probably will lie below that for other types of liability with equal expected loss. One standard concern of insurers, moral hazard (the risk that insured parties will increase their exposure to liability judgments),[159] is abated considerably in libel insurance for high-care press enterprises given these entities' non-award incentives to control their exposure to liability, through both *ex ante* regulation of their activities and *ex post* investment in contesting litigation. So long as insurers are willing to distinguish between high-care and low-care media enterprises,[160] this should limit the former's insurance costs for libel liability.

4. Behavioral Effects: Level of Activity and Level of Care

Another element in analyzing the effect of *New York Times* is the potential behavioral response. If the potential non-award costs of libel litigation rise sufficiently to induce increased defense expenditures and at the same time reduce the attractiveness of insurance against such costs to high-care press enterprises will those enterprises modify their behavior to avoid suit? Would they take more care in screening information, or would they avoiding certain kinds of statements or certain kinds of stories?[161] Neither response seems likely except in extremely small doses.

The marginal return from increased care, like the marginal return from defense expenditures, might be thought to rise if potential non-award costs of libel litigation increase more rapidly than expected award costs decrease. The analogy, however, is inapposite. To hold, the analogy's terms must be comparable: while litigation costs are critical to litigation investment, the question relevant to the return on investment in care is whether expected costs from *false critical statements* (rather than from *litigation*) increase after *New York Times*. This requires data on the total expected costs (award, non-award, defense, and risk costs) associated with false statements critical of public figures. If total costs decline for high-care enterprises after *New York Times,* the litigation-derived incentive to use care will be reduced. Declining costs from such false statements are at least plausible because the incidence of suit by public figures declines under the actual malice rule and because the number of suits is not a direct function of the number of false statements either before or after *New York Times.* False, critical statements prompt some suits; others are triggered by the promise of recompense; and still others by criticism, false or true.[162]

Given present information on the costs associated with *New York Times,* there is no firm basis for predicting a change, and especially not for predicting an increase, in the average level of care among high-care news media. *New York Times* may well have prompted a change, however, in the variance of care taken by the press in making different types of critical statements. On the one hand, the media may worry less about public figures who seem unlikely to place high non-monetizable value on reputation and especially those whose monetizable value also is low.[163] Statements about these public figures now may be scrutinized less than was the case before *New York Times*. On the other hand, by raising the stakes for cases in which suit is most likely, such as accusation of serious wrongdoing by politicians,[164] *New York Times* may encourage additional care in those cases. Although not certain, these seem the most likely changes in high-care press behavior.

The alternative response to altered liability is a change in the level of activity. One such change, decreased speech, is the principal focus of First Amendment concerns. This is the "chill" so often referred to in discussion of First Amendment values.[165] The likelihood of a change in the level of speech activity after *New York Times* depends, *inter alia,* on the public's demand for speech critical of public figures, the capacity of any given enterprise to capture that public value, and the cost of producing the information at a given level of care.

The calculus of production of critical speech is complicated by the fact that the production of critical information probably has substantial common costs with production on noncritical information about public figures, which in turn has substantial common costs with production of information generally respecting public issues. The presence of substantial common costs may make the marginal cost of producing critical speech relatively low for those that are in the business of reporting on public issues, a description generally applicable to high-care press enterprises. The adjustment of these enterprises' relative investment in critical and other speech will be responsive to the marginal costs and price elasticities of demand for each.[166]

For high-care press enterprises, criticism of politicians is the only category for which a decrease in speech is a possible reaction to *New York Times,* given the likely incidence of suit by actual or would-be officials for reasons extrinsic to the ultimate judgment and the cost of such suits. Several authors have argued that this sort of reduction in speech has indeed occurred and have offered some anecdotal support for this proposition.[167] It is, however, not at all clear that press speech critical of highly visible political officials has changed much since *New York Times*. One could speculate as to the reasons for apparent constancy in the quantum of speech critical of politicians. For instance, demand for such speech may be relatively price inelastic and thus affected less by changes in its cost than other speech. The oft-noted adversarial relationship between press and government may reflect a strong demand for privately produced critical information, perhaps a consequence of the fact that positive information is supplied by government in ample quantity. Such speculation, however, also provides no firm basis for conclusions respecting levels of press activity.

In sum, then, for high-care press enterprises *New York Times* produced ambiguous, and possibly beneficial, effects. Award and non-award costs probably declined. The increase in potential costs (especially potential non-award costs) drove up defense costs per suit and possibly in total. High-care press enterprises probably bear increased risk costs with respect to libel suit *defense,* but the change in risk costs for *liability* is uncertain and may have declined. No substantial behavioral effects can be established with confidence and perhaps none has occurred.

5. Big and Little, Better and Best: Special Effects

These various effects, it should be noted, will not affect all high-care enterprises the same. The categorization employed here segregates media enterprises principally by their average level of care and the influence of a reputation for veracity on the demand for and cost of the enterprise's product. As elaborated earlier, a publication's pre-suit credibility among the three monitor groups largely determines the non-award harm threatened to or suffered by defendant during libel litigation.[168] Credibility is not, however, the sole determinant of potential non-award harm.

In addition, non-award harm will be affected by factors that dictate how reduced credibility translates into reduced income. These other determinants of an enterprise's loss from reduced credibility are the availability of substitute sources of information, the shape of the enterprise's marginal revenue curve, and its level of earnings; better available substitute sources of information will increase consumers' responsiveness to changes in perceived veracity.[169] Given estimated economies of scale in newsgathering and dissemination,[170] it seems likely that national-audience publications will have better substitute sources than locally oriented media and thus will be more affected by changes in perceived credibility. Similarly, the steeper an enterprise's marginal revenue curve and the higher its earnings from the publication at issue, the greater the likely reduction in returns from any given decrease in demand.[171]

The shift in non-award incentives after *New York Times,* then, has its greatest affect on large-circulation, high-care, national media enterprises. Because of the threat of large costs from adverse judgment, these enterprises will bear the heaviest burden in defense costs and related strategic activity. Other high-care enterprises may get a "free ride" on the back of the large national news media's investment in discouraging suit and recovery.[172] The cost and duration of this ride will depend on the extent to which the large national firms' investment yields a perception among potential plaintiffs that libel litigation against any high-care defendant is expensive and generally nonremunerative. Indeed, as developed below, other media enterprises may come along for the ride as well.

D. Low-Care Enterprises

Ironically, the principal beneficiaries of *New York Times* on balance may be those media enterprises that use relatively little care in reporting, succeeding more by virtue of their style and capacity to shock, titillate, or intrigue consumers. At first blush, this may seem odd: these enterprises are likely both to generate a substantially greater proportion of false statements and to lose a substantially greater proportion of cases than will high-care defendants under a negligence or strict liability test.

Given the burden placed on plaintiffs under the *New York Times* rule, however, these media enterprises may be protected by the actual malice standard against adverse judgment considerably more often than high-care media. Even if publishers of these media are largely indifferent to the truth of their stories, proving that fact with convincing clarity along with the falsity of the statement is another matter.[173] Seldom will it be possible to demonstrate knowledge of falsity, and no mind-probe is available to measure concern or indifference; moreover, solid evidence of subjective doubt about a story's truth may be more difficult to come by in respect to enterprises that do not in fact care much about truth.[174] Low-care enterprises still should lose more cases, and a greater proportion of cases, than high-care enterprises. But the actual malice rule and precedents implementing it should confer a substantial benefit on these media in aiding their escape from liability.[175]

As the proportion of judgments against low-care media enterprises declines, the incidence of suit against them should fall correspondingly.[176] Indeed, if plaintiffs do not distinguish between the cost of suit (or probability of success) against high- and low-care enterprises, the number of suits might decline more than proportionately to the drop in recoveries, as the low-care defendants will not make the same investment in defense as enterprises with high non-award stakes.[177] The average award will rise, but that is the natural corollary of reduced probability of suit: a greater stake is necessary to justify the investment in litigations.

The low-care enterprises might face a more than commensurate increase in the size of potential damage awards if the shift to a fault-based standard encouraged an increase in punitive damages against defendants who seem to exercise peculiarly little care. The *New York Times* rule, in limiting recovery to cases of knowing or reckless untruth, does make the set of all recoveries much more congruent with the set of recoveries for which punitive damages might be available.[178] It does not, however, appear to have generated an increase in total punitive damages paid out by media defendants.[179]

Low-care media, thus, probably face lower total costs—award costs, non-award costs, and defense costs—after *New York Times* and may respond by decreasing care or increasing the amount of speech activity.[180] To the extent that these enterprises' coverage is skewed toward some group of public figures—for instance, entertainers—those individuals are likely to be subject to more, or less accurate, critical comment after *New York Times*.

E. Hybrid Media

The most interesting case is that of press enterprises that combine a reputation for veracity with a need to compete in an entertainment market. Protection against possible liability may be especially important for these news-entertainment hybrids. Combining the attention-getting instinct of entertainment-oriented media with the claim to veracity of the legitimate press, critical statements by these enterprises may be particularly damaging. As a result, both the likelihood of suit and the size of potential damage awards will be relatively high.[181] Moreover, insofar as the audience for libel affects the degree of harm,[182] the news-entertainment hybrids generally will benefit from *New York Times'* insulation more than standard high-care news enterprises.

Like high-care enterprises, hybrid media also will have very high non-award stakes in libel litigation, often exceeding those of high-care press enterprises. This may seem counterintuitive, as the monitor groups probably respond less to credibility variations for hybrid media than high-care media. Plainly, demand for the hybrids' product should be less affected by their credibility; after all, by definition demand for these media is substantially dependent on their entertainment value. (Contrast *60 Minutes* with the *Wall Street Journal*. My guess is that the ratio of production values to credibility as a demand determinant is considerably higher in the former). Similarly, managers, employees, and sources may be less concerned about credibility where entertainment values are recognized to loom larger, although the distinction between these groups' response to hybrid and high-care media is less certain. Even with proportionately smaller responses to signals of reduced credibility, however, the total dollar value of the changes in cost and income could be much larger for hybrid media. This most clearly is true for changes in demand, given that hybrid media appear to enjoy higher returns[183] and that substitute (entertainment) products are readily available.

These media, thus, should invest heavily in defense and litigation avoidance strategies.[184] While *Times'* benefit of insulation against liability has substantial value for hybrid media, they will pay a high price for it. These enterprises also should bear heavier noninsurable risk costs than other media, because they combine a disincentive to settle, high potential damage awards, and greater potential moral hazard in exposure to liability, born of greater financial rewards for surprising information about well-known individuals.

The behavioral implications of *New York Times* for these firms are unclear. The high stakes of libel litigation may increase the marginal return from behavioral adjustments in speech most likely to produce litigation (increasing care in some statements or decreasing the amount of critical speech), but the protection against damage awards may dominate an increase in other costs for most speech by these enterprises, leading perhaps to a decrease in the average level of care. For at least the better known hybrid media, the competing interests, defined by high returns from aggressive, critical speech and high risks from such speech, seem roughly balanced. So long as they maintain that balance, dramatic changes in their behavior are unlikely.

VII. CONCLUSION

The change in *New York Times* to an actual malice standard for public figure libels substantially altered the incentives of some press defendants to resist suit. This change most affects the highly respected, successful, national news publications the *New York Times* Court was trying to protect. The actual malice rule does protect these defendants by reducing the number of adverse judgments against them and possibly also reducing the sum of costs associated with speech critical of public figures. But by raising the potential costs of adverse judgments for these defendants, the *New York Times* rule induces them to make investments in litigation defense and related activities that consume a large portion of the savings conferred by the more press-protective rule. Elected government officials, the group of plaintiffs with which *New York Times* was directly concerned—indeed, the group whose potential power over the press lay at the heart of the decision[185]—are within the class of plaintiffs least likely to be deterred from suit by the rule.

Although these conclusions about the effect of the actual malice rule indicate that the Court probably misperceived some of the consequences of its decision, they do not necessarily suggest that the decision was unwise nor that some better rule is easily identified. Evaluation of the overall effect of the *New York Times* decision and its desirability requires careful disaggregation of factors that dictate the quantity and quality of information about public affairs that is produced. It also requires judgment as to the value of various changes consequent to *New York Times*. Any conclusion on this score is apt to be controversial if only because the necessary complexity of the analysis provides many opportunities for disagreement over premises as well as derivations from them. Analysis based on First Amendment concerns and analysis based in tort may lead in different directions on any of these issues. Both, however, should build on the common ground of recognition that the rule's effects flow in substantial measure from the inherent tension generated by a liability rule that is so highly press-protective that its invocation puts directly in issue a valuable asset of the press: its credibility.

ACKNOWLEDGMENT

I am indebted to Joseph Brodley, Ira Lupu, Mark Nadel, Richard A. Posner, Glen O. Robinson, Lawrence G. Sager, Warren Schwartz, Steven Shiffin, Kenneth Simons, and participants in the Boston University Law Faculty Workshop and the Georgetown University Law and Economics Workshop for helpful comments on a draft of this article, and to Meg Golodner and Susan Silberberg for research assistance.

NOTES

1. 376 U.S. 254 (1964).
2. For an extensive history of the development of libel law, *see generally,* C. Gregory & H. Kalven, *Cases and Materials on Torts* (1st ed. 1959).
3. *See, e.g.,* Beauharnais v. Illinois, 343 U.S. 250 (1952), (Justice Frankfurter's majority opinion stated: "[We] are precluded from saying that speech concededly punishable when immediately directed at individuals cannot be outlawed if directed at groups with whose position and esteem in society the affiliated individual may be inextricably involved. [Libelous] utterances not being within the area of constitutionally protected speech, it is unnecessary, either for us or for the State courts, to consider the issues behind the phrase 'clear and present danger.' Certainly no one would contend that obscene speech, for example, may be punished only upon a showing of such circumstances. Libel, as we have seen, is in the same class."); Chaplinsky v. New Hampshire, 315 U.S. 568 (1942), (Justice Murphy stated for the majority: "There are certain well-defined and narrowly limited classes of speech, the prevention and punishment of which have never been thought to raise any Constitutional problem. These include the lewd and obscene, the profane, the *libelous,* and the insulting or 'fighting' words." [Emphasis added]).

4. F. Schauer, *Free Speech: A Philosophical Enquiry* (1982); Kalven, "The Metaphysics of the Law of Obscenity," 1960 *Sup. Ct. Rev.* 1; Magrath, "The Obscenity Cases: Grapes of *Roth*," 1966 *Sup. Ct. Rev.* 7.

5. *See, e.g.,* Walker v. Bee-News Publishing Co., 240 N.W. 529 (1932); Oklahoma Publishing Co. v. Givens, 67 F.2d 207 (1925); *see also* W. Prosser, *The Law of Torts* 596–604 (2d ed. 1955); Franklin, "Winners and Losers and Why: A Study of Defamation Litigation," 1980 *Am. B. Found. Res. J.* 455 [cited as Franklin, Winners and Losers].

6. *New York Times,* 376 U.S. at 264–265; *see also* Franklin, Winners and Losers, *supra* note 5, at 458.

7. *New York Times,* 376 U.S. at 279–80.

8. *Id.*

9. *See, e.g.,* Bezanson, "Libel Law and the Realities of Litigation: Setting the Record Straight," 71 *Iowa L. Rev.* 226 (1985); Cranberg, "Fanning the Fire: The Media's Role in Libel Litigation," 71 *Iowa L. Rev.* 221 (1985); Lewis, "*New York Times v. Sullivan* Reconsidered: Time to Return to the Central Meaning of the First Amendment," 83 *Col. L. Rev.* 603 (1983); Smolla, "Let the Author Beware: Rejuvenation of the American Law of Libel," 132 *U. Pa. L. Rev.* 1 (1983); Soloski, "Who Sues for Libel?," 71 *Iowa L. Rev.* 217 (1985).

10. *See, e.g.,* Anderson, "Libel and Press Self-Censorship," 53 *Texas L. Rev.* 422, 435–36 (1975) (discussing high jury verdicts in libel cases); Barrett, "Declaratory Judgments for Libel: A Better Alternative," 74 *Cal. L. Rev.* 847, 857 (1986); Goodale, "Survey of Recent Media Verdicts, Their Disposition on Appeal, and Media Defense Costs," in Practicing Law Institute, *Media Insurance and Risk Management* (1985) [this book will be cited as *Media Insurance*]; Kaufman, ch. 1, *supra;* Lewis, *supra* note 9, at 608; Smolla, *supra* note 9, at 2–7.

The rise in cost of libel litigation since 1975 has been described as "an uncontrolled firestorm," Goodale, *supra,* at 86–89. For example, in the recent case, Westmoreland v. CBS 596 F. Supp. 1166 (S.D.N.Y. 1983), 601 F. Supp. 66 (S.D.N.Y. 1984), *aff'd,* 752 F.2d 16 (2d Cir. 1984), *cert. denied sub nom.* Cable News Network, Inc. v. U.S. District Court, 105 S. Ct. 3478 (1985), combined costs exceeded $10 million prior to settlement. *See* "A General Surrenders," *N.Y. Times,* Feb. 19, 1985 at A22, col. 1. *See also* Kaufman, *supra* ch. 1 ("it has been estimated that defense costs amount to 80% or more of the dollars spent by insurers of the media in libel cases. . . . [O]ne representative from a leading insurance carrier has estimated that defense costs in the average litigated case (at least in larger cities) have perhaps doubled in the last four years."); Lewis, *supra* note 9, at 609 (noting that CBS spent between $3 and $4 million for legal fees in Herbert v. Lando, 441 U.S. 153 (1979)).

The plaintiffs' ultimate financial rewards are small. The great majority of libel cases against media defendants are dismissed before trial, and few plaintiffs who succeed in securing a favorable jury verdict are able to sustain the verdict on appeal. *See* Franklin, "Good Names and Bad Law: A Critique of Libel Law and a Proposal" 18 *U.S.F. L. Rev.* 1, 4–5 & n.23 (1983) [cited as Franklin, Critique of Libel Law]. The proportion of cases in which plaintiffs ultimately prevail against media defendants is estimated to be no more than 5 to 10%. *Id.*

11. *See, e.g.,* Barrett, *supra* note 10; Bezanson, *supra* note 9; Bezanson, Cranberg & Soloski, ch. 3, *supra;* Cranberg, *supra* note 9; Kaufman, *supra* ch. 1; Lewis, *supra* note 9; Soloski, *supra* note 9.

12. Kaufman, *supra* ch. 1.

13. Bezanson, *supra* note 9, at 228; Bezanson, *supra* ch. 3; Soloski, *supra* note 9, at 219–220.

14. Cranberg, *supra* note 9, at 221; Soloski, *supra* note 9, at 219–220. *See also* R. Smolla, *Suing the Press* 186–87 (1986).

15. Bezanson, *supra* ch. 3.

16. *Id.*

17. Different figures are suggested by the various empirical studies. *See, e.g.,* Bezanson, *supra* ch. 3; Franklin, Critique of Libel Law, *supra* note 10 at 4–5; Franklin, "Suing Media for Libel: A Litigation Study," 1981 *Am. B. Found. Res. J.* 795, 800 [cited as Franklin, Litigation Study]; Kaufman, *supra* ch. 1. For tort litigation generally, *see* R. Posner, *Federal Courts* (1985).

18. *See, e.g.,* Epstein, *infra* ch. 5; *see also* Franklin, Winners and Loser, *supra* note 5; Franklin, Critique of Libel Law, *supra* note 10; Franklin, Litigation Study, *supra* note 17; Sheer & Zardkoohi, "An Analysis of the Economic Efficiency of the Law of Defamation," 80 *Nw. U. L. Rev.* 364, 369 (1985).

19. Epstein, *infra* ch. 5.

20. *Id.* For other related explanations for increase in jury awards, *see* Franklin, Critique of Libel Law *supra* note 10, at 10–11; Smolla, *supra* note 9, at 6–7; Note, "Punitive Damages and Libel Law," 98 *Harv. L. Rev. 847* (1985).

21. Epstein, *infra* ch. 5; Franklin, Critique of Libel, *surpa* note 10, at 13–14.

22. Professor Epstein argues that risk aversion should lead to an *increase* in the settlement rate, given the uncertainties of litigation and the magnitude of the damage award stakes involved in post-*New York Times* libel litigation. Epstein, *infra* ch. 5. The settlement rate for at least one important class of libel suits—those against news media—appears, however, to be quite low relative to other sorts of litigation. *See* Bezanson, *supra* ch. 3; Franklin, Critique of Libel Law, *supra* note 10, at 12, n. 56.

23. *See* note 10, *supra.*

24. Franklin, Winners and Losers, *supra* note 5. "Westmoreland Takes on CBS," *Newsweek,* Oct. 22, 1984, at 61 [cited as *Newsweek,* Westmoreland]. The press' record is considerably better after all appeals have run than it is when jury verdicts alone are examined. *See* note 10 *supra.*

25. *See, e.g.,* Gertz v. Welch, Inc., 418 U.S. 323 (1974). *See also* T. Carter, M. Franklin & J. Wright, *The First Amendment and the Fourth Estate: The Law of Mass Media* 495–96 (3rd ed., 1985); Franklin, Winners and Losers, *supra* note 5, at 498; Franklin, Litigation Study, *supra* note 17; Smolla, *supra* note 9, at 4–6. The Supreme Court's recent decision in Dun & Bradstreet, Inc. v. Greenmoss Builders, Inc., 472 U.S. 749 (1985), makes it easier for plaintiffs to secure presumed or punitive damages in some cases. But judges remain less receptive than juries do to large libel damage awards.

26. *See, e.g.,* Landes & Posner, "Adjudication as a Private Good," 8 *J. Legal Stud.* 235 (1979).

27. *See* Katz, Judicial Decisionmaking and Litigation Expenditure: An Economic Approach (May 1985; unpub.).

28. Epstein, *infra* ch. 5.

29. *See supra* notes 11–16 and accompanying discussion.

30. *See* Bezanson, *supra* note 9 at 228; Franklin, Critique of Libel Law, *supra* note 10 at 5; Soloski, *supra* note 9 at 220.

31. *See* Franklin, Critique of Libel Law, *supra* note 10 at 32; *Newsweek,* Westmoreland, *supra* note 24.

32. *See supra* notes 26–27 and accompanying discussion.

33. *See supra* notes 11–16 and accompanying discussion. *See also* discussion *infra* parts III, IV, V, VI.

34. Restatement (Second) of Torts §559 (1977); W. Prosser, *The Law of Torts* 739–744 (4th ed. 1971).

35. *See, e.g.,* C. Gregory & H. Kalven, *supra* note 2; W. Prosser, *supra* note 34.

36. This effect may not produce a readily seen footprint. The absolute level of post-libel earnings may not decline from the pre-libel level; and if a decline occurs, the cause may be obscure. The common supposition, however, was that post-libel earnings would be lower than they would have been but for the libel.

37. *See, e.g.,* Galanter, "Why the 'Haves' Come Out Ahead: Speculations on the Limits of Legal Change," 9 *Law & Soc. Rev.* 95 (1974); Landes & Posner, *supra* note 26.

38. Of course, injury to reputation is also of concern to other businesses and individuals who trade on trust. Thus, a bank must worry about reputational repercussions arising out of actions for misuse of depositor's funds; but news media are special in the libel context because they trade on trust in the business of providing information.

39. *See, e.g.,* authorities cited at note 37, *supra*. Other commentators also have noted disparate time-discount rates and attitudes toward risk as factors differentiating parties' interest in the outcome of a given litigation. *See, e.g.,* R. Posner, *Economic Analysis of Law* 524–25 (3d ed., 1986). Although these factors might be present in media libel litigation, the discussion here focuses on different causes of divergence in the parties' interests, causes less integrally related to evaluation of the money transferred in the instant litigation.

40. For some news media, features other than the quality and quantity of information may be so important that it is more accurate to say that these media also, or even principally, are in the business of selling entertainment. *See infra,* notes 173–184 and accompanying text.

41. *See* Wilde & Schwartz, "Equilibrium Comparison Shopping," 46 *Rev. Econ. Stud.* 543 (1979); *see also Newsweek, supra* note 24.

42. Anecdotal evidence on this point is presented *infra* at note 57.

43. For discussion of error and optimality in other business decisions, *see, e.g.,* Schwartz, "Products Liability, Corporate Structure, and Bankruptcy: Toxic Substances and the Remote Risk Relationship," 14 *J. Legal Stud.* 689 (1985).

44. *See* B. Owen, *Economics and Freedom of Expression: Media Structure and the First Amendment* 34–37 (1975).

45. The problem of inference based on thin data, of course, is not peculiar to this context. For various views of the role of probability and inference in law, *see* "Symposium: Probability and Inference in the Law of Evidence," 66 *B.U.L. Rev.* 377–952 (1986).

46. This indeed may be the source of the "availability heuristic" observed by psychologists and labelled as cognitive error. *See, e.g.,* Kahneman & Tversky, *Subjective Psychology* 430 (1972); Tversky & Kahneman, "Judgments Under Uncertainty: Heuristics and Biases," 185 *Science* 1124 (1974).

47. A normal distribution of error predictions across truth-sensitive consumers would produce a bell-shaped curve of divergent predictions. The judicial confirmation of a truth-error need not lead every consumer to shift his error-rate estimate upward, but it should not lead any consumer to shift his estimate downwards. The probabilistic result, then, is an overall upward adjustment in the predicted error rate. At the margin, this adjustment will lead some consumers to value the news product at less than its cost.

48. *See infra* notes 134–184 and accompanying text.

49. Cranberg, *supra* note 9, at 221. *See also* "Absence of Malice," *Newsweek,* February 4, 1985, at 52.

50. *See* discussion of error rate expected by consumers, *supra* notes 43–48 and accompanying text.

51. The difference between the cost of reputation effects among peers and that of reputation effects among consumers is akin to the difference between insider information (which usually anticipates public information) and public reactions (which follows). Although a smaller proportion of the consumers or outside investors are aware *ex post* than the proportion of media peers or corporate insiders, the change in the outsiders' evaluation of the veracity of a news enterprise or of the value of corporate stock will be greater as that group begins with less information about the enterprises, so that any new information is relatively more influential.

52. It should be noted that under pre-*New York Times* law, punitive damages awards had effects comparable to the adverse judgment in a public figure case after *New York Times*. The overlap between pre-*New York Times* punitive damages awards and "actual malice" findings under the *New York Times* standard, however, is incomplete. Moreover, the award of punitive damages probably always has been less visible to press monitors than the judgment itself; the cost of obtaining information about matters other than the win or lose judgment is higher, making other signals of press performance marginally less effective.

53. *See* discussion in section III A, *supra*.

54. *Id.*

55. This assumes an anthropomorphic reaction to institutions. *See Gertz*, 418 U.S. at 339–341. *See also* G. Allison, *Essence of Decision: Explaining the Cuban Missile Crisis* 9–11 (1971) (describing rational individual actor model).

56. For reasons indicated *infra*, the actual meaning of *New York Times* is probably known to the monitor groups, in part because it is well publicized in connection with high-visibility libel trials. *See infra* notes 82–83, 92–94, 151 and accompanying text. Professor Warren Schwartz rightly notes that, in addition to increasing the cost of adverse judgments to media defendants, *New York Times* decreases the affirmative benefit such defendants derive from favorable judgments. While this will limit the increase in defendants' non-award stakes, its effect should be modest so long as monitor groups expect the defendant to behave in a manner that minimizes the probability of losing libel suits. The stronger this expectation, the lower the affirmative gain from a favorable judgment and the greater the potential non-award cost of an adverse judgment. *See infra* notes 140–184 and accompanying text.

57. For instance, the *Washington Post*'s circulation figures show a decline of roughly 5% following the decision of the Court of Appeals to reinstate the jury verdict against the *Post* in the moderately publicized *Tavoulareas* case. *See* Tavoulareas v. Piro, 759 F.2d 90 (D.C. Cir. 1985). [I have not examined circulation figures for the *Post* following its subsequent appellate successes in this case, *petition for reh'g den., vacated for reh'g en banc,* 763 F.2d 1472 (1985); *judg't below aff'd,* 817 F.2d 762 (D.C. Cir. 1987) *(en banc).*] Circulation of the *Post*'s only daily, local competitor rose just over 5% (on a much smaller base) over the same period.

The *Post*'s circulation also declined about 5% following the original jury verdict against the paper in the *Tavoulareas* case in July 1982. Ten months later, the district court set aside the jury verdict and rendered judgment *n.o.v.* for the Post. 567 F. Supp. 651 (D.D.C. 1983). Between the two adverse judgments (the jury verdict in 1982 and the appellate decision in 1985), the *Post*'s circulation increased more than 6%.

It is difficult to place much reliance on figures such as these without controlling for potential seasonal variations in circulation an other, non-libel-related effects, and without examination of a much larger sample of cases and comparable pre-*New York Times* data. The infrequency of libel judgments against press defendants since *New York Times* makes strong empirical support for any proposition regarding the effects of such judgments unlikely. Although the anecdotal evidence at this stage is comforting, the propositions advanced in the text are grounded in intuition, not data.

58. *See* Bezanson, ch. 3; Kupferberg, "Libel Fever," *Colum. J. Rev.*, Sep.–Oct., 1981, at 36; "What the Jury—and Time Magazine—Said," *Newsweek*, Feb. 4, 1985, at 58. For a very different account of media behavior, at least where some possibility of suit exists (and arguing that failure to print retractions is a principal contributing cause of libel suits), *see* Bezanson, "The Libel Suit in Retrospect: What Plaintiffs Want and What Plaintiffs Get," 74 *Calif. L. Rev.* 789, 792 (1986); Cranberg, *supra* note 9, at 221–222; Soloski, *supra* note 9, at 220.

59. *See* Franklin, Critique of Libel Law, *supra* note 10, at 12, n. 56.

60. *See* Simon, "Libel as Malpractice," 53 *Fordham L. Rev.* 449, 452 (1984); *Newsweek, supra* note 54, at 58.

61. *See* T. Schelling, *The Strategy of Conflict* (1960).

62. As a rule, the direct costs associated with settlement are considerably less than those associated with litigation to judgment. While a number of factors—most notably, different assessments of the likely outcome of litigation by plaintiff and defendant—may impede settlement, that should remain the preferred vehicle for resolution of parties' disputes given its cost advantage. For samples of the extensive literature exploring settlement-versus-litigation decisions, see authorities cited *supra* notes 26 and 27 and *infra* note 70.

63. Franklin, Litigation Study, *supra* note 17, at 800; Smolla, *supra* note 9, at 13.

64. Kaufman, *supra* ch. 1. Though settlement is usually less visible than an adverse judgment, it may be much more visible in libel that in other contexts. *See infra* text at notes 82–83.

65. Franklin, Critique of Libel Law, *supra* note 10 at 14–16; Sheer & Zardkoohi, *supra* note 34, at 374–380.

66. An especially lucid introduction to the concept of agency costs, and to several interesting applications, is Pratt & Zeckhauser, "Principals and Agents: An Overview," in J. Pratt & R. Zeckhauser, eds., *Principals and Agents: The Structure of Business* 1 (1985).

67. Two important assumptions might be implicit in this account of systematic media overinvestment in contesting libel suits. First, because managers are imperfectly monitored (e.g., by shareholders and outside directors), they will commit more corporate funds to protect the press enterprise's reputation than the other members of the enterprise would agree is ideal. That is, the managers will spend a corporate dollar in reputation protection when the expected yield of that dollar (money saved from subscribers, employees, and sources as a result of the favorable outcome of litigation multiplied by the increased probability of such an outcome consequent to this marginal investment) is, say, 10 cents to the managers and 20 cents to the corporation. If managers were well monitored, they would invest only until the marginal dollars equalled their expected marginal benefit to the corporation.

It is clear that self-interested over-investment in libel litigation by managers will leave shareholders worse off. It is not, however, clear whether it in fact advantages managers. That depends on a second assumption regarding the efficiency of capital markets. The agency-cost analysis can build on an assumption that capital markets do not operate efficiently, in which case the managers will be able to arrogate to themselves real wealth from shareholders (and perhaps from other members of the corporate organization). *See, e.g.*, Bebchuck, "Toward Undistorted Choice and Equal Treatment in Corporate Takeovers," 98 *Harv. L. Rev.* 1693 (1985); Coffee, "Regulating the Market for Corporate Control: A Critical Assessment of the Tender Offer's Role in Corporate Governance," 84 *Colum. L. Rev.* 1145 (1984).

If, however, the capital markets operate efficiently (in the strong sense of that term), the shareholders discount *ex ante* (in approximately the correct amount) the return expected on their investment in light of the managers' propensity to waste corporate funds when personally advantageous. In such circumstances, enterprise managers in the ordinary case would be unable to secure a real wealth transfer; their potential gain from self-interested action contrary to the interests of the shareholders generally would be less than their gain from action congruent with shareholders' interests and, in all events, would already be taken into account by the shareholders (whose relative disinclination to invest in circumstances where agency costs are high would impose higher capital costs on such firms and thus constrain the availability of funds to support self-interested behavior). *See, e.g.,* Fama, "Agency Problems and the Theory of the Firm," 88 *J. Pol. Econ.* 288 (1980); Jensen & Meckling, "Theory of the Firm: Managerial Behavior, Agency Costs, & Ownership Structure," 3 *J. Financial Econ.* 305 (1976); Macey & McChesney, "A Theoretical Analysis of Corporate Greenmail," 95 *Yale L. J.* 13 (1985).

For examples of the literature expressly arguing the issue of capital market efficiency, *see* Fama, "Efficient Capital Markets: A Review of Theory and Empirical Work," 25 *J. Fin.* 383 (1970); Grossman & Stiglitz, "On the Impossibility of Informationally Efficient Markets," 70 *Am. Econ. Rev.* 393 (1980). An excellent survey and discussion of the arguments respecting market efficiency is Gordon & Kornhauser, "Efficient Markets, Costly Information, and Securities Research," 60 *N.Y.U. L. Rev.* 761 (1985).

68. The exact relation between any given investment and the consequent change in outcomes depends on the base probability of plaintiff success (given some probability distribution respecting the court's determination of critical fact and the state of applicable precedent). *See* Landes & Posner, *supra* note 26.

69. This conclusion is consistent with findings published in Bezanson, ch. 3. No rigorous comparison, however, to pre-*New York Times* data has yet been made.

70. *See, e.g.,* Landes & Posner, *supra* note 26; Priest & Klein, "The Selection of Disputes for Litigation," 13 J. *Legal Stud.* 1 (1984); Shavell, "Suit, Settlement, and Trial: A Theoretical Analysis Under Alternative Methods for the Allocation of Legal Costs," 11 *J. Legal Stud.* 55 (1982).

71. *See* authorities cited *supra* note 70.

72. *See e.g.,* Landes & Posner, *supra* note 26.

73. *See* Goodman, "An Economic Theory of the Evolution of the Common Law," 7 *J. Legal Stud.* 393 (1978).

74. *See* Landes & Posner, *supra* note 26; Priest, "Selective Characteristics of Litigation," 9 *J. Legal Stud.* 399 (1980).

75. Landes & Posner, *supra* note 26.

76. This assumes that damage award stakes and non-award stakes vary independently.

77. This assumes that, as to one or more elements of litigation expenditure, litigants reap declining marginal utility past some absolute level of investment not related to litigation stakes. Thus, for example, beyond some point it adds less and less to one's probability of success to continue advancing additional legal arguments on a given issue to the judge. *See* Landes & Posner, *supra* note 26.

78. *See* Bezanson, *supra* ch. 3; Soloski, *supra* note 9, at 219–220.

79. For example, the plaintiff in the *Tavoulareas* case, cited at note 57, *supra,* stated that he had spent $4 million to secure the $2 million judgment that now has been overturned a second time. The facts of and jury reaction to the *Tavoulareas* case are discussed in R. Smolla, *supra* note 14, at 182–97.

80. Bezanson, *supra* note 58, at 791–795; Bezanson, Setting the Record Straight, *supra* note 9, at 228–229.

81. For other positive relations of consumer demand to perceived cost, in circumstances for which negative correlations with actual cost still hold, *see* "Liebenstein, Bandwagon, Snob and Veblen Effects in the Theory of Consumer's Demand," 64 *Q.J. Econ.* 183 (1950).

82. This follows either from the efficient response to truth-sensitive, marginal consumers or from the personal interest of journalists (assuming that capital markets cannot reduce to zero agency costs from divergence of journalists' and consumers' new interests).

83. Although other factors, such as the level of competition faced by the press defendant, will affect the magnitude of defendant's non-award stakes (*see* discussion *infra*, part VI), these additional factors will not significantly affect the publicity given a libel case. The competitor who wishes to see a rival enterprise saddled with a large damage judgment and severely injured reputation does not have markedly different incentives regarding publicity for the libel suit than do non-competing publications unless the competitor is uniquely situated to influence the legal proceeding or to inform a group of its rival's potential consumers who otherwise would remain ignorant of the libel suit. Given the unlikelihood of these events, general newsworthiness considerations may be expected to dominate the publicity from competing and non-competing publications alike.

84. *Cf.* R. Posner, *supra* note 39, at 522–25. There will, of course, be some non-award stakes in the pre-*New York Times* world, and some of these may properly be classified as not involving direct financial interests. *Cf.* Leff, "Injury, Ignorance, and Spite—The Dynamics of Coercive Collection," 80 *Yale L. J.* 1 (1970). But the expectation here is that these will be dominated, as in the typical tort case, by direct financial incentives.

85. *See, e.g.,* R. Posner, *supra* note 39, at 534.

86. *See* Schwartz & Mitchell, "An Economic Analysis of the Contingent Fee in Personal-Injury Litigation," 22 *Stan. L. Rev.* 1125 (1970). *See also* Coffee, "Understanding the Plaintiff's Attorney: The Implications of Economic Theory for Private Enforcement of Law Through Class and Derivative Actions," 86 *Colum. L. Rev.* 669 (1986).

87. *See* Coffee, *supra* note 86.

88. A variety of practices historically has restrained competition among lawyers, including limitations on entry to the market for supply of lawyers' services, advertising constraints, prohibitions on certain fee agreements, and even collusive price-setting for some services. Although some of these have been relaxed after decisions such as Bates v. State Bar of Arizona, 433 U.S. 350 (1977), In re Primus, 436 U.S. 412 (1978), and Zauderer v. Office of Disciplinary Counsel, 471 U.S. 626 (1985), a number of these restrictions on full competition remain. *See, e.g.,* Ohralik v. Ohio State Bar, 436 U.S. 447 (1978). *See also* McChesney, "Commercial Speech in the Professions: The Supreme Court's Unanswered Questions and Questionable Answers," 134 U. Pa. L. Rev. 45 (1985).

89. Findlater, "The Proposed Revision of DRS-103(B): Champerty and Class Actions," 36 *Bus. Law* 1667, 1669 (1981).

90. The *Tavoulareas* case, cited at note 57, *supra,* is illustrative. The *Washington Post* had, at least by implication, charged the principal plaintiff, William Tavoulareas, who was President and Chief Executive Officer of Mobil Oil Corporation, with improperly using Mobil's resources to benefit his son. The article did not explicitly state that the behavior it suggested was questionable had resulted in any loss to the Corporation. It did, however, at least arguably provide a basis for belief that Tavoulareas had engaged in improper self-dealing. Tavoulareas had considerable interest in keeping a reputation for honesty. Plainly, the Post article's charge was inimical to his continued successful operation as head of Mobil. The dollar worth of the harm to Tavoulareas is not easily calculated, but he both felt strongly that the article harmed his reputation and was in a financial position to underwrite litigation that might not be a good investment for a party whose sole interest

was a right to the damage judgment recovered, if any. *See* discussion of the Tavoulareas case in R. Smolla, *supra* note 14, at 182–97. It should be added that the Mobil Oil Corporation apparently picked up the expenses for the litigation. Barrett, *supra* note 10, at 859.

91. *See* Franklin, Critique of Libel Law, *supra* note 10, at 12 (arguing that "lawyers specializing in the [libel] area would have little upon which to build a successful practice based on the contingent fee").

92. The two most highly publicized libel trials of the last few years, Sharon v. Time, Inc., 599 F. Supp. 538 (S.D. N.Y. 1984), and Westmoreland v. CBS, 596 F. Supp. 1170 (S.D.N.Y.), *aff'd*, 752 F.2d 16 (2d Cir. 1984), *cert. denied sub nom.* Cable News Network, Inc. v. U.S. District Court, 472 U.S. 1017 (1985), were both brought by the plaintiff's attorneys, Shea & Gould and The Capital Legal Foundation, respectively, without direct compensation from their clients. *See* Adler, "Annals of Law: Two Trials, Part II," *The New Yorker*, Jun. 23, 1986, at 34.

93. The change in large measure traces to judicial decisions holding formal prohibitions to be unconstitutional. *See* In the Matter of R. M. J., 455 U.S. 191 (1982); Bates v. State Bar of Arizona, 433 U.S. 350 (1977). More narrowly tailored restraints have received a mixed reception from the courts. *See, e.g.,* Zauderer v. Office of Disciplinary Counsel, 105 S. Ct. 2265 (1985); Ohralik v. Ohio State Bar, 436 U.S. 447 (1978).

94. *See, e.g., supra* note 92.

95. *See* A. Dershowitz, *The Best Defense,* (1982); F. Bailey, *The Defense Never Rests* (1971).

96. *See* Bezanson, *supra* note 9, at 228; *but see* Franklin, Critique of Libel Law, *supra* note 10, at 12.

97. *See, e.g.,* R. Smolla, *supra* note 14, at 200 (describing the ideologies of the opposing camps in *Westmoreland v. CBS,* cited *supra* note 10).

98. Examples include Floyd Abrams, James Goodale, and now David Boies. Observation of the non-parallel development of opposing sides of the libel bar can be found in Franklin, Critique of Libel Law, *supra* note 10, at 11–12. Professor Franklin opines, however, that recent developments may presage emergence of a more expert plaintiff's libel bar.

99. Of course, the opportunity for publicity lowers the real cost of representation to the defense lawyer as well as the plaintiff's lawyer; but the asymmetric interests of defendant and plaintiff means that the defense lawyer can hold out for direct payment that, together with revenue derived from the publicity generated by the case, will, in contrast, be well above the defense attorney's reservation price. Plaintiff's attorney, in contrast, will be compensated principally from publicity, without a similar dollar compensation from his client in many cases.

100. 376 U.S. at 294 (Black, J., concurring).

101. 376 U.S. at 260, n. 3.

102. *Id.* at 278–279.

103. *See* Lewis, *supra* note 9, at 608.

104. *See* Curtis Publishing Co. v. Butts, 388 U.S. 130 (1967).

105. Public figures/officials account for 60% of the libel plaintiffs who sue the media. *See* Smolla, *supra* note 9, at 20–21; Soloski, *supra* note 9, at 218.

106. *See supra* notes 68–83 and accompanying text.

107. *See supra* notes 69–81 and accompanying text.

108. *Id.*

109. Not only do office-holders frequently move from one position in government to other, often more important, positions—Jimmy Carter, Gerald Ford, Lyndon Johnson,

John Kennedy, Richard Nixon, and Ronald Reagan are visible examples of movement up the electoral ladder. Additionally, given the electoral advantage enjoyed by incumbents, *see, e.g.,* Beth, " 'Incumbency Advantage' and Incumbency Resources: Recent Articles," 9 *Cong. & Pres.* 119 (1981–1982); Lott, "Brand Names and Barriers to Entry in Political Markets," 51 *Pub. Choice* 87 (1986), holding one electoral office greatly increases the prospects for holding the same office in the future. The same increase in probability for further exercise of power also characterizes appointive office, witness Elliot Richardson and Caspar Weinberger, for examples.

110. *See, e.g.,* W. Ashworth, *Under the Influence: Congress, Lobbies, and the American Pork-Barrel System* (1981); Lowenstein, "Political Bribery and the Intermediate Theory of Politics," 32 *U.C.L.A. L. Rev.* 784 (1985); Wright, "Money and the Pollution of Politics: Is the First Amendment an Obstacle to Political Equality?," 82 *Colum. L. Rev.* 609 (1982).

111. *See, e.g.,* D. Mayhew, *Congress: The Electoral Connection* (1974); Aranson, Gellhorn & Robinson, "A Theory of Delegation," 68 *Cornell L. Rev.* 1 (1982); Lee, "Marginal Lobbying Cost and the Optimal Amount of Rent-Seeking," 45 *Pub. Choice* 207 (1985).

112. Presidents Johnson, Nixon, and Ford are ready examples of individuals who became quite well-to-do following (or, perhaps, in some cases during) public service. *See, e.g.,* Lindsey, "Busy Gerald Ford Adds Acting to His Repertory," *N.Y. Times,* Dec. 19, 1983, at A 16, col. 1.

113. *See* W. Keeton, D. Dobbs, R. Keeton & D. Owen, *Prosser and Keeton on Torts* §116A, at 843 (5th ed., 1984) [cited as Prosser & Keeton]; Franklin, Critique of Libel Law, *supra* note 10, at 11.

114. This seems especially likely to be true at the local level. One possible example is the small-town mayor whose libel claim was at issue in Ocala Star-Banner Co. v. Damron, 401 U.S. 295 (1971). *See* Schauer, "Public Figures," 25 *Wm. & Mary L. Rev.* 905, 910 (1984).

115. Indeed, this may explain a significant proportion of public figure libel suits. In particular, it may help explain some of the well-publicized suits by former military officers, *e.g.,* Westmoreland v. CBS, *supra,* and Herbert v. Lando, the full citation for which is unnecessarily long but which can be accessed through its Supreme Court phase, 441 U.S. 153 (1979).

116. *See* Franklin, Litigation Study, *supra* note 17. The same statement could apply to entertainers, albeit less so than to public officials. Although entertainers are not elected, notoriety and public exposure certainly play a large role in the success of an entertainer's career. Advertisers who invest in a television program and producers who invest in a play or movie often rely on the popularity of particular entertainers to draw viewers and produce revenues. An entertainer's popularity, therefore, directly influences the financial returns to him or her. An entertainer's popularity generally will be reflected in his or her immediate earnings, but popular approval has a separate value to future income. The entertainer, like the public official, relies on the work he or she does now, even if it is not very lucrative in terms of direct payments, to bring higher income later.

117. *See, e.g.,* Alioto v. Cowles Communication, Inc. 623 F.2d 616 (9th Cir. 1980).

118. Sharon v. Time, Inc., 599 F. Supp. 538 (S.D. N.Y. 1984). Although Sharon might be seen as a retired general, his inclusion within the "politician" category is generally accepted. *See, e.g.,* Deming & Kubic, "What Next for Sharon?: Using the Trial to Keep His Political Ambitions Alive," *Newsweek,* Feb. 4, 1985, at 57.

119. *See supra* notes 80–83 and accompanying text. *See also* Bezanson, *supra* note 9, at 231. Note that there may be harm from letting the suit die, yet the politician has the capacity either to explain that electoral victory is sufficient vindication or to decide that

after libel and electoral loss the added cost of harm to his reputation from dropping the suit is *de minimus*.

120. This was the explanation provided by (now former) Congressman Richard Kelly, charged with accepting bribes in the FBI's "ABSCAM" operation. *See N.Y. Times*, Jan. 8, 1981, §II, at 13, col. 1.

121. *See, e.g.*, Lakian v. Globe Newspaper Co., 399 Mass. 379 (1987) (unsuccessful gubernatorial candidate); "Lakian Cites Positive Effect of Settling WXKS Libel Suit," *Boston Globe*, Apr. 26, 1984, at 34, col. 1 (same plaintiff); Kennedy, "King Asks SJC to Order Trial in Suit Against Globe," *Boston Globe*, Feb. 6, 1987, at 82, col. 3 (former Governor and unsuccessful candidate for reelection). *See also* Franklin, Critique of Libel, *supra* note 10, at 2.

122. *See* Note, Punitive Damages, *supra* note 20, at 856. This is not inconsistent with a success rate for aspirants less than that for incumbents. *See* Franklin, Litigation Study, *supra* note 17, at 809 (elected officials are "proportionately more successful at winning and keeping verdicts than any other large group." *Id.* at 808–809). Those who place higher value on the *publicity* from filing media libel suits presumably will, as compared to others, be more inclined to file cases that have lower probabilities of yielding a successful judgment. In this regard, Glen Robinson suggests that a useful distinction can be drawn between *promotional* libel suits and *defensive* suits. The former class consists of suits that grant an electoral advantage other than simply combatting the ill effects of the libel. At first blush, these suits would appear to divide incumbents from aspirants to elective office, with promotional suits better adapted to an aspirant's interests and defensive suits better adapted to an incumbent's. The division of these suits along plaintiff class lines, however, is difficult, as incumbents also are apt to find promotional suits useful—*New York Times* seems illustrative—and aspirants may find defensive suits necessary more often than incumbents. I find Glen's suggestion attractive, but I have not yet found an appropriate device for integrating the categorization into the analysis of libel litigation.

123. *Supra* notes 69–79 and accompanying text.

124. *See* Franklin, Litigation Study, *supra* note 17, at 813.

125. *See e.g., Gertz*, 418 U.S. at 339–340; Miskovsky v. Oklahoma Publishing Co., 654 P.2d 587 (Okla.), *cert. denied*, 459 U.S. 923 (1982).

126. *See, e.g.*, R. Adler, *Reckless Disregard* 41 (1986). The *Sharon* case, *supra* note 90, is exemplary. This case is discussed in detail in R. Adler, *supra* (along with the *Westmoreland* case), and in less extended fashion in R. Smolla, *supra* note 14, at 80–99.

127. *Supra* note 92 and accompanying text. *See generally* R. Adler, *supra* note 126.

128. Of course, there is a peculiar difficulty here in digging proof of this out of data; guess-work suggests this answer in particular cases. *See, e.g.*, R. Adler, *supra* note 126, at 24; Smolla, *supra* note 14 (Smolla's title for chapter 4 of his book is indicative: *"Ariel Sharon v. Time Magazine:* The Libel Suit as Political Forum, International Style"); Deming & Kubic, *supra* note 118.

129. *See, e.g.*, Burnett v. National Enquirer, 144 Cal. App. 3d 991, 193 Cal Rptr. 206 (1983).

130. *See, e.g., Tavoulareas, supra* note 57, and discussion, *supra* note 90. Note that the court of appeals did not decide whether Tavoulareas was a public figure and, thus, had to meet the actual malice test; the court found that, if Tavoulareas is a public figure, the test was met in his case.

131. *Supra* notes 107–130 and accompanying text.

132. Note the frequent reversals, —*e.g., Tavoulareas, supra* note 57 (trial court reversed the jury verdict on motion for judgment *n.o.v.;* a panel of the D.C. Circuit reversed

the *j.n.o.v.* on appeal; the panel's decision was vacated, and the court *en banc* affirmed the judgment of the trial judge); *Miskovsky, supra* note 123 (court reversed jury verdict because trial court erred in submitting matter to jury)—and the frequent reductions in damages, *e.g.,* Pring v. Penthouse Int'l, Ltd., 695 F.2d 438 (10th Cir., 1982), *cert. denied,* 462 U.S. 1132 (1983) (trial judge reduced the punitive damages by half, and the Tenth Circuit set the award aside); Burnett v. National Enquirer, 144 Cal. App. 3d 991, 193 Cal Rptr. 206 (1983)(jury awarded $300,000 compensatory damages and $1.3 million punitive damages; trial judge reduced compensatory damages to $50,000 and punitive damages to $750,000; court of appeals reduced punitive damages to $150,000), *appeal dismissed,* 465 U.S. 1014 (1984).

133. For efforts to speculate, *see* Franklin, Litigation Study, *Supra* note 17; Lewis, *supra* note 9; Smolla, *supra* note 9. For an analysis of the desirability of *New York Times* under an approach *not* calling for similar data, *see* Schauer, *supra* note 114. *See also* Cass, "The Perils of Positive Thinking: Constitutional Interpretation and Negative First Amendment Theory," 34 *U.C.L.A. L. Rev.* 1405, 1455–65 (1987).

134. The changes associated with the *New York Times* legal standard will vary for different media. The simple formula for comparison of pre- and post-*New York Times* conditions requires summation of the costs (or benefits) listed above: award costs (A), non-award costs (N), defense costs (E), risk costs (r), costs of investment in care (C), and costs of reduced speech or benefits of increased speech (Q). While a summation of these costs before *New York Times*—(1) $A^b + N^b + E^b_d + r^b + c^b + Q^b$—and after—(2) $A^a + N^a + E_d^a + r^b + C^b + Q^b$—will represent the terms to be compared, actual comparison will not be easy because the terms are interrelated and because the change in any term need not be the same for all media. Even description of the relationships in their most general form suggest the difficulty.

So, for example, award costs (A) will be a function of several factors: the operative legal rule (after *New York Times,* L^a, or before *New York Times,* L^b; this term might be conceived of, as in Priest & Klein, *supra* note 70, as the proportion of a given set of disputes that would be resolved in plaintiff's favor, other things being equal); the relative investments of the plaintiff and defendant in the litigation (E_π and E_d, respectively); and the facts of the case (F, which might be conceived in terms of the location of a case within a dispute set arrayed horizontally from the case most clearly favoring defendant to that most clearly favoring plaintiff). Thus, (3) $A = \S$ L, E, E_d, F, with A correlating positively with L, E_π, and F, and negatively with E_d.

While a value can be assigned to L exogenously, both E_π and E_d, as well as F, are endogenous variables. Litigation costs are influenced by expected award stakes, $\bar{A}$ (assumed equal for both parties to litigation), by each party's expected non-award stakes ($\bar{N}_\pi$, $\bar{N}_d$), by assessment of the probable outcome at any level of investment ($\bar{p}$, defined as the expected probability of plaintiff's success, with $1-\bar{p}$ denoting the probability of defendants' success), and the risk costs associated with the litigation (r_π, r_d). Formally, (4) $E\pi = \S \bar{A}$, $\bar{N}_\pi$, $\bar{p}_\pi$, r_π, with $\bar{p}_\pi$ being plaintiff's expectation of success; (5) $E_d = \S \bar{A}$, $\bar{N}_d$, $\bar{p}_d$, r_d, with $\bar{p}_d$ being defendant's expectation of plaintiff's success. These terms that define the magnitude of expenditures also exhibit endogenous relations, with the probability of success dependent in part on relative litigation investment—(6) $p = \S$ L, F, E_π, E_d—and expectations respecting opposing parties' litigation investments (E_π, E_d) influencing the reciprocal investments.

The array of factual circumstances that gives rise to litigation also is influenced by the parties. First, the set of potential disputes any media enterprise faces is partly determined by its investment in care. Second, the likelihood that any dispute will result in litigation is partly determined by the potential plaintiffs non-award stakes and also partly by the potential plaintiffs' expectation respecting the media enterprise's investment in litigation. The greater the enterprise's investment in care, other things equal, the more likely F will have a lower mean (more favorable to defendant). The greater the news enterprise's expected investment in litigation, the higher the mean level of F. And the higher the mean non-award stake of potential plaintiffs, other things being equal, the lower the mean level of F. Thus, (7) $F = \S\ C$, $\bar{E}_d$, $\bar{N}_\pi$, λ, where λ is a random variable.

While these relationships can be presented in more detail, additional detail will entail substantially more complexity. Moreover, the one consistent relationship, $L^a < L^b$, will not significantly clarify the outcome of most equations under pre-*New York Times* and post-*New York Times* law. For efforts to formalize similar relationships and consideration of some of the complexities inherent in them, *see* Denzau, "Litigation Expenditures as Private Determinants of Judicial Decisions: A Comment," 8 *J. Legal Stud.* 295 (1979); Landes & Posner, *supra* note 26; Priest & Klein, *supra* note 70.

135. *See* authorities cited note 10, *supra*.

136. *See* Franklin, Litigation Study, *supra* note 17, at 810. This effect is dependent on the relative rates at which suits and judgments decrease in number and those at which defense costs and judgments rise in magnitude.

137. *Cf.* Landes & Posner, *supra* note 26; Shavell, *supra* note 70.

138. *See, e.g.,* Shavell, "On Liability and Insurance," 13 *Bell J. Econ.* 120 (1982) [cited as Insurance]; Shavell, "Strict Liability vs. Negligence," 9 *J. Legal Stud.* 1 (1980) [cited as Liability].

139. *See supra* notes 34–67 and accompanying text.

140. In attempting to sort out the various media enterprises, a definitional problem must be addressed. The assumption here is that these enterprises differ in their stake in libel suits and, further, that this difference is related to enterprises' varying sensitivity to the effect of libel litigation on the enterprise's reputation for veracity. It is not, however, clear what best correlates with sensitivity (or with a reputation for veracity). I frame the divisions in terms of average levels of care in reporting. Two other factors suggest themselves readily as alternative determinants of likely reaction to libel prospects: (1) the frequency of false reports, of (2) the frequency of recklessly false reports. I assume that these alternative factors are positively correlated (at a very high level of correlation) with the average level of care within an enterprise. I also assume that the level of care correlates well with reputation. Finally, insofar as there is divergence among these various factors, I think that average level of care would better indicate the media enterprise's own assessment of its reputation and of its interest in libel litigation. On the choice of average rather than marginal levels of care, *see infra*, text following note 142.

141. Of course, high-care media are sensitive to profit constraints. Anyone who doubts that can look to Rupert Murdoch's takeovers of enterprises such as *The Times of London*. Nonetheless, owners of high-care media, especially in closely-held corporations, may seek to attain a higher lever of veracity than the consumer market rewards. This preference may be justified by the savings from lowered input costs (managers, employees or sources) or it may be a taste for which the owner is willing to pay in lower profits. In this regard it may be noteworthy that many news enterprises remain family-owned, closely-held ventures. The choice among efficient-profit-maximizing owner-taste and agency-cost explanations is a difficult one that I do not reach here.

142. This point can, of course, be made with respect to any large organization. *See, e.g.,* Arrow, "Control in Large Organizations," in K. Arrow, *Essays in the Theory of Risk-Bearing* 223 (1971); Cass, "Allocation of Authority within Bureaucracies: Empirical Evidence and Normative Analysis," 66 *B.U. L. Rev.* 1 (1986); Pratt & Zeckhauser, *supra* note 66. The point also is made poignantly in the descriptions of reporters' and editors'

conduct that formed the background for the *Sharon* and *Westmoreland* suits. *See* R. Adler, *supra* note 126; D. Kowett, *A Matter of Honor* (1984); R. Smolla, *supra* note 14.

143. Franklin, Litigation Study, *supra* note 17, at 810; Smolla, *supra* note 9, at 12–13.

144. The damages awarded in the *New York Times* case itself, for instance, were $500,000, the equivalent of roughly two million dollars today. And at least another $2.5 million (1964 dollars) was at issue in related suits and could reasonably be expected to have been assessed against the *New York Times*. *See* Smolla, *supra* note 9. (Concurring in *New York Times*, Justice Black states that suits against the *New York Times* in Alabama asked for a total of $5.6 million, of which $1 million already had been awarded. 376 U.S. at 294–95.)

145. The change in expected marginal yield from defense expenditures wrought by *New York Times* is akin to the change that accompanies movement from a strict liability standard to a negligence standard. *See* Cooter, "Prices and Sanctions," 84 *Colum. L. Rev.* 1523 (1984).

146. Although the data are not clear on this point, some of the sources reporting recent trends in libel litigation seem to indicate that overall defense expenditures are rising for media enterprises. *See* Barrett, *supra* note 10; Goodale, *supra* note 10; Kaufman, *supra* ch. 1.

147. *See supra* notes 53–75 and accompanying text. This formulation of the defense calculus assumes risk neutrality.

148. During the *Sharon* trial, for example, non-subscription sales of *Time* magazine fell by 14% from the prior two months (slightly more when compared to the average of the prior six months). In the two months following the verdict, in which *Time* was found to have made a false, libelous statement and to have acted negligently, but not with actual malice, the publication's non-subscription sales declined an additional 5%. During the trial and post-trial period, single-copy sales of *Time*'s chief competitor, *Newsweek*, rose 5%. The *caveat* given in note 57 *supra* applies here as well.

149. *See supra* note 80–83 and accompanying text.

150. *See* R. Adler, *supra* note 126; Lewis, *supra* note 9.

151. Thus, for example, *Time* as well as *Newsweek* gave extensive coverage to the *Sharon* case. Although it may at first seem anomalous that a press enterprise would publicize libel actions against it, a fairly straightforward cost-benefit analysis explains this conduct. If the press-defendant were a monopolist of the news regarding the law suit, there would be substantial gain from suppressing the information. The existence of competing news outlets, however, reduces substantially the likelihood that libel suits against high-care press enterprises will go unnoticed. The rational, profit-maximizing defendant, aware that most of the information regarding the suit is publicly available, will calculate the number of its readers (and other monitors) who are expected to remain ignorant of the suit unless publicized by the defendant, and weigh the harm from disclosing the suit to these monitors against the benefit of telling the defendant's side of the story and the benefit of seeming sufficiently concerned about reporting all important stories to include in its publication information not unambiguously favorable to the defendant. Presumably, the monitors most sensitive to the fact that the suit has occurred, and those most sensitive to the quantity of information provided by the defendant publication, already will know of the suit. The additional publicity given by the defendant, thus, is not likely to be terribly costly to defendant and frequently will be outweighed by its benefits.

At the same time, the incentive for other press enterprises aggressively to publicize suits against a competitor is less than may at first blush appear. Two factors reduce the gains to be had from this publicity. First, there is some possibility for negative spillover effects: some monitors of the non-sued media enterprises will react to news of the suit against the competing enterprise by discounting the value not just of the competing publication but of all news media. The point can best be made by analogy. Airlines do not advertise their services by emphasizing comparative safety, relating the advertising carrier's safety record to those of his competitors. The airlines avoid this strategy because, while it may shift passengers from a less safe carrier to a more safe carrier, that effect may be dominated by the reduction in use of all air carriers consequent to the increased perception that air travel (generically) is unsafe. Second, aside from the effects of publicity in any given case, tacit collusion could reduce such publicity. If there are relatively few media competitors in a given "class" and if these competitors expect to be sued with roughly comparable frequency, they might tacitly agree to publicize such suits less vigorously than self-interest in the individual case would dictate. It is not evident that in the case of media libel suits either of these publicity-decreasing factors plays much of a role. To the extent, however, that press libel defendants and their competitors do not differ greatly in the publicity given to a libel suit, these factors, as well as those regarding the defendant noted above, may be implicated.

152. *See, e.g.,* American Security Council Educ. Found'n v. FCC, 607 F.2d 438 (D.C. Cir. 1979), *cert. denied,* 444 U.S. 1013 (1980); and sources cited in R. Cass, *Revolution in the Wasteland: Value and Diversity in Television* 1–2, 20–22, 171–72, nn. 32–43 (1981).

153. Indeed, Sullivan was not directly (or, perhaps, even indirectly) the subject of the advertisement at issue in *New York Times,* which declared:

> [A]s the whole world knows by now, thousands of Southern Negro students are engaged in widespread non-violent demonstrations in positive affirmation of the right to live in human dignity as guaranteed by the U.S. Constitution and the Bill of Rights. . . . In their efforts to uphold these guarantees, they are being met by an unprecedented wave of terror by those who would deny and negate that document which the whole world looks upon as setting the pattern for modern freedom. . . .
>
> In Montgomery, Alabama, after students sang "My Country, 'Tis of Thee" on the State Capitol steps, their leaders were expelled from school, and truckloads of police armed with shotguns and tear-gas ringed the Alabama State College Campus. When the entire student body protested to state authorities by refusing to re-register, their dining hall was padlocked in an attempt to starve them into submission. . . . Again and again the Southern violators have answered Dr. King's peaceful protests with intimidation and violence. They have bombed his home almost killing his wife and child. They have assaulted his person. They have arrested him seven times—for "speeding," "loitering" and similar "offenses." And now they have charged him with "perjury"—a felony under which they could imprison him for ten years. . . .

376 U.S. at 246–58.

Concern that this sense of idealogical and regional conflict permeated the libel litigation at issue in part explains the Court's decision to place its holding on relatively broad constitutional grounds. *See, e.g.,* Lewis, *supra* note 9, at 608 (stating that Justice Brennan's opinion for the *New York Times* Court "took an extraordinary step to make sure that the Alabama courts would not find some new way to punish *The Times* when the case went back down to them").

154. *See* Bezanson, *supra* ch. 3; and authorities cited *supra* note 144.

155. *See, e.g.,* K. Arrow, *supra* note142; Shavell, Insurance, *supra* note 138.

156. *See* Barrett, *supra* note 10, at 858.

157. *See* Worrall, "Libel Policy Deductibles and Limits," in *Media Insurance, supra* note 10, at 147, 143–57.

158. *See* Lankenau, "Comparison of Three Leading Insurance Policies," in *Media Insurance, supra* note 10, at 195, 236–37.

159. *See, e.g.,* Shavell, "On Moral Hazard and Insurance," 93 *Q. J. Econ.* 541 (1979).

160. *See* Lankenau, *supra* note 158, at 161–63. Although insurance companies do seem to distinguish between high-care and low-care companies in setting premiums (and not just on the basis of past losses), some companies that might be characterized as super-high care will find that their expected losses still will be well below the cost of insuring against them. This point simply applies the standard observation that insurance rating by class disfavors the least risky member of the class. This also might explain the historic disinclination of *The New York Times* to purchase libel liability insurance.

161. *See, e.g.,* Franklin, Critique of Libel Law, *supra* note 10, at 14–16; Schauer, "Fear, Risk, and the First Amendment: Unravelling the 'Chilling Effect,' " 58 *B.U. L. Rev.* 685 (1978); Sheer & Zardkoohi, *supra* note 18, at 374–79.

162. *See* Lewis, *supra* note 9, at 621–22.

163. Thus, reduced press care in statements regarding low-level officials, for example, may be a consequence of *New York Times. See* Schauer, *supra* note 114.

164. *E.g.,* Garrison v. Louisiana, 379 U.S. 64 (1964) (criminal prosecution for alleged libel of district attorney). *See* Franklin, Litigation Study, *supra* note 17. *See also* Smolla, *supra* note 9, at 2.

165. *See, e.g.,* United States v. Robel, 389 U.S. 258 (1967); Aptheker v. Secretary of State, 378 U.S. 510 (1964); *see also* G. Gunther, Constitutional Law 1148 (11th ed., 1985); Note, Punitive Damages, *supra* note 20, at 856.

166. Although the setting is different, the calculus for a profit-maximizing new enterprise will resemble that of a firm utilizing Ramsey prices. *See* Baumol and Braunstein, "Empirical Study of Scale Economies and Production Complementarity: The Case of Journal Publication," 85 *J. Polit. Econ.* 1037 (1977).

167. *See, e.g.,* Barrett, *supra* note 10, at 855–61; Smolla, *supra* note 9; Abrams, "Why We Should Change the Libel Law," *N.Y. Times,* Sep. 29, 1985, §6 (Magazine), at 34, 93. *See also* authorities cited in Schauer, "The Role of the People in First Amendment Theory," 74 *Calif. L. Rev.* 761, 767 n.35 (1986).

168. *See supra* notes 148–149 and accompanying text.

169. *Newseek*, Westmoreland, *supra* note 24, at 66.

170. *See* B. Owen, *supra* note 44, at 34–37 (discussing local limits on these economies of scale, given geographic segregation of local news sources, demand for local news, and advertiser demand for geographically-restricted (local) audiences).

171. *See* G. Stigler, *The Theory of Price* 333–36 (3d. ed., 1966).

172. *Cf.* Landes & Posner, "Legal Precedent: A Theoretical and Empirical Analysis," 19 *J. L. & Econ.* 249 (1976).

173. One of the relatively few examples of successful press libel litigation, the *Burnett* case, cited at note 129 *supra,* illustrates the difficulty. *See* discussion in R. Smolla, *supra* note 14, at 100–17.

174. It is unlikely, for instance, that enterprises such as *The National Enquirer* or *The Star* would generate the sort of internal documentation of concern over the veracity of a story such as *Time* did with respect to the story about Ariel Sharon or CBS in its "Benjamin Report" did with respect to its story about William Westmoreland, both with less than wholly salutary effect from the media enterprises' point of view. *See* R. Adler, *supra* note 126.

175. Indeed, even where malice, in both its common and *New York Times* senses is present, the law may offer considerable protection to publishers of less than unimpeachable scruple. *See, e.g.,* Falwell v. Flynt, 797 F.2d 1270 (4th Cir. 1985) (affirming a judgment

against Hustler Magazine publisher Larry Flynt for intentional infliction of emotional distress, but finding that this tort was subject to same actual malice requirement as defamation; the article in question had been found non-defamatory as parody, hence not reasonably construed as stating facts), *rev'd* 108 S.Ct. 876 (1988).

176. This follows from standard assumptions about economically-motivated litigation, *see, e.g.,* Epstein, *supra* note 18; Sheer & Zardkoohi, *supra* note 18; and authorities cited *supra* note 70.

177. *See* discussion *supra,* text at notes 124–131. *Cf.* Lankenau, *supra* note 158.

178. *See, e.g.,* authorities cited in Note, *supra* note 20, at 854 n. 43. The precise degree of congruence between *New York Times* actual malice and common law malice is not clear, but plainly the *New York Times* standard increases the overlap between liability for defaming a public figure and liability for punitive damages.

179. *See* authorities cited *supra* note 10. Much of the concern over punitive damages in media libel cases has focused not on the amounts actually collected from media libel defendants, but rather on the amounts prayed for in plaintiffs' complaints. *See, e.g.,* Note *supra* note 20, at 847. Discussion of libel suits by reference to their ad damnum clauses has been criticized in Barrett, *supra* note 10, at 857 n. 59.

180. *See, e.g.,* Epstein, *infra* ch. 5; Schauer, *supra* note 114; Shavell, Liability, *supra* note 138 (making same point for tort defendants generally when faced with decreased expected costs of harm-producing activity).

181. *See, e.g.,* Friendly, "CBS Settles Large Libel Suits by Public Officials in 2 Cities," *N.Y. Times,* Oct. 21, 1982, at 15, col. 5 *See also* Friendly, "Investigative Journalism Is Changing Some of Its Goals and Softening Tone," *N.Y. Times,* Aug. 23, 1983, at 8, col. 1.

182. Under a rule of common law libel widely accepted until the middle of this century, each copy of a publication that was sold or distributed constituted a separate defamatory act. Although few American jurisdictions currently follow this rule, the size of the audience for the defamatory publication still influences determination of the degree of damage from the defamatory remark. *See, e.g.,* Prosser & Keeton, *supra* note 113, at 797–801.

183. *See, e.g.,* R. Cass, *supra* note 152, at 61, and authorities cited *id.* at 188 n. 10.

184. For descriptions of media behavior consistent with this proposition, *see* R. Adler, *supra* note 126 (describing CBS' strategy in responding to General Westmoreland's complaint).

185. *See* Brennan, "The Supreme Court and the Meikeljohn Interpretation of the First Amendment," 79 *Harv. L. Rev.* 1 (1965); Cass, *supra* note 133; Kalven, "The New York Times Case: A Note on 'The Central Meaning of the First Amendment,' " 1964 *Sup. Ct. Rev.* 191; Schauer, *supra* note 114.

5

WAS *NEW YORK TIMES* v. *SULLIVAN* WRONG?

Richard A. Epstein

I. NO MORE DANCING

Twenty years ago in his classic article, "The New York Times Case: A Note on 'the Central Meaning of the First Amendment,' "[1] the late Harry Kalven recounted a conversation about the then recent Supreme Court decision in *New York Times v. Sullivan*.[2] Alexander Meiklejohn, the father of modern First Amendment theory, had said that *New York Times* "was an occasion for dancing in the streets." Kalven joined in that judgment, even though elsewhere in that same article he noted the difficulties in speculating about the precise course that the First Amendment law would take after this epochal case. His own guesses included, for example, a prediction that the Supreme Court would expand the *New York Times* privilege to cover matters of public interest and concern. Here he was at best a partial prophet, for the Court first flirted with[3] and then rejected[4] this test in the decade that followed. Nonetheless, Kalven's uncertainty about the ultimate contours of *New York Times* did nothing to temper his glee and enthusiasm for the decision. For him the great principle of *New York Times* was that there was no such thing as seditious libel. Criticism of the government was to be regarded as protected from both criminal punishment and private defamation suits, while false statements of fact about public officials received a qualified privilege rendering them actionable only in cases of "actual malice," carefully circumscribed in *New York Times* to cover only statements published "with knowledge that it was false or with reckless disregard of whether it was false or not."[5] Kalven's piece was both a masterly analysis and an unrestrained celebration of a great historical event. His overt pleasure in the outcome was both uncommonly frank and refreshing in academic writing. In 1964, the world was a better place after *New York Times* was decided.

A generation has now passed, and the dancing has stopped. In retrospect, Kalven's optimism and enthusiasm seem to have been misplaced. It is a commonplace observation that the concern, not to say anxiety, about the threat that defamation actions hold out to freedom of speech and the press has grown mightily, especially in the last decade. If the

only uncertainties with *New York Times* lay in its transitional rules and
marginal ambiguities, then exactly the opposite should have happened.
There should have been a flurry of cases to clarify loose ends in the
years immediately following the decision, followed by a period of stable
tranquillity. The trend has been just the reverse, for without question
the law of defamation is far more controversial today than it was a
decade ago,[6] even though there has been little significant change in the
framework of the substantive law. In recent years, the onslaught of
defamation actions is greater in number and severity than it was in the
"bad old days" of common law libel, as is evidenced by data collected by
the Libel Defense Resource Center, which shows a steady increase in
defamation suits notwithstanding *New York Times*.[7] There are today a
number of proposals for legislative reform, all of which seek to provide
alternative forms of relief to the present law, and most of which envision
the use of the declaratory judgment on truth as a supplement or alternative to the constitutional tort.[8]

The question on everyone's lips is: What went wrong? Why a winter
of discontent after a springtime of unrestrained joy? In part the problems
may have little to do with any of the rules of defamation. The law of tort
is far more active today than it was a generation ago, as we have
witnessed a continued expansion of liability and escalation of verdicts in
such areas as medical malpractice and products liability. The shifts in
defamation could simply reflect the larger social trends in other areas,
and have little to do with what the Supreme Court did to the law of
defamation itself.[9] There are many reforms that should be made in the
conduct of discovery, and in the handling of civil litigation generally,
which would have a substantial effect upon the law of libel.

Yet there is also profit in focusing on the law of defamation itself as a
source of the present discontent, and it is that possibility that I shall
explore here. Given the unforeseen expansion in liability for defamation,
one could argue that the *New York Times* rule is wrong because it did
not go far enough. In an odd sense, abolishing the law of defamation
against public officials *in its entirety* would provide a belated vindication
of the Black and Douglas position in *New York Times,* that the First
Amendment establishes an absolute ban against all libel actions.[10] This
way of framing the question presupposes that the right response to the
present uneasiness is to limit defamation actions even further. It regards
the interest of the press as dominant, so that once we can identify a
chink in its legal armor, the proper response is to afford the press still
greater protection by edging closer to the absolute privilege.

II. THE DEFAMATION TRIANGLE

Today's frequent calls for increased protection of the press are difficult to evaluate in a vacuum. The *New York Times* case is not wanting in a rich profusion of rules that touch virtually every aspect of the common law of defamation. Before one can examine the possibilities of reform it is useful to outline the basic structure of the law of defamation.

The logic of defamation creates a tangled web because it necessarily involves at least three parties—the plaintiff, the defendant, and a third party—who interact in a wide array of circumstances. Often the cast of characters contains a far more extensive list of individuals and entities, as when a newspaper (and its staff) makes false statements about a group (and each member) to its readership (of thousands, if not millions). The tripartite division of the tort largely dictates the elements of the standard defamation action.[11] The plaintiff must allege the publication of a false statement of fact, that the statement was made of and concerning the plaintiff, and that the statement has deterred the plaintiff from entering into or maintaining advantageous relationships with third parties. Statements so actionable may in turn be overridden by privilege. Some privileges are private, as between a prospective employee and a reference for an employer. Others pertain to the public sphere. *New York Times* addresses the privilege of fair comment as it applies to public officials. That privilege could extend to public figures, or even to all matters of public concern. In addition there are general privileges to utter defamatory remarks while petitioning public officials, to reprint "record libels" (i.e., accurate reports of public documents whose contents are known by the author to be false), or to utter defamation in the course of an official proceeding. Any of these privileges in turn could be absolute or qualified (i.e., overridden by proof of malice), as the circumstances dictate. The record libel and legislative privileges are typically absolute, while those of fair comment and the right to commit libel while petitioning the government are typically qualified.

A sound law of libel depends upon getting the right rules for each element of the tort and integrating the elements into a coherent whole. It is far from obvious today which of these pieces is defective, or whether defects that exist cut in the same direction. Lots of different permutations are possible for the law of libel; necessarily there are lots of different ways to be wrong. Indeed the simple law of probability suggests that when the permutations are many, the possibility of hitting the right one is slim. The key to understanding the law of libel is to view it as an integrated whole, in which the choice of one rule on one issue is heavily influenced by the rules adopted on another question. To make the point in its simplest fashion, the basic rule of liability cannot be chosen independent of the rules of damages, both compensatory and punitive. The failure to understand these interactions is, in my view, the source of the institutional distress that has emerged in recent years.

III. CONSTITUTIONALIZE THE TORT?

Thus far I have said nothing about *New York Times* as a constitutional decision. But the proper constitutional response is in large part a function of the difficulty in understanding how the constituent elements of the tort mesh with each other. If the tort of defamation represents a delicate balance, then the Supreme Court should tread carefully where so many common law judges have trodden before. My point is not that the first amendment has nothing to do with the common law of defamation. Quite the opposite, it clearly does. Yet to subject the common law to constitutional scrutiny only defines the scope of the judicial task. It does not even begin to state the proper solution. To understand what is right or wrong with the course the Supreme Court took in *New York Times,* it is necessary to retrace the path taken to see where, if at all, it made a wrong turn.

The defamation allegedly made by the New York Times was an advertisement sponsored by 64 prominent citizens under the heading "Heed Their Rising Voices." The ad, which appeared on March 29, 1960, contained a description of events in Montgomery, Alabama, at the height of Alabama's racial and political unrest. The ad said that the police had been ringing the campus, when in truth they were only deployed nearby. It said that padlocks had been used to keep all the students out of the dining hall, when in fact a few had been excluded because they were not properly registered. It said the students sang "My Country 'Tis of Thee" when in fact they sang the National Anthem. It said that Martin Luther King had been arrested seven times, but in fact he had been arrested only four times. The ad said the police had assisted King's enemies in bombing King's house when in fact they had sought to find the perpetrator. The ad said King was charged with a felony when the charge was a misdemeanor. The plaintiff, Sullivan, was a Montgomery City Commissioner, whose individual responsibilities included supervision of the Police Department as well as the Fire Department, the Department of Cemetery, and the Department of Scales. Many of these events occurred before Sullivan had taken office, but he claimed that the reference to police in the ad would lead persons to think of him as the government official in charge of the Police Department.

Simply reading the facts of the case reminds us how dramatically racial relations in the United States have changed for the better over the past 25 years. The events of the late fifties and early sixties are hardly conceivable today. The case also reminds us that men like Kalven may have danced to two separate melodies.[12] First, there was the doctrinal concern with the freedom of speech, for which the decision remains a landmark. Yet at the time the decision was, if anything, viewed more as a victory for the civil rights movement, guaranteeing a federal presence to offset the official power structure at the state level, which was an unholy bulwark for segregation and white supremacy in all areas of public and private life. The desire to reach the right result in *New York Times* had as much to do with the clear and overpowering sense of equities arising from the confrontation over racial questions as it did with any strong sense of the fine points of the law of defamation. The source of many of the modern problems with the law of defamation is that the *New York Times* decision was influenced too heavily by the dramatic facts of the underlying dispute that gave the doctrine its birth. In consequence the decision has not stood the test of time well when applied to the more mundane cases of defamation arising with public figures and officials.

One key to understanding the decision therefore is to ask how closely the first amendment issue was tied to the immediate political dispute before the court. In order to get a sense of that question, it is necessary to step back from the case and to ask how and why the private tort of defamation should be bound up with the Constitution at all. Before the *New York Times* case, defamation had been long regarded as the province of common law courts. The first step toward change had taken place a long time ago when the prohibitions of the first amendment were held to apply to the states.[13] But what was their force? To read Blackstone, one could easily conclude that freedom of press meant only that prior restraint by administrative officials was unconstitutional.[14] In *Near v. Minnesota ex rel. Olson*[15] that constitutional concern with prior restraint by the executive branch was lifted from its original moorings and extended to prohibit prior restraint by judges in a court of equity acting in response to a petition to abate a public nuisance. Yet Chief Justice Hughes' 5–4 opinion justified the removal of prior restraint by explicitly noting that defamation actions were available to public officials *after* publication:

Public officers, whose character and conduct remain open to debate and free discussion in the press find their remedies for false accusation in actions under libel law as providing for redress and punishment, and not in proceedings to restrain the publication of newspapers and periodicals.[16]

The passage does not contain the slightest hint of any constitutional infirmity in private tort actions for defamation. Indeed the hard problem raised in *Near* is whether court injunctions give rise to the same problems as censorship by administrative boards. One evident difference between the two systems is that administrative officials on a specialized censorship board will be chosen only on the basis of what they believe about censorship.[17] It is accordingly easier to stack a board devoted to a single issue than a court of general jurisdiction, which must deal with the full range of common law and equitable matters. The decision in *Near* must rest on the (good) sense that *any* form of prior restraint offers such possibility of abuse that it is best rejected.

The debate over prior restraint necessarily sets the stage for the analysis of common law defamation actions. As understood in *Near,* prior restraint and common law actions were substitutes for one another. The injunction can be removed from the plaintiff's legal arsenal precisely because the common law action remains. Yet once the two are recognized as substitute forms of social control, it becomes hard to say that one mode of control is subject to constitutional restraint while the other remains wholly beyond constitutional review. The Constitution speaks about freedom of speech, and liability rules can tread upon that freedom as much as direct regulation can.[18]

Once the boundary between legislative and judicial action was crossed in *Near,* then the line between ex ante and ex post remedies could not form a decisive bulwark against constitutional intervention. Yet by the same token, the decision to prevent all forms of prior restraint limits the extent to which constitutional restriction on private actions can and should take place. If private suits are wholly banned along with direct public restraints, then there is no prohibition on lying, for that in a word is what deliberate defamation is. It is hard to find in any theory of freedom of speech a theory that in principle protects the deliberate lie, just as it is inconceivable that any general theory of freedom of action could be pressed into service to reject the prohibitions against murder, rape, and theft. Freedom is not the same as anarchy, whether we deal with words or with actions. In both cases it speaks not only of individual rights of action but of correlative individual duties as well. Freedom, as countless efforts to "balance" interests have made clear, is a presumption in favor of speech or action, but it is one that can be overriden when the conduct regulated involves the use of force or misrepresentation.

Defamation often involves the latter so in principle it becomes fair game for some forms of state control. Where prohibitions ex ante are ruled out of bounds, then some liability ex post must be tolerated. The question is, what are its proper limits?

This issue came to a head in the *New York Times* decision. Before the case there was a quiet satisfaction with the basic common law rules of defamation, so much so that the issues left lurking in *Near* never became the subject of a direct judicial challenge. Yet the decision in *New York Times* shows that it is as easy to pervert common law rules as it is to pervert direct regulation. The New York Times had a tiny circulation in Alabama. The references it made to Sullivan were if anything indirect and obscure, and may well have improved his local standing, on the doubtful assumption that they had any effect at all. Yet the Alabama courts were prepared to sustain a judgment of $500,000 (in 1964 dollars) for this plaintiff, with the prospect of similar suits waiting in the wings. It is perhaps an exaggeration to say that this round of law suits would have bankrupted the Times, but any such judgments would have represented a deep miscarriage of the common law process. Harry Kalven thought that the common law rules would tolerate this result. I disagree. My sense is that tried anywhere outside the deep South, the plaintiff would have been sent home packing. The common law was sound; its application was not.

So what should be done in the United States Supreme Court? Here the task was complicated because the Court's powers of review were limited by the principles of federalism. The United States Supreme Court could not simply demonstrate that Alabama had misapplied its own substantive law. It had to show that its misapplication violated some rule of federal constitutional law. In order therefore to save the Times, it became necessary to constitutionalize some portion of the common law of defamation. Yet there is good sense in that endeavor, for one critical function of any constitution is to provide protection in moments of crisis, even those precipitated by common law adjudication.[19] There is a strict federal duty to police the line between permitted and prohibited speech. Let the major premise be that defamation should be actionable on the ground that freedom never encompasses the right to say false and harmful things about another individual. Nonetheless the states cannot be allowed to define defamation as they please. If they could, they might expand the boundaries of the tort until it covers what, in strict theory, belongs within the domain of protected speech.[20] The states cannot, either through their courts or their legislatures, circumvent the constitutional prohibitions by deft manipulations of common law rules.

In principle this argument is very powerful, and suggests that virtually the entire law of defamation, at least as it relates to matters of public interest and concern, could be subject to constitutional revision. Indeed I think there is no stopping point short of that large proposition. Yet there are crucial questions of technique. In particular, there are two other points that loom large in the discussion of *New York Times* itself.

The first point is that nothing in this broad principle says that the common law rules crafted over many centuries struck the wrong balance between speech and reputation. There may be ample reason for federal constitutional *review* of common law principles, but it need not follow that there is any parallel presumption for constitutional *rejection* of state common law principles. If anything, our prior intuitions should be just the opposite, for the common law operates from a deep conviction in the importance of freedom of speech (as it does with freedom generally). How else could one explain the general satisfaction with the law of libel before *New York Times,* and the extensive protection generally afforded criticism of public works and public figures? [21] We should therefore expect a very high level of congruence between what the first amendment requires and what the common law has provided. If there is any presumption, it should be in favor of the constitutional permissibility of the common law rules. The necessary protection should be provided, where possible, without disrupting the good sense of the common law rules in ordinary cases.

The second point is one of tactics. The great step in *New York Times* was to breach the wall between prior restraint and tort liability. Entering into the common law turf is, however, no simple task. The law of defamation is a highly complex body of rules. Federal judges should be at least aware of the possibility that these common law rules contain a greater inner coherence than first meets the eye. The proper strategy therefore is to enter upon these fields with caution. To save the New York Times from possible financial ruin might be reason enough to begin the constitutional journey, but it does not dictate the entire course of the journey. Once it is recognized that the Alabama decision in *New York Times* was a common law aberration, the right Supreme Court strategy should have been to colonize as little as possible of the common law turf in its initial foray. This call for procedural prudence has important consequences for the ultimate shape of the law. At one level the Court might have intervened by saying to the Alabama Court:

> We think that the common law rules of defamation have clear constitutional implications. When we reverse your judgment below, we seek to impose upon you no standard that you have not accepted, both as a general matter of common law rule, and in the course of

this case. Nonetheless we think that lip service to a common law standard is one thing; its faithful application in controversial cases is quite another. Mere pretext will not do. On our examination of this extraordinary case, it seems clear that you did not follow your own rules.

The other course of action starts with the assumption that the Supreme Court is under a constitutional duty to fashion a law of defamation (at least as regards public officials) from the text of the first amendment. Here the intervention upon state courts is far greater because now in effect the Court has to say:

In this case we do not have to decide whether Alabama has properly applied the common law as it existed within its jurisdiction. As far as we are concerned the balance between freedom of speech and the protection of individual reputation is solely a matter for this Court and this Court alone to decide. We think that the Constitution gives us sufficient material to refashion the entire law of defamation. It is that task which we undertake today.

IV. THE NARROW PATH

In a decision fraught with long-term institutional ramifications, the Court clearly took the second course. Yet it was quite possible to have disposed of this case without reaching the one issue for which *New York Times* has become so famous—its actual malice rule. In particular there were at least two far narrower grounds for intervention available to the Court, which would have neatly disposed of the case without changing the entire structure of the common law.

First, the Court could have constitutionalized the "of and concerning" requirement. There is a great sense that if speech says bad things about a large number of persons it loses its force and its credibility about any single person. The broader the class of persons about whom a falsehood is made, the greater the likelihood that the intended audience will know or at least intuit that the statement does not capture the relevant distinctions between individuals. These broad group denunciations therefore carry with them the seeds of their own futility; defamatory speech cannot succeed where the audience to whom it is uttered is left unmoved. To refer generally to the police or even more generally to state authorities or Southern violators is to refer to everyone and no one at the same time, which is what the ad did.[22] It is not to say that X of the police force did some wrongful act. There is clearly a delicate line between defamation of a huge part of the public and defamation of a small identifiable group. The standard common law decisions placed this gray area roughly between twelve and twenty persons.[23] That number could be right or wrong. But we have here a statement which refers to hundreds if not thousands of individuals. There is no need to struggle with the fine points. A summary judgment dismissing this cause of action, coupled with a general statement ordering all state and federal courts to enter similar judgments in other actions brought on the strength of this advertisement, would have ended the Times' travail. And if there had been any disregard at the lower levels, a simple summary reversal at the Supreme Court level would have stopped the issue dead in its tracks, while holding open the possibility of malicious prosecution actions against those parties who chose to continue with their suits after *New York Times*.

A second strategy was also available in the case. The $500,000 in general and punitive damages was entered without the slightest showing of any actual damages. In many defamation cases the use of general damages is appropriate because it is quite often impossible to reconstruct the ever-expanding web of influence that false statements can spin. The third parties who have been misled by the falsehood decide not to do business with the plaintiff but cannot be tracked down.[24] Nonetheless the recognition that there must be general damages does not provide an open season for a trier of fact to award whatever damages seem nice. Here the want of any precise measure shows the need to identify sensible surrogates for the anticipated damages. The focus of the statement upon the plaintiff and the size of the local circulation of the libel are the obvious tests, and both of these weighed very heavily against Sullivan's case. The Supreme Court with but little imagination could have struck down the entire verdict on the ground that Alabama clearly misapplied the law of general and punitive damages in the case.

In addition, the Court could have intervened on the ground of truth, which is regarded as a defense at the common law.[25] Nonetheless the common law rules exhibit two strange discontinuities. First, the ounce of falsehood is able to destroy the pound of truth. Thus any statement that is wrong on matters of inessential details is treated as though it were false altogether, so that marginal mistakes are allowed to condemn essentially truthful accounts.[26] But one could argue, as with other tort doctrines, that only the *incremental* harm attributable to the false portions of the statement is actionable, and not the total harm attributable to true and false portions alike. At this point the level of intervention has increased because the rationale for the constitutional decision breaks from the common law rule. But it does so in ways consistent with the general theories of tort liability. In any event, this principle clearly works wonders on the facts of *New York Times* because most of the errors in the advertisement were on matters of detail. The $500,000 judgment is manifestly unsupportable.

Second, one could argue, even as a constitutional matter, that the burden on truth should be on the plaintiff, as has finally been held in the recent case of *Philadelphia Newspapers v. Hepps.*[27] Again this requires the Court to go beyond the common law, but there are strong reasons for the warrant, at least in a world with the strict liability rule. Initially the idea of truth as *justification* strikes a discordant note in the law. In the usual case justifications are never absolute, but are themselves defeasible if their appropriate limits have been exceeded.[28] No one doubts that self-defense is a good justification for the infliction of a deliberate harm. Yet the nature of the justification is limited to the wrong that brought it into being, so that self-defense may be overriden by a showing of excessive or deadly force.[29] But truth is said to be absolute, which suggests it is error to regard it as a defense to defamation at all. Instead the real staying power of defamation, notwithstanding the fact that it has nothing to do with physical harm, is that it falls neatly within the general libertarian prohibition against the use of force and misrepresentation in human affairs. That is just what is at stake when defamation is rightly understood as false statements made to a third party to the discredit of the plaintiff.[30] Without the falsehood there is at most a hard case for invasion of privacy that has generally and rightly foundered.[31] It follows therefore that a proper understanding of falsehood would make truth a necessary requirement of the prima facie case, in which instance the ordinary burden of proof should fall upon the plaintiff to show falsity.[32] In *New York Times* the appropriate burden of proof probably would have not been decisive on most of the statements in the ads, but the proper allocation of this burden is of clear importance with respect to future cases, where the issue of truth or falsity may be harder to resolve.

V. ACTUAL MALICE: A RETURN TO FUNDAMENTALS

The *New York Times* case is, however, most remembered for the point that it did not need to decide, and which it may have wrongly decided: that proof of actual malice (i.e., knowledge that the statement is false or that it is made with reckless disregard for its truth) is required for a public official to bring a defamation action against a media defendant. The proposition stands in very sharp opposition to the majority common law position on the same question, which drew a line between statements of fact, for which liability was strict if the statements were false, and statements of opinion, which were generally privileged absolutely because they are incapable of being either true or false.[33]

In making the case for or against the actual malice privilege, the Constitution does not arm us with any knowledge or technique unavailable to the ordinary common law judge. The question is how those tools are put to use. In order to get a sense of what privilege, if any, should be accorded to false statements about public officials, it is useful to step back a bit and to recall why defamation is actionable at all, given the popular saw that "sticks and stones may break my bones but words will never hurt me." Here, moreover, the argument is the same within a system of common law as it is under the Constitution, because both start from the same general presumption that freedom of action (and freedom of speech) is protected unless it is shown to become an evil to others—not merely because others dislike it, but because it takes what they own.

That words can work the taking can be seen simply enough by reverting to the set of examples that show how narrow the gap is between speech and conduct. Case one: I take a thing from you which you own. It is an act of trespass. But what about variations on the simple theme? Suppose I put a gun to your head so that you will hand it over to me? I haven't said anything, but that is because everyone understands the assertive nature of the basic conduct. Now assume that the words: "Your money or your life" are added. Here is a threat. But go further, and suppose that I leave the domain of coercion and enter the domain of persuasion. I tell you I need the thing because I am sick. Now it is a gift if my statement is true, but it is a taking of the thing if the statement is false; and it matters little if we introduce the complexity of third persons. If I use force to compel you not to do business with X, then there is tortious behavior. When I utter words to that same effect, false words, there is also a removal from individuals of their right to dispose of their property and labor as they choose. Now my falsehoods prevent persons from engaging in the voluntary transactions in which they would otherwise participate. The range of these transactions is very wide, including all personal and social arrangements as well as those of a more strictly economic character. But in each case a strong theory of freedom generates individual rights of association, and recognizes that these are infringed by defamation as well as by physical means. The concerns with trespass and defamation come from the same source. The key difference is that it is usually easier to duck a libel than a bullet. But this point only shows that some wrongs are more serious than others; it does not show that defamation should not be actionable simply because the use of force provides a greater peril to the social order.

The general tendency in defamation cases has always been for a powerful rule of strict liability. I think this result rests upon commendable moral instincts here as it does with physical injuries.[34] Defamation is made to third persons about the plaintiff, so that prima facie the plaintiff is in no way responsible for the commission of the wrong and typically could do very little, if anything, to protect himself. As the defendant is prima facie the sole actor, the rule that places powerful incentives against his misconduct will be one which tends to deter the abuse that will otherwise take place. Where the plaintiff is not a stranger to the process and stands to benefit from it, a sensible body of privileges softens liability, as with references that prospective employers request in employment cases.[35] Understood in this fashion the parallels between defamation and the rules of trespass to land are very close. With trespass to land the strictness of the older common law rules rests upon the idea that the plaintiff landowner is wholly passive and the intruder is very active. The balance can shift of course, as when the landowner invites the defendant upon the property or plants a trap in order to harm him. The situation is surely simpler with the ordinary trespass because it involves only two parties, not three or perhaps many more. Nonetheless one can see in both trespass and defamation different applications of a unified concern with liberty and property.

VI. SHOULD WE BAR DEFAMATION ACTIONS BY PUBLIC OFFICIALS?

The critical question for *New York Times* is whether this account of the tort of defamation should extend without modification to false statements made about public officials. Here nothing about the merits of the individual case encourages abrogation of the tort or special protection of the defamer. People take public office at a risk to their serenity and composure; while they can respond in kind, there is nothing which says that the response will be effective, especially if it is about matters that are not well known, so that the world at large is in a genuine quandary as to who is telling the truth. Elections can be lost by an assertion of marital infidelity or bribery; careers can be ruined by charges of criminal misconduct. Reputation is not some lifeless abstraction, but the summation of all the possibilities for gainful interactions—economic, social, and political—with others that are stripped away by false statements. Specific rebuttals from the defamed party offer some protection but they are often too little, too late.

So why not allow the action for defamation? Here the argument is best stated in terms of error costs. There is a danger that if the false statements are punished, then the true statements will not be made at all. Self-censorship will substitute for government censorship, so that speech will not be free, open, and robust. The "breathing room" required for speech will disappear. The important point to note about this argument is that it recognizes only the error costs that run in one direction: those which lead to the reduction in the quantity of speech. If this is all there were to the analysis, then it would be hard to find anything which could allow the Supreme Court to stop short of the Black and Douglas position of no tort liability for the defamation of public officials. If the law desires only to maximize breathing room, then it must run to this extreme; it must afford absolute immunity from private defamation actions by all public officials.

New York Times stops short of that extreme position. What drives it back in the opposite direction? One way to see the problem is to ask what the world would look like if public officials could never sue for defamation. The first point is that we could not assume that primary conduct would remain unchanged by the radical difference in legal response. Defamation suits impose a price on those who make false statements about others. Repeal of the law of defamation dramatically reduces that price, given that all administrative and injunctive remedies have already been ruled out of bounds.[36] The cost to the defamer does not become zero, because those who engage in widespread defamation run the risk of ruining their own reputations and inviting retaliation by others. We should not expect an infinite supply of lies. Still the utter want of any restrictions against defamation does create the classical economic externality (I lie and you suffer) and the consequent misallocation of resources. The party who makes the statement keeps all the benefits and bears part but not all of the costs. The result is that the level of false statements will rise until private benefit equals private marginal cost. The presence of the powerful externality insures that an equilibrium position is reached where marginal social benefit is less than marginal social cost. A world without any protection against defamation is a world with too much defamation, too much misinformation—in a word, too much public fraud.

The point can be recast by taking literally the familiar observation that the first amendment is designed to protect a marketplace of ideas. This marketplace, no less than any other, presupposes that there are certain private moves that are simply not permitted. A belief in markets for ordinary goods requires government protection (funded by taxes) against theft and fraud. A belief in the marketplace of ideas requires the same protection. Some protection against defamation is part of the total package.

It follows therefore that even with public officials there are two types of error in devising the rules of defamation. There can be too much defamation or too little. The task is to find that set of rules which minimizes the costs of the two forms of error taken together. This proposition is not only of abstract concern but relates directly to those issues that go to the core of the first amendment. The traditional justifications for the *New York Times* rule on absolute malice stress the need to encourage free and robust debate. Nonetheless, it seems clear that the absolute privilege will not give rise to the best kind of public debate.

There are at least two sources of anxiety. First, the rules of defamation are important not only for the way in which they decide cases that arise. They are also important in the way in which they shape the primary decisions to enter into political discussion and debate. It does not seem far-fetched to assume that some honest people are vulnerable to serious losses if defamed. The greater their reputations, the greater their potential losses. If the remedies for actual defamation are removed, or even watered down, one response is for these people to stay out of the public arena, thus opening the field for other persons with lesser reputations and perhaps lesser character. The magnitude of this effect is very hard to measure, but there is no reason to assume that it is trivial. Distinguished men and women invest substantial sums in their reputation. They have the most to lose if the price of participating in public debate is the loss of all or part of that reputational capital.

The second cost relates to the public at large. The level of discourse over public issues is not simply a function of the total amount of speech. It also depends on the quality of speech. If there is no law of defamation, then the mix between truthful and false statements will shift. More false statements will be made. The public will then be required to discount the information that it acquires because it can be less sure of its pedigree. The influence of the press will diminish as there will be no obvious way to distinguish the good reports from the bad, in part because no one can ever be held legally accountable for their false statements. It is very hard to conceive of how the world would really look if there were no law of defamation. But one cannot assume that newspapers and public officials would behave with the same degree of caution as they do under the *New York Times* rule, or as they did under the common law rules.

One can get some sense of the extreme nature of total immunity by turning the constitutional inquiry on its head. There seems to be no obvious first amendment violation if the Court were to adopt the Black and Douglas position. But on reflection why is the point so obvious? Suppose one were to argue that the absolute ban on defamation action imposed an intolerable tax upon honest individuals who wanted to speak their mind but were afraid to do so. Is the issue now so clear? There have been first amendment cases which have protected the first amendment rights of nonspeakers, of workers who are opposed to union political positions to which they are forced to contribute, and of college students who are opposed to the use of student fees to support a public interest law firm that takes positions in opposition to their own.[37] The argument is that the tax makes people pay for what they oppose, which is inconsistent with any idea of freedom. But the difference between the express tax on the one hand and the implicit tax created by the abolition of all tort protection is not clear in principle. It has little place in first amendment theory, which has generally found in taxation,[38] regulation,[39] and modification of liability rules (as in *New York Times* itself) impermissible limitations upon freedom of speech.

The issue, if anything, becomes clearer when the question is set against ordinary property notions. I have argued elsewhere that it is an unconstitutional taking of property for the state to pass a rule which simply abolishes all common law rights against trespassers to land.[40] In effect that "small" change in legal rules would make all property held in common. In my view, there is good reason to think that reputation, rightly understood, is one of the bundle of property rights and liberty that all individuals enjoy. If the analysis given above is correct, then the action of defamation protects the rights of disposition in property and labor against the false statements of others. The abolition of the action generally amounts to a taking of the property for which insufficient compensation is tendered, given the disastrous overall consequences of the no liability rule. No cash compensation can be paid over to all persons, while the insertion of all reputations into the common pool so diminishes the value of human and physical resources that most everyone is left worse off in consequence.[41] The only way to prevent that form of taking is to retain some level of common law protection. I doubt very much whether the Supreme Court would find this line of argument appropriate, although it has flirted with the idea that reputation is protected under the due process clause, at least against defamation by public officials.[42] Analytically, however, there is no such thing as a free constitutional lunch. Just as the contraction of the rights of speech raises first amendment issues, so their indefinite *expansion* raises constitutional issues as well. There is an evident need to find the workable intermediate position in the law of defamation.

VII. THE ACTUAL MALICE COMPROMISE

The Supreme Court's recognition of the undesirable consequences of an absolute immunity rule led it to the actual malice rule as a compromise between the strict liability and no liability positions. Nonetheless, in dealing with liability rules the middle position may well be inferior to one of the two extremes. That point seems true here, for I think it can be shown that the Supreme Court has miscalculated both the costs and benefits of its own actual malice rule. Initially the rule offends the sense of justice because it makes innocent persons bear the harms that have been inflicted upon them by other persons, including those who have acted with negligence or even gross negligence. Indeed my own view is that the proper rule in defamation is strict liability, as it was at common law,[43] so that the deviation between the present law and the ideal is even greater than it might seem to others. The question, then, is what public interest can justify the deviation from these ordinary standards of liability?

I take it that in a world of error-free determinations there would be no case whatsoever, because then there would be no risk that innocent persons will be chilled from their exercise of protected speech and no risk of overcompensation for persons in fact defamed. This proposition remains true whether we worry about the internal operation of the legal system or the calculations made by private parties. The error-free world of litigation could only exist in a world of zero transaction costs, and in that world private parties would be able to make perfect predictions of how courts would respond to false statements. The subjective evaluations of truth and falsity would therefore come into alignment with the judgments of judges and juries.

The need for the actual malice rule therefore depends critically upon the error rate in litigation, which in turn complicates the analysis that any private parties make before publication. We can assume, I think, that the error rate in litigation is high, so that private decisions on publication are, consequently, clouded. The theory of *New York Times* is that a malice rule reduces the level of false positives (i.e., cases in which liability is found where none should be imposed) to a level that satisfies the first amendment. That it increases the number of false negatives (i.e., cases in which no liability is found when some should be imposed) simply becomes a cost to be borne for making good the constitutional commitment to freedom of speech.

It is doubtful, however, that the total situation is improved by the adoption of the actual malice rule. My argument on this point takes two parts. First, it is possible that the actual malice rule has made the situation worse for media defendants than it would be under a sensible strict liability rule. Even if these costs to the media were the only relevant issue, the older common law might be superior. In broaching this possibility I am going against the wisdom of the media professionals, who candidly prefer the actual malice rule to any regime of strict liability. For that reason alone I should be hesitant in raising this ironic twist, because most professionals do know their self-interest. But even if this dramatic conclusion is false, the factors in the analysis may well show that the media systematically overestimates their net benefits from the actual malice rule.

More critically, however, the final judgment about the desirability of the *New York Times* rule rests upon the *social* consequences of the rule. The common law principle of strict liability is supported by strong legal theory, so that any deviation from it should be justified by the net social benefits produced. Any complete evaluation therefore must take into account both the costs and benefits to plaintiffs and to the public at large under alternative legal regimes, as best we can do it. Expanding the field of vision, however, only makes the case for the actual malice rule less defensible, for plaintiffs and (probably) the public are losers as well. The argument ranges over a number of issues. Let me develop the particular facets of the case. These include liability and damages, litigation costs, uncertainty costs, and reputational effects. I shall take them in order.

Liability and damages. The nature of liability rules has powerful influences upon the way in which parties litigate their suits. In general, any liability system must make two critical choices. The first concerns the likelihood of success of the plaintiff's action, and this typically varies with the theories of liability adopted. Strict liability cases are uniformly more likely to succeed than those which require actual malice. The second element that the system controls is the level of damages awarded once liability is established. In the simplest model the damages could be low, as with actual damages, or high, as when punitive damages apply. In more complex models the level of actual damage could be allowed to vary with the strength of the plaintiff's case. Yet for the moment the central points can be made by confining attention to cases with two standards of liability and two measures of damages. On this assumption, four combinations of liability and damage rules have to be taken into account in assessing the complete situation. It seems possible to eliminate two of these fairly quickly, as the case law has always done. Thus it is highly unlikely that anyone would advocate a strict liability rule coupled with punitive damages. The high probability of success when coupled with the high level of damages yields a sanction for speech far in excess of the harm that it causes. The objection based upon overdeterrence of speech, both good and bad alike, seems evident without further comment. *New York Times* does allow punitive damages for public officials, but only when actual malice is proved.

By the same token one runs the risk of serious underdeterrence if there is a rule that provides a low probability of success (when actual malice must be proved) coupled with a low (or even zero) payoff once defamatory falsehood is established. Most people have the sense that if the defendant has acted in a terrible and malicious manner, courts ought not to trim damages in his favor; the risk of underdeterrence is too great. Even the Supreme Court has moved toward this view in a sense, for *New York Times* does not identify any obvious case where punitive damages could be denied once actual malice is established. Instead, taken as written, the opinion seems to say that whenever actual malice is established the plaintiff is entitled to recover both actual and punitive damages. It is conceivable to adopt (as at common law) mixed systems where actual damages are routinely allowed for defamation, and punitive damages come in only where malice is established, but that does not seem to be the current situation.

Postponing consideration of this mixed strategy, two strategies remain: strict liability and low damages; actual malice and high damages. The key question is which strategy better controls for the risk of error in defamation cases. In one sense there is no obvious answer to that question a priori. To see the point note that, as a first approximation, the net cost of the defamation laws to a defendant are simply a product of the two numbers—the probability of plaintiff's success and the level of damages awarded. It is easy to think of numbers in which first one and then the other system has greater total effect. In strict liability the probability of recovery is relatively large and the damages can be kept relatively small. With actual malice the probability of recovery is relatively small and damages are relatively large. It takes little mathematical sophistication to realize that if success is more likely with strict liability, and damages are more generous with actual malice, it becomes uncertain whether the total liabilities, which equal the product of loss and damages, are greater under the strict liability rule or the actual malice rule. The tipping point depends upon the relative magnitudes of the different variables.

The point has important implication for the soundness of the decision in *New York Times*. If it turns out that actual malice liability is greater than strict liability, then the *New York Times* rule has the odd and unfortunate consequence of increasing the expected costs of defamation actions to media defendants, all in the name of protecting freedom of speech. It is therefore important to analyze the relationship between the relevant variables, while remaining aware that there is very little hard data available on the question.

Consider first the question of probabilities. Here my own instinct is that the difference between success in strict liability and in actual malice is likely to be smaller than expected at first blush. The key variable that separates strict liability from the actual malice rule is the defendant's knowledge that the statement made is false, or his reckless disregard of whether it is true or false. In ordinary strict liability actions for physical harm inflicted upon strangers, any new knowledge barrier would be an effective limitation upon liability, for most defendants do not even know the identity of the persons whom they hurt by accident. But it is the rare defamation action where the words spoken just happen to defame a person of whom the defendant has no knowledge.[44] It is every bit as rare that words innocent on their face are rendered defamatory by some extrinsic facts known to the audience of the defendant's statement but unknown to the defendant himself.[45]

In the usual case the defendant names the plaintiff; in the usual case the defendant knows that the statement is defamatory and that it will hurt the plaintiff. That is one of the reasons why it is made, perhaps in the belief that the plaintiff's behavior warranted the hurt so inflicted. Ordinarily, the actual malice issue is not decided against a backdrop of innocent and inadvertent conduct. It becomes quite plausible for a plaintiff to assert that given what the defendant did know about the facts of the case, and about the sources from which these facts were acquired (persons with underground connections or with grudges to settle), it was incumbent upon him to take further steps to insure that the statement was truthful.[46] To be sure this statement may look like a simple assertion of ordinary negligence—a failure of ordinary investigation— which is of no avail to the plaintiff. But the skillful lawyer may often be able present these facts so as to make it clear, or at least arguable, that more is involved. The defendant had notice of the harm inflicted and made a conscious decision to stop the inquiries before he was perfectly satisfied that the statement which harmed the plaintiff was true. The line between ordinary negligence and recklessness may sound bright in principle, but it is easily grayed by stressing what the defendant had to know when critical decisions were made. The plaintiff's lawyer may also be aided by a marked change in sensibilities that has developed elsewhere in the law. In particular, plaintiffs may take some comfort from the carrying over of the modern law of products liability, where simple notice of a problem, coupled with a considered failure to change past practices, has been regarded, probably wrongly, as evidence sufficient to support a verdict of punitive damages.

The plaintiff's case is also fueled by a strong sense of equity. Why should this plaintiff be sacrificed on the alter of free speech when the defendant's words were both false and harmful? These tendencies can of course be checked by diligent judges, but there is enough play in the joints that a fair number of cases may well get through. There is no question that the probabilities of plaintiff success are diminished by the hurdles of the Supreme Court's actual malice rule. Some observers think that defendant's chances of being granted summary judgment on actual malice are very great. Numbers as high as 90 percent have been mentioned in conversation, but hard data to either confirm or contradict that assertion is difficult to find. The number may be that large, or it may be somewhat smaller.

The hard question is, how does one evaluate such a 90 percent figure even if it turns out to be true? Here the question can only be approached in the round. One key question concerns the total frequency of suit. These seem to have increased apace in the post-*New York Times* period, along with much other tort litigation. The data of the Libel Defense Resource Center hints at a threefold increase in the number of litigated cases, which may parallel the increase in total cases brought. The increase in total number of cases therefore suggests that the reduction in total libel suits is not as great as the extreme 90 percent figure suggests. In addition, the cases which pass the hurdle are not randomly selected. They are more likely to be the major cases where the plaintiff is willing to spend the money in discovery and investigation to get to the heart of a case. So even if 90 percent of the cases are stopped before trial, 90 percent of the potential exposure, measured either in dollars or publicity, is not.

One critical issue, then, concerns the source of the increase in cases. If that increase is attributable solely to general changes in litigation style, then the *New York Times* rule plays a major role in reducing the total number of cases brought. But in part the number of cases brought may well be a function of the types of damages that are demanded under the actual malice rule. One critical feature of *New York Times* is that it blurs the line between actual and punitive damages. Once the plaintiff has overcome the obstacle of actual malice, both compensatory and punitive damages are recoverable. A court or jury is not dealing solely with a wrongful statement, but with a pre-selected defendant whose conduct varies from the highly reprehensible to the quasi-criminal. To make matters worse, media defendants are not engaged simply in idle gossip. Typically they print these stories to boost sales and to obtain a private profit. The gains attributable to defamatory stories are difficult to quantify, and no one expressly advocates that the restitution measure of damages, based on a theory of unjust enrichment, should be systematically applied on a case by case basis. The difficulties of trying to figure how much one defamatory story increased the sales of a national newspaper or television show are formidable indeed. Nonetheless, the influence of defendant's gains cannot be ignored in trying to get some sense of the behavior of judge and jury alike. A bad defendant has made a killing at the expense of an innocent plaintiff. Why not haul out the lumber and swing away? The occasional mammoth jury award of $25,000,000 or more shows this tendency in action.[47] The increase in expected awards may therefore be a response to the larger sense of culpability that the media defendant is found to bear. No one suggests that this attitude will be shared by all juries and judges, but the relevant probabilities are undeniably changed if it is held by some. A ballpark estimate might suggest that compensatory and punitive damages would increase by, say, 60 percent. Indeed the review of the cases conducted by the Libel Defense Resource Center notes that the amount of jury awards far outpaced inflation, and was even more rapid than the parallel increases found in both medical malpractice and product liability cases. These findings must be adjusted to reflect the substantial reduction in award levels that routinely occur as the cases wind their way through the review and appellate process. Nonetheless, there is every theoretical reason to believe that, holding other factors constant, the abandonment of strict liability in favor of actual malice will induce a systematic increase in damage awards, which in turn might induce more plaintiffs to bring suit. It is very difficult to measure their relative extent, but by the same token it is not obvious, a priori, that the total payments from defendants to plaintiffs are reduced by the rule.

The relationship between liability rules and damage levels deserves a further observation, for there is no reason to assume that the two numbers, probability and severity, vary independently over their separate ranges. Juries and judges may think strategically about the proper calculation of awards. If they know that many defendants escape scot-free (i.e., if the probability of liability under actual malice is low), then they might deliberately raise the damage awards in order to compensate for that error. After all, the key defendants are *institutional* players who are necessarily involved in multiple incidents of arguable defamation. In some cases raising damages could be a conscious reaction, and in others it need not. But in all cases the effect may be the same. The rise in damages paid removes much of the protection that the actual malice rule wants to provide to a defendant. We can say that the more the plaintiff's probability of recovery is reduced, the more likely it is that damages in the cases that remain will increase. The total level of damage payments may not be substantially reduced.

Litigation costs. The case against the actual malice rule of *New York Times* is strengthened when litigation costs are taken into account. One obvious point is that there is simply more to litigate once actual malice is critical to liability. Under the common law rules the question of liability for defamation tended to turn largely on external facts. It was easy to determine whether or not a newspaper published a certain statement; generally it is not too difficult to find out whether it is defamatory.

The question of whether it was false is more problematic. In the *Westmoreland* case, for example, the issue of truth raised enormous problems. The events took place decades before the suit was brought, and the facts placed in issue spanned continents and years. Any thorough examination of the case required at a minimum a review of all contacts between President Johnson and General Westmoreland, and spread beyond it to the papers and recollection of others. Even more routine defamation cases could require a jury to understand the point behind certain complex business transactions. Truth can be a messy business where the statements are not about discrete persons at particular times and places. In practice, moreover, we should expect that litigation will be most prevalent where the uncertainty over truth is at its highest.[48] But it is risky to generalize from the most difficult cases that vex judge and jury alike. Truth and falsity may be touch-and-go in some cases, and one should not endow the common law with more clarity than it possesses. Still, for the general run of cases, finding truth does not raise intolerable burdens for the parties or the courts. If it did, then one could not try ordinary misrepresentation and fraud cases, and we would have to question the entire range of common law litigation, which typically presupposes the serviceability of its fact-finding efforts. Even within the libel context, falsehood must be ascertained before liability is established under *New York Times*. Short of the absolute immunity on liability, *any* system of defamation will have to address the issues of publication, defamation, and truth. We can survive such difficulties.

Actual malice, however, now shifts the inquiry from the external facts to the internal state of mind. Suits brought against the media typically turn on the state of mind of many people, not of one single person. Each of these persons must be subject to depositions and interrogatories, so that the elephantine rules of civil procedure now increase the burdens on both sides in a defamation case. There is no obvious way to rule out-of-bounds the very evidence on mental state that the *New York Times* rule decrees is central to the question of liability, as the Supreme Court recognized in *Herbert v. Lando*,[49] itself an epic piece of litigation that has been prolonged by attention to the actual malice question. The ability of a well-heeled or determined plaintiff to hound a defendant in discovery is an inescapable fact of life under the present law. It was a smaller risk in common law trials that were conducted on strict liability principles.

The difficulties of proof under an actual malice standard have a powerful influence on the overall behavior of the media. Defendants worry about the total costs of their speech, both defamatory and nondefamatory, and take into account the costs that they pay their lawyers as well as the costs they pay the plaintiffs. To be sure, the two types of costs operate in different fashion: the costs to the plaintiff are transfer payments, which in and of themselves generate neither social losses nor gains. They are typically justified as redress for individual wrongs or for the incentives they create against further misconduct. Legal fees are not transfers, but represent the private consumption of real resources— lawyers, experts, and others who would seek other employment if these suits were not brought. Defendants make these payments in order to avoid greater payments to the plaintiff and other losses associated with losing legal cases. Their hope is that if the defense is successful it will deter other plaintiffs from bringing similar suits, a vital concern for media defendants who are repeat players in defamation actions. "Millions for defense and not a penny for tribute" contains the germ of a rational institutional defendant's strategy, serviceable in many instances when long-term incentives are taken into account. Yet it represents an unhappy social strategy, given that litigation expenses are deadweight social losses, whereas transfer payments are not.

The important point here is to note the relationship between litigation expenses and the shape of the substantive rule. It is easy to be incautious and to assume that the costs of litigation are solely a function of the expected losses. Nothing could be further from the truth. The key point depends upon the relationship between probability of loss and anticipated damages. To begin at the limit, if recovery is certain there is no incentive for any defendant to resist payment. It will have to pay damages in any event, and therefore should act rationally in order to economize on litigation costs. On the other hand, when the probability of success is zero, the parallel conclusion holds. Why should the plaintiff bring a lawsuit if the return is known to be negative? (There are bluffing complications which I ignore.) Let the probability move towards 50 percent and uncertainty of outcome becomes very great. In addition, the uncertainty in total payoff is even greater because damages in actual malice cases are large relative to those in strict liability suits. There is now something worth fighting over, and private parties, out to maximize their private returns, will now find, especially under the American system of costs, that there is a greater anticipated payoff to very large litigation expenses. Stated otherwise, high uncertainty/high stakes games generate high litigation expenses for plaintiffs and defendants alike. The low uncertainty/low stakes games get resolved at far lower cost. It follows therefore that even if total liabilities under the two legal regimes are the same, the total litigation costs to a defendant may well be greater under the actual malice standard. A defendant would have to pay more for defamation under the *New York Times* rule than he would have to pay under a common law rule of strict liability, where probability of loss is greater and the amount in controversy is smaller. Even if the total liabilities under strict liability were greater than those under actual malice, it is quite possible that the difference in administrative costs would tend to narrow the gap further, and might even reverse the direction of the inequality.

Uncertainty and risk aversion. The matter is complicated still further because the defendant's costs under *New York Times* are increased by risk aversion, that is, by the simple observation that most people regard uncertainty itself as a cost. Generally risk aversion drives both sides to settlement precisely because each receives gains when an uncertain liability is replaced by a certain sum. It follows therefore that any legal rule which increases the uncertainty in outcomes can only have the effect of diminishing the utility of the parties that are governed by it. As with administrative costs, risk aversion is a feature that strikes at plaintiffs and defendants alike. In particular, the uncertainty under actual malice may be greater, especially in those big cases that dominate defamation litigation. Uncertainty again shifts the balance toward the strict liability rule.

Reputational effects. We have thus far looked at the gains and losses to the press from the point of view of its total exposure in litigation. Yet it is quite clear that a complete analysis would ask one to take into account the effects that the law of defamation has on the ability of the press to collect revenues and to obtain influence in the world at large. To see how the law of defamation works in this context, it is useful to analogize the situation here to that found in the ordinary law of consumer warranties. In many businesses sellers are quite eager to have a strict liability rule for their products. That eagerness will not express itself in litigation, after the loss has occurred, where the cost-minimizing strategy is to seek ways to escape payment. But it becomes quite clear ex ante, where the defendant has to trade off the ability to gain sales against the possibility of having to pay damage awards. Here the major function of the strict liability rule is to bond the defendant, and therefore to increase the willingness of people to purchase its product even when they lack any precise information as to how it is manufactured or marketed.[50] If for example the common law retreated from its strong presumption that sellers typically warrant that their wares are free from contamination and adulteration, superior manufacturers could stand to lose from the shift, as they would now be required to devise other ways to extend their cost-effective warranties to a large class of distant and disorganized consumers.[51] The public would lose as well because it would now be required to incur the search and inspection costs that the warranties otherwise reduce.

A simple model of the media shows the importance of the warranty conception as well. Newspapers and television stations are normally unable to enter into direct contracts with their customers. Yet they can be seen as bonding themselves to public reliability through common law defamation actions brought by injured persons. Where these actions make clear whether the statement was true or false, and provide some financial compensation as well, the public gains greater confidence that what they read is true and reliable. In consequence they pay more for the information so provided. The actual malice rule, in effect, is a rule in which the law regards bad information as favorably as good information so long as it was produced only with gross negligence. It is tantamount to a rule that a merchant can escape the consequences of selling contaminated goods so long as he did not mean to hurt his consumers. Ex ante, consumers as a class tend to lose, as do producers.

It is important to note that the consequences are not the same for all producers. Superior producers have lower costs of complying with strict liability rules than do inferior ones. The shift in liability rules therefore works an implicit subsidy of the inferior goods at the expense of the superior ones. That result would be regarded as quite indefensible in ordinary product markets, and it should be so regarded in defamation cases as well.

It may be said that superior media institutions have the remedy in their own hands, for all they need do is to announce to their customers that they are prepared to litigate cases under the traditional common law rules, without requiring proof of actual malice. Yet that approach creates complications of its own, for the media institution that follows this course of action cannot bind the prospective plaintiff to a regime that contemplates strict liability and limited damages. Those plaintiffs, and there will be some, who prefer to try the case under the actual malice rule will elect that remedy. As there is no feasible bilateral contract between the defamation plaintiff and the media defendant, the unilateral declaration, even assuming that it were otherwise practical, does not bring about a sensible strict liability system. The election conferred upon any persons so defamed would tend therefore to increase the costs of libel to the firm as plaintiffs will elect their remedies to maximize their own gains from litigation. There is no obvious reason to believe that the increased sales revenues would offset the increased costs of defending libel actions. The barrier of high transaction costs again makes its presence felt in an area long thought to be dominated by constitutional issues.

It follows therefore that the actual malice rule creates unanticipated difficulties for the revenue end of the business as well as for the liability end of the business. The normal pattern of strict but limited warranties that has proved itself stable in ordinary product markets was at work with the common law of defamation, where suits by injured plaintiffs gave indirect but effective protection to both readers and superior producers. When people say that "you can't trust the newspapers any more," they simplify the situation by treating trust as a simple "yes/no" variable. But behind that ordinary perception lies the greater truth that the level of trust declines with the relaxation in liability rules. We can now say that the reputational losses to the media seem greater under the actual malice rule than under the strict liability rule. Again the balance shifts closer towards a strict liability rule, looking at matters solely from the defendant's point of view.

VII. THE SOCIAL PERSPECTIVE

The picture is still not complete, for thus far we have viewed the situation from the standpoint of the defendant. Yet if absolute immunity is not wholly desirable, then it is because of the position of the plaintiff and the public at large. Recall that even the Supreme Court in *New York Times* did not treat the want of recovery in cases of actual harm as an end desired for its own sake, but only as a bad which was designed to purchase other greater goods. Here this overall social judgment involves a comparison of the total gains and losses for plaintiffs and defendants alike under both regimes. In figuring out the total gains and losses, the amount of money transferred between plaintiffs and defendants simply washes out, for what is gained by the one side is lost by the other. What remains therefore is the rest of the picture.

To start with litigation costs, the effects of the actual malice rule are uncertain. In those cases where actual malice forms an impenetrable barrier, the costs will be reduced, but the plaintiff will be denied all relief for the wrong. In other cases the plaintiff may sue for collateral reasons —publicity and saving face—without the hope of obtaining any judicial relief. In still others the plaintiff will be prepared to spend additional funds in search of the larger payoffs that victory in an actual malice case might provide. On balance the situation is unclear, but total litigation costs may well rise. Needless to say, the levels of uncertainty will increase in a system of this complexity as well.

The greatest cost of the present system is that it makes no provision for determining truth. When a defendant wins a case on actual malice, there is no correction of past errors, and no sense of vindication for the plaintiff who can complain bitterly that he lost on a technicality that was of no concern to him. Indeed it is not surprising that the plaintiff's level of frustration is so great in defamation cases precisely because of the frequency with which the defendant avoids the only issue that matters to the plaintiff—falsehood, which could allow rehabilitation of the plaintiff's reputation.[52] The public, too, is a loser because the present system places systematic roadblocks against the correction of error. If it is important for the public to know that Jones has been a faithless public official, it is equally important for the public to know that Jones has been a diligent public official falsely accused by the press. The centrality of truth is of critical importance to any overall assessment of the system. Even if a system that turned on truth were more expensive to operate than one which rested upon actual malice, which is far from obvious, it would still provide information of far greater social value. More cases might be brought, but they would serve an important public purpose.

VIII. PATHS FOR REFORM

So the question remains what, if anything, should be done in order to change the situation. In my own view the optimal strategy involves a return to earlier principles in which strict liability rules are used to determine liability. I have no question as a matter of general principle that any plaintiff should be entitled to a determination in court that a statement made by the defendant was false with respect to him. (I take it as a correlative that pure statements of opinion should never be subject to liability.) Even if not a penny is paid over, the determination of falsehood, unclouded by any examination of the defendant's motive, is like the restitution of a thing taken by the defendant. To use the simple analogy, if a defendant takes the plaintiff's land, a court may choose (mistakenly) to deny interim damages, but it must surely order restoration of the thing taken. Judging from the recent cases involving Sharon and Westmoreland, the money was almost secondary to the question of whose reputation would survive the trial, the plaintiff's or the defendant's. It is an easy guess that Time magazine would have preferred a substantial monetary payment to Sharon, without any admission of falsehood, than the verdict which left its own reputation for accurate and reliable reporting tarnished. A rule that hurts the reputation of unreliable members of the press creates useful differential advantages for their competitors, and it helps elevate the entire level of public discourse and debate. If this change and this change only were made, it would markedly improve the structure of the law.

More substantial changes might be considered as well. Thus once strict liability rules are the norm, there is little reason to keep with the very high damages that plaintiffs have requested, and in some instances have obtained. Most present proposals provide that the plaintiff who receives declaratory relief must forgo all opportunity to recover damages.[53] That approach still leaves a fair sting in the libel remedy, but does not compensate for the interim loss before the judgment was entered and the residual loss that remains after correction has been made. My own sense is that some damage award does remain appropriate under a strict liability regime, but that it should be carefully circumscribed. In part the desired reduction in award levels will be obtained simply because the element of actual malice is removed from the case; juries and judges are far less likely to be inflamed if the only evidence they see relates to the statement made and its consequences for the plaintiff's welfare. What the change in attitudes does not supply can be supplemented by continued judicial scrutiny of excessive damage awards, even if there are no other structural changes in the law.

Nonetheless, further movement in the control of damages might be appropriate. The record to date suggests that no plaintiff has ever actually recovered a libel award in excess of $1,000,000. A sensible statute might impose a fixed maximum on recovery in all libel cases, so as to minimize the residual uncertainty about the stakes of litigation. As no final judgment in a libel case seems ever to have been entered for more than $1,000,000, that figure offers one possible maximum, and lower numbers are surely conceivable—some might say imperative— as well. Alternatively it might be possible to find some fixed rule that calibrates the award to the revenues obtained by the defendant. It has been suggested for example that the plaintiff's award should never exceed three times the cost of a page of advertisement[54] (or alternatively a minute of advertising time). The precise number or formula could be subject to endless debate, but the fixed upper limit has many attractive features.

There is still the question of whether actual malice has any role to play in the ordinary defamation case. One possible plaintiff's response to the strict liability rule is to join punitive damage counts to actual damage counts. The punitive damage counts could then be abandoned, but only after extensive discovery into motive, and perhaps after the use of that evidence at trial. Yet the strength of the strict liability rule is that it keeps out all the evidence which the plaintiff's new strategy could let in. To forestall that possibility, it seems desirable to adopt a rule that simply says that public officials can *never* recover punitive damages from media defendants. The gains achieved in reducing both administrative costs and general uncertainty would be very substantial. Yet the rule would give undeserved relief to certain defendants who have pursued systematic and willful campaigns of defamation against innocent persons. It might be thought overbroad by some. If the return to actual malice is thought unacceptable, it is possible to fashion some intermediate position that allows punitive damages only for repeated and systematic defamation which the defendant refuses to correct or retract even after clear and convincing evidence of falsehood has been presented to him by the plaintiff. The irony here is that a rule such as this was on the books in Alabama, only to be manipulated to improper ends in the state court.[55] The point of the retraction statute is that it organizes and channels the inquiry into malice. By putting the burden on the plaintiff to make the formal written request, it becomes easier to evaluate the defendant's state of mind, not from an overall examination of the original events but from the more limited inquiry into defendant's responses to the plaintiff's request. Once the retraction is made, it operates like the judicial determination of truth. By formalizing the negotiations between the parties, the retraction statute makes it possible to look at one set of events for actual damages and a distinct set for punitives, and hence obviates the risk of confusing the compensatory and punitive parts of the case.

On balance, it is a very close question whether a total ban on punitive damages is preferable to a sensible retraction statute. But ironically, one clear defect of the actual malice requirement of *New York Times* is that by making basic liability turn on subjective intentions, it blurs the line between actual and punitive damages and thereby unwittingly simplifies the recovery of the latter.

IX. WAS *NEW YORK TIMES* RIGHT?

The question remains whether on balance *New York Times* was rightly decided. To be sure, the case was correctly decided on its facts. The Supreme Court had to stay the hand of the Alabama law of defamation. But as a matter of principle the decision is far more dubious. It is one thing to condemn the common law of defamation as it was applied in a single case, and it is quite a different thing to condemn the basic set of common law principles in their entirety. Here the ultimate judgment is extremely hard to reach because the choice of a liability rule influences the conduct of plaintiffs and defendants alike, before, during, and after litigation. At root therefore the great problem with *New York Times* is that the choice of legal principles rests heavily on certain elusive, empirical issues. What are the costs of error and of administration, under alternative legal rules? What are the incentives upon the press to investigate important matters of public affairs, or of prospective plaintiffs to participate in public affairs? The explicit empirical evidence, which reports jury verdicts and maybe settlements, is wholly inadequate to estimate the relevant empirical issues, so that the question reduces to one of intelligent guesses about difficult matters. In general I start with two such presumptions. The first is that simple rules are to be preferred to complex ones in organizing human affairs. The second is to look with some skepticism upon the claims of any group or individual that their activities are so special that they should be exempt from the general legal rules that govern relations between persons. The discussion of defamation takes us down so many byways that it is difficult to know whether these presumptions should be displaced. I believe they should not. On balance, the common law rules of defamation (sensibly controlled on the question of damages) represent a better reconciliation of the dual claims of freedom of speech and the protection of individual reputation than does the *New York Times* rule that has replaced it. Now that the exigencies of the immediate case and of the segregation crisis that brought it to the fore have passed, the sensible constitutional conclusion is to abandon the actual malice rule in *New York Times*. In its institutional sense, *New York Times v. Sullivan* was wrongly decided.

NOTES

1. Kalven, *"The New York Times Case: A Note on the Central Meaning of the First Amendment,"* 1964 S. Ct. Rev. 191, 221 n.125.
2. 376 U.S. 254 (1964).

3. Rosenbloom v. Metromedia, Inc., 403 U.S. 29 (1971).

4. Gertz v. Robert Welch, Inc., 418 U.S. 323 (1974).

5. *New York Times,* 376 U.S. at 280.

6. See, e.g., Marc Franklin, "Winners and Losers and Why: A Study of Defamation Litigation," 1980 *Am. B. Found. Research J.* 457 (details the operation of the system from 1976 to 1979, without any special sense of urgency).

7. While exact data is difficult to come by, the Center has noted, for example, that in the ten years before *New York Times* there were only 55 media libel cases that went to trial—34 in state court and 21 in federal court. Of these the plaintiff won 40, and obtained an average verdict, unadjusted for inflation, of about $129,000, a sum which was skewed by the award of more than $3,000,000 in Butts v. Curtis Publishing, 351 F.2d 702 (5th Cir. 1965), *aff'd sub nom.* Curtis Publishing Co. v. Butts and Associated Press v. Walker, 388 U.S. 130 (1967). The verdict was entered in the pre-*New York Times* era. The total amount of the final judgments awarded was far less, although the precise numbers are not reported in the Center's survey. In *Butts,* for example, the trial judge ordered a remittitur of $460,000, which was accepted by the plaintiff. This pattern, whereby extensive jury awards are sharply trimmed on appeal, has continued into the post-*New York Times* era. Since 1980 the average jury award has been slightly over $2,000,000, with three verdicts over $25,000,000. Again the pattern of massive reduction from verdict to final judgment seems to hold, with the average judgment being something under $100,000. (It is not clear whether the verdicts in the three very large cases were reduced to final judgment in the same time period.) Between 1980 and 1984, 81 trials were reported, which averages out to about 16 a year, compared with only 5 per year in the pre-*New York Times* days. Several of the modern suits have been of the epochal Westmoreland or Sharon variety, where defense expenses can mount easily into the millions of dollars. Evidence on the number of suits filed is not presented in the studies done by the Center, but the number of summary judgments on the "actual malice" issue is surely very great, perhaps amounting to more than 80% of the suits brought. The legal expenses of suit, rather than the total payout in final judgment, is clearly of paramount importance to media defendants. These figures are derived from papers delivered at a conference held in June of 1986; the conference was entitled "The Cost of Libel: Economic and Policy Implications," and was sponsored by the Gannett Center for Media Studies and the Center for Telecommunications and Information Studies, Columbia University Graduate School of Business. *See* Randall Bezanson, "The Libel Litigation Process: What the Parties Want, and What the Parties Get" *Wm. & Mary L. Rev.* (forthcoming); Henry Kaufman, Trends in Damage Awards, Insurance Premiums and the Cost of Media Libel Litigation (unpublished manuscript on file with *The University of Chicago Law Review*). When these papers were presented at the conference, there was general agreement that these numbers accurately represented the present situation.

8. *See, e.g.,* Three Proposals for Libel Law Reform (unpublished manuscript on file with *The University of Chicago Law Review*). The three proposals are California Senate Bill 1979 (the Lockyer bill); H.R. 2846, 99th Cong., 1st Sess. (1985) (the Schumer Study Bill); and an unpublished proposal developed by Marc Franklin.

9. *See* Smolla, "Let the Author Beware: The Rejuvenation of the American Law of Libel," 132 *U. Pa. L. Rev.* 1 (1983).

10. *New York Times,* 376 U.S. at 293 (Black, J., concurring). Justice Goldberg took the same line. *Id.* at 297 (Goldberg, J., concurring).

11. For a summary, see *Restatement (Second) of Torts* §§ 558–623 (1977); 2 F. Harper, F. James & O. Gray, *The Law of Torts,* §§ 5.0–.30 (1986).

12. See his writings on the interaction. Harry Kalven, *The Negro and the First Amendment* ch. 1 (1965).

13. *See* Gitlow v. New York, 268 U.S. 652 (1925).

14. "The *liberty of the press* is indeed essential to the nature of a free state; but this consists in laying no *previous* restraints upon publications, and not in freedom from censure for criminal matter when published." *4 W. Blackstone, Commentaries* *151. For a qualified endorsement that Blackstone's view was incorporated into the first amendment, see Leonard Levy, *Emergence of a Free Press* 281 (1985).

15. 283 U.S. 697 (1931).

16. *Id.* at 718–19.

17. Blackstone hints at the problem when he writes: "To subject the press to the restrictive power of a licenser, as was formerly done, both before and since the revolution [of 1688], is to subject all freedom of sentiment to the prejudices of one man, and make him the arbitrary and infallible judge of all controverted points in learning, religion, and government." *4 W. Blackstone, Commentaries* *152.

18. The close substitution between liability rules and direct regulation exists elsewhere as well, as with the law of eminent domain. For discussion of this point, see Richard A. Epstein, *Takings: Private Property and the Power of Eminent Domain* ch. 8 (1985).

19. *See* Blasi, "The Pathological Perspective and the First Amendment," 85 *Colum. L. Rev.* 449 (1985).

20. "At the simplest level, it is, of course, correct that the Court cannot permit the concepts of state law to control constitutional scrutiny. If the constitutional principle, for example, is that the state may regulate X, the principle can become illusory if the state is left free to define X as it will." Kalven, *supra* note 1, at 201.

21. For discussion of the absolute protection afforded critical opinion and review of public officials and public figures at the common law, see Carr v. Hood, reported in note to Tabart v. Tipper, 1 Camp. 350, 354, 170 Eng. Rep. 981, 983 (K.B. 1808); J. Spencer Bower, *Actionable Defamation* (1908). The operative common law line between harsh criticism of published works and improper criticism of the author's private life and personal character was also well observed. *See* Triggs v. Sun Printing & Publishing Ass'n, 179 N.Y. 144, 71 N.E. 739 (1904); Veeder, "Freedom in Public Discussion," 23 *Harv. L. Rev.* 413 (1910).

22. Note that the references contained in paragraph six of the ad, including those that referred to the seven arrests and the intimidation, did not refer expressly to anything that happened in Montgomery, but followed two other related paragraphs. *See* 376 U.S. at 292 (appendix). Paragraph four began: "In Tallahassee, Atlanta, Nashville, Savannah, Greensboro, Memphis, Richmond, Charlotte, and a host of other cities in the South, young American teenagers, in the face of the entire weight of official state apparatus and police power, have boldly stepped forth as protagonists of democracy." *Id.* The reference to Southern violators follows this paragraph, which undercuts any claim that the charges made were exclusively or even largely about Montgomery.

23. *See, e.g.,* Nieman-Marcus Co. v. Lait, 13 F.R.D. 311 (S.D.N.Y. 1952); 2 F. Harper, F. James & O. Gray, *supra* note 11, § 5.7.

24. *See, e.g.,* Ellsworth v. Martindale-Hubbell Law Directory, Inc., 68 N.D. 425, 280 N.W. 879 (1938).

25. *See Restatement (Second) of Torts, supra* note 11, § 582.

26. *See, e.g.,* Sharpe v. Stevenson, 34 N.C. (12 Ired.) 348 (1851).

27. 106 S. Ct. 1558 (1986).

28. *See generally* Epstein, "Pleadings and Presumptions," 40 *U. Chi. L. Rev.* 556 (1973) (discussing legal rules of presumptions and exceptions).

29. On the structure of justification generally, see *id.;* on its application to self-defense, see Epstein, "Intentional Harms," 4 *J. Legal Stud.* 391, 410–20 (1975).

30. *See* Youssoupoff v. Metro-Goldwyn-Mayer Pictures, 50 T.L.R. 581 (C.A. 1934).

31. *See, e.g.,* Sidis v. F-R Publishing Corp., 113 F.2d 806 (2d Cir. 1940).

32. The same conclusion need not carry over to cases litigated under *New York Times,* for it is far from obvious that the plaintiff should be put to the burden of proving falsehood after he has been made to overcome the substantial hurdles on actual malice. *See* Philadelphia Newspapers v. Hepps, 106 S. Ct. 1558, 1567–69 (1986) (Stevens, J., dissenting).

33. See Ollman v. Evans, 750 F.2d 970 (D.C. Cir. 1984) (en banc), for the adoption of this proposition, and for some sense of the difficulties at the margin.

34. *See* Epstein, "A Theory of Strict Liability," 2 *J. Legal Stud.* 151 (1973).

35. *See, e.g.,* Gardner v. Slade, 13 Q.B. 796 (1849).

36. Therefore the case is not comparable to one that proposes the adoption of an automobile no-fault system to replace the common law damage action, for in the latter situation systems of comprehensive insurance and direct regulation of traffic behavior exist that are absent here.

37. *See* Wooley v. Maynard, 430 U.S. 705 (1977) (rights of nonspeakers); Abood v. Detroit Bd. of Educ., 431 U.S. 209 (1977) (forced union contributions by workers); Galda v. Rutgers, 772 F.2d 1060 (3d Cir. 1985) (student fees), *cert. denied,* 106 S. Ct. 1375 (1986).

38. *See, e.g.,* Minneapolis Star v. Minnesota Comm'r of Revenue, 460 U.S. 575 (1983); Grosjean v. American Press Co., 297 U.S. 233 (1935).

39. *See, e.g.,* Thomas v. Collins, 323 U.S. 516 (1944); Schneider v. State, 308 U.S. 147 (1939).

40. *See* R. Epstein, *supra* note 18, ch. 16.

41. *See id.* chs. 14 & 15.

42. *See* Paul v. Davis, 424 U.S. 693 (1976).

43. *See, e.g.,* E. Hulton & Co. v. Jones, 1910 A.C. 20.

44. *See, e.g., id.* Here the facts suggested that the defendant had indeed known the plaintiff, although the point was held immaterial as a matter of law.

45. See, for example, Braun v. Armour & Co., 254 N.Y. 514, 173 N.E. 845 (1930), where the defendant listed the plaintiff as one of the dealers who sold its bacon products. The plaintiff was a Kosher butcher.

46. See, for example, Tavoulareas v. Washington Post Co., 763 F.2d 1472 (D.C. Cir. 1985), for a taste of some of the complexities that can arise.

47. The Libel Defense Resource Institute report three such awards since 1980. *See* Kaufman, *supra* note 7, at 4.

48. For a general discussion of this point, see Priest & Klein, "The Selection of Disputes for Litigation," 13 *J. Legal Stud.* 1 (1984).

49. 441 U.S. 153 (1979).

50. *See* Bishop, "The Contract-Tort Boundary and the Economics of Insurance," 12 *J. Legal Stud.* 241 (1983).

51. For the present provisions on this subject, see U.C.C. § 2–318 (1977).

52. The point is stressed at great length in Bezanson, Cranberg & Soloski, "Libel Law and the Press: Setting the Record Straight," 71 *Iowa L. Rev.* 215 (1986).

53. For three such proposals, see *supra* note 7.

54. Stephen Brill, the editor of the American Lawyer, made the point in commenting on this paper.

55. Alabama law denies a public officer recovery of punitive damages in a libel action brought on account of a publication concerning his official conduct unless he first makes a written demand for a public retraction and the defendant fails or refuses to comply. Alabama Code Tit. 7 §914. The Times did not publish a retraction in response to the demand, but wrote respondent a letter stating, among other things, that "we . . . are somewhat puzzled as to how you think the statements in any way reflect on you," and "you might, if you desire let us know in what respect you claim the statements in the advertisement reflect on you." Respondent filed this suit a few days later without answering the letter.

New York Times, 376 U.S. at 261. Clearly the letter from the Times does not amount to a failure or refusal to retract; it is merely an inquiry for further information, leaving the ultimate question open. Here, moreover, the Times was correct in the opinion it gave that the plaintiff was wrong in his application of the "of and concerning" requirement.

6

REFINING THE DOCTRINE OF *NEW YORK TIMES v. SULLIVAN*

Mark S. Nadel

In *New York Times v. Sullivan,* the Supreme Court dramatically changed the complexion of American libel law. After observing that "uninhibited robust" debate on controversial issues inevitably produces occasional erroneous statements, the Court concluded that the First Amendment's protection of such debate required that the press be accorded reasonable breathing space to make such errors, even when their carelessness damaged the reputations of public officials.[1] As long as defamatory material is not disseminated with malice,[2] the Court held that any damage that material causes to public officials is part of the cost of a vigorous marketplace of ideas.[3] With this landmark ruling, the Supreme Court sought to alleviate the "chilling" effect of libel law on public debate.[4]

With such protection against even those damages caused by negligent press conduct, a privilege unique among democratic nations,[5] the American press would be expected to be free from most of the burdensome costs of libel. Ironically, however, *Sullivan* appears to have increased libel costs by indulging the instinct of the press to engage in behavior which antagonizes potential plaintiffs, thereby encouraging them to sue and thus to increase the cost of resolving libel complaints. Hence, despite the apparent significant decrease in libel damage awards since *Sullivan,* the increase in litigation which it has indirectly encouraged has raised total litigation costs and thereby the cost of libel insurance. These increases appear to have discouraged robust debate to a greater degree than damage awards ever did.[6]

Suggestions have been offered about how members of the press could drastically reduce such costs by voluntarily improving their procedures for handling libel complaints. Yet there is reason to doubt that the press will heed these informal requests. Few in the press were willing to provide adequate financial support or editorial respect to the National News Council and, only about forty newspapers employ ombudsmen despite their apparent value. Some in the press are even said to ridicule *The New York Times* for its policy of prominently featuring a corrections column.[7]

This article discusses a more formal remedy: how the law of libel could be reformed to achieve such ends by refining the *Sullivan* doctrine in two respects. The first would require the press to concede error or at least some degree of uncertainty when replying to a libel complaint concerning any statements for which *Sullivan* protection was going to be asserted. The second would permit the press to recover reasonable attorneys' fees when a libel plaintiff could not prove that an uncorrected alleged defamation was false.

While the first refinement, in isolation, might well abridge the wide First Amendment protection articulated in *Sullivan,* the combination of both changes would provide greater protection for the press and of vigorous debate than the status quo. If a legislative body believed that to be so—that the pair served to decrease the total cost of resolving libel complaints without chilling the press—and the Supreme Court accepted that conclusion then a statute embodying the pair would not be unconstitutional for it would not represent an abridgement of the freedom of the press. Freedom would in fact be expanded.

I. UNEXPECTED EFFECTS OF THE *SULLIVAN* DOCTRINE

Although the *Sullivan* doctrine is intended to discourage public figures[8] from waging lawsuits by substantially diminishing their chances of success, other effects of the ruling appear to have more than neutralized that disincentive. By giving the press stronger legal protection against damage awards it has reinforced the instincts of those in the press to stand firm on questionable stories and deal rather unsympathetically, if not arrogantly, with potential plaintiffs.

As Gil Cranberg, co-author of a University of Iowa libel study has noted, defensiveness in the face of criticism is part of the human condition, but it is particularly exaggerated within the news media. News media are organizations "conditioned to resist pressure," Cranberg observes and thus a "siege mentality develops in which demands for retraction or other vindication can be regarded as forms of pressure, signals to circle the wagons."[9] To build morale among reporters, editors, and producers, media owners may often stand behind their editorial staff even when the staff has refused to publish a correction of an apparent error. The legal protection afforded by *Sullivan* has bolstered the ability of media owners to display this destructive attitude.

In fact, *Sullivan* may even encourage such behavior by presenting a curious choice to media firms that have made such defamatory errors. *Sullivan* makes it easier for a media firm to seek a courtroom victory rather than risking public embarrassment by conceding such errors. The likely result is that such a victory will be misunderstood by the majority of its audience as a vindication of the firm's reputation, since they will view it as a confirmation of the original story.[10]

Obviously this was not the *Sullivan* Court's intent. While the decision was designed to protect the pocketbooks of those firms, it was not intended to encourage them to ignore completely their responsibility to clarify or correct errors or misleading statements which had damaged the reputations of others as well as misinformed the public.

The reactions of injured parties to the tactics of the press is not surprising. As John Soloski, another co-author of the Iowa study explains, many libel plaintiffs do not sue to collect damages, but merely to elicit a concession of error.[11] When these parties complain to the media firms, and those firms, armed with *Sullivan* protection, give only a cold shoulder, the injured parties are often further antagonized. This is why Randall Bezanson, the third co-author of the Iowa study, observes that many plaintiffs feel compelled to retaliate formally by bringing a lawsuit against their accuser: plaintiffs feel that they win by suing.[12]

Meanwhile, evidence that media firms stubbornly refuse to correct negligent errors or misleading statements, in reliance on *Sullivan,* may well encourage juries to make excessive damage awards and force media firms to spend more time and money appealing such awards to appellete courts, albeit with great success.[13] It is likely that *Sullivan*'s aberration from general principles of tort law, which require a negligent actor to pay for the damages he or she causes to innocent victims, does not sit well with juries.[14] Understandably, it must be hard for them to accept a rule that permits the sloppy work of a powerful media firm to damage the reputation of a public figure while permitting the firm to escape scot-free without even apologizing for the harm done.

As a consequence of this situation, massive litigation expenses are incurred before and during the trial, and on appeals, and these are rarely recovered.[15] Thus while *Sullivan* has protected the press against numerous damage awards, it is not very much help with litigation costs, which greatly dwarf the cost of damage awards. In fact, it has been estimated that approximately 80 percent of the cost of libel lawsuits is the cost of litigation,[16] including the cost of answering the question of whether there was malice, although neither side may really care.

In summary then, the problem with the law of libel today is that *Sullivan* has reinforced the tendency of the media to stand firm and antagonize those who accuse them of errors. This increases the likelihood that plaintiffs will feel compelled to sue in retaliation. By encouraging formal adversarial confrontation, *Sullivan* has produced a situation where plaintiffs feel that they win by suing, while libel defendants, because of the cost of litigation, lose even when winning. *Sullivan* protects the press against the chill of large damage awards, but it does not provide effective protection against large and wasteful legal costs.

Time magazine's defense of former Israeli Defense Minister Ariel Sharon's libel suit is a good example. Rather than immediately conceding that it had made a factual error in its report, or at least conceding uncertainty in the face of apparently negligent journalism, *Sullivan* gave *Time* the opportunity to try to vindicate itself in court. The structure of *Sullivan* encouraged *Time* to spend $5 million to try to win the case by proving that it lacked malice—an issue of no particular interest to Sharon or society—rather than making the concession which it eventually made anyhow.[17] Substantial expenses would have been saved if there had been greater pressure on *Time* to negotiate the substance of its admission rather than using the *Sullivan* defense to try to vindicate itself in court.

CBS appears to have had a much better reason for seeking to defend itself against General William Westmoreland's recent libel suit. Although its own internal investigation of the alleged libelous story found that the network had failed to satisfy its own journalistic standards, CBS still felt that the thesis of its documentary program—that there had been a high level conspiracy to distort information about North Vietnamese troop strength—was accurate. Nevertheless, the opportunity to use the *Sullivan* defense appears to have encouraged it to waste $6 million and vast human resources on litigation, rather than being pressured to take the much less expensive route of conceding that its thesis was its own informed opinion, but not clear fact.[18]

II. THE BENEFITS OF CONCEDING ERRORS

Some justify the tactics discussed above by claiming that they protect journalistic freedom and integrity,[19] but this seems to be mere rationalization. Such behavior is wasteful of resources and does not help the public get access to the best information. *Sullivan* should not protect such behavior, but rather *Sullivan* should be modified so that, while it continues to protect the press against damage claims for the inevitable errors that will be made, it also discourages the press from acting in a manner that encourages litigation. It should encourage the press to concede error or admit uncertainty when mistakes or distortions have occurred.

The public is aware that no one is perfect and that errors are as inevitable in the pursuit of good journalism[20] as they are in any other endeavor and that opinions are just that, opinions. The public might even admire one with the courage to acknowledge errors and to revise opinions as new facts arose. In addition, when *The Detroit Free Press* and *The Detroit News* assigned full-time editors to oversee corrections and announced those corrections in prominant places in their newspapers, the circulations of those papers increased.[21] Furthermore, controversial assertions made by a media firm that admitted its errors would likely have more credibililty than those made by a firm that never acknowledged mistakes. It is perhaps partially because of its corrections policy that *The New York Times* remains probably the most respected newspaper in the world.

The official correction policy of the *American Lawyer*[22] is another that appears particularly worthy of emulation. That policy is "to publish corrections as soon as possible in a way that is never less prominent . . . than the original mistake . . . [and] never sugarcoated in euphemisms (such as 'clarification')." In addition, since it is also the publication's policy to give credit to the entire editorial staff by placing all their names on the masthead, it promises that it "will likewise often try to tell [its] readers who made the mistake." Presumably, this policy would also require a correction when a reporter's opinion had been presented as if it were a statement of fact.

Yet most alleged errors made by the press are not clear factual errors; rather they concern questions of interpretation or implication, or factual matters whose truth or falsity is very difficult to ascertain.[23] In these cases, however, the press should be willing to qualify its assertions, thereby admitting some doubt. Where a story draws conclusions based on admitted facts, the story should make it clear that those conclusions may be the opinions of experts, but they are not facts. Admittedly, some conclusions follow so obviously from a list of facts that it seems silly to qualify the conclusion, yet those in the press should recognize that in such cases the obvious conclusion will easily be drawn by audiences without any help.

Sullivan's goal of protecting robust debate requires that the press be permitted to make assertions about public figures that might not be convenient to confirm due to constraints on time or resources. Yet, it is unclear how vigorous dialogue would be hampered by a requirement that such assertions be corrected later if they turned out to be false or clarified if they turned out to be misleading, such as phrasing an opinion as if it were a fact. If anything, such a rule would likely improve the free flow of accurate information to the public, one of the primary purposes of freedom of expression.[24]

The primary drawback to such a procedure would be the extra words that the press would be required to include to clarify stories. Statements that an accused public figure denied all charges of wrongdoing might be considered unnecessary to a member of the press who had faith in credibility of all his or her sources, but since it is impossible to be completely sure of anyone, a good journalist should always remain a bit cautious about what the facts really are, at least until all sides have given their full stories. As for the cost of including the extra words, it has always been true that controversy attracts attention, so giving more attention to a matter of controversy should not do significant harm to the press.

Media firms would not only improve their credibility by conceding errors and uncertainty, but they would also provide the public with more accurate information as well as reducing their libel costs, by removing many plaintiffs' motives to sue.

III. REFINEMENTS TO THE LAW OF DEFAMATION

If many in the media have too much pride to pursue their own best interests in this area then legislation should be passed to limit the *Sullivan* defense to its original purpose. Refinements could be made in the tort law of defamation to discourage the *Sullivan* defense from being used to protect the reputation of an undeserving member of the press and to further discourage firms from pursuing litigation in preference to more constructive negotiation, all without abridging the constitutional dimensions of *Sullivan*.

Legislation could be written to limit the use of the actual malice standard to two situations: cases where media firms faced potentially large damage awards for accidental or negligent defamation of public figures; and cases where media firms believed that they had presented true stories, but found those stories to be too difficult or expensive to prove in court. Such a refinement would not be inconsistent with the spirit of the *Sullivan* decision and its progeny and would appear to be achievable with two refinements of present tort law.

The first statutory refinement would be to require a defendant desiring to use the actual malice defense to concede publicly that it had made an error or was at least uncertain about the statement at issue. If a mutually acceptable concession could not be negotiated, the libel defendant would be required to admit that "Although a story of ours included the following assertions, we are not completely certain of their accuracy," followed by a list of the assertions for which it desired to defend itself on the ground that it lacked malice. Such a concession would be required to be included in its answer to an initial legal complaint and could refer to the specific assertions for which libel was charged or to the story as a whole and could be subject to liberal amendment at the discretion of the judge.

While media defendants would not be legally obligated to publish or broadcast any concessions, it would be hoped that the more ethical media defendants would do so voluntarily, as would at least some of those competing with the defendant in its market.[25] *Sullivan* would continue to enable good journalists to escape extreme financial penalties for occasional errors, but when they erred or mislabeled an opinion they would be pressed to admit such and so their reputations would suffer, as well they should. Media owners would find it even more expensive to permit those who had erred to avoid their responsibility to correct their errors and presumably the "my country right or wrong" attitude would give way to the increased combined weight of journalistic ethics and financial costs.

Some in the media and many media defenders might regard this refinement to be an unconstitutional abridgement of *Sullivan,* by claiming that the decision was intended to give the press complete protection against any statutory duty concerning stories about public figures written without malice. Yet one may also interpret *Sullivan* as only protecting the press against financial penalties for making careless and damaging errors about public figures, not protecting them against the trivial cost of some form of apology. It should be remembered that *Sullivan* did not completely prohibit libel suits by public officials although many believe that this is what the First Amendment demands.[26]

If the First Amendment permits the press to be punished for malicious errors then it is not clear that it would prohibit rules which strongly pressure the press to admit uncertainty about assertions that it considered difficult to prove in court. Such rules would not seem to chill vigorous dialogue, but rather would supplement caustic debate with clarifications, which permit the public to stay better and more accurately informed.

In addition, as presently interpreted, *Sullivan* has not provided the press with any protection against the substantial litigation costs that have burdened and chilled the press. If a statutory refinement were added to diminish the chill, it is hard to understand why the Supreme Court would necessarily reject it as an abridgement of the First Amendment. It is quite possible that the Court would review the *Sullivan* rule and hold that the constitutional protection provided by the First Amendment went only so far as to protect libel defendants in the two cases mentioned above.

Some might complain that a rule requiring a libel defendant to confess some degree of uncertainty about an alleged libel would severely damage its litigation position. Such an admission would make it next to impossible to convince a jury that the statement was true. Yet when media firms use the actual malice defense they do not face the burden of convincing the judge or jury that their assertions are true; they need prove only that they were not reckless or dishonest in believing the assertions to be true. The plaintiff would retain the burden of proving that the alleged libel was false and that it was asserted with malice.

A more significant drawback in the proposed rule, however, is that it would require a concession from a media firm that felt certain that its story was true, but believed it would be too difficult or expensive to prove it so in court. While the required concession would force the media firm to admit only uncertainty, not actual error, it is arguable that even the slight diminution of reputation caused by such a concession would represent an unacceptable abridgement of the constitutional protection articulated in the *Sullivan* decision.[27]

There are two responses to this point. The first is that any resulting harms, in addition to being minimal, would not likely be permanent. If the original statement were true, then it is likely that sufficient facts would eventually become available so that the truth of the alleged libel could even be proven in court at some later date. At that point, any former libel defendants could restate the reputed libel and discuss their earlier stories and libel case. Presumably they would quickly garner credit for their earlier scoops and thereby restore any former damage to their credibility. If they were sued for libel again they would likely be able to gain a quick dismissal based on the new evidence or take advantage of the second proposed refinement in the law, discussed below. Media firms that had made assertions that were true, but too expensive to prove in court, would also benefit from this protection.

Yet even if the first part of the statutory modification would, in isolation, abridge the constitutional protection of expression that does not mean that such a provision would be struck down by the courts if it were combined with another provision so that the pair benefited libel defendants and free speech to a much greater degree than it harmed it. Such a modification in the law of libel would have a good chance of withstanding constitutional scrutiny.

The second statutory refinement in the law of defamation would benefit libel defendants by discouraging potential plaintiffs from initiating groundless libel lawsuits.[28] It would do so by *requiring* a judge to award reasonable attorney's fees to a libel defendant whenever the plaintiff could not prove, with convincing clarity, that an alleged libel was false and remained uncorrected despite the media firm's receipt of a legal complaint. This would save media firms the costs of defending many of the groundless and harassing lawsuits which they currently face—by discouraging them from being brought in the first place—and thus alleviate a part of the problem of costly litigation never addressed by *Sullivan.*[29]

This problem has arisen because many public figures and officials are able to bring defamation suits at little or no cost to themselves.[30] Attorneys usually take these cases on a contingency fee basis. They receive a portion of the amount collected if they win rather than an hourly fee. Some lawyers seem willing to subsidize the cost of groundless lawsuits rather than risk the alienation and loss of their clients by refusing to sue.[31] Others may take such cases to increase their visibility with free publicity. If the defendant's legal fees might also have to paid, however, most groundless suits would probably be deterred. Attorneys could advise their clients that if they initiated such suits they would risk the demoralizing and likely result of being ordered to pay damages to the subjects of their wrath.

One objection which could be raised to this provision is that, as a practical matter, courts would not give defendants attorney's fees unless plaintiffs could also recover such fees under comparable circumstances. Yet, this complaint ignores two aspects of the attorneys' fee provision. First, the provision would not be phrased to permit a discretionary award to the prevailing party, as most attorneys' fee provisions are,[32] but rather grant attorneys' fees automatically if the plaintiff did not meet its burden of proving the falsity of the uncorrected alleged libel.

Second, the rule would not stack the deck unfairly against plaintiffs, but rather even the stakes involved in the trial. At present, a libel plaintiff who is victorious collects damages and, assuming the standard contingency fee arrangement, ends up way ahead after the legal fees are deducted. A victorious libel defendant, on the other hand, collects nothing, and ends up significantly worse off after paying litigation costs. A one-sided attorney's fee rule therefore would simply balance the stakes.[33]

This provision, meanwhile, would rarely, if ever, harm plaintiffs who had actually been defamed. As they would be in full possession of all the relevant facts concerning the truth of the alleged defamations and how those facts might be proven,[34] it is hard to believe that many actual victims of defamation would not be able to prove falsity, even if the matters of negligence and defamatory effect were unclear. The clear directive of the *Sullivan* doctrine is that public figures should make their responses in public debate, outside the courtroom. It would seem to follow that they do not belong in costly courtroom litigation unless they can present clear proof of falsity.

The First Amendment should protect the media against even the cost of litigating lawsuits brought by public figures, as long as they are willing to quickly correct or concede uncertainty about all statements that public figures are able to prove to be false.

SUMMARY

The refinements in the *Sullivan* rule of libel law discussed above should benefit both media firms and plaintiffs, with libel attorneys as the only losers. Many groundless libel suits would be eliminated and many of those initiated would produce relatively quick concessions of error.[35] Only when libel plaintiffs sought excessive damages from negligent media firms would costly litigation ensue over the existence of malice. The cost of libel insurance would likely fall significantly. Thus the press would finally enjoy the full promise of *New York Times v. Sullivan*—freedom to pursue America's profound national committment to uninhibited, robust, and wide open debate on public issues, without the fear of heavy financial penalties for accidental errors.

ACKNOWLEDGMENTS

This piece was written before the author took his present position and it reflects solely his own opinions, not those of OTA. The author would like to thank David Anderson, Randall Bezanson, Steven Brill, Ronald Cass, Jonina Duker, Marc Franklin, Mike Moore, Eugene Nadel, and Eli Noam for helpful comments on earlier drafts of this article.

NOTES

1. 376 U.S. 254, 271–72 (1964).

2. Malice is defined in this context as actual knowledge that the material was false or a reckless disregard for its truth. Id. at 279–80.

3. Id. at 272–73.

4. Id. at 277–78.

5. See P. Lahav, *Press Law in Modern Democracies* (1985).

6. In a study by the Libel Defense Resource Center (LRDC) the average final award for the successful libel lawsuits in 1954–64, after appeal, was $29,153.89 (or $107,577.85, adjusted for inflation). The corresponding figures for 1964–77 were $18,613.14 (or

$49,510.95, adjusted for inflation). See Kaufman, *supra* ch. 1, which provides statistics showing the increase in libel insurance. See also Baer, "The Party's Over," *The American Lawyer*, (Nov. 1985), at 68; two speeches by Eugene Roberts, Executive Editor of the *Philadelphia Inquirer*, one delivered at the William Allen White Award event at the University of Kansas, Feb. 8, 1986; the other, delivered as the Kenneth Murray Lecture at the University of Michigan, March 28, 1986 recounting a few specific instances where fear of a libel lawsuit led to the suppression of a story.

7. See, e.g., Bezanson, Cranberg & Soloski, "Libel Law and the Press: Setting the Record Straight," 71 *Iowa L. Rev.* 215 (1985). See N. Isaacs, Untended Gates: *The Mismanaged Press*, 113–46 (1986); McIntyre, "Repositioning a Landmark: The Hutchins Commission and Freedom of the Press," 4 *Critical Studies in Mass Communications* 136, 148 (1987); R. Adler, *Reckless Disregard* 152 (1986).

8. The Court quickly expanded the protection afforded by Sullivan to include protection against libel suits brought by any public figures, not just public officials. See, e.g., Curtis Publishing Co. v. Butts, 388 U.S. 130 (1967); Associated Press v. Walker, 388 U.S. 130 (1967). See, also, Gertz v. Robert Welch, Inc., 418 U.S. 323 (1974).

9. See Cranberg, "Fanning the Fire: The Media's Role in Libel Litigation," 71 *Iowa L. Rev.* 221, 222–23 (1985).

10. The proposition that the press must win a libel case even though its negligent conduct has severly damaged the reputation of a public official is one that is even difficult for fairminded judges to impart to juries. Still, the press deserves at least some of the blame for failing to educate the public about the intricacies of the *Sullivan* concept.

11. See Soloski, "The Study and the Libel Plaintiff: Who Sues for Libel?" 71 *Iowa L. Rev.* 217, 220 (1985).

12. See Bezanson, "Libel Law and the Realities of Litigation: Setting the Record Straight," *id.* at 226, 229.

13. Reversal rates seem to run at about 90% over the past few years. See Kaufman, ch. 1.

14. See, W. Keeton, et al. *Prosser and Keeton on Torts* (5th ed. 1984).

15. On rare occasions, a media firm will sue a libel plaintiff for the cost of litigation. Steven Brill, publisher of *The American Lawyer*, however, has recovered damages from plaintiffs on three occasions. Comments by Steven Brill, Columbia University conference on libel, Jun. 13, 1986.

16. See, "Lankenau, Living With the Risk of Libel," *Folio Magazine* (Nov. 1985) at 171.

17. The jury found that *Time* was negligent as did many other journalists, see, e.g., Brill," Say It Ain't So, Henry," *The American Lawyer* (Jan./Feb. 1985) at 1. For a short summary of the case closer to *Time's* perspective, see, "Of Meaning and Malice," *Time*, (Jan. 21, 1985) at 58. The decision refusing to grant a summary judgment is Sharon v. Time, 599 F. Supp. 538 (1984). The cost of litigation is estimated by Lankenau, *supra* note 16, at 171. *Time* finally issues a correction in its January 21, 1985 edition, at 59, but still "stands by the substance of the paragraph in question."

18. The investigation, known as the Benjamin report, was released but never published; it is discussed in some detail in Kowett, *A Matter of Honor* 202–24, 266–74, (1984). Kowett also gives a detailed description of the events leading up to the trial. Lankenau, *supra* note 16, discusses the cost of libel litigation. Despite the conclusions of the Benjamin report, CBS News president Van Gordon Sauter decided to "stand by" the broadcast and not to apologize (*see* Kowett, at 220–24) although he could have done both.

19. See, Adler, *supra* note 7, at 15.

20. Sullivan, 376 U.S. at 271–72.

21. See Wilkerson, "To Err is Human, but To Correct Sells Papers," *N.Y. Times,* Nov. 21, 1986, at A16.

22. See Memo from Steven Brill to All Am-Law Publishing Corp. editorial people, regarding general rules and guidelines, Mar. 8, 1986, at 1. See also N. Isaacs, *supra* note 7, at 145.

23. See Franklin, *infra* ch. 7.

24. See, e.g., Abrams v. United States, 250 U.S. 616, 630 (1919) (Holmes, J., joined by Brandeis, J., dissenting).

25. This might be a vain hope, however, for, according to Adler, "professional solidarity," which includes "refusing to contradict, or even question anybody else's [story] has virtually eliminated the very diversity that it was the purpose of the framers, in the First Amendment, to protect." Adler, *supra,* note 7 at 18.

26. Among the many who have believed that public officials should not be permitted to sue for libel are Justices Black and Douglas. Sullivan, 276 U.S., at 293 (Black and Douglas, JJ., concurring)

27. In *Sullivan,* 376 U.S. at 279, the Court clearly stated a desire to protect those who might find it too expensive or otherwise too difficult to prove in court the truth of their statements. The addition of an opportunity to collect attorneys' fees would more than compensate them for any psychic loss due to a requirement that they concede their failure to be able to prove the truth of various statements in their story. It is suggested here that a more valuable tool for these defendants would be the right to win attorneys' fees, as discussed below.

28. It has been estimated that such nuisance suits may constitute 50% of all defamation suits. See, Weber, "Editors Surveyed Describe Half of All Libel Suits as 'Nuisance' Cases," *ASNE Bulletin* 38 (Jan. 1986); Franklin, "Good Names and Bad Law: A Critique of Libel Law and a Proposal," 18 *U.S.F.L. Rev.* 1, 6 n.27 (1983).

29. As Steven Brill has noted, "I've written, and I mean it, that I would give away most of my *Times v. Sullivan* freedoms for the simple freedom of being able to have those who sue us at the *American Lawyer* for libel, pay our legal costs after we win." Comments offered at the Columbia University conference on libel, Jun. 13, 1986.

30. See Bezanson, supra note 12, at 228. The use of contingency fee arrangements is standard practice in tort litigation.

31. Clients often have a strong desire to bring such suits out of anger or frustration, whether or not the charges made against them are accurate. Many believe that the mere act of bringing suit lends credibility to their position, regardless of the outcome. *Id.*

32. Most statutes granting attorneys' fees grant them to the prevailing party at the discretion of the court. The best known of such statutes is probably the one that is part of the civil rights act. See 42 U.S.C. sec. 1988 (1986).

33. Since the attorneys' fee provision would only apply to cases involving *Sullivan* and therefore public figures, it would be very likely that such public figures would have significant personal resources for satisfying attorneys' awards.

34. This differentiates plaintiffs in defamation cases from other plaintiffs. Most tort plaintiffs are not sure of all the facts and thus do not know who is at fault and whether they can provide sufficient proof. They do not have certain knowledge of the truth.

35. According to the Iowa Study, those defamed in the media often contact the media before contacting an attorney. Thus the press often has the opportunity to resolve the dispute with a correction, where appropriate, without costly litigation. See Cranberg, *supra* note 9, at 221. Nevertheless, the study found that only about 15% of claims are settled out of court. Bezanson, *supra* note 29.

A requirement that negligence be conceded before the *Sullivan* defense could be invoked would create a stronger incentive to concede error earlier. Presumably this would lead to a settlement rate much closer to the approximately 95% overall rate for tort litigation. See, Priest & Klein, "The Selection of Disputes for Litigation," 13 *J. Legal Stud.* 1, 2 (1983).

7

THE FINANCIAL IMPACT OF LIBEL REFORM ON REPEAT PLAYERS

Marc A. Franklin

In the libel area, increased attention has recently been given to questions of legislative action ranging from those that simply shift fees to those so broad as to look like proposals for libel "reform."[1] As these complex proposals are unveiled, it is sometimes difficult to see how the proposed changes will actually operate. The goal of this paper is to provide a systematic way in which the repeat players—newspapers and broadcasters in particular—can think about how they will fare under each proposal. Although I analyze matters from the perspective of the media, it will be relatively easy to see how each plan will affect plaintiffs. The overall impact of these proposals on the public is beyond the scope of this paper and is addressed elsewhere.[2] Although noneconomic issues are critical to any discussion of libel reform, and perceptions of fairness, "chilling," and political reality may carry the day, it is important that the repeat players, who will undoubtedly have much to say about any proposed reform, understand the financial impact of proposed changes.[3]

This paper identifies the costs defendants incur under the current libel system, and then assesses the direction and magnitude of changes in these costs produced by three related but distinct reform proposals.

The discussion supplies no numbers for three reasons. First, at this early stage it is more important to develop an approach than to achieve a result. Second, we can expect that a set of numbers obtained in confidence from a few unidentified media operations will have little relevance for most of the others. Numbers supplied by a large newspaper may have little relevance to a small newspaper, or at least will be perceived that way. Broadcasters may find even less affinity. Third, and perhaps most important, each newspaper is likely to have the relevant figures for its own operation or to be able to obtain them. The primary purpose of this paper, then, is to provide a formula for calculating the costs of proposed reforms, one that each repeat libel play may adjust for its own situation.

I. THE CURRENT SYSTEM

As a first approximation, we may say that the economic costs *(E$)* of defending a libel action today consist of a broad category called legal expenses *(L$)* plus those amounts that defendants pay out on claims *(P$)*. In an effort to make this analysis as concrete as possible, we exclude more speculative costs, such as any long-run rise or fall in public confidence in the press that might accompany any change in the legal rules. In each case it is important to subdivide these two items so that we can trace their rise and fall under various proposed reforms. At this first stage, however, we can say that $E\$ = L\$ + P\$$.

A. Legal Expenses

Legal expenses break down into five categories. One involves the amounts now spent on such items as hiring specialists to advise the staff on libel or having some or all articles reviewed prior to publication. These expenses are not attributable to any specific claims, but rather to general libel overhead. These will be called legal overhead *(Lo)*.

Although this expense is likely to vary widely, according to the size and focus of the publication, we will assume, unless otherwise stated, that the libel overhead for any particular newspaper will not be altered substantially by any of the proposals. Standard practice will certainly not change until it is clear how any new proposal will operate. And even if absolute privilege were to become law, most publishers would still endeavor to be accurate. Some might suggest that the elimination of a damage sanction would cause even the most conscientious publishers to spend less on accuracy than they do now. Others would respond that this economic approach fails to recognize the value most publishers put on their reputations for accuracy.

The other four subdivisions of legal expenses are tied to specific libel claims. These consist of (1) expenses allocated to investigating and litigating questions related to the alleged error of the statement;[4] (2) those allocated to the fault question, including the determination whether the plaintiff is public or private;[5] (3) those allocated to all other legal issues and defenses involved in the claim, such as state rules of special damages and the statute of limitations; and (4) those allocated to negotiations arising from the dispute. These will be called *Le, Lf, Lm,* and *Ln* respectively, for "error," "fault,"[6] "miscellaneous," and "negotiation."

In any single case the relative proportions of the four types of legal expenses will vary greatly. If the error becomes clear shortly after publication, little need be spent in litigating the falsity of the charges.

But that same case may involve substantial costs related to litigation over whether the error resulted from actual malice.[7] In some cases, however, the error issue assumes center stage, though not to the exclusion of the fault question. The course of discovery may dictate that questions of error and fault be explored together, rather than concentrating on one of them.[8]

Since most states follow the negligence rule for private plaintiffs,[9] the fault inquiry in these cases should cost less on average than cases brought by public plaintiffs—unless the private plaintiff attempts to show actual malice in an effort to recover general and punitive damages. Thus, in cases brought by public plaintiffs the legal expenses devoted to actual malice are likely to be larger on average and to be a larger percentage of total legal expenses than in cases brought by private plaintiffs.[10]

Over a long period, most newspapers will find that the types of legal expense fall into predictable proportions. Although some larger media may find themselves in very expensive disputes over falsity, such as the Sharon and Westmoreland cases, smaller media are unlikely to be in the same position. For them, at least, it seems likely that the costs of litigating fault will far exceed those incurred in litigating falsity.

Although miscellaneous legal expenses may dominate most of the simpler libel claims, they are not likely to loom large in absolute dollar terms because the issues often can be raised on motions to dismiss. Although an issue involving special damages or the statute of limitations may produce only "miscellaneous" expenses, if the defense is successful, the case is likely to be a very small one. Moreover, miscellaneous expenses tend to be eclipsed in any gigantic case, in which either error or fault questions, or both, will dominate.

Finally, negotiations of some sort are likely to occur in every case under the current system. Persons upset with an article will attempt to have it corrected, which may lead to further discussion over whether an error occurred and, if the newspaper is persuaded that it erred, how to correct the error. Despite their frequency, negotiation expenses are unlikely to loom large in any single case. To sum up so far, we can say that $L\$ = Lo + Le + Lf + Lm + Ln$.[11]

B. Payouts

We know that the media are successful in some 90 percent of the cases that are litigated to conclusion.[12] In the few that are lost, defendants make some payment that must be included in our calculations. Payouts that result from judgments *(Pj)* may include both compensatory and punitive damages.

Although some claims lead to settlements in which no money changes hands,[13] newspapers do sometimes make payments *(Ps)* as parts of settlements.[14] The amount of money changing hands in any single libel case will be attributable either to judgment or settlement. Over a period of time the total payouts may include both and can be symbolized as $P\$ = Pj + Ps$.

One would expect payments to be made more often in negligence cases than in actual malice cases because it is easier to recover under negligence law.[15] The amount of actual injury damages in such cases[16] would appear to be independent of whether the libel occurred through negligence or actual malice.[17] If so, compensatory damages should be substantially higher on average in the fewer successful public plaintiff cases, which will include general damages, than in the private plaintiff cases in which the plaintiff does not show actual malice. The damage disparity should be greater in those states in which punitive damages are available.[18]

When we look at current small legislative changes in personal injury law, we can see that proposals to limit general damages or to cap or eliminate punitive damages[19] will have much less effect on libel defendants than on other defendants because so few libel defendants pay damages. Still, such legislation may affect the bargaining range in settlement discussions and might dissuade some plaintiffs—or their attorneys if the contingency fee is used[20]—from suing at all.[21] Overall, then, the total costs of libel under the current system over any period of time can be seen to be:

$$E\$ = L\$ \ [Lo + Le + Lf + Lm + Ln] + P\$ \ [Pj + Ps].^{22}$$

C. Recovery of Expenses

From this total of the costs of the current system, we must subtract outlays that are recouped or avoided. These are likely to be achieved in either of two ways.

1. Countersuits

If the defendant has prevailed in a case that was brought to harass or without any chance of success, the defendant may attempt to recoup its expenses—either by seeking legal fees as part of the judgment in the original case, or by bringing a separate action for malicious civil prosecution.[23] Success under either of these routes would reduce net legal expenses by the defendant. Because this recoupment has been successful in only a few cases,[24] we can omit it here in the interest of simplicity without much loss of accuracy.[25]

2. Insurance

It is not possible, however, to neglect the other major way in which newspapers may avoid the full economic brunt of the current libel system, including its potential annual fluctuations—libel insurance. Those who carry libel insurance are likely to view the costs of libel in terms of premiums and deductibles. In fact, the basic approach developed here addresses the problems of both insured and uninsured defendants because, for most publications, insurance premiums, over time, will approximate a balanced flow of the expenses actually incurred.[26]

II. THE IMPACT ON COSTS OF THREE REFORM PROPOSALS

A. Introduction

We turn now to a consideration of three proposals for reform—the Lockyer bill,[27] the Schumer bill,[28] and the Plaintiff's Option Libel Reform Act.[29] All provide a declaratory judgment option whose exercise bars a damage action.[30] Although the proposals vary greatly, they all create two-track systems with several basic features in common that might be addressed at the outset. All offer the plaintiff the chance to obtain a declaratory judgment by proving with convincing clarity that the defendant's defamatory statement was false. In that proceeding no damages are available, fault plays no part, and the winning plaintiff generally recovers legal expenses.[31] All the proposals offer a statute of limitations of one year,[32] but most plaintiffs attracted to a declaratory approach will move quickly to obtain one of the great benefits of the action—an early resolution.

In the discussion that follows, we are concerned with the impact that each of these new proposals will have on existing law and on defense costs. We are especially eager to determine whether those who today have only a choice between suing for damages and filing no suit will behave differently when they have the added option of suing for a declaratory judgment. The second goal is to determine the cost impact of these shifts. Schematically, this may be set out as in table 7.1 (with the operational questions set in each box).

It is important to recognize that "no suit" does not mean that the aggrieved person does nothing at all after the article in question appears. This category now includes at least three separate groups: (1) those who in fact do nothing; (2) those who complain and negotiate but, getting no relief, give up; and (3) those who negotiate successfully for either a retraction, a reply, money, or some combination thereof. The first course of action produces virtually no defense costs; the second produces minor negotiation costs and perhaps some costs involved in exploring the claim. The third, however, involves negotiation expenses and perhaps some payouts in settlement. This may also include the costs of using space in the newspaper or buying space elsewhere for retractions or replies, and the "costs" of embarrassment in admitting some kinds of errors.

Each newspaper will best be able to subdivide the current "no suit" category that it confronts. To the extent that initial negotiations do not produce a settlement before suit is filed, these expenses are included as part of the damage action. Where a complaint is filed and allowed to lapse without much further action, the damage claim may involve fewer defense costs than a situation classified as "no suit."

A brief overview of the table 7.1 at this point suggests that the critical question in terms of flow and costs will be how many current seekers of damages will switch to the declaratory action. The more who do so, the lower the total legal expenses incurred in case 1 cases; but the higher the expenses in case 2, which today is zero. The extent of the switch may be controlled by changes that an individual proposal makes in the damage action. Case 3 will come into existence if the shifting of fees deters current suits or if the declaratory alternative induces more settlements without suit. Case 4 will exist only if fee shifting provisions make feasible damage suits that are not now feasible—a highly unlikely situa-

TABLE 7.1: The Impact of the Proposals on the Current System (Generic)

PROPOSED SYSTEM	CURRENT SYSTEM	
	Suit for Damages	*No Suit Filed*
Suit for Damages	1. How many will continue to seek damages?	4. How many who do not now sue will?
Suit for Declaratory Judgment	2. How many who now seek damages will switch to dj?	5. How many who do not now sue will seek dj?
No Suit	3. How many who now seek damages will not sue?	6. How many will still not sue?

tion. Case 5 will be crucial if many who do not sue today are induced to bring actions for declaratory judgments. This would substantially raise the costs here from its current figure of zero. Finally those who did not sue under the old system and do not sue under the new system (case 6) may decrease in number because of the new alternative of case 5; but the costs associated with case 6 may increase since some claimants will fare better in pre-suit negotiations than they do today.

We turn now to more specific analysis of the likely directions and magnitudes of the possible movements. Before turning to specific proposals we consider some general questions that are raised by all three.

B. Common Questions Under All Three Proposals

1. Total Claims

The first question is to try to determine how many, under the current system, are suing for damages and how many are in one of the "no suit" groups.

It seems unlikely that all who see themselves as victims are suing today. Most try to get corrections.[33] Some who fail, angry at the media for the story on their subsequent treatment or both, go to a lawyer to initiate a suit.[34] If the lawyer will take the case on a contingency fee,[35] the case will be brought. If not, what will the complainant do? This is likely to depend on the severity of the perceived harm or injustice, the financial status of the complainant, and the lawyer's advice about the chances for ultimate success.[36] The complainant who is discouraged by an accurate explanation of the obstacles may decide to forget the whole matter. To the extent that plaintiffs today consult lawyers who systematically overestimate the chances for success,[37] the current system is producing more weak cases than might be expected.

There is also the situation in which, even after the adverse odds are explained, the complainant concludes that the act of bringing suit itself may be helpful in rehabilitating a hurt reputation.[38] Finally, some may sue simply because there is no other way to clear their names. If they can at least get to trial and get a special verdict, they may be able to clear their names even if the jury does not find the requisite fault.[39]

Those now suing. The number of eligible[40] persons now seeking damages who will be induced to shift to the declaratory action will depend in large part on the motives for suit, the strength of the case, the attractiveness of the declaratory action, and on what changes, if any, make the current damage action less attractive. The Lockyer bill, for example, does not affect the damage action,[41] but other approaches make the damage action less attractive to some or all prospective plaintiffs.[42]

Those not now suing. How many of the current "no suits" are likely to become declaratory judgments under a new system? Different media are likely to have different rates here. Publications that enrage those who think themselves defamed might find virtually no rise in total suits against them under any two-track system if today's suits are based on anger and frustration. But publications generally perceived to be "responsible" might face more litigation. Complainants who perceive error but are not upset by the newspaper's style or content or its dispute resolution tactics and who do not want to press weak legal claims would now have a way to test their claims of error.

The patterns might vary from the status quo (no suers switch to declaratory actions and all current non-suers behave exactly as they have been) to one extreme (all current suers continue to seek damages and all current non-suers bring or threaten declaratory actions) or another (all current plaintiffs switch to declaratory actions and all current non-suers take no action whatever). It is much more likely, of course, that some plaintiffs will switch from damage actions and that some who do to sue today will decide to bring the declaratory action. We must then compare any savings from fewer damage defenses with the new costs incurred in defending the declaratory actions, adding the role of fee shifting[43] In fact, however, many cases that start on the declaratory track will not run the full course.[44]

2. Changes in costs

The crux of the matter, though, is not how many persons switch from one regime to another, but whether the total costs incurred under the new system are lower than those incurred under the current one. The first question here is whether a case litigated under the declaratory judgment system will cost less than one litigated under the current system. The exclusion of fault may reduce that legal expense to zero. But what will happen to the costs of litigating falsity? The central empirical question here is whether falsity litigation in case 2 will cost less than it would in case 1. Two features suggest lower cost: a plaintiff who cannot get damages may not push the matter as hard as where damages are available; and a defendant who is not at risk for damages may not put the same resources into defending the accuracy of a story. The opposite argument is that a media organization's reputation for accuracy will require as rigorous and expensive a defense of a story as that now made in a damage action.

The large responsible media, remembering the Sharon and Westmoreland cases, assert that they will not save costs in a declaratory judgment system because the gigantic cases tend to center on falsity and will cost the same as they do now. Does this perception accurately reflect the situation of most big media or are a handful of massive cases distorting the perceptions? Even if the large media do not save much in the falsity phase of the case, might they still save enough by the elimination of fault questions to more than cover the costs of the new cases brought in case 5 by the current non-suers?

Although it seems likely that there will be some savings from the elimination of the fault question and the low likelihood that the falsity litigation will cost more when damages are not at stake than when they are, still it might be that in some cases it would be cheaper for the defendant to obtain summary judgment on the fault question in a damage action than to litigate solely the falsity question in a declaratory framework. But overall this seems an unusual case.

It seems highly unlikely that the small media will find themselves embroiled in the massive falsity disputes. Their cases tend to involve local matters that, no matter how hard to sort out with confidence, are unlikely to produce long trials over falsity. It is important to recognize that just as large and small media may have different concerns under the current system, they may gain different types and levels of benefits from proposed changes in that system.

Finally, the timing of the election is such that the plaintiff who is interested primarily in litigating falsity may make the election without knowing how the alleged error occurred. Without a choice, the plaintiff will begin the action to see what discovery will produce. Under a two-track system, the plaintiff who finds declaratory action more congenial will forgo what might have been a successful damage action in order to obtain the quicker and surer declaratory judgment. This timing may cast doubt on defendants' concern that plaintiffs with strong damage actions will continue to bring them and that only those with weak damage actions will switch to declaratory actions.

3. Settlements

Experience suggests that few libel defendants emerge unscathed from high-publicity cases. Either the story is shown to be false,[45] or certain practices of the defendants are shown to be less than admirable,[46] or the plaintiff actually obtains an award that is upheld on appeal.[47] Even if no wounds are inflicted, the financial and psychic costs of discovery may be so great that most newspapers will prefer to shift as many cases as possible from the damage track. For each case settled, the risk of payout

(P$) drops to zero or to a known settlement figure, and legal expenses are conserved.

What keeps newspapers from settling more cases? In cases in which the error is recognized shortly after publication—called here clear error *(Ec)*—why does the case proceed? Is it because the plaintiff is dissatisfied with the timing or placement of any retraction? Does the plaintiff assert that the correction has not undone enough of the initial harm? Are the parties unable to agree on the role of fault or on a financial settlement? Is it that the plaintiff's goal was to harass or seek a big recovery, so that any retraction offered or made was virtually irrelevant to the decision to sue? Or did the defendant choose to defend a damage action on the assumptions that the requisite fault could not be shown and that it was better to incur the legal expenses and the very low risk of payout than to admit the error publicly? The answers will vary with the plaintiff, the publication, and the specific situation.

When the allegation of error is disputed *(Ed)*, the newspaper cannot retract.[48] A reputable publisher involved in such a dispute can avoid a suit today only by a settlement that gives the plaintiff a chance to state his or her side or by an article that reports the differing views and how difficult it is to establish the truth. If these do not satisfy the plaintiff, and the plaintiff is ready to pursue the case, the defendant must hope to win quickly on lack of fault or on a miscellaneous defense because the error question seems to present a matter for trial.

Two-track settlements. Under a two-track system, the analysis of settlements becomes more complex. In the systems in which the plaintiff's option controls,[49] the plaintiff must weigh the attractiveness of the damage action against the value of the opportunity to prove falsity. A plaintiff who could be sure of the opportunity to litigate falsity would have more leverage in negotiations than he has today. But just as information about falsity may lie more with one party than the other,[50] so too with information on the fault question. In most cases, the plaintiff will have no independent knowledge about how an error occurred— even an error that is now clear.

The preliminary negotiations may be critical in directing the plaintiff. If the error is clear and the defendant is prepared to make an acceptable retraction, the plaintiff will get as much as he might have were he to use the declaratory track. Indeed, he will get more, since an admission of error will come sooner and be more convincing than a judicial declaration of error after litigation. Whether the newspaper will admit the error and hope to end the matter or try to trade the retraction for a total settlement may depend on the rules that control the damage action—a subject on which the proposals differ.

If the error is disputed, the plaintiff must realize that the declaratory action may fail. The damage action presents the same risk plus several other hurdles. The newspaper, on the other hand, will recognize that retraction is not available as a remedy, and that if plaintiff pursues either of the two remedies the case may be extended. A plaintiff who is intent on clearing his name is likely to pursue the declaratory road. This will keep legal costs low[51] and be likelier to achieve the goal sought. A plaintiff who realizes that the path is going to be difficult, that the result is uncertain, and that the need for clearing his name is not as important as reaching the same audience with his side of the dispute, might be receptive to the opportunity to state his views in a column or letter soon after the statement that caused the dispute.

4. Defaults

The three proposals all envision a contested declaratory proceeding that culminates, if there is no settlement, in a judgment that falsity was or was not established. Under each proposal, however, there is the possibility that the defendant, no longer liable for damages after the plaintiff's election,[52] may simply default in the declaratory action. This would allow the plaintiff to obtain a default judgment of falsity, which would render the defendant liable for the plaintiff's reasonable legal fees.[53] These fees are likely to be low in the default situation.

What has the plaintiff obtained in such a situation? Will the public that learns about the outcome treat the default as an admission of error? Might there be other explanations, such as the inability of a small newspaper to afford to defend a case of disputed error? The proposals do not address the issue. Would the defendant's default undermine the plaintiff's efforts to clear ·his name? Some bargaining on the default question may be possible where the plaintiff's election controls. Where, as in the Schumer bill,[54] the defendant can convert a damage action into a declaratory action and then default, the plaintiff can do nothing to avoid that outcome. The analysis of settlement and default dynamics will be specific to each proposal.

5. Insurance Practices

Another set of common questions is whether the introduction of a two-track system would change either the way in which media libel insurance is written or the size of the premiums. This might depend on how readily new costs or savings can be predicted. That in turn will depend on how the declaratory action operates and what changes are made in the damage action. These will be discussed shortly. In any event, there may be much slippage between what new legislation says, and how it works.

If the legislation appears to have the potential to increase costs, insurers might raise premiums. If it seems clear that one goal of the legislation is to reduce overall defense costs, insurers may adopt a wait-and-see attitude or may be reassured about the jurisdiction's libel climate and reduce premiums quickly. I will assume that the introduction of any of the three proposals will not, by itself, produce any substantial shift in insurance underwriting practices or premiums until some experience has been obtained.[55]

C. The Lockyer Bill

The bill introduced by California[56] State Senator Bill Lockyer permits any public official or public figure who claims to be the subject of a media defamation to bring an action for a declaratory judgment that the statement was defamatory and false.[57] Fault and common law malice are irrelevant, damages are not recoverable, and seeking this relief precludes seeking damages.[58] In the declaratory judgment action, the prevailing party is to recover reasonable attorney's fees except when the judge finds an "overriding reason" not to follow the prevailing party rule;[59] the defendant proves that it "exercised reasonable efforts to determine that the publication or broadcast was not false and defamatory";[60] the defendant published a correction no later than 10 days after the action as filed;[61] or when a losing plaintiff is found to have to have brought and maintained the action with a "reasonable chance of success."[62] The existing damage action is unchanged.

In comparing costs, we start with the current system's regime under which all costs and risks are incurred in defending damage actions or in negotiations conducted under threat of a suit for damages. Under the Lockyer bill, case 1 in table 7.1 would remain the same for all plaintiffs who continued to sue under the proposal, but the total would decrease as plaintiffs instead chose to seek declaratory relief or not to sue. (There is no reason why any former suers should move to total inaction under the Lockyer bill because no losing plaintiff in a damage action would owe legal fees to the defendant. But some current damage seekers will now be in a position to bargain effectively for retractions and other relief, under case 3, without suit.) The major question then is how many will switch from case 1 to case 2.

Since no change in the rules or fee structure of damage actions has occurred, the inducement to shift from damage actions to declaratory relief will have to be found in the attractions of the new action. The clearest attraction is the far greater ability to obtain a judgment on falsity. Since no damages are recoverable in such an action, the fee-shifting provisions will be important to those who would find it burdensome to have to bear even these reduced costs.

Are the fee-shifting provisions strong enough to encourage marginal plaintiffs to switch to the declaratory action? Although the general rule awards reasonable fees to the prevailing party in the declaratory action, exceptions cloud this picture for successful plaintiffs and will cause extra litigation and negotiation.[63] If the defendant exercised reasonable efforts to avoid falsity before the publication (something the plaintiff may not readily know) or if the defendant retracted no later than 10 days after the action was filed, each side will bear its own fees if the plaintiff wins the action. It seems probable that the more the error is disputed, the more likely it is that reasonable care will be found to have been taken. Even if these two specific defenses do not apply, the court may bar the successful plaintiff from recovering fees if it finds an "overriding reason" to do so.[64] Thus, the fee provisions are unlikely to be a strong inducement to the plaintiff to switch from the damage action. To the extent the defendant must reimburse the plaintiff, we may call these amounts *"Fp."*

The other side of the coin is, of course, that if the plaintiff brings a declaratory action (but not a damage action) and loses, the bill's general rule would require the plaintiff to reimburse the defendant's reasonable legal expenses *(Fd)*. Will this deter plaintiffs from choosing the declaratory action? This is unlikely. The most significant fee provision is the fourth,[65] which permits a shift against a plaintiff who has proceeded without a reasonable chance of success. If the statement is defamatory, the plaintiff might be held to have had a reasonable chance for success so long as a colorable, even if unsuccessful, case of falsity could be made out. In any event, a losing plaintiff may be able to avoid reimbursing the defendant under the "overriding reason" provision, especially if the defendant is prosperous and the plaintiff is an ordinary citizen.[66] All in all, the extent of fee shifting is hard to predict, but it would seem to add little incentive to plaintiffs to choose the declaratory route if they are not already so inclined.

Table 7.2 suggests the likely impact on defense costs of plaintiffs who do switch from damage actions to the declaratory alternative under the Lockyer bill. (Recall that negotiations may occur before the decision to switch is made.)

The settlement payments are not zero because a switch does not mean that no money will be spent in settlements. One can imagine a case in which the plaintiff may think that the requisite fault can be established but in which the error may be hard to prove. The plaintiff might be willing to go the declaratory route if the defendant, to avoid the expense of defending and possibly losing a conventional damage action, were willing to agree to a payment (perhaps of special damages?) if plaintiff proved falsity.

In the second column, those who do not sue today are not likely to seek damages under the Lockyer proposal (case 4) because it does nothing to make the damage action any more attractive—either substantively or by fee shifting. On the other hand, some who do not sue today may find the declaratory relief attractive (case 5). Depending on the pre-suit negotiations, some of these current non-suers may wind up in case 6 rather than case 5. Those who can show clear error may not have to sue at all because the defendant, knowing that a declaratory action will reveal the error, may choose to settle the case before suit is filed. Or the defendant may wait to see if the plaintiff is persistent enough to file that action. Either way, these new plaintiffs will impose new costs on defendants. If the error is disputed, the dispute is more likely to fall under case 5 than 6, unless the parties can agree to a reply or nonretraction device. The immediate question is the impact of these new plaintiffs. A summary of their role under the Lockyer bill can be seen in table 7.3.

The situation under the Lockyer proposal may be summarized as follows in table 7.4.

My sense is that apart from the bare incentive it offers in the opportunity to seek a declaration of falsity, the Lockyer bill does little to induce plaintiffs to switch from the damage action to the declaratory action. To the extent plaintiffs do switch to case 2 there will be overall savings in litigation costs—in most cases—that may not be offset by the total of costs imposed by new plaintiffs (case 5) or by the added negotiating costs incurred generally, primarily in cases 3 and 6.

TABLE 7.2: Lockyer Bill

Impact of Plaintiffs Who Switch to Case 2 of Table 7.1 on Current Expenses

EXPENSE	COMMENTS
Lo =	At most little change.
Le probably =	Still in every case—possible large-small media difference.
Lf far lower	Zero except for pre-suit work.
Lm ?	Saves some defense research but adds disputes over fees.
Ln higher	Increased negotiation.
Pj to zero	All risk is gone.
Ps lower	Lower range for bargaining—but not zero.
Fp higher	A new item that might matter in clear cases.
Fd slightly higher	New *offset*—unlikely to be significant.

In terms of the formula, the question for defendants under the Lockyer bill is whether:

Savings $[Lf + P\$ + Fd] >$ New Costs $[Le + Ln + Fp]$.

As we have seen, [67] the nature of the error may determine the course of the bargaining. The earlier explanation of why cases of clear error are unlikely to go to judgment becomes even stronger when we add the possible obligation to reimburse the successful plaintiff, unless the defendant can establish that its behavior before publication protects it. [68] Each

---

TABLE 7.3: Lockyer Bill

Impact of New Plaintiffs on Current Expenses (Cases 5 and 6 of Table 7.1)

EXPENSE	COMMENTS
$Lo =$	At most little change
Le far higher	Major new expense
$Lf =$	Low before and now
Lm ?	Low before—now includes litigation over fees
Ln higher	Increased negotiation
Pj to zero	Very low before and zero now
Ps slightly higher	More settlements—but low $
Fp higher	A new item that might matter in clear cases
Fd slightly higher	New *offset*—unlikely to be significant

TABLE 7.4: The Impact of the Lockyer Proposal on the Current System

LOCKYEAR PROPOSAL	CURRENT SYSTEM	
	Suit for Damages	*No Suit Filed*
Suit for Damages	1. Same costs per suit	4. No suit now if none before
Suit for Declaratory Judgment	2. Each dj case cheaper than former damage suit	5. New costs incurred
No suit	3. A few bargainers will settle without suit	6. A few bargainers will get more than before

newspaper can best judge for itself how its clear errors occur and how it
will fare under this part of the Lockyer fee rules. If the alleged error is
disputed, as noted earlier,[69] negotiations may take a different course
under the Lockyer bill but will still occur. The existence of the dispute
makes it likely that the defendants will be able to prove reasonable care
before publication and avoid having to reimburse a successful plaintiff.

D. The Schumer Bill

Representative Charles Schumer's (D., New York) study bill[70] begins,
as does the Lockyer bill, with the option permitting both public officials
and public figures to obtain declaratory judgments of falsity on clear and
convincing evidence, without regard to fault, and bars a plaintiff who
seeks declaratory relief from seeking damages.[71] The critical difference
is that if the plaintiff elects the conventional damage action the defendant
may override that election by unilaterally converting the plaintiff's damage claim into one for declaratory relief.[72] The case would then proceed
as if the plaintiff had made that election originally.[73]

The Schumer bill (tables 7.5 and 7.6) provides that in both the declaratory action and the damage action the prevailing party shall recover
reasonable attorney's fees except (1) that the court may reduce or
disallow the award if "it determines that there is an overriding reason to
do so"[74] and (2) no fees may be awarded against a defendant that proves
that it exercised due care to avoid making the false and defamatory

TABLE 7.5: Schumer Bill

Impact of Plaintiffs who Switch to Case 2 on Current Expenses

EXPENSE	COMMENT
$Lo =$	Very little change.
Le probably $=$	Still in every case—possible difference between large and small media.
Lf far lower	Possibly zero for public plaintiffs.
Lm ?	Lower on law; higher on fees.
Ln slightly higher	A few more options for claimant.
Pj to zero	All risk is gone.
Ps far lower	Very little room for money claims.
Fp higher	New item—more wins for P since D can elect DJ for public P.
Fd slightly higher	New *offset*—unlikely to be significant.

statement or shows that it retracted not later than 10 days after an action was filed.[75] Finally, the Schumer bill makes the damage action less attractive by barring the award of punitive damages.[76] Since only one libel plaintiff in ten has been prevailing in reported damage actions,[77] the chance to recover fees is unlikely to make the damage action more attractive to prospective plaintiffs, especially when combined with the new declaratory option.

But are damage actions likely to survive under the Schumer bill? It seems that the public[78] plaintiffs likeliest to bring damage actions are those most confident about showing the requisite fault. But defendants will know more about how the error occurred and will be most likely to convert to declaratory actions the plaintiffs' self-selected strongest damage cases.

Plaintiffs are unlikely to bring weak damage actions, because of both the fee provisions and the creation of the alternative action. But if a plaintiff were to miscalculate and bring a weak damage action, how might the defendant respond? Would it convert the action anyway to save itself from the risk of an unjustifiable loss, or from concern that perhaps *it* is miscalculating, or to avoid the disruptions that discovery might bring to the newspaper? Or would it accept the damage action and hope to win and to recoup litigation expenses? My sense is that media organizations (and their insurers) are risk averse in the extreme under current libel law and would take any chance to avoid exposure to damages, even where punitive damages are barred.[79]

If I am right that the Schumer approach will lead to the virtual[80] demise of damage actions, it becomes fairly easy to predict its impact on

---

TABLE 7.6: Schumer Bill

Impact of New Plaintiffs on Current Expenses (Cases 5 and 6)

EXPENSE	COMMENTS
$Lo =$	At most little change.
Le far higher	Major new expense.
$Lf =$	Low before and now.
Lm ?	Low before—now includes fee litigation.
Ln higher	Increased negotiation.
Pj to zero	Very low before and zero now.
Ps slightly higher	More settlements—but low $.
Fp higher	A new item that might matter in clear cases.
Fd slightly higher	New *offset*—unlikely to be significant

defense costs. If all cases went the full declaratory route, a defendant would eliminate damage exposure and legal expenses related to fault. The new costs in defending declaratory actions would include added expenses for negotiation and for determining falsity in cases brought by current non-suers.

Although it is hard to predict how fee shifting will operate when it includes an exception for "overriding reason,"[81] it seems likely that here, as with the Lockyer bill, the defendant will have to reimburse fees when the plaintiff establishes falsity—unless the defendant can come within the other escape hatches such as due care before publication or a quick retraction after suit is filed.[82] On the other hand, it is unlikely that many losing plaintiffs will have to reimburse.[83] The incentive effects of the fact that the damage action has been made unattractive (by eliminating punitive damages and by imposing the risk that unsuccessful damage plaintiffs may have to reimburse defendants) are unimportant because of the Schumer defendant's unilateral ability to avoid damage exposure.

It appears, then, that the effect of the Schumer bill will be to switch virtually all public plaintiffs into case 2. (Any plaintiffs left in case 1 who prove actual malice will recover less on average than they do now because of the elimination of punitive damages.) Some plaintiffs who sue today on a contingency fee basis might decide not to sue (case 3) because of the danger of having to reimburse a successful defendant. Others in case 3 may now be able to bargain more effectively for retraction or reply because of the new declaratory option. But since the defendant can now unilaterally avoid all damage liability, it is hard to see how the defendant need pay much in settlements.

Plaintiffs who do not sue under current law have no reason to bring a damage action under the Schumer bill (case 4) because it is no more attractive substantively. The only possible new basis for suit would be the possibility of recovering fees. But the fact that so few plaintiffs now win these cases, the lack of punitive damages, the risk of having to reimburse if unsuccessful, and the current availability of contingency arrangements suggest that no new damage cases will appear.

But certainly some plaintiffs who now do not sue are likely to take advantage of the declaratory option (case 5) if they cannot reach agreements under case 6. Because of the similarity of the fee provisions, the analysis here should be the same as that earlier for cases 5 and 6 of the Lockyer bill.[84] (The defendant's ability to avoid a damage action under the Schumer bill is irrelevant here because we are dealing with plaintiffs who do not seek damages today and who have no reason to change that now, as discussed in connection with case 4.)

Surely the savings related to actual malice and to payouts must exceed the new costs related to negotiation and falsity in cases 5 and 6. Bargaining is quite restrained here because the defendant can unilaterally avoid damage actions. Still, there may be some room for bargaining for retractions or for opportunities to reply, to avoid a potentially extended and uncertain declaratory action. In addition to losing leverage in terms of the damage action, the plaintiff also cannot negotiate to avoid the defendant's default in the declaratory action. It seems clear that:

Savings $[Lf + P\$] >$ New Costs $[Ln + Le]$.

The effect on each of the six cases appears in table 7.7.

The crucial difference between the Schumer bill and the Lockyer bill will be in the number in cases 1 and 2. Under the Schumer bill the vast majority will switch to case 2. To the extent that it costs less to litigate in case 2 than in case 1 (the savings will be somewhat less under Schumer because of the bar on punitive damages), the Schumer bill will yield greater total savings to defendants. The costs incurred in cases 5 and 6 should be about the same under both—but less likely to wipe out the savings otherwise produced by the Schumer bill. In addition, negotiated settlements will surely involve fewer and smaller payouts under the Schumer bill than under the Lockyer bill.

E. The Plaintiff's Option Libel Reform Act (POLRA)

This proposal[85] gives the plaintiff the controlling choice, as does the Lockyer bill, but extends it to all plaintiffs and makes it available against

TABLE 7.7: The Impact of the Schumer Proposal on the Current System

SCHUMER PROPOSAL	CURRENT SYSTEM	
	Suit for Damages	*No Suit Filed*
Suit for Damages	1. Very few public *Ps*. Lower average payouts	4. No reason to sue now if not before
Suit for Declaratory Judgment	2. Very large category— each case costs less than case 1	5. New costs incurred
No Suit	3. A few bargainers will settle without suit	6. Slightly more bargaining

all defendants. Discovery on falsity is barred.[86] The proposal goes beyond the two bills in making the damage action less attractive by requiring all plaintiffs to show falsity and actual malice with convincing clarity and by eliminating punitive damages.[87]

The proposal provides, as does the Schumer bill, that losers in both the declaratory action and the damage action generally owe the winners reasonable legal fees, subject to four exceptions.[88] In damage actions, an unsuccessful plaintiff who has suffered special damages and who had a reasonable chance of success need not reimburse.[89] The other three exceptions involve the declaratory action: (1) the losing plaintiff need not reimburse unless he proceeded without a reasonable chance for success or failed to present his evidence to the defendant before suit;[90] (2) a plaintiff who has succeeded on the basis of evidence not presented to the defendant beforehand cannot recoup legal fees from the defendant;[91] and (3) if the defendant has made an appropriate retraction after the declaratory action was filed, the defendant is the prevailing party thereafter.[92] Since fee shifting is not subject to an "overriding reason" exception or to one based on prepublication conduct, it should play a more predictable role here than under either the Lockyer or Schumer bills—and cost less to determine.

A newspaper may find it more difficult to calculate the consequence of this proposal than of the other two. Since the Lockyer bill simply cleared a new path, the first question was how many would choose the new path instead of the damage route. Under POLRA, in addition to measuring that effect, we must also determine how many more will switch to the declaratory route because of the changes made in the damage action. Since the two declaratory actions are essentially the same (except for fee provisions),[93] it seems clear that however many persons would choose the Lockyer declaratory path over the damage action, more would do so under POLRA (see tables 7.8 and 7.9).

The differences in fee shifting strengthen that contrast. Plaintiffs who succeed in the declaratory action are more likely to get their legal expenses reimbursed under POLRA than under the Lockyer bill because POLRA contains no exceptions for "overriding reason" or prepublication care. Moreover, it protects most losing plaintiffs who have offered their evidence of falsity to the defendant early in an attempt to get a quick resolution.[94] (A further provision to encourage early showing of evidence of falsity bars from reimbursement even a successful plaintiff who has not shown the evidence of falsity to the defendant.[95])

By making the tort action less attractive and the recovery of fees more likely in the declaratory action in case of success and avoidable in case of failure, POLRA should encourage plaintiffs to switch to the declaratory path (case 2). Moreover, that course is more widely available than under the other two bills because it is not limited to public plaintiffs or to media defendants.

The plaintiffs who would continue to sue for damages (case 1) would presumably be those who may think they have a good case on actual malice (and who want to pursue it), as well as those bent on harassing or intimidating the media. This may mean that the average costs of defending the remaining damage actions will be higher than they are

TABLE 7.8: POLRA Proposal

Impact of Plaintiffs Who Switch to Case 2 on Current Expenses

EXPENSE	COMMENTS
Lo =	Very little change.
Le probably =	Still in every case—possible large-small media difference.
Lf far lower	Zero except for pre-suit work.
Lm ?	Less legal defense—but more fee litigation.
Ln slightly higher	More options for plaintiff.
Pj to zero	All risk is gone.
Ps lower	Lower range for bargaining—but not zero.
Fp higher	New item—extent depends on how many use DJ and the outcomes.
Fd slightly higher	New *offset*—potentially significant but uncertain.

TABLE 7.9: POLRA Proposal

Impact of New Plaintiffs on Current Expenses (Cases 5 and 6)

EXPENSE	COMMENTS
Lo =	At most little change.
Le far higher	Major new expense.
Lf =	Low before and now.
Lm ?	Low before—now includes fee litigation.
Ln higher	Increased negotiation.
Pj to zero	Very low before and zero now.
Ps slightly higher	More settlements now.
Fp higher	A new item that might matter in clear cases.
Fd slightly higher	New *offset*—unlikely to be significant.

today when plaintiffs have no choice. But the costs will often be recoverable, especially from solvent individuals or groups whose suits fail.

Will the plaintiff success rate increase over the current 10 percent? Although the self-selection that will result from creating a two-track system suggests a higher rate, several factors cut the other way. The first is the greater difficulty of winning the action because of the requirement of actual malice. Second, as noted earlier,[96] solid information about actual malice is rarely available to the plaintiff when the election must be made. As a result, some plaintiffs who might succeed today will forgo the damage route under POLRA. Thus, as with the Lockyer bill, it is not clear why the current success figure should change.

So far as case 3 is concerned, the effect under POLRA should be essentially the same as that under the Schumer bill. Some plaintiffs who sue today on a contingency fee might decide not to sue because of the danger of having to reimburse a successful defendant. Others in case 3 may now be able to bargain more effectively for retraction or reply because of the new declaratory option. Under POLRA, the plaintiff's bargaining leverage will resemble that under the Lockyer bill more than that under the Schumer bill because the plaintiff controls the election.

Plaintiffs who do not sue under current law have no reason to bring a damage action under POLRA (case 4) because it is substantively less attractive than the current damage action. Only the possibility of recovering fees might tip the balance in favor of suit. But, as with the Schumer bill, the fact that so few plaintiffs now win these cases, the lack of punitive damages, the risk of having to reimburse if unsuccessful, and the likely availability today of contingency arrangements for strong cases suggest that no new damage cases will appear.

How many current non-suers are likely to take advantage of the declaratory option (case 5)? This will depend to some extent upon the impact of the fee-shifting provisions, which is more predictable than under either of the other proposals. A plaintiff who is confident about falsity and who is willing to show his evidence to the defendant can be assured of winning and recovering fees—or of obtaining an appropriate retraction. Complainants will also be aware of the risk of having to reimburse, if unsuccessful, for failure to reveal evidence—or for having brought or maintained the case without a reasonable chance of success. Of course, the defendant is aware of the same points and may settle some of these cases before suit (case 6). The impact of new plaintiffs is suggested in table 7.9

The usual question is whether the major costs saved by not having to defend so many damage actions, together with the reduced risks in those damage actions that are still brought (offset by the new burden of reimbursing successful plaintiffs), outweigh the new costs attributable to the declaratory action and the added negotiation and settlement costs that come from providing plaintiffs with the new alternative. To the extent that failing suits are brought to harass, defendant may obtain substantial reimbursements of fees; to the extent plaintiffs switch to declaratory relief, the saving will come in lower expenses related to fault. In terms of the formula, the question is whether

$$\text{Savings } [Lf + P\$ + Fd] > \text{New Costs } [Le + Ln + Fp].$$

The overall analysis is presented in table 7.10.

If, on average, litigating declaratory actions is cheaper than litigating current damage actions, and if enough plaintiffs switch from the damage action to the declaratory action, this may more than make up for the new costs introduced by those plaintiffs who do not now sue (case 5) and the added negotiation expenses generally. The incentive to settle cases of clear error may be stronger here because the fee-shifting provisions focus on postpublication conduct. The defendant's incentive to settle cases of disputed error may be stronger here because losing defendants are more likely to owe fees than under the two bills.

CONCLUSION

At this point, it might be helpful to take another look at the six boxes from a comparative standpoint to see the points at which the reform

TABLE 7.10: The Impact of the POLRA Proposal on the Current System

POLRA PROPOSAL	CURRENT SYSTEM	
	Suit for Damages	*No Suit Filed*
Suit For Damages	1. Fewer suits by all *Ps*. Lower average payouts	4. No reason to sue now if not before
Suit for Declaratory Judgment	2. Each case cheaper than former damage suit	5. New costs incurred
No suit	3. A few bargainers will settle without suit	6. A few bargainers will get more than before

proposals differ from current law and from each other. (In table 7.11 *L* stands for Lockyer, *S* for Schumer, and *P* for POLRA.)

Unless the Lockyer bill manages to divert a substantial number of plaintiffs away from damage actions, it is not clear that it will achieve cost savings for defendants. It seems clear that such savings will be achieved under the Schumer bill and it seems likely that the POLRA proposal will achieve savings though in a lesser amount than under the Schumer bill.

Plaintiffs will certainly be better off under all of these proposals than under current law. Under the Lockyer proposal, plaintiffs as a class make no tradeoffs to obtain their new advantage. Under POLRA, some

TABLE 7.11: The Impact of Each Proposal on the Current System

PROPOSAL	CURRENT SYSTEM	
	Suit for Damages	*No Suit Filed*
Suit for Damages	1. Number of cases: Most under *L* Fewest under *S* *P* in between Rate of recovery: *P* lower than *L* and *S* Size of recovery: *L* highest *S* lowest—private *Ps* *P* in between Fee shifts: *L* none More under *P* than *S*	4. No reason to sue now if not before
Suit for Declaratory Judgment	2. Number of cases: Fewest under *L* Most under *S* *P* in between Fee shifts Uncertain under *L* & *S* Most under *P* DJ suits cheaper for small media, possibly not so in giant cases	5. New costs incurred in all plans Most fee shifts in *P*
No Suit	3. Settlers better off under *L* and *P*. Some large payments	6. Weak damage cases—more retractions, not many or large payments

plaintiffs give up substantial damage claims. Under the Schumer bill public plaintiffs may lose their damage claims entirely.[97] Although the impact on plaintiffs is not a mirror image of the effect on the defendants, it is not hard to predict how different groups of plaintiffs will react to each of the three proposals.

Finally, it is worth reemphasizing that this paper has stressed defense costs to the virtual exclusion of all other criteria. This was done not because these questions are the only ones or even the most important ones but because it seemed useful to try to provide media organizations, which are certain to play a vital role in the political process, a way of assessing this one impact on their operations. Some media organizations may find the impact on their costs conclusive. Others will use it as the starting point for their own much broader analysis of today's libel law, touching such matters as the impact of declaratory approaches on press credibility and on public attitudes toward the press.

It appears from the analysis that declaratory proposals that discourage resort to damage actions and encourage resort to declaratory actions will cost media no more than the current system now costs, and may produce substantially lower costs for all the media or at least for smaller media. If these predictions are accurate, the economic concerns of media should not stand in the way of serious considerations of alternatives to the current libel regime.

APPENDIX A

The people of the State of California do enact as follows:

SECTION 1. The Legislature finds that the current judicial mechanism for redress of defamation of a public official or public figure by a media defendant fails to provide justice for either party.

The current remedy of a suit for money damages produces an unacceptable risk of suppression of free speech and public access to vital information.

Concurrently, the plaintiff in such an action is rarely interested in monetary redress, but rather seeks vindication of his or her reputation.

It is, therefore, the intent of the Legislature to provide a concurrent remedy to a suit for money damages which avoids costly and protracted litigation on the issue of defamation of a public figure or public official, and establishes a remedy which truly protects the defamed individual and at the same time encourages the robust exchange of ideas which is so vital to our democracy.

SEC. 2. Section 48.6 is added to the Civil Code, to read:

48.6. (a) A public official or a public figure who is the subject of a publication or broadcast made in a newspaper, magazine, radio or television broadcast, or any other print or electronic media, may bring an action for a judgment that the publication or broadcast was false and defamatory.

(b) Notwithstanding any other provision of law, it shall be no defense to an action brought under this section that a publication or broadcast was made without malice or ill will or any other improper motive or negligence.

(c) In any action brought under this section, the plaintiff shall be required to prove by clear and convincing evidence that the publication or broadcast was false and defamatory.

(d) No damages may be awarded in any action brought under this section, whether or not those damages are for compensation or for punishment and by way of example. Any person who commences an action for relief under this section shall be barred from asserting or pursuing any other claim or cause of action arising out of the publication or broadcast, and shall be deemed to have waived the right to assert any such claim.

(e) In any action arising under this section, the court shall award reasonable attorney's fees to the prevailing party except as follows:

(1) The court may reduce or disallow attorney's fees if there is an overriding reason to do so.

(2) No attorney's fees shall be awarded against a defendant that proves that it exercised reasonable efforts to determine that the publication or broadcast was not false and defamatory.

(3) No attorney's fees shall be awarded against a defendant that published a correction or retraction no later than 10 days after the action is filed.

(4) No attorney's fees shall be awarded against a plaintiff unless it is proved that the action was brought or maintained without a reasonable chance of success.

(f) An action under this section shall be subject to the period of limitations of Section 340 of the Code of Civil Procedure.

APPENDIX B

A BILL

To protect the constitutional right to freedom of speech by establishing a new cause of action for defamation, and for other purposes.

Be it enacted by the Senate and House of Representatives of the United States of America in Congress assembled,

SECTION 1. ACTION FOR DECLARATORY JUDGMENT THAT STATEMENT IS FALSE AND DEFAMATORY.

(a) CAUSE OF ACTION.

(1) A public official or public figure who is the subject of a publication or broadcast which is published or broadcast in the print or electronic media may bring an action in any court of competent jurisdiction for a declaratory judgment that such publication or broadcast was false and defamatory.

(2) Paragraph (1) shall not be construed to require proof of the state of mind of the defendant.

(3) No damages shall be awarded in such an action.

(b) BURDEN OF PROOF. The plaintiff seeking a declaratory judgment under subsection (a) shall bear the burden of proving by clear and convincing evidence each element of the cause of action described in subsection (a).

(c) BAR TO CERTAIN CLAIMS. A plaintiff who brings an action for a declaratory judgment under subsection (a) shall be forever barred from asserting any other claim or cause of action arising out of a publication or broadcast which is the subject of such action.

(d) ELECTION BY DEFENDANT.

(1) A defendant in an action brought by a public official or public figure arising out of a publication or broadcast in the print or electronic media which is alleged to be false and defamatory shall have the right, at the time of filing its answer or within 90 days from the commencement of the action, which ever comes first, to designate the action as an action for a declaratory judgment pursuant to subsection (a).

(2) Any action designated as an action for a declaratory judgment pursuant to paragraph (1) shall be treated for all purposes as if it had been filed orginally as an action for a declaratory judgment under subsection (a), and the plaintiff shall be forever barred from asserting or recovering for any other claim or cause of action arising out of a publication or broadcast which is the subject of such action.

SEC. 2. LIMITATION ON ACTION.

Any action arising out of a publication or broadcast which is alleged to be false and defamatory must be commenced not later than one year after the first date of such publication or broadcast.

SEC. 3. PUNITIVE DAMAGES PROHIBITED.

Punitive damages may not be awarded in any action arising out of a publication or broadcast which is alleged to be false and defamatory.

SEC. 4. ATTORNEY'S FEES.

In any action arising out of a publication or broadcast which is alleged to be false and defamatory, the court shall award the prevailing party reasonable attorney's fees, except that—

(1) the court may reduce or disallow the award of attorney's fees if it determines that there is an overriding reason to do so; and

(2) the court shall not award attorney's fees against a defendant which proves that it exercised reasonable efforts to ascertain that the publication or broadcast was not false and defamatory or that it published or broadcast a retraction not later than 10 days after the action was filed.

SEC. 5. EFFECTIVE DATE.

This Act shall apply to any cause of action which arises on or after the date of the enactment of this Act.

APPENDIX C: THE PLAINTIFF'S OPTION LIBEL REFORM ACT

SECTION 1. ACTION FOR DECLARATORY JUDGMENT THAT STATEMENT IS FALSE AND DEFAMATORY.

(a) CAUSE OF ACTION.

(1) Any person who is the subject of any defamation may bring an action in any court of competent jurisdiction for a declaratory judgment that such publication or broadcast was false and defamatory.

(2) Paragraph (1) shall not be construed to require proof of the state of mind of the defendant.

(3) No damages shall be awarded in such an action.

(b) BURDEN OF PROOF. The plaintiff seeking a declaratory judgment under subsection (a) shall bear the burden of proving by clear and convincing evidence each element of the cause of action described in subsection (a). In an action under subsection (a) a report of a statement made by an identified source not associated with the defendant shall not be deemed false if it is accurately reported.

(c) DEFENSES. Privileges that already exist at common law or by statute, including but not limited to the privilege of fair and accurate report, shall apply to actions brought under this section.

(d) BAR TO CERTAIN CLAIMS. A plaintiff who brings an action for a declaratory judgment under subsection (a) shall be forever barred from asserting any other claim or cause of action arising out of a publication or broadcast which is the subject of such action.

SEC. 2. LIMITATION ON ACTION.

(a) Any action arising out of a publication or broadcast which is alleged to be false and defamatory must be commenced not later than one year after the first date of such publication or broadcast.

(b) It shall be a defense to an action brought under SEC. 1 that the defendant published or broadcast an appropriate retraction before the action was filed.

(c) No pretrial discovery of any sort shall be allowed in any action brought under SEC. 1.

(d) Actions brought under SEC. 1 shall be accorded highest priority in setting dates for trial.

SEC. 3. PROOF AND RECOVERY IN DAMAGE ACTIONS.

(a) In any action for damages for libel or slander or for false-light invasion of privacy, the plaintiff may recover no damages unless plaintiff proves falsity and actual malice by clear and convincing evidence.

(b) Punitive damages may not be awarded in any action for libel or slander or false-light invasion of privacy.

SEC. 4. ATTORNEY'S FEES.

(a) GENERAL RULE. Except as provided in subsection (b), in any action arising out of a publication or broadcast which is alleged to be false and defamatory, the court shall award the prevailing party reasonable attorney's fees.

(b) EXCEPTIONS.

(1) In an action for damages brought by a plaintiff who sustained special damages, the prevailing defendant shall not be awarded attorney's fees unless the action is found to have been brought or maintained without a reasonable chance for success.

(2) In an action brought under SEC. 1, a prevailing defendant shall not be awarded attorney's fees unless the plaintiff has brought or maintained the action without a reasonable chance for success or has failed to present evidence to the defendant before the action was filed.

(3) In any case brought under SEC. 1, in which the plaintiff has prevailed on the basis of evidence that plaintiff did not present, or formally try to present, to the defendant before the action was filed, the plaintiff shall not recover attorney's fees.

(4) In any case brought under SEC. 1, in which the defendant has made an appropriate retraction after the filing of suit, the plaintiff shall be treated as the prevailing party up to that point, and the defendant shall be treated as the prevailing party after that point.

SEC. 5. EFFECTIVE DATE.

This Act shall apply to any cause of action that arises on or after the date of the enactment of this Act.

ACKNOWLEDGMENT

I would like to thank my colleague Mark Kelman and my research assistants, Fred H. Cate and Thomas C. Rubin, for their helpful comments. Support for this paper came from the Stanford Legal Research Fund, made possible by a bequest from the Estate of Ira S. Lillick, and by gifts from Roderick E. and Carla A. Hills and other friends of the Stanford Law School.

NOTES

1. E.g., H.R. 2846 (99th Cong. 1st Sess.) (1985), the Schumer study bill, reprinted in Appendix B; Cal. S. B. 1979 (1986), the Lockyer bill, reprinted in Appendix A; Franklin, "A Declaratory Judgment Alternative to Current Libel Law," 74 *Calif. L.Rev.* 809 (1986), containing a proposal that is reprinted in Appendix C.

2. E.g., Barrett, "Declaratory Judgments for Libel: A Better Alternative," 74 *Calif. L. Rev.* 847 (1986); Cendali, "Of Things to Come—The Actual Impact of *Herbert v. Lando* and a Proposed National Correction Statute," 22 *Harv. J. Legis.* 441 (1985); Franklin, *supra* note 1.

4. Although all three proposals require the plaintiff to establish falsity, see text *infra* following note 30, and states must impose this burden in most, if not all, libel cases, Philadelphia Newspaper Co. v. Hepps, 475 U.S. 1134 (1986), the term "truth" may still be important. For example, a defendant who seeks summary judgment on this issue may find that demonstrating the statement's truth is the most effective way of showing that the plaintiff will be unable to prove it false.

5. Among the noneconomic costs beyond the scope of this paper are the effects on staff morale of being engaged in extensive pretrial activities.

6. I assume that strict liability will not be imposed on media defendants under an extension of Dun & Bradstreet v. Greenmoss Builders, Inc., 472 U.S. 749 (1985).

7. E.g., Burnett v. National Enquirer, Inc., 144 Cal. App. 3d 991, 193 Cal. Rptr. 206 (1983), appeal dismissed for want of jurisdiction, 465 U.S. 1014 (1984).

8. E.g., Westmoreland v. CBS, Inc., 596 F.Supp. 1170 (S.D.N.Y. 1984); Sharon v. Time, Inc., 599 F.Supp. 538 (S.D.N.Y. 1984). Despite suggestions for carefully structured discovery from Justice Brennan, dissenting in part, in Herbert v. Lando, 441 U.S. 153, 180 (1979), most are not so conducted.

9. Gazette, Inc. v. Harris, 229 Va. 1, 325 S.E.2d 713, 726 n.3 (1985). Although some private plaintiffs try to prove actual malice in order to recover a larger amount of damages, e.g., Gertz v. Robert Welch, Inc, 680 F.2d 527 (7th Cir. 1982), cert. denied, 459 U.S. 1226 (1983), many rely on negligence principles. See the cases cited in Bloom, "Proof of Fault in Media Defamation Litigation," 38 *Vand. L. Rev.* 247 (1985) and Franklin, "What Does 'Negligence' Mean in Defamation Cases?" 6 *Comm/Ent L. J.* 259 (1984).

10. If smaller media tend to be sued more frequently by plaintiffs who are called private (and who do not try to prove actual malice), it may mean that the legal expenses devoted to the fault question may be a lower portion of that newspaper's total legal expenses than it would be for larger media. See statement of Charles Nutt, Executive Editor of the Bridgewater (N.J.) *Courier News* at Symposium sponsored by ABA-ANPA Task Force, March 21, 1986 (smaller papers are finding that persons they write about—local bankers and important persons in town—are being called private). See, e.g., Bank of Oregon v. Independent News, Inc., 29B.Or. 434, 693 P.2d 35, rehearing denied, 298 Or. 819, 696 P.2d 1095, cert. denied, 474 U.S. 826 (1985).

11. Another way to look at legal expenses is by stage of disposition. Thus, rather than

breaking the expenses down by issue, one could break them down according to cases that were won on motion to dismiss, on summary judgment, after trial, or after appeal, or were lost, or were settled. Although this will help measure the strength of the plaintiff's case, it will not be helpful in tracing the reasons for spending defense money. Nor will it permit comparisons with alternative systems that emphasize the role of falsity. Finally, this breakdown is harder to categorize because, for example, motions to dismiss may be granted after some substantial discovery has occurred. Although the same discovery might address questions of both falsity and fault, this seems easier to unravel than procedural overlaps.

12. Franklin, "Suing Media for Libel: A Litigation Study," 1981 *Amer. B. Found. Research J.* 795, 803; Bezanson, "Libel Law and the Realities of Litigation: Setting the Record Straight," 71 *Iowa L. Rev.* 226, 228 (1985) ("[l]ess than ten percent of media libel cases are won in court").

13. E.g., Bezanson, supra note 12, at 228 ("another fifteen or so percent are settled, usually without money changing hands"). Sometimes the parties agree that one or both will contribute some amount to charity. Thus, the settlement between Charles Rebozo and the *Washington Post* (after ten years of litigation) included a published statement that the newspaper "did not state that Mr. Rebozo committed a criminal act, and it was not intended to convey that implication." Both parties agreed to make contributions to charity. *N. Y. Times,* Nov. 5, 1983, at 13 col. 3. In addition to the legal expenses incurred before that point, there may be some further costs in loss of respect depending on whether the settlement involved an admission of serious error. See *infra* note 22.

14. Franklin, *supra* note 15, at 800 n.12.

15. On the other hand, in the vast majority of reported cases the plaintiff is treated as public. Franklin, *supra* note 12, at 825.

16. The limit is "actual injury damages," Gertz v. Robert Welch, Inc., 418 U.S. 323, 349–50 (1974). See also Time, Inc. v. Firestone, 424 U.S. 448 (1976).

17. The relationship between the source of the error and the harm done by the error depends on the facts. There seems little to say on this abstractly.

18. Punitive damages are available in most states, Bender, "Public Policy Limitations on Insuring Punitive and Actual Damages," in J. Lankenau (ed.), Media Insurance and Risk Management 337 (PLI 1985).

19. Strasser, "Changing Law in Handling of Liability Claims," *Nat'l L. J.,* Apr. 28, 1986, at 1 (reporting on new statutes in ten states).

20. Bezanson, *supra* note 12, at 228 ("Roughly eighty percent [of libel plaintiffs] engage lawyers on a contingency fee arrangement").

21. It does seem unlikely, though, that these limitations would discourage many plaintiffs who were motivated primarily by the possibility of recovering damages. Moreover, damage limitations would not discourage plaintiffs who were suing to clear their names or those who were suing primarily to harass defendants. Although defendants might decide to spend less on legal defense if the outer limits of exposure were more predictable, it seems unlikely that the outer limits will be pulled in so far as to make this kind of calculation central to any decision.

22. This formula excludes several economic costs such as the possible impact on advertising volume or rates from lower circulation caused by editorial decisions motivated by libel law. It also excludes the impact of judicial findings of libel on the value of the newspaper in any future sales negotiations. Cf. Brand, "Denver Post Corrects Story on Continental Airlines," *Editor & Publisher* 80 (April 19, 1986) (lengthy front page editorial statement correcting an earlier front page story). Will this enhance or hurt the paper's credibility in the community? How might this be translated into economic terms?

23. Countersuits in libel cases are much discussed today, but courts and lawyers have so far shown an ambivalent attitude toward the device. Strasser and Lauter, "Tables Turned in Libel Trial," *Nat'l L. J.*, Nov. 19, 1984, at 3.

24. Successful efforts include Beary v. West Publishing Co., 763 F.2d 66 (2d Cir.) cert. denied, 474 U.S. 903 (1985) and Daily Gazette Co. v. Canady, 332 S.E.2d 262 (W.Va.1985).

25. Each newspaper will use its unique experience in making calculations—here, that it actively and successfully pursues this course. If it spends money seeking this result but failing, these expenses should be added to miscellaneous expenses.

26. Legal expense *(L$)* can be seen to be the sum of the insurance premium *(Ip)* plus the deductible or retention *(Id)* plus any sum that exceeds the maximum coverage under the policy *(Im)*. This last item can be entirely made up of very large legal expenses or might be made up of both legal expenses and some payout. In addition, now that at least one libel insurer requires insureds to bear 20 percent of the legal expenses after any deductible (Il), these amounts must also be included in legal expenses. This yields a formula for economic costs of insured media in which legal expenses and payouts are no longer separate items. Since some of these costs involve annual expenditures and perhaps limits per year or per case, extended time frames should be used. Thus, the economic costs of libel law for an insured newspaper are $E\$ = Ip + Id + Im + Il$.

27. See Appendix A.

28. See Appendix B.

29. See Appendix C. This proposal was suggested in Franklin, "Good Names and Bad Law: A Critique of Libel Law and a Proposal," 18 *U. S. F. L. Rev.* 1 (1983) and presented in statutory form in Franklin, *supra* note 1.

30. Although there has been some discussion of the role of retraction statutes in libel reform, e.g., Cendali, *supra* note 2, this device, which exists in some form in over 30 states (B. Sanford, *Libel and Privacy* 663 [1985]), has not gained wide support as a reform. These statutes are not perceived to help plaintiffs who are primarily interested in clearing their names in cases in which, after publication, the facts are still in serious dispute. Although this might lead the parties to settle for a reply by the plaintiff in the newspaper, it does not provide the plaintiff with the admission or adjudication being sought. In such a case the plaintiffs' only alternative is to resort to the conventional damage action. As suggested in the text, declaratory proposals may induce retractions and replies.

31. Appendix A § 2(b), (d)-(e); Appendix B §§ 1(a) (2)-(3), 4; Appendix C § 1 (a) (2)-(3), 4.

32. Appendix A § 2 (f); Appendix B § 2; Appendix C § (2)(a).

33. Soloski, "The Study and the Libel Plaintiff: Who Sues for Libel?" 71 *Iowa L. Rev.* 217, 219–20 (1985) (half of the future plaintiffs go to media before seeing an attorney; others go to media after seeing an attorney).

34. *Id.* at 220.

35. Eighty percent do so. Bezanson, *supra* note 15, at 228.

36. Greed cannot explain lawyers' overstatements about the chances for success in libel cases against media. Since most are using the contingent fee, they may have been unaware of the statistics in this area and been analogizing to other tort areas. The cases studied took place before the well publicized results in the Westmoreland and Sharon cases. See *supra* note 8.

37. One explanation may be that lawyers enjoy libel cases and are willing to subsidize them. This might be due to the intrinsic legal interest in the cases or to the recognition that libel cases tend to get wide publicity and will put the lawyer's name before the community—perhaps as a champion of ordinary citizens against unpopular media. See *infra* note 40 for an additional comment.

38. Bezanson, *supra* note 12, at 228 ("'The second reason plaintiffs sue is that they win, although they do so by *their* standards, not the judicial system's").

39. E.g., Lubasch, "Time Cleared of Libeling Sharon But Jurors Criticize its Reporting, *N.Y. Times,*" Jan. 25, 1985, at 1 (jury found falsity but did not find actual malice); Trumbull, "Nauru President Loses Libel Suit Against Gannett Paper on Guam," *N. Y. Times,* Nov. 1, 1985, at 1 (jury found falsity in suit by Hammer DeRoburt but did not find actual malice).

Some surveys suggest that, at least from the defendant's and insurance perspectives, a high percentage of cases are nuisance cases. Weber, "Editors Surveyed Describe Half of All Libel Suits as 'Nuisance' Cases," *ASNE Bulletin* 38 (Jan. 1986), and Franklin, *supra* note 29 at 6 n.27 (quoting Larry Worrall). This is accurate if it means that the story is true, or is clearly nondefamatory, and the case is being brought to harass. But if it means also that victims of defamatory falsehoods have almost no chance of proving the required fault, many would not call these nuisance cases.

40. The Lockyer and Schumer bills offer this option only to public plaintiffs. Appendix A § 2 (a); Appendix B § 1(a) (1). This might mean extra litigation expense to determine eligibility if an arguably private plaintiff wanted to invoke the declaratory remedy—with the oddity that the plaintiff would be claiming to be public. It seems unlikely that a defendant would want to expose itself to damage litigation under a negligence standard when the plaintiff is willing to forgo damages entirely. But if the plaintiff's eligibility is jurisdictional, the parties cannot effectively waive the point.

Under the Schumer bill litigation might also arise if the plaintiff chose to seek damages. When the defendant sought to convert the action into one for declaratory relief, the plaintiff would assert that the case was not covered by the statute because the plaintiff was private.

41. See Appendix A.

42. See Appendix C.

43. The magnitude of any shift of costs will largely depend upon the identity of the defendant and whether it is the sort plaintiffs may wish to sue for damages for other reasons.

44. See text *infra* following note 49.

45. See *supra* note 39.

46. See The CBS Benjamin Report (1984), an examination by a CBS official of the procedures followed in producing the program that led to General Westmoreland's defamation action against CBS. Cf. Galloway v. FCC, 778 F2d 16 (D.C.Cir. 1985) (detailing, in the context of a distortion claim, procedures followed in a CBS program that led as well to a defamation claim).

47. Burnett v. National Enquirer, Inc., 144 Cal. App. 3d 991, 193 Cal. Rptr. 206 (1983), appeal dismissed for want of jurisdiction, 465 U.S. 1014 (1984). Rather than retry the punitive damage aspect of the case, the parties settled for an undisclosed sum.

48. The costs in staff morale and in the loss of public confidence in the editorial process would render this course unacceptable despite some short-run economic gains in the specific case.

49. These are the Lockyer bill and the POLRA proposal.

50. In most cases the plaintiff who objects to the published version of a story knows information to the contrary.

51. As discussed, the legal costs will be lower case by case under the declaratory judgment approach unless it would have been a case in which a damage action would have been dismissed at an early stage. The cost of the defense in the damage action must include any appeal needed to preserve or obtain that dismissal.

52. Under all three approaches, plaintiff's election of the declaratory route prevents a later damage action. See Appendix A § 2(d); Appendix B § 1(c); Appendix C § 1(d).

53. Although all the proposals have a general rule that would make the loser liable for the winner's attorney's fees in the declaratory action, the loser in a default situation might escape such responsibility under the Lockyer and Schumer bills. See Appendix A § 2(c); Appendix B § 4(1)-(2).

54. See Appendix B § 1(d).

55. Questions will inevitably arise over the role insurers are to play in the question of how much to put into the defense of a declaratory action. If, under the Schumer bill, the insurer had the controlling power to exercise the election, it could be sure of avoiding exposure to damages. This would affect only the insurers's risk of paying judgments or of making payments to settle cases—events that occur in only a small percentage of all claims. Any payments would be small so long as the defense controls the election. Would this be offset by increased litigation costs in the declaratory actions? As my conclusion suggests, insurers should be most reassured by the Schumer bill.

56. It must be recognized that how proposals to change state law will operate depends on the special features of that state's law, especially the role already played by retraction.

57. Although the text of the Lockyer bill appears to cover both media and nonmedia defendants, the preamble suggests that only media defendants are covered. Compare Appendix A § 1 with the preamble. This presents no difficulty in this paper because of our focus on media cases.

58. Appendix A § 2(b), (d)-(e).

59. *Id.* at § 2(e)(1).

60. *Id.* at § 2(e)(2).

61. *Id.* at § 2(e)(3).

62. *Id.* at § 2(e)(4).

63. Legal expenses incurred in resolving disputes over whether fees are recoverable are considered to be miscellaneous expenses *(Lm)*.

64. Appendix A § 2(e)(1).

65. Id. at § 2(e)(4).

66. See *infra* note 81.

67. See text *supra* following note 44.

68. Appendix A § 2(e)(2).

69. See text supra following note 50.

70. H.R. 2846 (99th Cong. 1st Sess.) (1985), reprinted in Appendix B.

71. Appendix B §§ 1(a)(2)-(3), 4.

72. *Id.* at § 1(d)(1).

73. *Id.* at § 1(d)(2).

74. *Id.* at § 4(1).

75. *Id.* at § 4(2).

76. *Id.* at § 3 (barring punitive damages).

77. See *supra* note 12.

78. See *supra* note 40.

79. Two scenarios might conceivably produce a damage action. The first case would be brought by a powerful plaintiff, eager enough to harass the defendant to be willing to pay both fees, if necessary, against a defendant who decides to stand up to the perceived harassment and "teach the plaintiff a lesson." This scenario will not occur frequently.

The second is one in which the public plaintiff has sustained large special damages as the result of a false statement and needs to try to recover them, even though evidence of fault is weak. The defendant might accept the damage action if it believes that some essential element is missing or that the evidence of fault is indeed weak, and that a successful motion to dismiss or a quick summary judgment might cost less than a declaratory action. In addition, of course, the paper might avoid having to admit error or having a court find error in the original story. This combination of a powerful incentive to seek damages and the hypothesized weakness, but not hopelessness, of the damage action, and the assumption about how surely, cheaply, and quickly the defendant can win the damage action seems rare.

80. The demise will probably not be complete because of the exclusion of private plaintiffs.

81. See Barrett, *supra* note 2 a, suggesting that this provision in the Schumer bill is meant to cover at least the case of the poor plaintiff with special damages who loses the damage action and the wealthy plaintiff who prevails against the poor media defendant in the declaratory action.

82. Appendix B § 4(2).

83. One might expect the invocation of "overriding reason" when a poor plaintiff reasonably tries, but fails, to prove falsity in a declaratory action against a large newspaper.

84. See text *supra* following table 7.1. The fact that the defendant's election controls under the Schumer bill is not important here since that power is no threat to a plaintiff whose case was so weak under current law that no suit is filed.

85. The genesis of this proposal is set out in Franklin, *supra* note 29. The text of the proposal is in Appendix C.

86. Appendix C § 2(c)-(d). The lack of discovery may make some resolutions swifter. On the other hand, it is likely to prevent the use of summary judgment in cases that, in retrospect, surely did not warrant using courtroom time. But cutting against this is the elimination of appeals from grants and denials of summary judgment. I think there will be a net saving here, but that is open to argument.

87. *Id.* § at 3(a).

88. *Id.* at § 4(a)-(b).

89. *Id.* at § 4(b)(1).

90. *Id.* at § 4(b)(4).

91. *Id.* at § 4(b)(3).

92. *Id.* at § 4(b)(4).

93. Compare Appendix A § 2(e) with Appendix C § 4.

94. Appendix C § 4(b)(2).

95. Id. at § 4(b)(3).

96. See text *supra* at note 50.

97. For an introduction to the discussion of these other aspects, see Barrett, *supra* note 2 and Franklin, *supra* note 1.

8

IS THE LAW OF DEFAMATION AS IT RELATES TO PUBLIC OFFICIALS AND PUBLIC FIGURES ECONOMICALLY EFFICIENT?

Alain Sheer
Asghar Zardkoohi

This Article considers the effects on investigative effort and self-censorship of the constitutional limitations the Supreme Court has placed upon the common law of defamation as it relates to falsehoods defamatory of public officials and public figures.[1] These limitations replaced the strict liability regime of the common law with a regime based upon the actual malice liability rule. The Court intended for this transformation to reduce the extent of self-censorship caused by the common law's strict liability approach.

This article's analysis of the new law of defamation is based on two fundamental assumptions: the first, that publishers organize their activities in order to maximize profit and thus apply profit maximization principles in deciding how much effort to make in investigating the accuracy of statements published and whether to self-censor; the second, that the social objective of the new law of defamation is to balance First Amendment and reputational interests. The analysis first evaluates the consequences of the strict liability and actual malice liability regimes upon publishers' decisions to investigate accuracy and to self-censor publications that concern public officials and public figures, and then compares the decisions induced by each rule with the decisions which would balance the social interests.

I. AN OVERVIEW OF THE LAW OF DEFAMATION

A. The Common Law

Before *New York Times v. Sullivan,*[2] defamation lawsuits were decided under principles of common law rather than constitutional law.[3] These principles required the plaintiff to prove both that the defendant had published defamatory statements and that he had suffered the specific type of injury needed to establish that the form of the defamation alleged was actionable.[4] If it was so established, the plaintiff could recover general, specific, and sometimes punitive damages. The common law of defamation recognized only truth and various privileges as defenses and did not allow the defendant to avoid liability by showing the absence of fault.[5] The common law rule was thus one of strict liability to the defendant.

Of the defenses available at common law the most important for the purpose of analyzing the present law of defamation is the privilege of fair comment. In most of the American jurisdictions which recognized it, the privilege of fair comment was interpreted as not excusing false and defamatory statements of fact.[6] The privilege of fair comment did not usually excuse falsehoods defamatory of either private individuals or public officials, and thus it represents the point of departure for the constitutional law of defamation.

On balance, then, the common law of defamation recognized and strongly favored the interest in protecting reputation. Under it defamatory falsehoods were not understood as contributing to the realization of other valid social objectives.

B. The *Sullivan* Case and the Conflict Between the First Amendment and the Common Law of Defamation

The Supreme Court first addressed the implications of the First Amendment upon the common law of defamation in the *Sullivan* case. The Court recognized a constitutionally based qualified privilege for the publication of defamatory falsehoods holding that the first amendment protects a publisher from liability for falsehoods defamatory of the official conduct of a public official unless the plaintiff proves by clear and convincing evidence that the statements were made with actual malice— that is, "with knowledge that [the statements were] false or with reckless disregard of whether [the statements were] false or not."[7]

The tests announced in *Sullivan* and the Court's discussion of them show its concern with balancing the competing interests implicated by the publication of statements critical of government. The Court recognized that, at the time the decision to publish is made, a statement criticizing government will often possess both a potential to injure reputation (because there is some probability it will prove to be false) and a potential to provide information valuable to society (because there is some probability it will prove to be true). The Court reasoned that the extent of self-censorship exercised by publishers under the prevailing liability regime determines the balance struck between these competing interests. On the one hand, even when publishers are granted immunity from the consequences of publishing false information, the First Amendment interest in the publication of truthful statements is advanced, because society is not deprived of the benefits of true statements, whose publication might be deterred by a threat of liability.[8] On the other hand, increasing the extent of self-censorship benefits society, because it avoids the effects of injuries to reputation that would arise when statements that prove to be false and defamatory are published.

The Court balanced the injury to reputation against the social value derived from publishing statements that subsequently would prove to be true. It concluded that the strict liability rule causes too much self-censorship and deprives society of valuable, accurate information about government, but that a rule of absolute immunity for defamatory false-hoods would cause too little self-censorship and injure reputation unjus-tifiably. It therefore announced a rule to accommodate the First Amend-ment interest in encouraging criticism of government and the state's interest in protecting the reputation of individuals: a public official can recover for a defamatory falsehood about his official conduct only if he proves by clear and convincing evidence that the statement was made with actual malice.

C. The Application of the Actual Malice Rule

The *Sullivan* Court did not have to decide, and in fact did not decide, "how far down into the lower ranks of government employees the 'public official' designation would extend for the purposes of this rule," and it did not "specify categories of persons who would or would not be included" or "the boundaries of the 'official conduct' concept."[9] That question was addressed in the line of cases that began with *Curtis Publishing Co. v. Butts.*[10] By holding in *Butts* that the actual malice rule applied in cases brought by public *figures*, not merely public *officials*, the Court expanded the First Amendment's ambit. In *Gertz v. Robert Welch, Inc.*,[11] the Court provided a test to distinguish public figures from private plaintiffs. The Court subsequently clarified this public figure test in *Time, Inc. v. Firestone,*[12] *Wolston v. Reader's Digest Association, Inc.*[13] and *Hutchinson v. Proxmire.*[14]

Butts and the companion case, *Associated Press v. Walker,*[15] dealt with statements about the conduct of people who—while not official—were of interest to the public. Butts, a nationally known football coach and athletic director at the University of Georgia, had allegedly partici-pated in a conspiracy to fix a football game. He was not an employee of the State of Georgia, although he directed the university's athletic pro-gram. Walker, a private citizen, allegedly had led a violent crowd in opposition to the enrollment of a black student at the University of

Mississippi. The Court, while holding that falsehoods defamatory of public figures were protected by the First Amendment and determining that both Butts and Walker were public figures, nevertheless decided in favor of Butts. However, it did decide against Walker.

The initial premises justified the decision to expand the application of the actual malice rule to include cases brought by public figures. The first was that " '[t]he guarantees for speech and press are not the preserve of political expression or comment upon public affairs. . .' [and therefore] freedom of discussion 'must embrace all issues about which information is needed or appropriate to enable the members of society to cope with the exigencies of their period.' "[16] The discussion of such issues is therefore protected by the First Amendment, even when the discussion concerns the actions of individuals who are not public officials. The second premise was that false and defamatory comments about such individuals, like falsehoods defaming public officials, are protected by the First Amendment because, as Justice Harlan explained, "a rational distinction 'cannot be founded on the assumption that criticism of private citizens who seek to lead in the determination of . . . policy will be less important to the public interest than will criticism of government officials.' "[17] Chief Justice Warren implicitly characterized individuals "intimately involved in the resolution of important public questions" as private deciders of public policy.[18] In *Butts* the Court concluded that First Amendment protection extended to falsehoods defamatory of private individuals who involved themselves in the resolution of important public controversies.

The *Gertz* case arose when the family of an individual who had been murdered by a policeman retained the plaintiff to represent them in a civil action for damages. The defendant published an article which described the trial as part of a plan to create a national police force sympathetic to a communist dictatorship and falsely identified the plaintiff as a central figure in the plan. The Court announced that the principal issue of the case was whether a newspaper or broadcaster that publishes defamatory falsehoods about an individual who is neither a public official nor a public figure may claim a constitutional privilege against liability for the injury inflicted by those statements."[19]

The *Gertz* Court held that the actual malice liability rule must be applied in defamation cases brought by public officials and public figures, while in state actions fault-based liability rules would be used to resolve cases brought by private plaintiffs. The meaning of the public figure test is of great importance because in conjunction with the public official test it limits the ambit of the First Amendment to which the actual malice rule applies. The Court described three classes of public persons: all-purpose, limited-purpose, and involuntary. Of these it considered the limited-purpose public figure category to be the largest and most important.[20] Limited-purpose public figures "thrust themselves to the forefront of particular public controversies in order to influence the resolution of the issues involved," and can be identified by "the nature and extent of [the] individual's participation in the particular controversy giving rise to the defamation."[21] The Court thus established voluntariness and public controversy as the elements of the limited-purpose public figure test. It did not, however, explain fully whether a public controversy is anything interesting to the public or whether voluntariness and public controversy are independently necessary characteristics of limited-purpose public figures.

The meaning and independent significance of the public controversy and voluntariness elements of the limited-pupose public figure test announced in *Gertz* were partially clarified in the *Firestone, Wolston,* and *Hutchinson* cases. The *Firestone* case concerned a defamatory falsehood about the ground on which a divorce had been granted. Although it did not settle the matter, the Court suggested that the respondent was not a public figure and that public controversy and voluntariness constitute independent elements of the limited-purpose public figure test.

The *Wolston* case arose from a book which falsely described the petitioner as a Soviet agent who had been indicted for espionage and then convicted of contempt. The Court held that voluntariness and public controversy were separate and independent elements of the public figure test. It found that the requisite voluntariness did not exist because the petitioner had not made an affirmative effort to persuade others to a particular viewpoint: he had "never discussed the matter with the press and [had] limited his involvement to that necessary to defend himself against the contempt charge."[22]

The *Hutchinson* case arose when the government agency that had sponsored the petitioner's scientific research was awarded Senator Proxmire's "Golden Fleece of the Month Award." The Court held that the petitioner was not a public figure, and by so holding it clarified the meaning of the public controversy element of the limited-purpose public figure test. *Hutchinson* did not place this controversy within the meaning of the public figure test because a concern about public expenditures was simply too broad to be a *Gertz* controversy. The Court also concluded that the requisite degree of voluntariness was absent.

Taken together *Gertz, Firestone, Wolston,* and *Hutchinson* suggest that: (1) voluntariness and public controversy are separate and independent elements in the limited-purpose public figure test; (2) the universe of public controversies is smaller than the universe of topics that are newsworthy or of general public interest; and (3) the requisite degree of voluntariness exists when an affirmative effort to persuade others has been made.

In sum, under the new law of defamation the plaintiff's status as a public official, public figure, or private plaintiff determines the rules that may be used to decide both liability and the type of damages that may be recovered. Public officials and public figures must overcome the actual malice liability standard because, unlike private figures, they voluntarily involve themselves in events at least arguably related to self-government. Public officials and public figures can recover compensatory and noncompensatory damages upon clear and convincing proof of actual malice. In keeping with the Court's requirement that the states apply some type of fault-based rule in cases brought by most private plaintiff's,[23] various states now decide these cases using simple negligence, negligence-actual malice, gross negligence, or actual malice rules.[24] Private plaintiffs can not recover noncompensatory damages absent proof of actual malice, and even then such recoveries can be forbidden at state option.

II. EFFICIENCY UNDER THE STRICT LIABILITY AND ACTUAL MALICE RULES

In developing the constitutional privilege for defamatory falsehoods, the Court addressed the question of the proper balance between the interest raised by the First Amendment and the state's interest in protecting reputation. It determined that the common law rule of strict liability over-protected reputations and caused too much self-censorship of probabilistic statements relevant to self-government. To provide additional "breathing space" the Court required that cases brought by public officials and public figures be decided under the actual malice liability rule instead of the strict liability rule. The question addressed here is whether the replacement of the strict liability rule with the actual malice rule changed the balance between the competing interests to society's advantage.

There are three steps to answer this question. The first, which is considered in subsection A, is to explain the basic economic model and the implications for it of the constitutional privilege for falsehoods defamatory of public officials and public figures. The second, discussed in subsection B, is to determine, using the economic model, the effects of the common law strict liability regime upon both private decisions to investigate accuracy and publish or self-censor and the balance achieved between the competing interests. The third step is to determine the effects of the actual malice rule upon private decisions and upon social efficiency.

A. The Economic Model and the Implications of Constitutional Privilege

1. The Economic Model[25]

A publisher's decision to investigate and publish or to self-censor a statement that he is aware may be defamatory depends upon the calculus of expected profit maximization. In this model, the publisher's expected profit is the anticipated revenue to be earned from publishing it (the product of the probability the statement is true and its market value if it is true, less the cost of investigating its accuracy and less the expected cost of the damages that would accrue if it were not, and a suit resulted and the publishers were judged liable).

By hypothesis, each element of the publisher's calculation depends on the extent of his investigation into accuracy. We assume that there exists a production function relationship between the level of investigative effort and the probability the statement is true such that increments in investigative effort increase the probability of truth and reduce the probability of falsity.[26] Such increments are costly, but they benefit the publisher, because they increase the market value or revenue to be derived from publication and they reduce the expected cost of liability.

In principle, to maximize expected profit the publisher must evaluate each of the elements of the profit equation at the margin.[27] Thus, once he has notice of a statement's defamatory potential, he maximizes profit by undertaking additional investigation until the marginal cost of further investigating accuracy equals the sum of the increase in value and the decrease in the cost of liability expected to result from the increase in the probability of truth associated with further investigation. The level of the profit the publisher would earn if he were to publish after undertaking the optimal level of investigation determines whether he will actually provide that level of investigation and publish.[28]

Functions representing these elements of the profit equation are depicted geometrically in figure 8.1. There, the incremental or marginal cost of additional units of investigation into accuracy is represented by the upward sloping *MC* function.[29] Whether committing additional resources to investigating accuracy will reduce the expected cost of liability depends partially upon the prevailing liability rule: under a strict liability rule this kind of marginal benefit is depicted by the *MB* function in figure 8.1.[30] Additional efforts at investigation are assumed to increase

FIGURE 8.1: The Basic Model

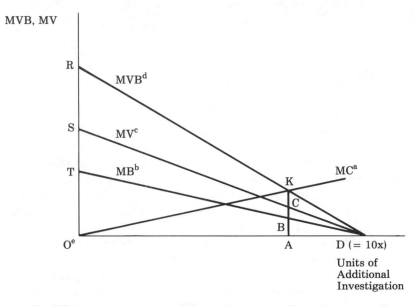

a. The *MC* function measures the change in the total cost of investigation that occurs when the publisher changes the level of additional investigation by one unit.

b. The *MB* function measures the change in the total expected cost of liability when the publisher changes the level of investigation by one unit, or changes the probability of truthfulness by the amount associated with a one-unit change in the level of investigation, and is subject to a strict liability limited to actual damages rule.

c. The *MV* function measures the change in the total expected value of publication that occurs when the publisher changes the level of investigation by one unit, or changes the probability of truthfulness by the amount associated with a one-unit change in the level of investigation.

d. The *MVB* function is the vertical addition of the *MB* and *MV* functions. It therefore measures the change in the sum of the total expected cost of liability and the total expected value of publication when the publisher, facing a strict liability limited to actual damages rule, changes the level of investigation by one unit, or changes the probability of truthfulness by the amount associated with a one-unit change in the level of investigation.

e. *O* represents the point at which the publisher has notice of a statement's defamatory potential and can begin to act to avoid liability for a defamatory falsehood.

the value expected from publication by reducing the probability of a statement being false.[31] This kind of marginal benefit is depicted by the MV function in figure 8.1. Finally, under the strict liability rule the sum of the marginal benefits function is the vertical summation of the *MB* and *MV* functions. In the figure, the sum of the marginal benefits function is labelled *MVB*.

Under a rule of strict liability the investment in additional investigation that will maximize expected profit is identified by the intersection of the *MC* and *MVB* functions. In the figure, the optimal level of additional investigation is *A* units when the rule is one of strict liability.

Establishing the level of additional investigation that will maximize profit does not, however, ensure that the publisher will in fact investigate to that extent and publish the statement: undertaking that level of investigation merely means either that the profit expected from publishing will be maximized or that the loss expected will be minimized. Because the publisher can avoid such a loss by not publishing, the next step in deciding whether to publish or not is to calculate the level of profit expected were the optimal level of additional investigation to be undertaken. The outcome of that calculation, which is simply expected revenue less the sum of the cost of investigation and the expected cost of unavoided liability, can also be determined using the functions depicted in the figure. There expected revenue is the area beneath the *MV* function to the left of *A* units of investigation, or area *OSCA*.[32] The cost of the optimal amount of additional investigation is the area beneath the *MC* function to the left of *A* units of investigation, or area *OKA* in figure 8.1. Under the strict liability rule, the expected cost of unavoided liability is the area beneath the *MB* function to the right of *A* units of additional investigation, or area *ABD*. Thus, when the optimal investigation is undertaken expected profit is area *OSCA* less the sum of areas *OKA* and *ABD* under the strict liability rule. If expected profit so calculated is positive, the optimal investment in investigation will be made and the statement will be published; if it is negative, the investigation will not be made and the statement will not be published. As depicted in figure 8.1, expected profit is positive, so publication will occur.

2. The Implication of the Constitutional Privilege for the Maximization of the Social Interest

The social objective in regulating the publication of statements about which there is some doubt is to maximize the net social benefit derived from publishing such statements. Achieving this objective involves balancing the expected value of publication to society and the expected cost of damage to reputation on the one hand with the cost of investigation on the other. The analytical procedure by which publishers decide the optimal extent of investigation and whether to publish or not is also the method by which society determines both the extent of investigative effort and of self-censorship which is optimal from its perspective. Thus, net expected social benefit will be maximized when published statements are beneficial and embody the level of additional investigation consistent with the equality of marginal cost and the sum of the expected marginal benefits to society.

It follows that when the sum of the marginal benefits function and the marginal cost function that direct private decisions about additional investigation and self-censorship are also the relevant functions from society's perspective, publishers will in their own self-interest reach decisions that maximize the net social benefit. There is no difference between the private and social marginal cost of additional investigation, and, under a strict liability rule, there is no difference between the private and social marginal benefit arising from reductions in the expected cost of liability. The constitutional privilege regarding defamation of public officials and public figures, however, implies that in such cases there is an important difference between the marginal social value of additional investigation and the marginal value of additional investigation to the publisher.

The Court distinguishes public officials and public figures from other public figures and from other plaintiffs within the ambit of the First Amendment because it recognizes that the marginal social value and the marginal private value of statements at issue in cases brought by public officials and public figures, but not in cases brought by other plaintiffs, almost always will differ. Thus:

> [t]he Amendment has a "central meaning"—a core of protection of
> speech without which democracy cannot function, without which,
> in Madison's phrase, "the censorial power" would be in the Gov-
> ernment over the people and not "in the people over the Govern-
> ment." This is not the whole meaning of the Amendment. There
> are other freedoms protected by it. But at the center there is no
> doubt what speech is being protected and no doubt why it is being
> protected.[33]

By requiring public plaintiffs to be advocates of public policy positions, that is, to be officially or voluntarily involved in the resolution of important public controversies, the Court identified the class of individuals about whom publications are likely to implicate what economic theory describes as an externality issue.[34]

Publications that concern public officials and public figures are usually relevant to self-government and, if true, likely to contribute to government decisions that benefit even those from whom publishers cannot obtain compensation. In such cases publishing probabilistic statements provides an expected external benefit to society.

On the other hand, when false and acted upon as though true, such publications impose an external cost upon society. Such an external cost arises, however, only when the underlying publication stands unchallenged. When defamatory falsehoods are challenged, society is put on notice not to treat them as true, which, one would expect, would call into play investigative forces originating in the news market. By noting that public officials and public figures possess meaningful access to the means of counterargument[35] the Court has implicitly indicated its willingness to rely on challenge and such corrective forces to forestall the imposition of external costs upon society. It is therefore unlikely that the publication of falsehoods defaming public officials or public figures will impose external costs upon society.

From these arguments, it can be seen that the publication of probabilistic statements concerning public figures and public officials are likely to contribute to the realization of important external benefits but not to the realization of external costs. The private incentive to publish may be affected adversely by the incidence of this self-government external benefit. The private profit expected from publishing a statement that implicates that benefit is less than the expected benefit of publishing it to society, even when—as we assume—the publisher can extract the full value of the publication from those who purchase it. In such cases, there will be more self-censorship than would be ideal from society's perspective, even before considering the implications of fault-based liability regimes.

B. The Social Efficiency of the Strict Liability Rule When the Self-Government External Benefit Is Implicated

The strict liability rule is the appropriate baseline for assessing whether the imposition of the actual malice regime advanced the objective of maximizing net social benefit. Thus, it is necessary to evaluate the efficiency consequences of the strict liability rule with respect to publications that implicate the self-government external benefit. The efficiency of that rule is developed in two steps, making use of the economic model in the form depicted in figure 8.2. The first addresses publishers' responses and social efficiency of a strict liability rule that authorizes the recovery of only compensatory damages, and the second step considers complications that arise when, as under the common law, noncompensatory damages may be recovered.

1. Efficiency Under a Strict Liability Rule With Only Compensatory Damages

In figure 8.2 the *MC, MB, MV* and *MVB* functions represent the marginal cost of additional investigation, the marginal benefit from reduc-

FIGURE 8.2: Strict Liability and Actual Malice

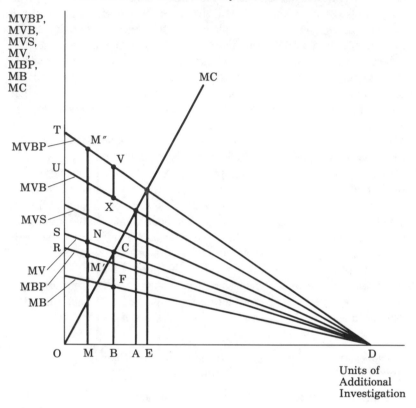

tions in the expected cost of actual injury, the marginal benefit due to increases in the expected value of publication to the publisher, and the sum of the publisher's marginal benefits function. The increment in the expected value of publication to society attributable to additional investigative efforts is labeled the *MVS* function. The *MVS* function is the sum of the *MV* function and the expected value of the external benefit. The function labeled *MVBP* is the sum of the marginal benefits function for society.

As in figure 8.1, when the rule is one of strict liability, an investment of *A* units of additional investigation maximizes the profit expected by the publisher, since at that level of additional investigation the *MC* and *MVB* functions intersect. That level of additional investigation, however, is not optimal from society's perspective because there the sum of society's marginal benefits function—the sum of the *MVS* and *MB* functions or the *MVBP* function—lies above the *MC* function. From society's perspective, *E* units of additional investigation maximizes net social benefit since at that level of additional investigation the *MC* and *MVBP* functions intersect. Thus, statements that implicate the self-government external benefit and that would be published under the strict liability rule will not be investigated as much as society would like. When only compensatory damages can be recovered the strict liability rule will therefore not maximize the net social benefit derived from statements whose publication it does not prevent because the publisher can not appropriate the value of the external benefit.

It is, however, also possible that under such a rule statements whose publication would advance the social interest will not be published. This possibility can be evaluated without resorting to geometric analysis. Because the publisher can not appropriate the value of the external benefit, in at least some circumstances the profit he expects from publication will be insufficient to make publishing worthwhile, even though society would prefer publication because it does realize the expected external benefit. In such cases, the strict liability rule will induce too much self-censorship of statements that may not be accurate.

It seems, therefore, that a strict liability rule authorizing the recovery of only compensatory damages will be inefficient: from the social point of view such a rule will call forth both too much self-censorship and too little investigation into those probabilistic statements that are published under it.

2. Efficiency Under a Strict Liability Rule With Noncompensatory Damages

To the extent that noncompensatory damage awards alter the values of the factors that guide private decisions to investigate accuracy and publish or self-censor, private decisions reached under a strict liability rule—one authorizing the recovery of noncompensatory damages— may differ from decisions made under actual damage limited strict liability rule. In principle, when noncompensatory damage awards are expected the marginal benefit of additional investigation, in the form of reductions in the expected cost of the publisher's liability, is greater than it would be if only actual damages could be recovered. Assuming that noncompensatory damages are equal to the value of the external benefit,[36] the function that represents the marginal benefit of additional investigation, including noncompensatory damages, is the *MBP* function in figure 8.2. It is the vertical summation of the *MB* function and expected noncompensatory damages. The sum of the publisher's marginal benefits function is therefore the function of MVBP in figure 8.2.

Under a strict liability rule authorizing the recovery of noncompensa-

tory damages, the level of investigation that maximizes the profit expected by the publisher occurs where the MC and the $MVBP$ functions
intersect. In figure 8.2, the privately optimal investment in additional
investigation is therefore E units. As the preceding subsection explained, E units of additional investigation also maximize net social benefit. Therefore, when the threat of noncompensatory damages does not
deter publication, the ideal regime from society's perspective is a strict
liability rule under which noncompensatory damage awards are equivalent in amount to the external benefit expected from the publication in
question.

The threat of noncompensatory damage awards may, however, deter
socially desirable publications. This is because the publisher can not
extract for himself the expected value of the external benefit, with the
result that expected profit from publishing may be negative when the
net social benefit of publishing is positive. In such cases a strict liability
regime under which noncompensatory damages may be recovered fails
to maximize net social benefit: it induces too much self-censorship, since
as an incentive to publish unappropriated expected value is not the same
as noncompensatory damages paid.

In summary, the introduction of noncompensatory damage awards
equal in value to the expected external benefit does not make the strict
liability rule efficient. That rule advances the social interest by inducing
the proper amount of investigation into accuracy of those publications
which it does not deter, but it also deters some publications which
society would prefer to be published. It therefore seems unlikely that
the common law which preceded *Sullivan* was efficient. That approach
did not generally distinguish between publications that implicated the
external benefit and those that did not, and even if it had, it provided no
mechanism to avoid undersirable self-censorship. On this analysis the
Court's conclusion that the common law approach provided insufficient
"breathing room" seems correct. Of course this conclusion does not
mean that the Court advanced the social interest by imposing the actual
malice rule in the place of the common law regime.

C. The Social Efficiency of the Actual Malice Rule When the Self-Government External Benefit Is Implicated

We now use the same economic model as in our evaluation of the
consequences of the strict liability regimes to determine the efficiency
consequences of the actual malice rule. The first step is to establish the
correspondence between actual malice, which the *Sullivan* Court described as publishing with knowledge of falsity or with reckless disregard

for truth or falsity, [37] and investment in investigation. The second step is to evaluate the private and social consequences of the actual malice rule.

1. Actual Malice in the Context of the Economic Model

The Court has explained that reckless disregard exists when a publisher has serious doubts about the accuracy of a statement but publishes it in spite of those doubts. Its holding in *Lando v. Herbert*[38] established that serious doubts can be inferred from the extent and results of the publisher's investigation, so that actual malice exists when the evidence of the publisher's investigation makes clear that the publisher's state of mind was inappropriate. Actual malice liability exists when, from his own perspective, the publisher's investigation was insufficient; it does not exist merely because the publisher should have had serious doubts about a statement's accuracy. The behavioral consequences of the actual malice rule can therefore be evaluated in the context of the economic model explicated in preceding subsections.

The consequences of the actual malice rule for investigation into accuracy and self-censorship can, however, be evaluated only after the meaning of actual malice in terms of the level of investigation at which liability is avoided has been established. Although the location of that threshold can not be identified with precision it is clear that it entails less investigation than is necessary to avoid liability under the negligence rule: in *Sullivan,* for example, the Court held that the *New York Times* had at most been negligent in publishing the advertisement defamatory of Sullivan, and that was not enough to make out actual malice.[39] The threshold of actual malice liability in terms of the level of investigation is therefore lower than under the negligence rule.

The comparative position of the investigative threshold of liability under alternative liability rules is an important determinant of the publisher's behavior under such rules. It determines the shape of the publisher's expected marginal benefit function, because it marks the level of additional investigation at which the marginal benefit in the form of reductions in the expected cost of liability becomes zero. Thus the expected marginal benefit function for the publisher, but not for society, is sensitive to the prevailing liability rule, and because the expected marginal benefit function is an element in the sum of the publisher's marginal benefits function, the shape of that aggregate function also is determined by the prevailing liability rule. It is in this way that the actual malice rule affects publisher's decisions whether to investigate and publish or self-censor. These decisions and the resulting social efficiency are discussed in the next subsection.

2. The Efficiency of the Actual Malice Rule

The functions depicted in figure 8.2 facilitate analysis of the behavioral and efficiency consequences of the actual malice rule. Except for two functions that are affected by the liability threshold of the actual malice rule, all the functions in figure 8.2 and the assumptions that underlie them remain as previously discussed. The first of the new functions is the publisher's expected marginal benefit function under the actual malice rule. Under that rule the benefit expected from further investigation is zero once the liability threshold has been reached or surpassed. That threshold lies below the negligence threshold, which occurs at the intersection of the MC and MB functions in figure 8.2,[40] and it is denoted as M units of additional investigation in figure 8.2. The publisher's expected marginal benefit function under the actual malice rule is therefore coincident with the MBP function for fewer than M units of additional investigation, and thereafter the marginal benefit of further investigation becomes zero. The publisher's expected marginal benefit function is line segment $RM'MD$ in figure 8.2. The second new function is the sum of the publisher's marginal benefits function. In figure 8.2 it is line segment $TM''ND$.

The level of additional investigation that maximizes the publisher's expected profit occurs at the intersection of the MC and the sum of the publisher's expected marginal benefits function under the actual malice rule, which is line segment $TM''ND$. Under the actual malice rule the publisher therefore maximizes profit by investing in B units of additional investigation. Although this level of additional investigation satisfies the actual malice standard, it clearly fails to maximize net social benefit, which, as discussed in preceding subsections, is maximized by E units of additional investigation. On this analysis, the actual malice rule induces publishers to investigate those statements that are published less extensively than society desires. Because E units of additional investigation would be provided by a publisher facing a strict liability rule under which noncompensatory damages may be recovered, it seems clear that with respect to those statements that would be published under either rule the actual malice rule is the less desirable rule.

There remains, however, the question of the extent of self-censorship induced by the actual malice rule. As depicted in figure 8.2, the publisher will find it profitable to publish under the actual malice rule, since expected profit equals area $SCBO$ (the revenue expected from publishing) less the sum of area OCB (the cost of B units of additional investigation) or area SCO (which is positive). In such circumstances, however, society prefers self-censorship, because the net expected social benefit derived from publishing is area $SCBO$ (the revenue expected by the publisher), plus area $TVXU$ (the expected value of the external benefit) less area BFD (the expected cost of unavoided liability), and less area OCB (the cost of B units of additional investigation), which under the conditions depicted in figure 8.2 is negative. Thus, in some circumstances the actual malice rule induces too little self-censorship.

The actual malice rule is thus an efficient rule under the postulated circumstances. It induces publishers to invest less in ascertaining the accuracy of published statements than is socially optimal. As a result, under the actual malice rule the probability of truth of those statements that are published will be undesirably low. In addition, the actual malice rule also induces publishers to engage in too little self-censorship. It is therefore inefficient on both counts.

CONCLUSION

The *Sullivan* case and its progeny have transformed the law of defamation. Where there formerly had been a rule of strict liability under which compensatory and noncompensatory damages could be recovered there is now a rule of actual malice which permits public officials and public figures to recover compensatory and noncompensatory damages. This article has analyzed the consequences of this transformation on the decisions of publishers and on the achievement of efficiency. It has treated both private decisions to investigate and publish probabilistic statements and the balance of the social objectives as economic problems. The publisher's objective was taken to be expected profit maximization, while the social objective was to balance the interest in publishing information relevant to self-government against the interest in protecting reputation. The impact of liability rules upon the achievement of these objectives was analyzed using an economic model which assumed that: (1) publications concerning public officials and public figures implicate an important external benefit; (2) publishers extract the full value of their publications from those who buy them; (3) the value of such publications to purchasers depends upon their expected accuracy; (4) investigating accuracy is costly; (5) noncompensatory or punitive damage awards equals the value of the external benefit implicated by such publications; and (6) the liability rules do not differ significantly in terms of administrative and other costs.

Under these circumstances neither rule maximizes net social benefit: when neither rule deters publication the actual malice rule induces too little investigation into accuracy while the strict liability rule induces the ideal investigative effort, but the actual malice rule also induces too little self-censorship while the common law approach induces too much. Thus the new law of defamation probably substitutes an imbalance in favor of publication for an imbalance in favor of reputation. This may be a useful second-best solution, because of the importance of the self-government external benefit implicated by publications concerning public officials and public figures.

NOTES

1. The concepts and arguments presented in this Article are derived from, and explained in much greater detail in Sheer & Zardkoohi, "An Analysis of the Economic Efficiency of the Law of Defamation," 80 *NW. U. L. Rev.* 364 (1985).

2. 376 U.S. 254 (1964).

3. The description of the common law presented here is both brief and necessarily general, and it does not reflect the variations in the law of defamation among the states. *See, e.g.,* Eaton, "The American Law of Defamation Through Gertz v. Robert Welch, Inc. and Beyond: An Analytical Primer," 61 *Va. L. Rev.* 1349, 1351–63 (1975). The purpose of this description of the common law is to provide a basis for evalauting how the new law of defamation changed the balance of interests.

4. *See* W. Prosser, *Law Of Torts* 751–64 (4th ed. 1971) [hereinafter Prosser]. To be defamatory, a statement had to injure the plaintiff's reputation or discourage others from associating with him. *Id.* at 739–44. The publication could be made negligently or intentionally. *Id.* at 774–76. Those to whom the statement was published must have interpreted it as referring to or being "of and concerning" the plaintiff. *Id.* at 749–51. We assume all elements of the cause of action here.

5. *Id.* at 776–96.

6. Sixteen states included within the privilege false statements of fact. C. Lawhorne, *Defamation and Public Officials* 152–65, 173 (1971).

7. *Sullivan,* 376 U.S. at 279–80.

8. *See* Gertz v. Robert Welch, Inc., 418 U.S. 323, 340 (1974).

9. *Sullivan,* 376 U.S. at 283 n.23

10. 388 U.S. 130 (1967).

11. 418 U.S. 323 (1974).

12. 424 U.S. 448 (1976).

13. 443 U.S. 157 (1979).

14. 443 U.S. 111 (1979).

15. 388 U.S. 130 (1967), reported *sub nom.* Curtis Publishing Co. v. Butts.

16. *Id.* at 147 (quoting Time, Inc. v. Hill, 385 U.S. 374, 388 (1967) and Thornhill v. Alabama, 310 U.S. 88, 102 (1940)).

17. *Id.* at 147–48 (quoting Pauling v. Globe-Democrat Publishing Co., 362 F.2d 188, 196 (8th Cir. 1966), *cert denied,* 388 U.S. 909 (1967)).

18. *Id.* at 164 (Warren, C. J., concurring).

19. *Gertz,* 418 U.S. at 332.

20. The all-purpose public figure class included individuals who "occupy positions of such persuasive power and influence that they are deemed public figures for all purposes." *Id.* at 345. But the Court intended this class to be small since "[a]bsent clear evidence of general fame or notoriety in the community, and pervasive involvement in the affairs of

society, an individual should not be deemed a public personality for all aspects of his life."
Id. at 352. With respect to involuntary public figures, the Court noted that "[h]ypothetically, it may be possible for someone to become a public figure through no purposeful action of his own, but the instances of truly involuntary public figures must be exceedingly rare." *Id.* at 345. Thus we consider in detail only the limited-purpose public figure class.

21. *Id.* at 352.

22. *Wolston,* 443 U.S. at 167.

23. *Gertz,* 418 U.S. at 346–48.

24. The simple negligence rule is exemplified by Stone v. Essex County Newspapers Inc., 367 Mass. 849, 330 N.E.2d 161 (1975). Taskett v. King Broadcasting Co., 86 Wash. 2d 439, 546 P.2d 81 (1976) is an example of the bifurcated rule approach, which involves a combination of the negligence and actual malice rules. The application of the gross negligence rule is exemplified by Chapadeau v. Utica Observer-Dispatch, Inc., 38 N.Y.2d 196, 341 N.E.2d 569, 379 N.Y.S.2d 61 (1975). Finally, Aafco Heating and Air Conditioning Co. v. Northwest Publications, Inc., 162 Ind. App. 671, 321 N.E.2d 580 (1974), *cert. denied,* 424 U.S. 913 (1976) represents the actual malice rule approach.

25. Economic theory characterizes the empirical settings in which injuries occur as either alternative-care or joint-care. *See, e.g.,* Landes & Posner, "The Positive Economic Theory of Tort Law," 15 *Ga. L. Rev.* 851, 880–83 (1981). The setting which is appropriate in a given case depends upon the abilities of the parties to the injury to avoid the injury. In joint-care situations efficiency requires that both parties make appropriate efforts to avoid injury, while in alternative-care situations efficiency requires that only one party attempt accident-avoidance. The difference is analytically significant, because only in the alternative-care setting can simple demand and supply functions be used to evaluate the efficiency of alternative liability rules.

We evaluate the efficiency consequences of the law of defamation using an alternative-care economic model. Both the Courts and commentators, at least by implication, suggest that defamation is properly analyzed in the context of such a model. In Curtis Publishing Co. v. Butts, for example, Justice Harlan began his discussion of liability rules by noting that "the basic theory of libel has not changed [over time] and words defamatory of another are still placed 'in the same class with the use of explosives or the keeping of wild animals.' " 388 U.S. at 152 (citation omitted). But he did not recognize assumption of risk or voluntary involvement as affirmative defenses, even though assumption of risk is generally a complete defense in cases involving wild animals and explosives. Moreover, some commentators have noted that the assumption of risk defense available in cases involving wild animals and explosives should be interpreted as a method to identify alternative-care cases in which the plaintiff can avoid the accident at lower cost than the defendant. We therefore analyze the law of defamation using an economic model in which the defendant rather than the plaintiff is the party able effectively to avoid injury to reputation.

26. We assume that additional investigation increases the probability of truth and decreases the probability of falsity at a decreasing rate. Thus, successive increments in investigation increase the probability of truth and reduce the probability of falsity by successively smaller amounts.

27. An economic problem is usually characterized as either an equilibrium problem or as an optimization problem. Profit maximization is an optimization problem. "Mathematically, the process of optimization can be formulated as finding a maximum (or minimum) of some desired (or undesired) criterion. . . . Economists have devised a variety of methods for optimization, turning upon the idea of 'marginal' quantities. . . ." J. Hirshleifer, *Price Theory and Applications* 20–21 (2d ed. 1984).

Incremental or marginal analysis concerns the change in a dependent variable attributable to a one-unit, or marginal, change in an independent variable. For example, since profit is defined as total revenue less total cost, both of which are dependent upon the level of output, profit is maximized when the last unit of output produced adds as much to cost (marginal cost) as it does to revenue (marginal revenue).

28. The expected profit calculation which determines publisher responses to liability rules reflects only the extent of additional investigation undertaken after the publisher has notice of a statement's defamatory potential, because only when the publisher has such notice does he have an opportunity to take appropriate measures to avoid injuring reputation. This is the meaning of the Court's announcement in Gertz v. Robert Welch, Inc., 418 U.S. 323 (1970), that in defamation cases its rules of liability apply only when the publication at issue "makes substantial danger to reputation apparent." *Gertz*, 418 U.S. at 348.

29. The marginal cost of additional investigation is the change in the total cost of investigation when one more unit of investigation is committed to determining accuracy. In figures 8.1 and 8.2, the total cost of a particular level of additional investigation is the area beneath the MC function to the left of that level of investigative effort.

30. We assume that additional investigation increases the probability of truth (and reduces the probability of falsity), but at a decreasing rate. Thus, successive increments in investigative effort increase the probability of truth (and reduce the probability of falsity) by successively smaller amounts. As a result, when the publisher cannot avoid liability, as is the case under the strict liability rule, additional investigation reduces the expected cost of liability by successively smaller amounts. The MB function depicts this relationship. It is drawn so that at D units of additional investigation the probability of falsity is zero. When fewer than D units of additional investigation are undertaken, the area under the MB function to the left of the investigative effort made is the avoided expected cost of liability, while the area to the right of it is the unavoided expected cost of liability.

31. We assume that purchasers value accuracy. By increasing at a decreasing rate the probability of truth increments in investigation therefore also provide successively smaller increments in the revenue expected by publishers. The MV function in figures 8.1 and 8.2 depicts this relationship.

32. For analytical simplicity and also because publishers frequently possess substantial market power we assume that publishers can extract from purchasers the full value of their purchases. The total revenue the publisher therefore expects to earn from undertaking additional investigation is the area beneath the MV function to the left of the additional investigation undertaken.

33. Kalven, *"The New York Times Case: A Note on 'The Central Meaning Of The First Amendment,' "* 1964 *Sup. Ct. Rev.* 191, 208.

34. External costs and benefits are the consequences of "the decisions of some economic agents . . . [which] affect other economic agents in ways that do not set up legally recognized rights of compensation or redress. . . .

"Consider pollution. An upstream use of water may degrade water quality, for example, chemical pollution may reduce potability for downstream consumers, or heat pollution may make the river less effective for down-stream cooling." *Supra* note 32, at 484.

35. Public persons "usually enjoy significantly greater access to the channels of effective communication and hence have a more realistic opportunity to counteract false statements than private individuals." *Gertz*, 418 U.S. at 344. *See also Butts*, 388 U.S. at 154–55 (the application of the actual malice rule in cases brought by public officials and public figures and of a rule more protective of reputation in other cases can be justified by considering the differences between these plaintiff classes with respect to official position or voluntary involvement and access to the means of counterargument).

36. Because there is no empirical evidence relating the level of punitive damages available under either rule to the expected value of the external benefit, the analysis advanced here can proceed only if such a relationship is assumed. Our assumption that punitive damages equal the value of the external benefit simplifies the analysis, and it provides a basis for conclusions about efficiency should a different, systematic relationship be discovered.

37. *Sullivan,* 376 U.S. 254 at 279–80.

38. 441 U.S. 153, 157 n. 2, 177 (1979).

39. See *Sullivan,* 376 U.S. at 280.

40. *See* Landes & Posner, *supra* note 30, at 876, 892–903.

9

REPUTATION AND RISKTAKING

Judith A. Lachman

REPUTATION

Living and dying alone on a desert island, incommunicado with the rest of the world, I can have no reputation, and hence no reputational injury. For the concept of reputation itself requires the existence of at least two persons: one who is the subject of the reputation and a second who regards the first.

Given the existence of this second person who regards me, I can enhance, diminish, or destroy my reputation by doing various things likely to precipitate adulation, disgust, or dismay. When I do these things —or, more generally, when I do anything at all or nothing at all—I can myself affect the reputation I hold. But there is a catch. My reputation, that is, the reputation that belongs to me in the sense that it is about me, is not something that I can hold onto at all. It is information about me, however good or bad it might be, that resides in the mind of someone else; indeed, no matter what I may myself think of myself, such information stored in my own mind cannot be reputation, by definition.

So, reputation, then, constitutes a curious sort of thing. It is information about a person that is typically not a fleeting thought but rather a more enduring one, and hence is a kind of capital asset—property of a sort.[1] Moreover, considered as a capital asset, it bears a subtle difference from tractors, stock options, plots of land, even from patents, which are also products of the mind. For my reputation is human capital, an asset like my health or education, that cannot, by a stroke of the pen, be given or sold to another, for whom it would then be her health, education, or reputation.[2]

Instead, my reputation is uniquely, nontransferrably mine, in the sense that it is about me; it is a capital asset that I can nurture or destroy; it may determine my livelihood, influence, pleasure or pain; it may be the key to power and wealth, to ecstasy or despair, perhaps even life or death—and it is totally in the custody of someone else.

REPUTATIONAL INJURY

If I want to improve my reputation there are probably things I can do about it; in an analogous fashion, if I want to shoot myself in the foot, literally or figuratively, I can do that, too. It is the way of things, however, that when it comes to reputational advance or diminishment, I do not hold a monopoly position: Others can do it to me, or for me, too; indeed, within some constellations of events, I may be quite powerless to stop them.

This, then, is reputational injury: it is a game that anyone can play, which only sounds disturbing when I come to realize that it is my reputation that is being played with. Others can do me in. Furthermore, as my reputation, my human capital, is being tossed about, I may be the monkey in the middle—unable to grasp my reputation to bring it aright again, unable to shield it from the winds of one person's destructive speech, and from the chill of another person's now-frostier regard.

What to do, when you appear to be injuring me as you speak about me? Were you targeting me with your automobile, I could swerve out of your way, drive more slowly, or venture out into the world only in my trusty armor-studded tank. In other words, when the injury isn't from words, there are things I can do to avoid it. Indeed, even if the injury emanates from truthful words, there may be things I can do to avoid that, too: I can live my life so that the truth, when known, protects me from the disapproval of others—as well as my trusty tank protects me from your automobile. That is, I can live my life in such a way that the reputation I have—if it is truthful information about me in the minds of others—is OK.[3] Even though information about me may be transmitted from you to others, if that information about me is truthful, it is the consequence of my own acts rather than the flights of your imagination which have led my reputation to plummet or to soar.[4]

Suppose I do something stupid, which you dutifully report, and which sends my reputation downward. What can I do to repair my reputation? I can do more that's better, and hope the additional news brightens the mental picture held of me by others, or even engage in interchange with those others in a more direct fashion.

Now suppose instead that the harm comes from a false statement about me: I have been slogging through life in my usual fashion, with only your tales of my wanderings, rather than my actual wanderings, haven taken a nasty twist. What can I do to repair my reputation, or must I just retreat to the sidelines and surrender in defeat? True, I can do those things that would have stood me in good stead had I been the cause of my own undoing, or I can run around trying to rehab my reputation with the regarders, one by one.[5] But it will most likely take greater self-improvement to improve myself enough, and greater around-running to those who now think ill (or iller) of me than would have been the case had I pursued my reputational destruction on the do-it-yourself plan.

In other words, a set of questions to be asked and answered begins with, Who can avoid what sorts of injuries and at what cost? In order to pursue this inquiry, the paper develops a conceptual framework encompassing the processes of creation and injury to reputation and of injury avoidance. As illustrated in the preceding paragraphs, libel law is characterized by a triangular relationship between the speaker, the hearer, and the subject which makes the processes of reputational change potentially complex. Whether one focuses on the creation, the maintenance, or the destruction of one's reputation, the resulting effect must occur, by definition, in the mind of someone else; this complicates the problem of injury-avoidance, as well as the legal rules and remedies that may come into play.

REPUTATIONAL INVESTMENT AND INJURY: SPEAKER, HEARER, AND SUBJECT

To advance her reputation, a person will do certain things and forbear from doing others. She does this in the belief that today's sacrifice will yield tomorrow's benefit—whether the future benefit be in the form of a greater personal esteem in the eyes of others, broader patronage of a business or purchase of its products, willingness of prospective employees to accept employment with her, or whatever. Whether the result be called "reputation," "goodwill," or another term, it is something of an enduring nature (for better or worse) and therefore a kind of capital asset.[6]

Although the person who so "invests" in reputation is indeed relying on the expectation of future benefit, she is casting her lot with an asset rather different in form from many others. For if the "investment" is successful, it may well be successful because of speech,[7] such as word-of-mouth advertising for services or a product or, perhaps, other less task oriented words of mouth. Moreover, unlike a stamping-press installed in a manufacturing plant, this asset cannot be controlled at the will of its owner nor be limited in its activity to the shop floor on which it is placed.

Instead, the seeker of a good reputation often must depend on the speech of some people, and on the listening and subsequent actions of others. For example, by doing kindly deeds, one develops a reputation resulting in friendships and contacts in the community; these favorable relationships lead in turn to others, and to invitations, community office-holding, enhanced esteem, and other desirable things. Or, having done something extra to produce a high quality service or product, she must wait for happy clients to speak its praises, and after that, for their acquaintances to come and buy.[8]

Once having made such an investment, however, a person has this asset, a reputation, which is by definition totally in the mind of someone else. Consequently, the maintenance and the protection of an existing reputation will generally depend on the actions of others at least as much as did the initial process of reputation creation. One way to influence the course of one's reputational investment is to do praiseworthy things which the reputation would then reflect, particularly in a world where trees are known by their fruit, where fruits are attached to trees, or whatever. So long as speakers speak truly and later actors base decisions only on what is true, one's reputation will rest in the hands of its investor or subject, even if various intermediaries must act in order to bring about this result.[9]

Where speakers speak falsely, however, this characterization no longer holds: what the subject has herself done or said is not what is transmitted, so that the resulting effect on reputation is less easily causally attributed to her. Moreover, actors who hear the falsity but behave in reasonable ways, assuming it to be true, may not be the persons to whom the reputational effect should be attributed.[10] This attribution problem may arise even though it is the steps taken by these "hearers" rather than by, say, a gossiper, that most immediately precipitate the injury at stake: If the hearer no longer buys a piece of real-estate when otherwise he would, or no longer patronizes the subject's business, nor invites her to his party, nor nominates her to a prestigious post, the hearer may be blameless (as, indeed, if the statements had been true); yet the subject is injured in a way that, but for falsity, would not have occurred.[11]

What is different here is falsity, not just the occurrence of injury: for alternatively, the gossiper might not have responded at all to the subject's activities, or might have gossiped to fewer friends. The subject who "invests" in reputation may have no right to a specific favorable result, but has a special basis for dissatisfaction when an intermediary injects falsity into process and result. Although the subject of the reputation has in some sense "signed up" for particular risks, as other investors do,[12] the risk of injury from falsity was probably not one of the risks on that list.[13] Ironically, it is the person, the speaker, whose intermediary role is often essential to the formation of reputation—

whose acts can lead also to reputational decline. And it is this critical change in function, from reacting to and speaking about what is true to the injecting of information which is false, that may change the speaker's causal role as well.[14]

But the speaker isn't the end of the story. Quite literally it requires a "hearer" or "regarder" too.[15] Were not the hearer influenced by the gossiper's tale, for example, then perhaps neither the efforts of reputational investment nor, alternatively, the introduction of false information would make any difference. Moreover, were the hearer to have (or even believe he had) complete and accurate information beforehand, then additional information, true or false, might be disregarded and injury circumvented once again.[16] Finally, a skeptical, distrustful hearer could conceivably check further before choosing to act.

Paradoxically, it is the receptiveness of the hearer to new information that creates for reputational investments the potential to pay off, but simultaneously permits the influence of false information that might be offered in its stead. Although some actions of hearers may be considered in themselves blameworthy,[17] their response to what a speaker says will often not be so readily set aside; instead their actions may function as the foreseeable results of the false statements to which they are exposed.[18]

In terms of reputational injury or avoidance, then, three candidates present themselves: the subject of the reputation, the speaker of false information, and the hearer who reacts to it. As suggested above, each of these actors potentially has an injury-or-avoidance role to play.

Judicial decisions, however, do not speak of the problem of libel in these terms. They talk instead about public officials and public figures as distinguished from private ones;[19] about fact as distinguished from opinion (if indeed that can be done);[20] about matters that are of public concern as distinguished from others that might not be;[21] and about other distinguishing features of a much different categorization of the world. Despite this different taxonomy, many aspects of libel law lend themselves to characterization in terms of the accident-or-avoidance conceptual framework, as illustrated in some examples below. Indeed, not only the changes in the law signaled by *New York Times v. Sullivan*[22] but also some of the anomalies and instabilities encountered in its wake can be analyzed within this conceptual scheme.

A. Public Officials, Public Figures, and Very Private Ones: The Subject of a Reputation as Possible Avoider of Injury

Police Commissioner Sullivan claimed he was injured by false statements made and published by others.[23] In a world of common law strict liability for libel, with its focus on "but for" causation and its implicit sense of what was within whose control, the speaker was the obvious pressure point[24]—the person to whom the injury-or-avoidance decision could properly be put. Apparently on the theory that false speech could be costlessly omitted by a speaker who willed it so, courts permitted recovery once the requisite showing of false defamatory publication had been made.[25] In other words, avoidance of falsehood by a speaker was perceived not to be very costly, and the subject- or hearer-avoidance possibilities were hardly taken into account.[26]

With the Supreme Court decision in *New York Times v. Sullivan*,[27] however, several new and different factors appear to have come into play, which ultimately affect the relative desirability of the speaker as a pressure point in the avoidance of reputational injury. First, the "constitutionalization" of libel law, reversing its previous outcast status, meant that any restrictions on speech, false or true, were worthy of some special examination, even if the restrictions were in the end upheld; it was a constitutional right that was then at stake.[28]

Second, the *New York Times* concern with the costs of litigation suggested that if false speech were not totally costlessly separable from the rest, then litigation costs—which already added a deterrent bang to the compensation-paying buck—would be costs affecting other speech as well.[29] Third, the Court pointed out why total and costless separability could hardly be assumed for speech such as that at issue in the case.[30]

Fourth, where individuals are petitioning or criticizing government freely, "uninhibited, robust, and wide-open debate" was seen by the Court to be a likely and beneficial result.[31] Speakers and hearers engaged in such debate (as well as subjects) are doing something publicly valued; where a speaker who would otherwise make such debate possible is silenced, the public cost of his declining to speak is particularly steep. All of these considerations serve to raise the perceived cost of speaker avoidance, and hence affect the relative desirability of the speaker as the person on whom the injury-or-avoidance burden should fall.

As if these changes were not enough, the Court introduced, in *New York Times* and subsequent decisions, another change in the common law landscape: it addressed special consideration simultaneously to the identity of the subject of the reputation, a factor which could add a thumb to the scales in any ensuing measurement of relative speaker-avoidance costs.

The subject of the reputational injury, if a public official, can make the choice of running for or accepting office in light of the fact that caustic comments or occasional unpleasant falsity may come part and parcel with the job.[32] Taking into account not only a snapshot of the moment but also the moving picture from which it was drawn, the Court has appeared willing to look backward in time to a moment when reputational injury to the subject could have been avoided simply by his choosing not to hold office at all.[33] Relevant to that decision, perhaps requisite to the office, was the proverbial thick skin that (to massacre the metaphors) allows otherwise hurtful speech to bounce off its subject without wounding.[34] Moreover, an office-holder who might be injured by false statements had some ability to "contradict the lie," or at least reduce its damage, as a consequence of the more regular access to the media that officeholding typically affords.[35]

All of these considerations serve to raise the perceived costs of speaker and hearer avoidance but lead subject-avoidance to be evaluated as being of lower cost. Once this is so, it should hardly be surprising if the "cheapest cost avoider"[36] were found not to be the speaker or hearer, but instead, the subject; and for many sets of circumstances— particularly those involving speech about public officials—such a result would seem to follow from *New York Times*.

But not always: When a speaker knows a statement to be falsehood, she would seemingly be better positioned to avoid falsity than she would be if such knowledge on her part did not exist. In contrast to her hearer, but also in contrast to the subject, she appears to have more control and hence greater ability to avoid injury than would otherwise be the case. Alternatively, if she speaks in a reckless disregard of truthfulness, the adoption of a bit more regard for such an issue seems to have been considered by the Court to entail relatively little cost.[37] Perhaps present also, but not articulated, is the idea that speech commenced on the basis of knowing falsehood or reckless disregard for truth would be of lesser public value in provoking uninhibited and robust debate.[38]

Consequently, it appears that the Supreme Court's reconceptualiza-tion of the process for production of speech and of the role of speech in the public life changed the relative desirability of speaker vis-à-vis others as avoiders of reputational harm. Moreover, where a public official is the subject of speech, the resulting recounting and reweighting of avoidance costs is particularly profound. With a public official plaintiff, a showing of a published defamatory falsehood constitutes but the beginning of a journey—the carrying of the plaintiff's burden—rather than its end. And what had before *New York Times* been a rule of strict liability is shrunken, for these plaintiffs, until a finding of liability at all becomes "the exception which makes the rule" of the more typical no-liability result.

For other plaintiffs, however, things might be different, as subsequent episodes of litigation came to suggest. While public figures might, for reasons resembling those for the officials, be given a heavier burden to carry as in *Curtis v. Butts,*[39] private figures—particularly those not involved with public issues—were returned to a status closer to that of the generic plaintiff in the pre *New York Times* era.[40] The Court said, in *Gertz v. Robert Welch, Inc.,*[41] that so long as the strict liability were avoided, states could, for private figure libel cases, choose forms of fault-based liability and yet be consistent with the Court's constitutional resolves.[42]

Without a public-interest thumb on the scales the avoidance costs to speaker and hearer were shrunken; and where a subject had in the past made no choice in favor of exposure to such reputational risks, nor could in the present command access to media as an avenue for reply, the subject's ability to avoid or mitigate injury was substantially less than that of speaker or hearer. Consequently, in private-figure cases, the burden of injury-avoidance appears more likely to fall on speaker or hearer, and to shift somewhat away from the subject of the reputation, at least as compared with cases involving public official and public figure plaintiffs.

Between these two situations and their corresponding treatments of public and private persons, the problem of "public issue" has uncomfortably resided, sometimes shifting to one end of the spectrum, sometimes shifting back to the other end. In some ways this is not surprising, for where discussion about a private figure arises in the context of a public issue, the two competing sets of considerations simultaneously come into play. The state interest in protecting reputation (not to mention the subject's liberty or property interest in protecting it himself) pushes the "cheapest cost avoider" computation in the direction of the speaker; yet the public value of debate on public issues would push the evaluation toward the opposite result. And, unlike the public figure, who in his choice of profession has effectively accepted exposure to the public, the private figure has had control over neither the snapshot nor the moving picture in which alternative choices could seemingly have prevented the injury.

Given these competing considerations, judicial sensitivity to factual context and perhaps even vacillating judgments might be anticipated results and those have indeed occurred. The *Rosenbloom* plurality decisions[43] extending *New York Times* protections to discussion of public issues was cut back in *Gertz* to a more conservative result. Then in *Dun & Bradstreet v. Greenmoss Builders,*[44] matters of "public concern" resurfaced, but this time to free plaintiffs associated with nonpublic matters from even the few strictures *Gertz* would have imposed.[45]

B. The Role of the Hearer: Changed and Changing

Reputational advancement or decline will likely happen only when the hearer's mind is open to information about the subject, whether the information is of a flattering or a defamatory kind. Consequently, where the hearer is not so open-minded, a plaintiff is less likely to suffer severe reputational injury from falsehood and a speaker is less likely, at least in relative terms, to be designated a recipient of the blame.

The less-responsive or nonresponsive hearer might be someone having greater knowledge or expertise than a particular speaker, in which case a speaker could be deliberately ignored, or might be someone who simply exercises skepticism when certain topics or kinds of exchanges happen to arise. Under other circumstances, a hearer's acts will be proscribed or will be subject to special statutory provisions that, in effect, require skepticism or even correction of false statements by a hearer, as illustrated below.

A hearer might be signaled to be skeptical by the context in which speech occurs: the importance of context is so salient, yet so obvious, that we may fail to articulate it much or even most of the time. When a strikebreaker in a unionization campaign is angrily labeled a "traitor," for example, the epithet is "merely rhetorical hyperbole," the Supreme Court has said.[46] In fact when the subject of such a labeling did sue for libel, the Court found it "impossible to believe" that any reader of the newsletter in question would have understood it "to be charging the appellee with committing the criminal offense of treason," and declined even to invoke the two-tiered analysis of *New York Times* and *Gertz*.[47] Similarly, in a case preceding the labor one, *Greenbelt Cooperative Publishing Association v. Bresler*,[48] a landowner who was involved in tough bargaining with the City Council was denounced as engaging in "blackmail"; to his allegations of libel, the Court replied that the term "blackmail" is but "a vigorous epithet" with its context providing the critical interpretive clues.[49] Just as a readily visible flight of stairs may give its own sufficient notice of a danger to those who would pass its way, so the charged atmosphere of, say, a unionization drive or political campaign, or certain other settings gives its own notice for a hearer to be on her skeptical guard.[50] Where such signals to skepticism are offered, avoidance of reputational injury apparently rests with the hearer, and a plaintiff's attempt to recover from a speaker may be pursued in vain.

Indeed, during most eras of our history being a skeptical hearer was probably more common than seems to be the case today, at least where the speaker in question is the institutional press. Objectivity of reporting, as well as the idea of news reporting to all, are relatively recent innovations in American journalism: From the time of the Revolution until the 1830s the press tended to be merely an atomistic cottage industry, comprised of individuals whose papers were each sponsored by a political party or commercial interest; a range of conflicting views of the world was the cacophonic result.[51] Moreover, the papers were often too dear for all but the wealthy and commercial classes to buy: the era of the low-cost, wide-circulation paper in America—and the opportunity for false reports to be read by many more people—was yet to come.

Subsequent eras were hardly better, were objectivity the measure of success. From a political or personal propaganda device, the press was transformed in the 1830s to "the newspaper as personal statement."[52] There followed the period of yellow journalism and, only in the twentieth century, the adoption of objectivity as both a standard for reporting and an ideology of the press.[53]

Yet, even as the goal of objectivity conferred the benefits of greater accuracy in the press, it simultaneously permitted greater harm to flow from inadvertent errors or omissions. If accuracy and objectivity beget believability, then hearers are more likely to respond to certain statements with the diminished regard that is reputational injury and a given falsehood may therefore do more harm. As one scholar has pointed out, "Back in the heyday of yellow journalism reporting was surely much worse than it is today, but it was also less harmful, because there was no presumption, or pretension, of accuracy."[54]

Despite such considerations, the responses of hearers to falsity are not totally unrestrained by law, for particular responses by hearers may have their own "rewards." Hearers who relay false statements may be liable for doing so; for example, those who give out false credit or insurance information or themselves act on such information may be subject to provisions of the Federal Fair Credit Reporting Act as well as other laws.[55] Due process rights of public sector employees, as well as the contract rights of others may require an employer to inquire further rather than rely on information received that may itself be false.[56] The legendary false shout of fire that causes panic in a theater,[57] as well as false news of the death of a family member[58] may not leave the hearer who makes such cries unscathed. Under these and other conditions, the actions of hearers may be circumscribed. Yet, the hearer as the chosen "pressure point" may still prevent liability: for not only hearer skepticism but also hearer behavior, where skepticism is absent, may serve to reduce or avoid the incidence of reputational injury.[59]

C. The Speaker

Because hearers must respond to speakers before reputational injury from libel can occur, the hearers constitute a possible pressure point at which legal rules might affect the occurrence of such injury. But publication of falsehood is also necessary for libel, and in that process the hearer hears because a speaker speaks. The speaker, too, is a possible pressure point—indeed, in periods, all too obviously so, as the pre-*New York Times* state law and the early Sedition Act attest.[60]

Yet, as with other acts giving rest to liability, when speech runs afoul of law, a decision to compensate for harm is simultaneously a decision to deter like incidents from occurring again.[61] Were the effect of such a decision to be the deterrence of false speech alone, one kind of issue would be raised, namely: How do we value, in public-interest terms, the utterance of false speech? "[U]ntruthful speech . . . has never been protected for its own sake,[62] the Court might answer, as it has done on occasion before in the context of commercial speech. Others might respond, however, that false speech on its own may have public value, if, for example, its occurrence enlightens the public about the existence of particular viewpoints held by those in the population, or serves as a safety-valve when greater harm might otherwise occur.[63] If liability for falsehood deterred only false speech, these public benefits that may accrue from false speech would surely be lost as well. The strict liability that antedated *New York Times* as well as the strict liability that may yet recur,[64] suggest that such losses, as weighed in by state common-law makers, may not be assigned substantial weight.

In situations such as those the earlier common law had addressed, it is likely that its proponents would point to the speaker as the best avoider of reputational harm; for if the false speech is not valued itself, nor is its disappearance associated with any other sort of loss, then the cost of injury avoidance which is accomplished by avoiding speech must be lower than would otherwise be the case. Moreover, if the benefits of speech accrue only to the speaker, and to him in his private role alone, the cost of avoidance is a cost he can't take into overall account as well a widget manufacturer might do.[65] Indeed, given the character of libel as involving the triangular relationship of subject, speaker, and hearer, and the necessary alienation of the owner of a reputation from the asset she seeks to protect, the speaker holds peculiar power in connection with this asset that the other two cannot control. Perhaps the common law's response to the control-in-the-triangle problem is not too surprising for its time.

With *New York Times v. Sullivan*, however, the conception about the independence of false and true speech changed, altering the injury-or-avoidance analysis in fundamental ways. As suggested earlier, *New York Times* characterized the occurrence of false speech not as an enterprise of its own, but as a byproduct on the way to the creation of something else: If the production of true speech cannot occur without some impurities, the deterrence of such impurities could deter the production of true speech as well.[66]

Consequently, the attempt to limit or compensate for speech that is false must be evaluated in the context of endangering speech that is true. If the latter were considered to be of no public value, the analysis might remain unchanged.[67] But if true speech has any public-interest value, then such benefits need to be taken into account, even if the eventual decision were that the particular benefit did not warrant the harm.

The *New York Times* case presented such questions in a peculiarly provocative way. Though the speech at issue was published in the form of an advertisement at a time that both libel and commercial speech were outside the First Amendment realm,[68] it concerned the conduct of public officials acting in their official roles: It thus implicated values that were simultaneously at the core[69] and beyond the reach of First Amendment protection of speech. If form or falsity were all that mattered, the costs of speaker avoidance would be only private ones, and the speaker might well be found to be the person best able to bear the costs of injury or its avoidance.

If, however, speech about the conduct of government officials were of value in itself, the relative avoidance-cost computation could well come out quite differently. And indeed, if the production of true speech were inextricably tied to the production of falsity, then the unprotected speech of libel could well fold in on the core.[70] True speech about the conduct of government could be had only at the risk of some falsity, perhaps false statements about those officials whose conduct was most important for the public to know. With commensurately high weight accorded to such political speech, the cost of speaker avoidance could well be deemed too high, in public-value terms. In terms of private costs, however, a speaker might well respond to the deterrence incentives if liability were forthcoming, with the result that not just false speech but true speech of special public value would be deterred.[71] This "chilling effect," while perhaps necessary as a practical matter for a speaker who would otherwise be liable, would constitute a compromise with what, in public-interest terms, should occur. The public interest in such speech therefore called for a high cost to be associated with speaker avoidance, and the relative desirability of speaker as avoider experienced a corresponding decline.

Two additional factors associated with speaker avoidance arose—one directly, one less so—in the decision of the *Times*. First, the costs of litigation and the fear of unwarranted liability were recognized by the Court as costs of speaker avoidance—even in situations where, if one had a crystal ball, no liability would have ensued.[72] Even in cases not imposing costs of liability, the prospects of litigation and liability could nudge speakers in the direction of avoiding speech that in retrospect need not have been avoided even under common law standards had they applied.

Second, the means of preventing falsity—such as additional research on the truthfulness of statements, which would impose additional costs on a speaker—were apparently considered too costly by the Court because of public-interest losses in the delayed or deterred publication of what would otherwise have been considered news.[73] Ironically, or perhaps not so after all, the *New York Times* had itself reported on the events discussed by participants in the advertisement it later published; so it could, by delving into its own files, have corrected some of the factual assertions of the ad.[74] To do so for each advertisement placed by others, however, would substantially raise the cost and delay the publishing of what is true, and the Supreme Court decision did not require this.[75]

So the production metaphor extends not only to falsity which might be inevitable (at any cost) but also to falsity whose foreclosure would entail high costs. The costs of avoidance that *New York Times* speakers are not required to bear include, apparently, some costs in the literal sense: Although speaking with "knowing falsehood or reckless disregard" is different,[76] the Court said, the costs of speech below that threshold are not ones the speaker would be required to bear.

Gertz v. Robert Welch[77] did not, as it happened, appear to raise all these issues, particularly those associated with intertwined truth and falsity and the avoidance of falsity which could, with expense, be disentangled from the truth. In *Gertz,* a magazine had hired a free-lance writer whose error-proneness it knew;[78] and then, the editor had added a rather courageous introductory note despite his lack of familiarity with the subject matter.[79] Even within *New York Times/Curtis v. Butts* framework for public officials and public figures, the editor's liability might have been an understandable result. (Indeed, the outcome on retrial, where Gertz successfully showed "actual malice" by the defendant, is consistent with the assertion offered here.) Instead, perhaps for its own reasons, the Court classed Gertz as a private figure and progressed to other things.[80]

Dun & Bradstreet v. Greenmoss Builders,[81] however, did entail issues associated with these kinds of avoidance costs, and thus might be viewed as the mirror image of *New York Times* in that regard. Moreover, *Dun & Bradstreet* offers a promising illustration of the applicability of the injury-or-avoidance framework to issues of reputational injury and speech. Indeed, given the Court's lack of sympathy for *Dun & Bradstreet* or its services,[82] it is surprising that greater analysis of the avoidance issues was not (in any terminology) pursued.

Dun & Bradstreet, a credit reporting agency, had issued a false report to five prospective creditors of a building company, and the company subsequently sued.[83] The agency, which would presumably be viewed as an expert and be held in negligence to the standard of its expertise, had hired a high school student to do important aspects of its work, at the impressive sum of $200 per year. From the perspective of injury avoidance, it is curious that a business which by its nature deals with reputations—else why would prospective business contacts purchase such information at all?—had entrusted the fate of its subjects to a seventeen-year-old for less than the price of a VCR. What this student employee did was not simple clerical work, but the analysis of state bankruptcy petitions, for which some additional education or training might seemingly have come in handy. When a mistake occurred, as well under such an arrangement it might, it seems hardly the sort of thing to be labeled a surprise. To the garden-variety negligence that probably was associated with the student's result[84] could be added negligent hiring and supervision, as well as other torts.[85]

But the facts might carry us farther, for the plaintiff's difficulties, and the defendant's contributions to them, did not end with the initial report. Although the builder learned of the false report of his company's bankruptcy on the day it was issued, and protested it immediately to Dun, the company did not issue its minimal "correction" notice until almost two weeks had passed.[86] Despite repeated requests from Greenmoss Builders, Dun refused to furnish the names of those to whom reports had been issued[87]—four firms beyond the one he knew. Finally, despite the furnishing of a specific form-statement which the builder suggested Dun use to reply to future inquiries, Dun continued to issue to other creditors a less than favorable report (though one without the false bankruptcy information). Negligence and perhaps intentional torts fell one after another upon the builder, even after the first report and his timely complaint to Dun.

Given the array of its decisions, and perhaps not-surprising accidents caused by Dun and its employees, there would appear to have been more than ample room to avoid injury had the company been so inclined. By contrast, the builder's avoidance prospects appear to have been quite limited: Since he could not obtain the names of the businesses to which the erroneous credit report had been sent, and since Dun continued to send out less-than favorable reports even after, he could hardly have practiced the sort of behavior for injury-avoidance that a *Gertz* Court would recommend. "The first remedy of any victim is self-help," the Court said, "using available opportunities to contradict the lie or correct the error and thereby minimize its adverse impact on reputation."[88] Indeed to the extent that were possible, he had already done so in his appeals to Dun & Bradstreet. Since his avoidance ability appears close to zero, the cheapest cost avoider would more likely be the speaker or the hearer so the Court's analysis might have turned back to one of them.

Though hearers may sometimes offer natural skepticism, in *Dun & Bradstreet* that would hardly have been expected to occur. The service offered by Dun & Bradstreet could command a high price precisely because subscribers wished to save themselves the cost and inconvenience of making similar inquiries on their own; Dun could meet the request in the form of a single report. And, because they were dealing with a company regularly in the business, the subscribers might with reason have relied on its expertise. Although the subscriber's acts might in some cases be themselves restricted by various laws, crucial decisions affecting the fate of the builder would likely be discretionary in nature, would depend on a multiplicity of factors, and therefore be particularly difficult to attribute in casual terms to a false-but-corrected or not-entirely-favorable report. Avoidance of the injury by the hearer would therefore be unlikely; and, if such a subscriber were obligated to become itself a credit agency gathering on its own a duplicate set of data, hearer avoidance would become at best a very costly longer-run result. It would, in fact, be exactly the type of cost Congress sought to prevent in its adoption of a regulatory framework for credit agencies, together with rights and remedies for those whom they would rate.[89]

Hearers such as those to whom the Greenmoss reports were sent would appear therefore to have somewhat limited abilities to avoid reputational injury here. Moreover, the number of hearers called upon to do so would grow with the number of false or deprecatory reports issued—even as the profits of Dun might rise directly with the number of such reports it sent out. Consequently, the greater the activity of the speaker, the more challenging the collective avoidance problem for hearers or subjects or both.

Dun & Bradstreet would therefore appear not simply as the party best able to accomplish injury-avoidance but would seem to be the only party in the triangle with much of a chance at all. If acting as the cheapest cost avoider, it would be best able to weigh the costs of reputational injury when such injury happens against the increased costs of preventing its occurrence altogether. Under such circumstances, the company could, for example, choose to hire an adult, whose sense of the import of the work might automatically draw forth greater care—and preferably someone with the background it takes to properly understand bankruptcy petitions. Dun might also find it worthwhile to double check that information in its files had already been double-checked; although stating that Dun's practice was to do so, no checking of the bankruptcy report had occurred for the Greenmoss file.[90] What would it cost Dun to have avoided the Greenmoss injury? A modicum of money, some supervisory time, and perhaps (though not necessarily) some delay in its reporting of credit information.

Although Dun argued its claim with reference to the First Amendment,[91] the relation if its speech to the considerations motivating the *Times, Curtis,* and *Gertz* decisions appears somewhat attenuated (particularly if compared in terms of its content as political speech). The inextricability of truth and falsehood seems more difficult to argue for *Dun:* since one is unlikely to find a bankruptcy petition without there being a bankrupt petitioner who goes with it, the Greenmoss type of problem could readily arise only in the presence of clerical errors or errors of comprehension—exactly what occurred with the young Dun & Bradstreet employee. Errors of the sort that occurred are more likely attributable to, and avoidable by, steps that also incur greater costs. So the second branch of *New York Times* would have to be the basis of a favorable appeal. Yet that too would be difficult to support in the *Dun* context. In *New York Times* the effort to extricate false information from true would have been costly in time as well as money, affecting the time at which news which was otherwise forthcoming would appear. In *Dun & Bradstreet,* the information would not otherwise have been forthcoming (certainly not without a hefty fee that would surely have covered costs) because the main thing the company had to sell was information that would not otherwise be available. Rather than publication, nonpublication was the essence of its business profitability, so the public interest costs borne by would-be readers and debaters of public issues would figure less prominently in its costs. Although there are publicly valued benefits associated with individual benefits of speech—self-expression being an example—such benefits were not the ones on which the Court had focused in *New York Times* or its progeny. In any event, such benefits are probably the only noneconomic costs to which Dun could have pointed; hence in the inquiry about relative ability to avoid injury, the credit agency would likely still have been termed the cheapest cost avoider.

In other words, given the framework supplied by *New York Times* and extended in subsequent cases, *Dun & Bradstreet* would appear to present a relatively strong case for speaker avoidance—perhaps even an easy case for some members of the Court.

Moreover, while litigation involving loss of personal reputation may be difficult when it comes to proof of actual damages, the business consequences of a firm like Greenmoss would generally be easier to assess. The inability of Greenmoss to present proof of its injuries, unlike the problem often facing individual subjects, arose precisely because of Dun's refusal to disclose where it had sent reports, and was thus a proof problem that was precisely of Dun's own making. A more limited decision in keeping with the framework built upon *New York Times* could readily have resolved critical issues in *Dun*.

The Court did in *Dun & Bradstreet* designate the speaker as avoider, but for reasons quite different from those suggested above. Instead of analyzing the case within the framework of *New York Times* and *Gertz*, the Court's plurality created a new below-*Gertz* category into which *Dun & Bradstreet* then fell. For cases in this category, not only would presumed and punitive damages be possible without proof of "actual malice" as *Gertz* would have required—and as the builder in *Dun & Bradstreet* very likely could have shown—but also the perceived lack of public concern with the speech at issue drew *Dun* out from under the *Gertz* analysis altogether.

The *Dun & Bradstreet* opinion thus expanded the framework of analysis founded upon *New York Times:* previously the strictures of *New York Times* libel recovery had applied to a limited set of persons, with the *Gertz* limitations seemingly applicable to all others. Rather than "slotting" *Dun* into one of these two categories, the court instead created a third one, applicable to situations in which the public "concern" was so little that even the *Gertz* limitations for private figure libel recovery should not apply.

Motivating the Court's plurality, I suggest, are two considerations which the injury-or-avoidance framework could readily have taken into account. First, the injury to the plaintiff was readily avoidable at minimal additional cost—or at least at a cost those justices thought such a business ought to bear. Seen perhaps more readily here than in other settings, the increased expenditure on employee service appeared to be a reasonable cost of injury avoidance. Second, because the purpose of the credit report was exchange of information in a business context, with neither the identity of the parties nor the substance of the transaction provoking special concern by the Court about the public value associated with freedom of speech, it was a relatively easier setting in which to permit an outcome that would make speech more costly.

In an injury-or-avoidance framework, however, these financial costs could have been taken into account explicitly, without need for further expansion of the taxonomy of *New York Times* tradition. Moreover, the nonfinancial costs which the opinion in *Dun & Bradstreet* found so untroublesome might be of greater concern in other cases, such as one involving core political speech; these "costs"—that is, the lost speech and the chilling effect—could instead be taken into account as the thumb on the scales, as discussed previously in this paper.

CONCLUSION

Reputation as a form of human capital can exist only in the mind of someone other than its "owner": no matter what I myself think of myself, that cannot be my reputation. It has to reside in the mind of someone else. Yet, when the injury of libel occurs, it is injury that happens to me—not to the person in whose mind the reputation exists, and whose change of heart or mind toward me constitutes the injury itself. And such injury typically occurs because of a statement by yet someone else. So the reputational injury of libel occurs in connection with a triangular relationship of subject, speaker, and hearer, just as the original reputational investment often does.

Who can avoid the reputational injury and at what cost is potentially rather tricky. The subject may not know that injury is about to occur; or even after the fact, that it has occurred until some later crisis appears. Moreover, because hearers respond to speakers, it can be the case that the speech itself causes no injury as it is spoken, but does so only when the hearer—in her mind or by particular acts—reacts to the speech. When she does so, *her* acts may be blameless, given the information on which she acted. In such situations, it would take cooperation by the speaker in order for the hearer to avoid the injury; at other times, it would take the speaker plus the subject; and in still other circumstances, each alone can do it.

The judicial decisions, of course, do not speak in these terms. Instead, in cases setting forth the reach of the First Amendment, they distinguish public officials and public figures from private figures; they talk about fact versus opinion; and occasionally counsel that politicians and judges should have a "hide that tough" and so forth.

Collectively, however, these decisions constitute a framework which is perhaps more readily explainable in terms of injury and avoidance: In debate about the conduct of government, its public officials, those subjects whose reputations are at risk, have already made certain choices (to accept appointment or run for office, to embark on a controversial policy perhaps); they have greater access to the media, thus reducing or preventing injury; and they may benefit from the public (hearer) skepticism that politics and political debate engender.

One alternative avoider is the speaker, deterrence of whose speech may, however, not only prevent falsity but prevent speaking altogether. Another avoider would be the hearer, with reliance on his avoidance possibly raising issues of the rights to know or to participate in self-government. But speaker avoidance, with its possible chilling affect, and hearer avoidance are both particularly costly. For a large range of such circumstances, it is possible that subjects are the persons best able to avoid or bear injury (at least, given the heavy costs associated with compromising freedom of speech). Yet, where the speaker knows a statement to be false or has reckless disregard for its truthfulness, *New York Times* says the speaker may be the injury-avoider of choice, even with a public official plaintiff. By contrast, for private figures, who have not thrust themselves into the "vortex " of a public debate or otherwise signed up for such added risks of reputational injury, and apparently considered less able to avoid or reduce injury, there is a lesser burden to be carried in shifting the injury costs to a speaker.

A speaker will not be held liable, however, where hearers bear special responsibility or are expected to act in particular ways. Referring to strikebreakers as "traitors" in the context of an acrimonious labor dispute, for example, does not precipitate speaker liability; hearers are not expected to believe that the subject actually engaged in acts compromising the security of the United States. In other circumstances, often set out by statute, hearers are restricted in the acts they can take in response. Sometimes liability for injury, or its avoidance, apparently falls on them.

All together, these features of the configuration of libel law seem to make sense within a framework in which the cost of injury is compared to the cost of its avoidance. Not only that, but the tensions and instabilities seem to make sense, too: for example, in *Rosenbloom v. Metromedia* only a plurality of the Court was willing to treat persons linked to "issues of public interest" with the severity accorded to public officials, and by the time of *Gertz v. Robert Welch,* even that tide had seemingly declined—only to resurge in a roundabout way in *Dun & Bradstreet*, when a plurality once again distinguished matters of "public concern." Given the relative avoidance and injury-bearing ability of subject vis-a-vis speaker—a closer contest where private figures are associated with public issues—it would seem to be a harder sort of choice, at least for those in the middle of the Court.

Although this inquiry has suggested some applications to libel law of the more familiar framework for analysis of tort law, taking into consideration both the costs of injury and the costs of its avoidance, what has been presented here is intended not as an end to the journey but rather its beginning—as a suggestion of a different approach to thinking about the public and private interests in reputation and those in freedom of speech.

ACKNOWLEDGMENTS

I am grateful for the conversations and comments shared by Bruce Ackerman, Guido Calabresi, Henry Farber, Donald Lessard, Lisa Lynch, Susan Rose-Ackerman, Theodore Schneyer, Frederick Schauer, Gerald Thain, Alan Weisbard, and Burt Weisbrod; for the excellent research assistance of John Copeland and Joseph Kryshak; and the research support of the University of Wisconsin Law Alumni Association and the Sloan School, MIT.

NOTES

1. See, e.g., Warren & Brandeis, "The Right to Privacy," 5 *Harv. L. Rev.* 193, 205 (1890): "In [the right to be defamed] there inheres the quality of being owned or possessed —and (as that is the distinguishing attribute of property) there may be some propriety in speaking of these rights as property." Moreover, other interests in reputation may be implicated as well. See, e.g., Wisconsin v. Constantineau, 400 U.S. 433, 437 (1971) (where individual's "good name, reputation, honor, or integrity is at stake," liberty interest is implicated, and state officials must therefore satisfy procedural due process requirements); cf. Reich, "The New Property," 73 *Yale L.J.* 733 (1964).

2. The concept of reputation as a capital asset is one of current interest in economics, although the focus has been primarily on the reputation of a firm as employer, e.g., Hart, "Optimal Labour Contracts Under Asymmetric Information: An Introduction," 50 *Rev. Econ. Stud.* 3 (1983) or on the reputation of particular products the firm sells to consumers, e.g., Rogerson, "Reputation and Product Quality," 14 *Bell J. Econ.* 508 (1983). On the decision to invest in such capital (though not in human capital) see, e.g., Shapiro, "Premiums for High Quality Products as Returns to Reputations," *Q. J. Econ.* 659 (1983). *Cf.* "Goodwill," in *Black's Law Dictionary*, note *supra* (goodwill means "every advantage,

every positive advantage, that has been acquired by a proprietor in carrying on his business"). *See generally* G. Becker, *Human Capital* (1964).

3. Nothing is, of course, guaranteed, including happiness with one's own reputation, even when truthful. Moreover, it is possible that what one does will affect not only the substance of reputation, but its extent or visibility as well. *See*, e.g., Gertz v. Robert Welch, 418 U.S. 323, 345 (1974). ("commonly, those classed as public figures have thrust themselves to the forefront of particular public controversies . . . [and thereby] invite attention and comment").

4. Actually, the causal aspects may be more complex, for example, where my reputation founders as a result of the publication of truthful but embarrassing facts. Such scenarios, however, would take us into the realm of privacy law, which is beyond the scope of this article.

5. Gertz v. Robert Welch, 418 U.S. 323, 344 (1974). ("The first remedy of any victim of defamation is self-help—using available opportunities to contradict the lie or correct the error and thereby minimize its adverse impact on reputation"); *cf.* Whitney v. California, 274 U.S. 357, 377 (1927) (Brandeis, J.) ("If there be time to expose through discussion the falsehood and fallacies . . . the remedy to be applied is more speech").

6. Like other capital assets such as buildings or equipment, the acquisition of reputation requires investment in an earlier period in order to receive the returns to that investment in later ones. The decision to make such an investment may be analyzed in a fashion similar to that of other investments, and indeed for some sorts of reputational investment, economists have done so. *See*, e.g., Shapiro, *supra* note 2.

7. Of course, reputation can often be enhanced or diminished in a situation involving only two rather than three parties. For example, the reader of this article may form opinions about its author without need of a third party's speech. Such a situation may be viewed as a special case of the analysis presented in the text in which the reader plays the roles of both speaker and hearer. Alternatively, it would be possible that the subject and speaker roles are both played by one person.

For libel to occur, however, there must be three or more persons, for by definition libel entails the publication of false information (*see* W. Prosser and W. Keeton, *Prosser and Keeton on the Law of Torts*, 795–97 (5th ed. 1984). Libel would not have occurred, for example, by means only of a letter of reply from a nonsubject to subject unless the letter had been shown to another. An opinion formed by the reader of this article, but not expressed to a third party, would fail to satisfy the publication criterion. *See*, e.g. New York Times v. Sullivan, 376 U.S. 254, 261 (1964) (individual libel defendants claimed that since they had not authorized use of their names in advertisement, they had not published the allegedly libelous statements in the ad).

8. *See*, e.g., Akerlof, "The Market for 'Lemons': Quality Uncertainty and the Market Mechanism," 84 *Q. J. Econ.* 488 (1970) 14 *Bell J. Econ.* 508 (1983); Shapiro, "Premiums for High Quality Products as Returns to Reputation," 98 *Q. J. Econ.* 659 (1983); Sattherthwaite, "Consumer Information Equilibrium, Industry Price, and the Number of Sellers," 10 *Bell J. Econ.* 483 (1979); Nelson, "Information and Consumer Behavior," 78 *J. Polit. Econ.* 311 (1970); Shapiro, "Consumer Information, Product Quality, and Seller Reputation," 13 *Bell J. Econ.* 20 (1982).

9. *See generally* H. Hart & A. Honore, *Causation in the Law* (2d ed., 1959); Calabresi, "Concerning Cause and the Law of Torts: An Essay for Harry Kalven, Jr.," 43 *U. Chi. L. Rev.* 69 (1975); Epstein, "A Theory of Strict Liability," 2 *J. Legal Stud.* 151, 160-89 (1973); Lachman, "A Theory of Causation in the Context of Speech-Related Harm, or, When Does Speech Cause Harm?" (unpublished ms. 1985).

10. This might be the case, for example, for hearers as members of the crowd in the

theater where Justice Holmes' speaker falsely shouts fire. Schenck. v. United States, 249 U.S. 47, 52 (1919). Loss of profits to the theater-owner might more properly be attributed to the shouter than to the crowd.

11. *See*, e.g., Time, Inc. v. Hill, 385 U.S. 374 (1967) (plaintiff, his wife, and 10-year-old daughter were ostracized from their respective friends and from the community at large as a result of the news magazine's story portraying plaintiff in a "false light"); *cf.* Greenmoss Builders, Inc. v. Dun & Bradstreet, Inc. 143 Vt. 66, 461 A2d 414 (1984), *aff'd* 472 U.S. 749 (1985), (even after correction of defendant's false credit report, plaintiff building company was refused loans by bank to whom false report had previously been issued).

12. Indeed, those investing in human capital also sign up for risks that other investors don't, since special risks and vulnerability attend investments in capital in human form. *See*, e.g., Razin, "Lifetime Uncertainty, Human Capital and Physical Capital," 14 *Econ. Inquiry* 439 (1976) (human capital, which can be lost by premature death, yields higher return than investment in nonhuman capital, consistent with the relative riskiness of these assets).

13. Although people in general may not sign up for such risks, politicians and public figures have been characterized by the Court as people who do in varying degrees sign up for them. *See*, e.g., New York Times v. Sullivan, 376 U.S. 254, 270 (1964): "debate on public issues should be uninhibited, robust, and wide-open, and . . . it may well include vehement, caustic, and sometimes unpleasantly sharp attacks on government and public officials." *See also* Curtis Pub. Co. v. Butts, 388 U.S. 130, 155 (1967) (public figures, persons who "thrust [their] personalit[ies] into the 'vortex of public controversy' come under the *Times* rule requiring showing of "actual malice" for recovery in libel) Harlan, J., (plurality opinion); Gertz v. Robert Welch, 418 U.S. 323, 345 (1974) (same). Paradoxically (or inconsistently) the Court has held that a wealthy and eminent socialite who holds a press conference to discuss her divorce has not signed up for the risks that had Wally Butts, the football coach in *Butts*. Time, Inc. v. Firestone, 424 U.S. 448 (1976).

14. *See* Lachman, *supra* note 9 at 19–20 (panicking by crowd after shout of "fire" in theater would likely be attributed to shouter who has cried out falsely; but if true, it would be attributed to the fire itself, to faulty electrical maintenance, or to an arsonist if fire had truly occurred.

15. It is possible that speaker and hearer are one person; this is a special case (though not a case of libel, since that would require publication to a third person). *See supra* note 6.

16. *See* New York Times v. Sullivan, 376 U.S. 254, 260 (1964) (no proof adduced at trial of case that plaintiff's witnesses actually believed statements in *Times'* political advertisement to be true).

17. *See* examples at *infra* note 59.

18. *See*, e.g., Greenmoss Builders, Inc., v. Dun & Bradstreet, Inc. 143 Vt. 66, 461 A2d 414 (1984) (building company denied loan following false report of applicant's credit status, and even after subsequent notice of correction), *aff'd* 472 U.S. 749; Ocala v. Star-Banner Co. v. Damron, 401 U.S. 295 (1971) (candidate for tax assessor lost election after newspaper reported that he had been indicted for perjury, when indictment was actually of his brother).

19. *See*, e.g., New York Times v. Sullivan, 376 U.S. 254 (1964) (public officials); Curtis Pub. Co. v. Butts, 388 U.S. 130 (1967) (public figures); Gertz v. Robert Welch, 418 U.S. 323 (1974) (private figures).

20. *See*, e.g., Ollman v. Evans, 750 F.2d 970 (D.C. Cir. 1984) (en banc) (statement

that plaintiff has "no status" in his academic field is opinion rather than fact, so recovery for libel is not possible), *cert. denied,* 471 U.S. 1127 (1985).

21. *See,* e.g., Rosenbloom v. Metromedia, Inc., 403 U.S. 29 (1971) (plurality opinion) (matters of "public interest" plaintiff must show "actual malice" in order to recover for injury from false statements); Greenmoss Builders, Inc. v. Dun & Bradstreet, Inc., 472 U.S. 749 (1985) (where defamatory statements "involve no issue of public concern," state law may permit awards of presumed or punitive damages without showing of actual malice).

22. 376. U.S. 254 (1964).

23. *Id.* at 257–60.

24. *See* Calabresi, *supra* note 9 (concept of pressure points). New York Times v. Sullivan, 376 U.S. 267 (1964) (strict liability for statements libelous per se); Gertz v. Robert Welch, 418 U.S. 323, 371 (1974) (White, J. dissenting) (reviewing common law of libel before *New York Times*).

25. Indeed, given the believed difficulty of showing the specific damage from the statement, a presumption of damage to reputation was allowed. Greenmoss Builders, Inc. v. Dun & Bradstreet, Inc. 472 U.S. 749, 765 (1985) (White, J. concurring); W. Prosser and W. Keeton *supra* note 7 at 795–797.

26. *See* New York Times v. Sullivan, 144 So.2d 25 (Ala. 1962), *rev'd* 376 U.S. 254 (1964).

27. 376 U.S. 254 (1964).

28. *Id.* at 271.

29. *Id.* at 279. *See* Schauer, "Fear, Risk and the First Amendment: Unraveling the 'Chilling Effect,' " 58 *B.U.L. Rev.* 685 (1978) (characterizing effect as one of "excess deterrence").

30. New York Times, 376 U.S. at 271–72, 278–79. *See also Gertz,* 418 U.S. at 340; text accompany *infra* notes 65–68 (discussing separability of false from true speech in terms of production metaphor).

31. *New York Times,* 376 U.S. at 270.

32. *See,* e.g., *New York Times,* 376 U.S. at 268 (" 'public men, are, as it were, public property,' and 'discussion cannot be denied and the right as well as the duty, of criticism must not be stifled' ") (quoting Beauharnais v. Illinois, 343 U.S. 250, 263–64 & n.18 (1952)). *See also* Monitor Patriot Co. v. Roy, 401 U.S. 265 (1971) (candidates for office within *New York Times* rule); *cf.* Ollman v. Evans, 750 F.2d 970, 993 (D.C. Cir 1984) (Bork, J., concurring), *cert. denied,* 471 U.S. 1127 (1985):

> Those who step into areas of public dispute, who choose the pleasures and distractions of controversy, must be willing to bear criticism, disparagement, and even wounding assessments. Perhaps it would be better if disputation were conducted in measured phrases and calibrated assessments. . . . [b]ut that is not the world in which we live, ever have lived, or are ever likely to know, and the law of the first amendment must not try to make public dispute safe and comfortable for all the participants. That would only stifle the debate.

33. *Gertz,* 418 U.S. at 344.

34. *See,* e.g., *New York Times,* 376 U.S. at 273:

> If judges are to be treated as "men of fortitude, able to thrive in a hardy climate," *Craig v. Harney,* . . . 331 U.S., at 376, surely the same must be true of other government officials, such as elected city commissioners. Criticism of their official

conduct does not lose its constitutional protection merely because it is effective criticism and hence diminishes their official reputations.

35. *Gertz,* 418 U.S. at 344.

36. Calabresi & Hirschoff, *Toward a Test for Strict Liability in Torts,* 81 *Yale L.J.* 1055 (1972); G. *Calabresi, The Costs of Accidents* 135 (1970). The cheapest cost avoider, the candidate for strict liability suggested by Calabresi, is the party who "is in the best position to make the cost-benefit analysis between accident costs and accident avoidance costs and to act on that decision once it is made." Calabresi & Hirschoff, *Strict Liability,* note 13, *supra.*

37. *Cf.* Schauer, *"Public Figures,"* 25 *Wm. & Mary L. Rev.* 905, 911 (1984):

The behavioral lesson of *New York Times* could have been taken one step further, for only by eliminating all remedies for defamatory statements can the law completely maximize the dissemination of truth. Yet, the fact that this step was not taken, even with respect to comment on the official conduct of public officials, demonstrates that maximizing the dissemination of truth does not enjoy a lexical priority over all other societal values. (footnotes omitted)

38. With respect to determining who is a public official or a public figure, *see* Rosenblatt v. Baer, 383 U.S. 75, 85 (1966) (public officials include "at the very least . . . those among the hierarchy of government employees who have, or appear to the public to have, substantial responsibility for or control over the conduct of governmental affairs") (footnote omitted); Gertz v. Robert Welch, Inc. 418 U.S. 323, 351–51 (1974) (public figures include those who have achieved "general fame or notoriety in the community"). *cf.* Hutchinson v. Proxmire, 443. U.S. 157 (1979) (mental hospital researcher who was state employee and recipient of federal research funding, was private figure).

39. 388 U.S. 130 (1967).

40. *See* W. Prosser and W. Keeton *supra* note 7 (presenting rationales for varying plaintiff burdens and relations of standards to one another).

41. 418 U.S. 323 (1974).

42. *Id.* at 347 (for private figure plaintiffs, states may "define for themselves" the appropriate standard of liability "so long as they do not impose liability without fault") (Powell, J.) (opinion of Court). *Cf. id.* at 350 (in later discussion about punitive damages, opinion mentions a "negligence standard" for private defamation actions). Dun & Bradstreet v. Greenmoss Builders, 105 S.Ct. 2939 600 (Powell, J.) (characterizing *Gertz* as having adopted a negligence rule for this class of private figure plaintiffs, rather than simply the "caveat against strict liability," *Gertz* 418 U.S. at 377 n. 10). But *cf.* Guilford v. Yale 128 Conn. 449, 23 A.2d 917 (1942) (defendant's duty to plaintiff, ranging from slight care to negligence to high degree of care, depends on relative gains to be had by each party).

43. Rosenbloom v. Metromedia, Inc., 403 U.S. 29 (1971).

44. Dun & Bradstreet v. Greenmoss Builders, 472 U.S. 749 (1985).

45. *Dun & Bradstreet* not only permitted the awarding of presumed and punitive damages to a private plaintiff—as had previously seemed largely foreclosed—but also presented the curious though unanswered question whether strict liability might once again be acceptable state law for such private person/private issue cases. *See id.* at 772, 773 (White, J. concurring in judgment).

46. Old Dominion Branch No. 496, National Association of Letter Carriers v. Austin, 418 U.S. 264, 285–86 (1974).

47. *Id.* at 268.

48. 398 U.S. 6 (1970).

49. *Id.* at 14; *cf.* Chaplinski v. New Hampshire 315 U.S. 568 (1942) (words which by their very utterance inflicted injury would not have done so had speaker offered a "disarming smile").

50. *See e.g.,* Ollman v. Evans, 750 F.2d 970, 1010 (D.C. Cir. 1984) (en banc) (Bork, J. concurring):

> It is significant . . . that the column appeared on the Op-Ed pages of newspapers. These are pages reserved for the expression of opinion, much of it highly controversial. . . . [that alerts] the reader that he is in the context of controversy and politics, and that what he reads does not even purport to be as balanced, objective, and fair-minded as he has a right to hope to be the case with what is contained in the news columns of the paper. The Op-Ed pages are known to be a forum for controversy, often heated controversy, analogous in many respects to the context of a labor dispute. . . .
>
> . . . By the time the reader comes to the [allegedly libelous assertion] he is most unlikely to regard that assertion as to be trusted automatically. It is an assertion of a kind of fact, it is true, but a hyperbolic "fact" so thoroughly embedded in opinions and tendentiousness that it takes on their qualities.

51. M. Schudson, *Discovering the News* (1978); J. Tebbel, *The Compact History of the American Newspaper* (1969). Moreover, before the advent of the regular reporting by professional reporters, publishers relied heavily on letters from traveling friends (correspondents, quite literally) and republished news from other publications. The resulting product was of varying quality and predictability. For example, *The New York Gazette and Mercury* reported that *The Hartford Post* reported "That he saw a Gentleman in Springfield, who informed him that he (the Gentleman) saw a letter from an Officer in Gen. Howe's Army to another in Gen. Burgoyne's, giving him to understand, war was declared on the sides of France and Spain against the MIGHTY kingdom of Britain." As the skeptical reader might expect, or at least wonder, this particular "news" wasn't true!

52. J. Tebbel, *supra* note 51. Moreover, "Americans understood that the newspapers of William Randolph Hearst were largely an extension of his personality, and so they took that into account. Why believe the *New York World* when it might be flatly contradicted by the *Herald-Tribune!* R. Smolla, *Suing the Press. Libel, the Media, & Power* 11 (1900).

53. M. Schudson *supra* note 51 at 61–106. "Indeed, the concept of reporting itself, as contrasted with writing what one can without stirring from the office, is only a late-nineteenth-century invention; and when it came to such things as White House press conferences, President Wilson in 1912 was clearly the first one on his block to have one." *Id.* at 139.

54. R. Smolla *supra* note 52 at 11. Largely a postwar invention, objectivity as ideology for the press (and as a standard of performance expected by the readers) has conferred the benefits of more accurate reporting of certain events, even as it has brought with it a greater potential for harm. M. Schudson *supra* note 51. If accuracy and objectivity beget believability, then hearers are more likely to manifest the diminished regard that is reputational injury, and a given falsehood may do more harm. "Back in the heyday of yellow journalism, reporting was surely much worse than it is today, but it was also less harmful, because there was no presumption, or pretension, or accuracy." R. Smolla *supra* note 52 at all.

55. Fair Credit Reporting Act of 1970, 15 U.S.C. §1681 *et seq.* Specifically, *see* §1681i (any inaccurate information must be promptly deleted from the records of the consumer

reporting agency), §1681n (civil liability for noncompliance), and §1681o (civil liability for negligent compliance).

56. Example of public employees' termination based on false information; (Roth) Green for first dissent; Union contracts, employment at will.

57. Schenk v. United States, 249 U.S. 47, 52 (1919).

58. *See* e.g., Johnson v. New York 37 N.Y. 2d58, 334 N.E.2d 590, 372, NYS.2d 63 (1975) (daughter of state mental hospital patient, after being negligently misinformed that her mother had died, recovered for emotional distress and costs of funeral and wake conducted before error was discovered).

59. There are a variety of laws limiting disclosure by hearers of information, whether it be true or false. *See* e.g., Freedom of Information Act Pub. L. 89–487, 80 Stat. 250, 251 (1966) (as amended and codified in 5 U.S.C. §552((7) (c)) (privacy exception); Higher Education Act of 1968, U.S.C. §1232g (Buckley Amendment, limiting disclosure of records maintained by educational institutions *cf.* S. Milson, *Historical Foundations of the Common Law* 341 (1969) (under Star Chamber's developing law of defamation, "[r]epetition was punishable, but mere listening was not").

For criticism of the extension of the *New York Times* rule to all public figures, see Schauer, *supra* note 34; Blasi, "The Checking Value in First Amendment Theory," 1977 *Am. B. Found. Res. J.* 521, 581–82 ("checking value" of First Amendment supports *New York Times* standard as applied to public officials but not as applied to public figures).

60. Sedition Act of July 14, 1798, 1 Stat. 596; the Act expired by its own terms in 1801, *id.*, but not before a series of indictments and convictions. *See* L. Levy, *Emergence of a Free Press (1985);* L. tribe, *American Constitutional Law* 632 (1978); *see also* Gertz v. Robert Welch, Inc. 418 U.S. at 369 (White, J. dissenting) (reviewing libel law).

It is noteworthy that the distinction between libel and slander, of medieval origin, arose from the Crown's desire to have an avenue for easier recovery in libel against those who criticized it, particularly by means of the newly invented printing press. Veeder, "The History and Theory of the Law of Defamation," 3 *Colum. L. Rev.* 546, 559–61 (1903).

Previous to the invention of the printing press, such comments had apparently not been so troublesome, if only because making written copies was a more labor intensive process of relatively less influence when few could read, and spoken criticism was apparently less enduring. Defamation, an action on the case for words, could be either spoken or written utterance and was one of the most common torts in the courts of the middle ages. *Id.* at 558; Donnelly, "History of Defamation," 1949 *Wisc. L. Rev.* 99, 100–101. Responding to a perceived litigation crisis the common law judges had cut back on the ability of libel plaintiffs to obtain recovery. *Id.* at 113–15. When the Crown chose to seek redress from the increase in offensive statements the printing press made possible, it was necessary to take an approach different from that of the common law courts. As the Star Chamber came to assume jurisdiction over defamation actions and also to enforce statutes against defamation, the distinction between written and spoken defamation became, first, a *statistical* one. S. Milson, *supra* note 59, at 342. This "emphatic" statistical linkage later became a rule. *Id.; see also* Veeder, *supra,* at 566–69 (attributing greater weight to rule of 1609 case *De Libellus Famosis* which borrowed from the Roman criminal law).

61. *See* Calabresi, "'Some Thoughts on Risk Distribution and the Law of Torts," 70 *Yale L.J.* 499 (1961) (discussing goals and their achievement in tort law, including compensation, deterrence, wealth, distribution, and loss spreading.

62. Virginia State Board of Pharmacy v. Va. Citizens Consumers Council, 425 U.S. 748, 771 (1976).

63. J. S. Mill, *On Liberty* 15 (1947) (false statement brings to public debate a "clearer perception and livelier impression of truth, produced by its collison with error"); R.

Nimmer, *Freedom of Speech* (1984) at 3–16, 3–17 (false speech may serve functions of enlightenment, self-fulfillment, and as a safety valve. *Cf.* Emery & Emery *supra* note 51 at 83 (mob stormed printer's shop in reaction to story of President Washington, published in 1776).

64. Dun & Bradstreet Inc. v. Greenmoss Builders, 472 U.S. 749 (1985).

65. *See* e.g., Escola v. Coca Cola Bottling Co., 24 Cal.2d 453, 150 P.2d 436 (1944) (Traynor, J. concurring) (setting forth theory of enterprise liability).

66. *New York Times,* 376 U.S. at 279.

67. My own reading of *Dun & Bradstreet* suggests a position by the plurality that comes surprisingly close to this position. See Dun & Bradstreet Inc. v. Greenmoss Builders, 472 U.S. 749, 762, 763 (Powell, J.); *cf. id.* at 771, 772 (White, J. concurring); *id.* at 775 (Brennan, J., dissenting).

68. Chaplinski v. New Hampshire, 315 U.S. 568 (1942); Valentine v. Chrestensen, 316 U.S. 52 (1942) (commercial speech).

69. See R. Bork, "Neutral Principles and Some First Amendment Problems," 47 *Ind. L.J.* 1 (1971); A. Meiklejohn, *Free Speech and Its Relation to Self-Government* 18–27 (1948).

70. *See* Kalven, "the Reasonable Man and the First Amendment," in *Free Speech and Association* 207, 234 (P. Kurland, ed. 1975)) ("one might develop a free-speech theory on the premise that we must overprotect speech in order to protect the speech that matters").

71. *See* Kalven, "The New York Times Case: A Note on the 'Central Meaning of the First Amendment,' " 1964 *Supreme Ct. Rev.* 1919; Schauer, "Public Figures," 25 *William and Mary L. Rev.* 905, 909 (1984) (characterizing *New York Times* approach as "strategic, immunizing some falsity from the reach of the law to encourage the dissemination of the maximum amount of truth" (footnote omitted).

72. *New York Times,* 376 U.S. at 279.

73. *Id.* at 271, 279.

74. *Id.* at 261, 263, 287.

75. *Id.* at 287–88.

76. *Id.* at 280. *See also* Garrison v. Louisiana, 379 U.S. 64, 75 (1964) ("the lie, knowlingly and deliberately published about a public official" is not constitutionally protected).

77. 418 U.S. 323 (1974).

78. *Id.* at 329.

79. *Id.* 327.

80. *Id.* at 352.

81. 472 U.S. at 749.

82. *Id.* at 605.

83. *Dun & Bradstreet* 472 U.S. at 751.

84. Here, I am assuming that a reasonably prudent adult would not make the mistake of attributing an individual's bankruptcy to the person's former employer instead. Whether a reasonable 17-year-old would do so would seemingly not be relevant so long as the youth was engaged in an adult activity. *See,* e.g., Hill Transp. Co. v. Everett, 145 F.2d 746 (1st Cir. 1944) (even where lower standard of care would otherwise apply because of youthfulness of actor, it could not be invoked so as to shield employer from liability in *respondent superior*); Dellwo v. Pearson, 259 Minn. 452, 107 N.W.2d 859 (1961) (overruling standard of care geared to age of actor, where actor engaged in adult activities.

85. *See generally* W. Prosser and W. Keeton, *supra* note 7.

86. *Dun & Bradstreet,* 472 U.S. at 751, 752.

87. *Id.* at 752.
88. *Gertz*, 418 U.S. 323, 344 (1974).
89. Fair Credit Reporting Act of 1970, 15 U.S.C. § 1681 *et seq.*
90. *Dun & Bradstreet*, 472 U.S. at 752.
91. *Id.* at 752, 753.

10

THE ECONOMICS OF LIBEL LITIGATION

David A. Hollander

Since the landmark decision in *New York Times v. Sullivan,*[1] courts and commentators have struggled with the question of what protection speakers should be given from liability for defamation: should speakers be shielded from liability through use of a fault standard, damage limitations, evidenciary burdens or through some other means? This paper sets out to analyze the utility or some of these approaches from an economic perspective. Part I develops a model of information production. This model, which focuses on how liability rules affect the professional media, demonstrates that such rules should be structured to induce the media to produce more information in order to help correct a failure in the market for information. Part I also examines some empirical evidence on the effect of both damage rewards and litigation costs on the production of information. We shall see that litigation costs have a far greater impact on information production than do damage awards. Part II compares the relative effects of three different types of protection against defamation suits—fault standards, limitations on damages, and fee shifting—and proposes a set of revisions of constitutional privilege centering on the use of awarding litigation costs to the prevailing party.

I. THE ECONOMICS OF INFORMATION PRODUCTION

A. Elements of the Market for Information

The market for information consists of information producers, information consumers, and information itself. The model of the market for information discussed below will assume that all information is produced by the professional media, who are responsible for most of the information we receive, and that rules affecting them are likely to have a major impact on the production of information. In addition, they—more than anyone—are likely to be aware of the rules of liability and to respond to changes in them.

Consumers, the second element of the market for information, purchase information directly, when they buy a book or newspaper, or indirectly, when they obtain their information from advertising supplied mainly by television and radio. Consumers demand information both for its entertainment value and to help them make decisions. The demand for the latter type of information is presumed to be a function of its accuracy and the nature of the decision to be made.

This model assumes that information production is determined by the laws of supply and demand. This, in turn, assumes that consumers desire accurate information and are willing to pay for it, and that the media respond to the various financial incentives provided to them. Either or both of these assumptions could be wrong: consumers may, for example, care far less for the accuracy or relevance of the news they purchase than for its entertainment value, and the media may determine their output based on their desire for awards and prestige or to serve a professional ethic that encourages the publication of newsworthy stories rather than any desire to maximize profits.[2]

The assumption that the media are responsive to financial incentives is independent from the assumption that consumers are willing to pay for useful information. Even if the news content or quality of a broadcaster's or publisher's output were of no concern to consumers and had no effect on sales, the level of news produced should still be influenced by the cost of producing it. In this case, we would be able to determine how various liability rules affect the production of information. We would be unable to determine, however, whether the media were producing the appropriate level of information in the absence of effective signals in the form of consumer demand.

Some members of the media have claimed that they are unresponsive to at least one financial incentive—the threat of litigation.[3] Even if this is true in the case of some publishers and broadcasters, it is unlikely to be true generally. Rather, the much more common claim by the media is that the threat of libel litigation results in self-censorship, numerous instances of which have been documented.[4] For smaller publishers or broadcasters, a libel suit can be disastrous. It seems implausible that they do not take into account the risk of being sued when deciding what to publish.

A number of commentators have argued that, although the media are sensitive to the threat of defamation suits, they are relatively unaffected by the level of consumer demand for investigative journalism. These commentators typically favor increased protection of the media on the ground that there is no countervailing economic incentive for the media to run the risk of litigation. One reason why the media may be unresponsive to pressure from consumers to publish potentially libelous stories is that they are sheltered from competition.[5] Newspapers, in particular, which are the most frequent targets of libel litigation,[6] are almost entirely without local competition.[7] Lack of competition, it is argued, frees timid publishers from the threat that more aggressive competitors will win their customers or advertisers by carrying stories that they refuse to publish. Moreover, the nature of the market for information allows the professional media great latitude in choosing the types of stories they will cover. In contrast to most other businesses, the media are able to reduce or eliminate the risk of tort liability (by refusing to carry offensive stories), without discontinuing their operations.[8] If true, this would mean that the media can determine their coverage of controversial stories largely without regard for consumer demand. It has also been argued that consumers are uninterested in "hard-hitting" stories and, therefore, decisions by the media to change the level of coverage of such stories would not affect their sales. One proponent of this view states that a newspaper "competing for circulation is more likely to fight the battle with comics, color photos, stock tables, or contests than with more daring treatment of potentially defamatory material. When a broadcaster's ratings slip, he is likely to respond by hiring a more congenial anchorman, or by replacing news and public affairs programming with entertainment, instead of opting for more aggressive journalism."[9] This argument implies that there is minimal financial pressure on the media to publish stories that may result in litigation.

While these views have some merit, there is still reason to believe that the production of information is affected by financial incentives. First, it seems doubtful that there is no consumer demand for investigative journalism. The success of such television programs as *60 Minutes* indicates that investigative journalism can be a profitable enterprise. That potentially defamatory stories are published despite the risk of litigation strongly suggests that there must be some financial incentive to do so. If ratings and circulations were unaffected by the boldness or timidity of the broadcaster or publisher, there would be no reason (except for the aforementioned professional ethic) to run the risk of any libel litigation.

Second, the relative absence of competition in local newspaper markets does not mean that publishers can afford to be unresponsive to the tastes of their customers. Even under conditions of monopoly, production is still determined by supply and demand. The effect of monopoly is to reduce the equilibrium output level from what it would be under conditions of perfect competition. Nonetheless, a monopolist will find it profitable to increase the demand for its goods. By making its product more desirable, a monopolist can charge higher prices for it, or increase sales to those who would have otherwise gone without the product.

Thus, even newspapers without local competition will have some incentive to publish stories that increase the demand for their product.

One final reason that economic analysis is an appropriate tool in this area is that the use of constitutional privilege necessarily presupposes that the production of information can be affected by altering the financial incentives given to the media. Its primary, if not exclusive, purpose is to increase the production of information. If it does not accomplish this, then its only effect is to shift part of the burden of producing news onto private shoulders, without any accompanying benefit. If we assume that constitutional privilege has its intended effect, we must also assume that the media and their consumers are responsive to economic incentives.

The third element of the market is information itself. In most respects, information is similar to tangible goods and commodities. Information varies in type and quality; it is often produced by large financial enterprises, sold wholesale (as by the wire services) and then retail. Information differs, however, from most other goods in an important respect: it is a *public good*. A characteristic of public goods is that their consumption by one does not diminish the ability of others to enjoy some or all of their benefits as well. Information is the classic public good; it can be enjoyed equally by one person or a million. Thus, free markets, unfortunately, cannot be relied on to produce the optimal level of public goods because the normal mechanisms that translate consumer preferences into goods and services break down. In the case of private goods (e.g., most tangible goods), persons must act on their preferences through market transactions in order to obtain the benefits of the goods. Would-be beneficiaries of these goods are forced to reveal their preferences by paying for them. The preferences of consumers for the goods are reflected in the perceived demand curve for them. Production of private goods in a perfectly competitive economy, in which the cost of the goods to consumers reflects the true social cost of producing the goods, is ideal in the sense that increased production could not be obtained except at the expenditure of resources valued more greatly by consumers than the incremental production.[10]

The benefits of public goods, in contrast, are more difficult to confine. "Free riders" can obtain the benefits of public goods without paying for them. Information production has a substantial free rider problem, basically because it is usually cheaper and easier to copy information than to create it. The ability of persons to copy information is only partially limited by the copyright laws. For example, once a news story is publicly disseminated, other members of the media can generally publish the same information as that contained in the original after only a short time lag.[11] In addition, the use of information, particularly political informa-

FIGURE 10.1: The Effect of Free Riders

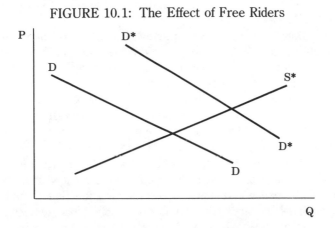

tion, by paying consumers may also have public good aspects. Decisions made by voters have far ranging impacts and we traditionally assume that such decisions are improved by an informed electorate. The benefits of the additional information obtained by a portion of the electorate accrue not just to that portion, but to society in general. The impact of the investigative work performed by the *Washington Post* and other major news organizations during the early seventies, for example, surely reached far beyond their customers. Because political information will benefit persons other than those who pay for it, the production of political information suffers from a substantial free rider problem.[12]

The effect of free riders is illustrated in figure 10.1. D^* is the demand curve representing information as a purely private good. The demand curve D represents the actual level of information demanded. The lower equilibrium level of the intersection of S^* (the supply curve) and D illustrates that production of information is less than that actually desired by consumers.

B. Effect of Constitutional Privilege on the Accuracy and Quantity of Information Production

Modifications of the liability rules for defamation are likely to affect both the quantity and accuracy of information produced. This section compares the effects of the various fault standards—strict liability, negligence, actual malice, and absolute privilege—and differing measures of recoverable damages on the production of information. For the sake of simplicity, I assume that the legal system operates costlessly and without error, imposing liability in full conformity with the relevant legal standards. The impact of costly litigation on the model is explored in section C.

Constitutional privilege increases the production of information by decreasing its cost. Both the requirement that fault be proved and the restrictions on recovery of presumed damages reduce the media's expenditures on legal costs. By lessening the cost of production, constitutional privilege shifts the supply curve to the right. A new equilibrium is established, at which more information is sold, and at a lower cost relative to that under strict liability. The more expansive the protections given to the media, the greater these effects will be.

The liability rules will also influence the level of accuracy of the information produced, although these effects are somewhat more complicated. This section assumes that accuracy is a function of the amount of money spent on care. This seems reasonable, since additional accuracy can by "purchased" by requiring such things as multiple sources for controversial allegations, electronic recording of interviews, additional editing stages, and so forth.

Under a system of strict liability, the media will be held liable for all damages caused by the publication of defamatory matter. The media would attempt to avoid some, although not all, of these costs. They will optimize their expenditures on care to minimize the sum of the net amount spent on error-preventive measures and on legal expenses.

In Figure 10.2, line C represents the amount spent on care. Line C' represents the net amount spent on care after deducting the additional profits realized by the higher level of quality.[13] Line I represents the injury caused by the publication of defamatory matter. The sum of lines C' and I is represented in line T.

FIGURE 10.2: The Effect of Care

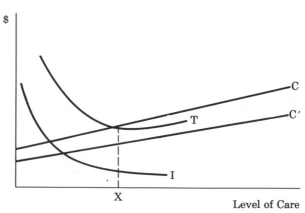

Under strict liability, the media will set care at X, thereby minimizing the total of expenditures on care and on defamation suits. The level of care that will be set under a negligence standard depends on how the standard is interpreted. Under one common formulation of the standard, put forth by Learned Hand, liability is imposed when the cost of increasing the level of care would be exceeded by the savings that the increase would bring in terms of reduced accidents.[14] It can be shown that the level of care required to avoid liability under this standard minimizes the sum of the amounts spent on care and the damage caused by the activity. Thus, the use of Learned Hand's negligence formula would induce the media to use the same degree of care that the strict liability standard would.[15]

The same cannot be said for standards that are more protective of the media, such as gross negligence, actual malice and absolute privilege. Under these standards, the media will be able to avoid the imposition of liability while employing less care than that required by negligence or strict liability. Within limits, the use of these standards will result in lower accuracy than would be used under negligence or strict liability.[16]

Alterations of the measure of recoverable damages will also affect the financial incentive to use care in the production of news. A requirement that the defendant pay the full measure of damage caused by the defamation (but no more) will result in the use of one degree of care. Limitations on the measure of recoverable damages will induce the media to use a lower degree of care, while allowance of punitive damages will result in the use of a greater degree of care.

It is sometimes suggested that the free interchange of information will by itself regulate the accuracy of information—i.e., that truth will eventually emerge from the "marketplace of ideas." This is based on a different sort of market analysis from that proposed here. The marketplace-of-ideas metaphor, which has been eloquently championed by Milton[17] and Mill,[18] can be summarized as follows: Truth is a product that is "bought" by persons who accept the validity of another's statements. The way to ensure quality in the marketplace for ideas is to allow competition. Eventually, falsehood will be rejected and truth will be accepted in its place. More recently, this idea has received support from Richard Posner, who has argued that truth and falsity are only labels that we attach to ideas that have been accepted or rejected by consumers of information.[19] Under this view, there is no need to protect the public from falsehood since they can protect themselves by rejecting defective information.

The marketplace-of-ideas model implies that an unregulated market would result in an optimal accuracy level. That model is predicated on a belief that truth will necessarily prevail over falsehood in open debate. This assumption, however, has been repeatedly challenged by numerous scholars: "Although elegantly stated, in contemporary society, Milton's belief is rather naïve. Defamation rejects his empirical precept. At least in the short run, falsity may well win out.[20] And Professor Alexander Meiklejohn, whose writings influenced the *New York Times* Court, has "never been able to share the Miltonian faith that in a fair fight between truth and error, truth is sure to win."[21] Even Mill recognized that "[h]istory teems with instances of truth put down by error."[22]

The marketplace metaphor is incorrect because the assumption that self-interest will induce people to accept true information over false, while plausible, is an oversimplification. It ignores the fact that consumers of information do not necessarily know whether information being offered to them is true or false. A consumer could rationally decide to accept information that was probably false on the ground that the benefit of accepting it (assuming it is true) is high and the harm from accepting it (assuming it is false) is low. For example, let us assume that a consumer has been given information that a certain brand of food is unsafe to eat. Even if this information is almost certainly false, the rational consumer might avoid that brand because the cost of accepting the information as true is fairly low (the difference in satisfaction from purchasing that brand and from purchasing the consumer's second choice) whereas the potential benefit, assuming the information were true, is quite high. Because of this effect, consumers will tend to act on a wide variety of information that is unlikely to be accurate.

C. Accounting for the Effects of Costly Litigation

The preceding analysis assumed that the legal system could operate perfectly, charging the media for the exact amount of damage they cause by publishing defamatory matter. This is a fairly common assumption in economic analyses, but in the present case it seriously skews the results. In reality, the legal system imposes on the media the expense of damage awards and the expense of defending themselves in court— which they bear win or lose—as well. This is particularly troubling when what the defendant has published is essentially accurate. The proper choice of a liability rule cannot be made without some understanding of how it is likely to affect litigation costs.

Litigation costs complicate the foregoing analysis in a number of ways. First, because plaintiffs must generally bear their own costs even if they prevail, many plaintiffs with small claims may find it unprofitable to bring suit. This may reduce the level of litigation below what is socially appropriate.[23] This problem cuts both ways. Since defendants must also bear their own costs—which can exceed the cost of making a cash settlement—plaintiffs whose claims lack merit may be tempted to bring "nuisance" suits, which would raise the level of litigation above the appropriate level. Moreover, as will be seen, there are a number of nonmonetary incentives to bring suit, which may also result in excessive litigation. Without the appropriate data, one cannot determine which of these effects is likely to prevail.

It is important to understand the role of litigation costs in libel cases because they greatly overshadow damage awards. Approximately 75 to 80 percent of the total cost of libel suits goes toward legal fees.[24] This is significantly higher than in other fields of civil litigation, including medical malpractice and product liability cases.[25] The expense of defending extraordinary libel cases can be staggering.[26] Even the costs of defending routine actions are significant, particularly in the aggregate.[27]

One can argue that the high cost of defense should not, by itself, be cause for concern. After all, the media's unparalleled expenditures have bought them an equally unparalleled success rate.[28] If the defendants prefer to pay more in defense costs and less in damage awards, one can argue, that is their business; so long as the overall level of protection is adequate, we need not specifically worry about litigation costs.

There are, however, a number of reasons why we should be concerned about litigation costs. One is that they are a deadweight loss to society. Unlike damage awards, which are simply transfers of wealth, litigation costs represent the consumption of resources. Although defendants may be indifferent to paying litigation costs or damage awards, society clearly is not. If litigation costs could be reduced, more resources would be available to compensate defamation victims without imposing a greater burden on the media.

Another, more significant problem posed by litigation costs is the effect they have in discouraging the production of valuable information. As will be shown below, a significant percentage of all defamation suits brought have no realistic chance of success under prevailing legal standards. Many of these probably involve stories that, while unflattering, are essentially accurate. The media cannot avoid these suits by being more careful, since such suits are brought regardless of the accuracy of the publication. While having no beneficial effect on accuracy,[29] these nonmeritorious suits discourage critical but accurate commentary. The easiest way for a publisher to avoid libel suits is to refuse to carry controversial stories. This is particularly troubling because the persons and organizations that have the power and motive to discourage unfavorable reporting are very often the ones about which society has the greatest need for information. This type of suit may "chill" the production of particularly valuable speech.

We have little direct evidence of a percentage of defamation suits or harassment suits in which the underlining story is essentially accurate because libel suits rarely reach the issue of truth.[30] There is, however, a fair amount of inferential evidence that the percentage is high. One reason that this may be the case is that persons who have been subjects of negative but accurate commentary can achieve a number of goals by bringing defamation suits, even if unsuccessful. The most obvious of these is the desire to punish the defendant for publishing an unpopular opinion, or to discourage the defendant and others from publishing unfavorable material in the future. A defamation suit may also serve to retaliate against a defendant who has angered the plaintiff by poor treatment either in the story itself, or by the defendant after the plaintiff has complained. These suits, commonly referred to as nuisance or harassment suits,[31] probably constitute a third to a half of all defamation suits. Another motive for bringing a suit is the belief that defending one's name in court will by itself produce a positive change in public opinion by substantiating the plaintiff's claim of falsity.[32]

It is important to note that a plaintiff will have just as much incentive to pursue the above goals regardless of the accuracy of the information. Indeed, the plaintiff may even have more reason to bring suit when the story is true, since may be more widely believed and thus be more damaging. Furthermore, plaintiffs can successfully pursue those goals even if they lose their suits. Because the defendants must bear their costs even if they win, libel litigation is an effective tool to harass the press. And, at least according to many plaintiffs, the act of bringing suit can persuade others of the validity of the plaintiff's cause regardless of the outcome of the case.

In addition, plaintiffs with a continuing interest in discouraging public criticisms of them have made very frequent use of the nuisance value of the defamation laws. Of course, an individual suit cannot be assumed to be nonmeritorious simply because the plaintiff wanted to deter negative media coverage, but it is likely that the disproportionate level of litigation by these plaintiffs is due at least in part to their litigious tendencies rather than to lack of care by the press.[33]

Much has been made of the alarming regularity with which plaintiffs in defamation actions have been awarded "mega-verdicts"—those in excess of $1 million.[34] This could imply that plaintiffs are bringing suits in the hope of receiving a large award. Were this the case, it might mean that plaintiffs are bringing weak cases simply in the hope of making money, rather than to harass the defendant. But the profitability of defamation suits is largely illusory. Plaintiffs in defamation actions win a lower percentage of cases than in any other area of tort law. The great majority of the awards that plaintiffs receive at trial are either reduced or completely eliminated upon appeal.[35]

Not only do plaintiffs lose most of their cases, but the awards that have been sustained on appeal have tended to be rather small. In Franklin's study, a total of $683,500 was awarded in 291 cases, including 37 that went through a trial and appeal. Thus, the average award per full trial comes to $18,472. The statistics in the LDRC study are only slightly better. They show a total of $829,500 awarded in 35 cases that had gone through trial (34 of which had gone through an appeal as well). The average award here was $23,700.

The ILRP Study found that successful litigants obtained an average of $80,000 in damage awards and that, after excluding two large awards, the average recovery "was only $20,600, a sizable portion of which went to fees and costs."[36] Moreover, a portion of these awards is not allocable to the decision to litigate. Plaintiffs with strong cases would have received some money in out of court settlements had they pursued that path. Only the excess of the awards received in trial over the amounts that the cases could have been settled for is properly attributable to the decision to litigate.

Compounding the low return to libel suits is the high cost of conducting them. The cost of bringing a simple defamation suit is estimated at between ten and fifty thousand dollars.[37] The more costly suits (those brought by the wealthy and famous) have increasingly been financed by plaintiffs on an hourly fee basis rather than on a contingency fee basis.[38] Such suits, which have little chance of success, have proved enormously expensive to bring.[39] These statistics support the contention that plaintiffs are not bringing these suits because it is profitable to do so. The plaintiffs in the ILRP Study corroborated this conclusion: "Only about one-fifth of the plaintiffs said that they sued to win money damages. . . . Most plaintiffs said that their chief objective was restoring reputation or punishing the media."[40]

One of the most intriguing (and overlooked) pieces of evidence of the extent of excess litigation is the percentage of claims that are litigated instead of being settled without trial. The ILRP Study found that only fifteen percent of cases brought against the media are settled out of court.[41] This contrasts markedly with the overall settlement rate for tort litigation, which is estimated at 50 percent.[42]

This disparity is also present in appellate rates. Various studies show that only a fraction of trial verdicts in other areas of tort litigation are appealed.[43] In contrast, virtually all defamation cases that reach trial are subsequently appealed.[44]

The most plausible explanation for this remarkable disparity in litigation rates seems to be that people are bringing defamation suits in order to pursue nonmonetary goals, such as harassing the defendant. To see this, it is necessary to understand how the decision to litigate or settle a dispute is made. In general, parties will litigate instead of settle if the plaintiff's estimate of his or her expected judgment exceeds the defendant's estimate by at least the sum of their legal costs.[45] Where both parties place the same estimate of the expected judgment at trial, the dispute will be settled. The low settlement rate of libel disputes can be explained as the result of nonmonetary benefits that defamation plaintiffs receive by going to trial. These benefits will create a divergence between the defendant's estimate of the expected cost of going to trial— damage awards—from the plaintiff's estimate of the expected reward from going to trial—damage awards plus nonmonetary benefits. The greater the divergence, the less likely is settlement. If we assume that the settlement rate for defamation disputes would be the same as that for other tort actions were it not for the ability of plaintiffs to receive nonmonetary benefits at trial, then it would seem that a high percentage of defamation cases are now being brought for reasons other than the recovery of damages. Many of these disputes are probably based on critical but essentially accurate speech.

D. The Social Impact of Constitutional Privilege

As noted, one effect of protecting speakers from defamation liability is to increase the production of information by decreasing its cost. We can be quite certain that this is beneficial: The market will naturally tend to underproduce information, because of the free-rider problem and, to a lesser extent, the monopolistic characteristics of many local markets. By "subsidizing" the media, constitutional privilege pushes the level of information production closer to what would prevail under conditions of perfect competition.[46]

The second major effect of certain of the protections is to decrease the accuracy of the information. Use of the actual malice standard or absolute privilege (but not negligence) will reduce the incentive to use care below that which would be used under strict liability. Similarly, restrictions on recoverable damages will result in lower accuracy. The reduction in accuracy that certain liability rules cause is clearly undesirable, and constitutes the major disadvantage of using constitutional privilege to subsidize the media.

One cost of excessive protection of the media is the loss of public faith in the credibility of the press. The real public benefit of defamation law comes from ensuring that certain standards of care are met. Increasing the accuracy of information benefits not just paying consumers (who presumably can bargain for whatever standards they wish) but free riders as well. Conversely, the major disadvantage of protecting the media against defamation suits is the risk of reducing the media's accuracy. This problem has not received the attention it deserves. Admittedly, the historical purpose of defamation law was to compensate the victim, not to protect the public from misleading information. But once we have decided that defamation law must be tailored to accommodate the public need for information, it seems inescapable that we must also be concerned with the effect defamation law has on accuracy. All of the benefits arising from an increase in the production of information are based on the accuracy of the information. Few people seriously believe that falsehoods contribute anything worthwhile to public debate.[47] On the contrary, falsehood is likely to result in the making of poor decisions by a misinformed public. By ensuring that reasonable care is used, defamation suits serve the public good:

> [A]n action for defamation at least partially ensures that only truthful information is disseminated. Since first amendment goals are not furthered by false information, restricting the flow of such information is permissible and beneficial. If undeterred, falsehood may inhibit debate and the democratic goals discussion is designed to serve. "Surely, if the 1950's taught us anything," wrote Justice Stewart, "they taught us that the poisonous atmosphere of the easy lie can infect and degrade a whole society." Liability for defamatory falsehoods encourages a publisher to investigate and ascertain the truth of potentially harmful statements before disseminating them.[48]

This analysis illustrates the fundamental problem with using constitutional privilege to correct failures in the market for information: constitutional privilege may replace the problem of under-production with that of suboptimal accuracy. Further expansions of this privilege that have been proposed—extension of the actual malice requirement for private figure plaintiffs, giving the media absolute privilege, and severe restrictions on damages—would exacerbate the problem of reduced accuracy.

This is not to say that these proposals would necessarily be counterproductive. The benefit from the higher level of information that would be produced under those proposals might well outweigh the harm caused by the decreased level of accuracy. Unfortunately, this tradeoff is difficult to evaluate.

II. MODIFICATIONS OF CONSTITUTIONAL PRIVILEGE

The preceding analysis suggests what defamation law should do. First, the law should foster the production of information by decreasing its cost. Second, the law should increase, or at least maintain, the media's incentive to be accurate. And third, the law should minimize the resources needed to enforce it. To some degree, these goals are inconsistent. The first and third goals could be achieved at the expense of the second by granting speakers absolute privilege, while the second goal would be furthered by returning to strict liability. It is hard to determine which of these goals should have priority in the absence of empirical data. It may well be, for example, that the level of care taken by the media is determined almost entirely by their sense of professionalism, and that their level of accuracy would not fall appreciably even if all defamation suits were barred. In such case, the social gain from increased information production would outweigh the minimal loss from decreased accuracy. On the other hand, it is possible that the degree of care used by the media is influenced greatly by the liability rules, in which case absolute privilege would result in a marked decline in standards. Theory alone cannot determine which of these is likely to be the case, and the data that could tell us do not exist.

A partial solution to this dilemma is to seek rules that increase the flow of information without significantly reducing its accuracy. Use of the negligence standard in place of strict liability is one example of such a rule, albeit of limited utility. Much more could be gained by rules that limited the financial impact of nonmeritorious suits without simultaneously restricting meritorious ones. Rules that disproportionately deter nonmeritorious claims are more likely to result in a net gain than are rules that deter both types of suits equally. Such rules would offer the possibility of significant improvements in the system of constitutional protections at minimal risk.

I now examine how well a number of liability rules, including those currently in force, advance the above goals. I place particular emphasis on each rule's comparative impact on meritorious and nonmeritorious claims. After reviewing a number of possible revisions of the law, I conclude that a set of rules based on fee shifting is most likely to increase the production of information without decreasing its accuracy.

Constitutional privilege gets mixed reviews. On the one hand, its major elements—the fault requirement and the limitation on damages in *Gertz* cases—do not protect the media from the threats that they face in the real world. Nor do they foster accuracy. The problem is that these rules were designed on the assumption that damage awards, rather than litigation costs, were the primary burden on defendants. Given the size of the awards in many libel cases, the concern about damages is not surprising.[49] Most of these awards are eventually reduced or eliminated, however, whereas the defendants must bear their litigation costs in any event. While the Supreme Court has acknowledged the chilling effect of litigation costs,[50] it had, until recently, made no effort to address this problem, and had even opposed the efforts of lower courts to make summary judgment more available to defendants.[51]

On the other hand, constitutional privilege is effective in shielding the media from much of the costs they would otherwise incur. The difficulty of prevailing under either the negligence or actual malice standards prevents most plaintiffs from recovering damages, and no doubt discourages many others from ever bringing action. Accordingly, the present rules do a good job in decreasing the cost of information. But to the extent that this is achieved by restricting the ability of legitimate claimants to receive compensation, the present rules also decrease the media's incentive to be accurate. In addition, the form of protection now offered is inefficient in that it requires substantial expenditures on litigation costs to operate.

One type of proposal to give the media greater protection involves extending the actual malice requirement to private-figure plaintiffs, or granting the media absolute privilege in some or all cases. Both proposals would encourage the flow of information by reducing or, in the case of absolute privilege, eliminating liability for defamation. But both proposals would seriously reduce the incentive of the media to use care. In addition, the continued use of unwarranted litigation as a means of achieving nonmonetary goals would still be possible under an actual malice standard. Those seeking to harass or punish the press would still be able to force defendants to pay the not-inconsequential cost of litigating at least through the summary judgment stage. And though many cases are dismissed at this stage under the actual malice standard, many others are not. Any harassment suit that puts the defendant to the expense of a full trial can be considered a success to the plaintiff regardless of outcome. Plaintiffs seeking to validate their claims of falsity would

also be able to do so under an actual malice standard. As noted in the
ILRP study, plaintiffs believe that they can partially vindicate themselves
simply by bringing suit. Increasing the fault requirement would not
remove this incentive, since victory on the merits is not essential to
those plaintiffs. In fact, the requirement that the plaintiff prove fault may
actually encourage this type of suit. Because most defense verdicts are
based on lack of fault, rather than truth of the publication, plaintiffs can
sue without "fear that their claim will ever be compromised by a finding
that what was said about them was true."[52] The extension of the actual
malice requirement would thus have much less impact on unwarranted
litigation than on legitimate suits. Only the use of absolute privilege
would end the use of unwarranted suits, and at a cost in accuracy that
may be unacceptable.

A second type of proposal is to limit recoverable damages. One
commonly suggested rule is to eliminate punitive damages.[53] Other
proposals go beyond that, and would limit damages to "provable injury
to reputation,"[54] actual pecuniary loss,[55] or to actual pecuniary loss plus
some fixed amount for compensatory damages.[56] These proposals are
aimed at reducing the wide latitude now enjoyed by judges and juries in
determining damages. Although the Supreme Court has attempted to
limit discretion by prohibiting awards of presumed damages where there
had been no showing of actual malice, this effort has not been successful.
The Court has taken a broad view of the "actual damages" that may be
awarded in *Gertz* cases.[57] Judges and juries may award damages for
humiliation and suffering, thus allowing the trier of fact to award damages
vastly in excess of any possible pecuniary injury suffered by the plaintiff.
Further, the limits on damages that do exist do not apply where actual
malice is shown.

Damage limitations might be useful if they deterred nonmeritorious
claims more than meritorious ones, but it is not clear that such would be
the case. Since the recovery of damages is not essential to those
bringing nonmeritorious suits, restrictions on damages might have no
significant effect on them. These rules might consequently deter a
disproportionate number of plaintiffs who are seeking only compensation
for injury. But other factors must also be considered. For example, it is
possible that the largest awards—those which would be disproportionately affected by damage limitations—are disproportionately made in
nonmeritorious cases. There is reason to believe that many excessive
awards are the result of jurors' antipathy toward the defendant and not
merely egregious error by the defendant. Like some plaintiffs, jurors
may be punishing defendants for taking unpopular positions rather than
publishing false information. Such antagonism would help explain why

defendants fare so much worse in front of juries than judges.[58] Curbing jury discretion to award damages could therefore disproportionately reduce the impact of harassment suits.

Another factor to consider is the effect of damage limitations on the ability of plaintiffs to bring small but legitimate claims. Most plaintiffs, who can rarely prove actual pecuniary loss,[59] might find it unprofitable to sue even when the evidence of fault and falsity was clear. Damage limitations might thus close out a great many plaintiffs with legitimate grievances. There are at least two ways of mitigating this risk. One is to award attorneys' fees to a successful plaintiff who has proved actual pecuniary loss. Another possibility is to allow plaintiffs to recover both their pecuniary loss and some fixed sum. In an interesting proposal by Steven Brill, plaintiffs would be entitled to recover for their pecuniary loss and an amount based on the advertising rates of the offending publication. A simpler alternative is to allow the recovery of pecuniary loss plus an amount picked by the trier of fact up to an arbitrary limit—$100,000, for example.

A third approach to protecting the press from unwarranted suits is to award attorney's fees to the prevailing party.[60] Fee shifting has a number of complex effects that are not easy to predict with certainty. Fortunately, a large body of good literature on this has appeared in recent years.[61] While these articles do not all reach the same conclusion, most conclude that fee shifting will have the following effects. First, assuming the plaintiff is risk neutral, fee shifting will increase the probability the plaintiff will bring suit if the suit's likelihood of success is above some critical percentage.[62] Second, also assuming the plaintiff is risk neutral, fee shifting will decrease the probability the plaintiff will bring suit if the suit's likelihood of success is below some critical percentage. And third, fee shifting increases the risk involved in bringing suit.[63]

The first effect will be desirable whenever the rate of litigation under the American system, where each party bears its own costs, is below the socially appropriate level. Unfortunately, we cannot determine what this level is without knowing the extent to which meritorious libel suits deter the publication of falsehood. If they have no deterrent effect, for example, then the socially appropriate level of litigation would be zero. In other words, it is possible that absolute privilege is the best alternative. But if we have decided that a cause of action for defamation is warranted on the basis of its beneficial deterrent effect, then it also follows that we should encourage the bringing of meritorious claims. This goal would be furthered by use of fee shifting.

The second effect will be desirable whenever the rate of litigation under the American system is above the socially appropriate level. We are on much firmer ground in believing that this would be beneficial. By hypothesis, nonmeritorious claims do not increase the incentive to use care, but instead chill the production of valuable speech. Discouraging these suits should result in a unambiguous social gain.

The third effect, that of increasing the risk associated with bringing suit, complicates the above analysis. Assuming that plaintiffs are risk averse, additional risk would tend to discourage suits, even for meritorious claims. Risk aversion should be strongest when the claim is small relative to the likely attorneys' fees. The effect of risk aversion counters the tendency of fee shifting to encourage meritorious claims, and might outweigh it.[64] The relative lack of enthusiasm that commentators have shown for fee shifting stems in part from fear that this risk would discourage too many legitimate claimants.[65] This concern should not be lightly dismissed, since the increase in risk could restrict access to the courts by legitimate claimants as effectively as use of protective fault standards.

Increasing the level of risk involved in bringing meritorious claims is a serious disadvantage of using fee shifting, one for which there is no simple solution. One proposal is to exempt from the payment of fees unsuccessful plaintiffs who have suffered special damages.[66] The utility of this is limited, however, by the low percentage of plaintiffs who can prove special damages. Most plaintiffs, particularly those of moderate means, would probably find the risk involved in bringing suit to be excessive, at least if their claims were not clearly meritorious.[67]

What is needed is a method of recovery for those who have been legitimately defamed, but whose claims do not justify the risk of paying the defendant's attorneys' fees. I suggest that the following set of rules provides an acceptable compromise between the competing goals of freeing the media from nonmeritorious litigation and allowing a means of recovery for defamation victims.

First, plaintiffs proving falsity but not fault on the part of the defendant would be entitled to recover their actual pecuniary losses, if any, plus reasonable attorneys' fees. For most plaintiffs, this would operate as a means for obtaining declaratory judgment. Plaintiffs who currently sue to set the record straight would be given an opportunity to do so. At the same time, since every defamation trial would result in a finding of truth or falsity, those bringing actions in cases in which the publication was accurate would suffer the added penalty of a judicial pronouncement on the invalidity of their claims.

Allowing a plaintiff who proves falsity to recover reasonable attorneys' fees goes far in reducing the risk involved in pursuing small but meritorious claims. Where only falsity is at issue, the litigation costs should be much lower than is now typical. In addition, since the plaintiffs should know whether the publication were true, they should be able to evaluate the risk of having to pay the other side's attorneys' fees well in advance of any discovery or litigation. Cases in which plaintiffs do not feel confident that falsity can be proved should not be brought.

Requiring defendants to pay reasonable attorneys' fees in these cases should not pose an unacceptable threat to the media. Where evidence of falsity is clear, defendants could and probably would concede the case at an early stage, thus granting the defendant the admission of error, which many plaintiffs seem to be seeking, and limiting damages to a negligible amount. Of course, many members of the media might simply decide to take the laudable step of attempting to satisfy aggrieved victims without litigation by a more judicious handling of complaints.

Second, a plaintiff who proves both falsity and fault amounting to at least negligence would be entitled to recover both reasonable attorneys' fees plus actual damages, as currently defined. This proposal would eliminate punitive damages and presumed damages, but would not eliminate a jury's discretion to award for humiliation, loss of reputation, etc. This would apply to both public and private figures, who would henceforth be subject to the same rules. This proposal does not go further in the restriction of recoverable damages for two reasons. First, it does not appear to be necessary. As noted, few large awards are sustained on appeal. Most of the costs of defamation suits go toward the defense, a problem addressed by the use of fee shifting. Second, there is the risk that restrictions on damage awards would deter legitimate claimants more than nonmeritorious ones. However, both of these propositions are subject to empirical verification. If it appears that damage awards pose an unacceptable threat to the media, then proposals to limit damages to fixed sums should be explored.

The requirement that the plaintiff prove negligence is based on the analysis in part I. A negligence rule provides the media with greater protection than strict liability, yet does not decrease their incentive to use care. The proposal requires proof of negligence rather than actual malice, in order to eliminate the possibility of reduced accuracy.

Third, a plaintiff who does not prove defamatory falsehood would be liable for the other side's reasonable attorneys' fees. This proposal should greatly reduce the burden on the media by deterring the bringing of claims in cases in which the publication was accurate. Those seeking to harass the press would be deterred both by the prospect of having to pay the defendant's attorneys' fees and by the knowledge that they would not be able to inflict punitive litigation costs on the defendant. This rule would protect the media from suits involving accurate publications which, according to the evidence in part I, constitute a significant proportion of all suits now brought.

CONCLUSION

The law of constitutional privilege provides insufficient protection to the media, to defamed persons, and to the public. The media continue to be threatened by the use of harassment suits, which may constitute more than half of the total number of defamation suits brought. Requiring the loser to pay the winner's reasonable attorneys' fees provides an attractive alternative to the present system. The loser-pays rule would eliminate the incentive to bring harassment suits, and would protect the media from the largest element of expenses associated with defamation suits. At the same time, this rule need not pose an insurmountable barrier in the path of those with legitimate claims. If this rule were coupled with appropriate fault standards and damage rules, the media would retain their incentive to be accurate, and defamed individuals would still have a chance to be compensated.

NOTES

1. 376 U.S. 254 (1964).

2. *See* Anderson, "Libel and Press Self-Censorship," 53 *Tex. L. Rev.* 422, 434 (1975): "Reporters and editors share a professional ethic that encourages them to seek to inform the public, even at the risk of libel litigation. This may even be institutionalized, so that it represents the prevailing ethic of a broadcasting organization; 'all the news that's fit to print' presumably includes some news that creates a danger of legal action. Although impossible to measure, this professional pressure to publish is probably the strongest force against self-censorship."

3. *See* e.g., Smith, "The Rising Tide of Libel Litigation: Implications of the Gertz Negligence Rules, 44 *Mont. L. Rev.* 71, 87 & n. 98 (1983) citing statement from counsel for the *Washington Post* that libel litigation has not changed its editorial practices.

4. For discussion of some of this evidence, see Franklin, "Good Names and Bad Law: A Critique of Libel Law and a Proposal," 18 *U.S.F.L. Rev.*, 1, 14–18 (1983) [hereinafter *A Critique*].

5. *See id.* at 14–15; *see also* Anderson *supra* note 2 at 433.

6. *See* Soloski, "The Study and the Libel Plaintiff: Who Sues for Libel?" 71 *Iowa L. Rev.* 217, 219 (1965) (finding that two-thirds of all media cases were brought against newspapers).

7. A 1972 study found that only 42 cities had competing daily newspapers. "Media and the First Amendment in a Free Society," 60 *Geo L. J.* 867, 892 (1972). A study done in 1976 found that this number had decreased to 39, out of 1550 cities studied. Sobel &

Emergy, "U.S. Dailies' Competition in Relation to Circulation Size: A Newspaper Data Update," 55 *Journ. Q.* 145, 146 (1978).

8. *See* Franklin, *A Critique, supra* note 2 at 15.

9. *See* Anderson, *supra* note 2 at 433.

10. This can be derived from the fact that, under conditions of perfect competition, firms set their output levels such that the marginal cost of producing an additional unit will exceed the social cost, as measured by its price, or the resources needed to produce it.

11. E. Kitch & H. Perlman, *Legal Regulation of the Competitive Process* 25, 28 (1972).

12. This differs from ordinary free riding in that nonpaying beneficiaries in these cases do not receive the goods themselves; rather, they receive secondary benefits created by use of the goods by paying consumers.

13. The analysis of libel law's effect on accuracy is complicated by the dual economic rule that accuracy plays in the production of information. Not only does the level of care used change the expected liability of a producer to third parties, it also changes the desirability of the product to its customers. Greater accuracy should increase demand for the product and, all other things being equal, profits. This should induce the media to use more care than they would if the only benefit from care were decreased liability. This is accounted for in line C' by netting out the incremental profits brought by higher accuracy from the cost of error-preventive measures.

14. United States v. Carroll Towing Co., 159 F.2d 169 (2d Cir. 1947).

15. The Hand formula imposes liability when the sum of accident costs and prevention costs could be reduced by using more care. A producer operating under this formula would spend no more on care than is required to avoid this liability. The degree of care that is just sufficient to enable the producer to escape liability under this negligence formula minimizes the total costs of care and accidents. This is the point that a firm under strict liability would choose.

16. The decline in the use of care would be limited by consumer demand for accuracy. The incentive to meet this demand is reflected in line C' in Fig. 10.2. The additional sales that can be obtained from improvements in accuracy would induce the media to use some care even if they were protected by absolute privilege.

17. J. Milton, Areopagitica (E. Rhys ed. 1946).

18. J. S. Mill, On Liberty (Harvard Classics 1921).

19. *See* R. Posner, *Economic Analysis of The Law* § 28.1, at 543–45 (2d ed. 1977); R. Posner, *The Economics of Justice*, 264–66, 287–99, 337–38 (1981).

20. Ingbar, "Defamation: A Conflict Between Reason and Decency," 65 *Va. L. Rev.* 785, 794 n.37 (1979).

21. Meikeljohn, "The First Amendment Is an Absolute," in *Free Speech and Association* 14 (P. Kurland ed. 1975).

22. J. S. Mill, *supra* note 18.

23. The "socially appropriate" level is a function of the social benefit derived from litigation—the deterrence of harmful behavior—and the social cost of litigation—attorneys, fees, court costs, etc. *See* Shavell, "The Social Versus the Private Incentive To Bring Suit in a Costly Legal System," 11 *J. Legal Stud.* 333, 334 (1982).

24. Worrall, "Negotiating the Libel Policy: Examination in Detail of One Policy," in *Media Insurance* 365, 373 (J. Lankenau, ed 1983); R. Smolla, *Suing the Press* 75 (1986). More recently, Worrall has estimated that up to 90 percent of the money spent by insurance companies on libel insurance policies goes to legal fees. *See* Baer, "Insurers to Libel Defense Counsel: 'The Party's Over.' " *The Am. Lawyer* 69, 70 (1985).

25. *See* O'Connell, "An Alternative to Abandoning Tort Liability: Elective No-Fault Insurance for Many Kinds of Injuries, 60 *Minn. L. Rev.* 501, 508 (1976) (estimating 72%

of expenditures going to litigation costs and overhead in medical malpractice cases and 62.5% going to litigation costs and overhead in product liability cases).

26. B. Sandford, *Libel and Privacy: The Prevention and Defense of Litigation* 8 (1985) (citing estimates that the cost of the Westmoreland suit against CBS was in excess of $6 million and that Time, Inc. reportedly spent more than $4 million defending itself against General Sharon's suit). ABC reportedly spent $7 million defending itself against a suit brought by Synanon, and CBS was said to have spent between $3 and $4 million defending itself in Herbert v. Lando. R. Smolla, *supra* note 24 at 75.

27. The "minimum cost in responding to a complaint is $2,500 and in defending a suit in court, $15,000–$20,000." Larry Worrall, quoted in *Broadcasting,* Nov. 17, 1980, at 63. *See also* Worrall, quoted in L. Kramer & C. Wright, "Up Against the Wall," *Wash. Journalism Rev.,* Sept–Oct. 1978, at 49, 51 ("even if the paper can show that there was no malice in a suit involving a public figure, it can hardly get the case thrown out on a summary judgment for under $5,000"). Defense costs escalate rapidly if the case is not dismissed on summary judgment. According to Congressman Charles Schumer of New York, an average libel suit now costs $150,000 to try. Baer, *supra* note 24 at 69. Much of these costs are attributable to the fact-intensive nature of a defense based on constitutional privilege, requiring extensive discovery. "Protracted discovery on both sides of the litigation and greater defense emphasis on trial preparation [have] tended to drive the costs of defending a case through trial to over $250,000 for relatively uncomplicated cases, over $400,000 for more factually complex cases.'" B. Sanford *supra* note 26 at 8 n.19.

28. Plaintiffs in defamation actions lost 75% of their cases at the trial level as well as losing 75% of their appeals. Franklin, "Suing the Media for Libel: A Litigation Study," 1981 *Am. B. Found. Research J.* 797, 802 [hereinafter cited as *A Litigation Study*]. The Iowa Libel Research Project (ILRP Study) similarly found that "plaintiffs win only ten percent of the cases pressed to judicial resolution, while the media win ninety percent." Soloski, *supra* note 6 at 218. This compares with an average loss rate of only 50% in most other tort actions. Priest & Klein, "The Selection of Disputes for Litigation," 13 *J. Legal Stud.* 1 (1983).

29. Nonmeritorious suits will not include greater accuracy unless by using greater accuracy the media were able to dismiss more of such suits on motions for summary judgment, thus avoiding a portion of the litigation costs they would otherwise face. This is unlikely. Actions taken prior to publication, when they can improve the story's accuracy, are unlikely to produce the convincing evidence of truthfulness that a motion for summary judgment requires. Indeed, truth is rarely the basis for a successful defense even at trial. *See* Franklin *A Litigation Study supra* note 28 at 820. The media are similarly unlikely to be able to obtain summary judgment on the issue of due care, regardless of the amount of care they take. The courts view due care as a question of fact to be decided at trial. (*See infra* note 50.)

30. In the Franklin study, only 4 of the 126 defense verdicts were based on proven truth or lack of proven falsity of the story. Franklin *A Litigation Study supra* note 28 at 820–26. This was corroborated by the Iowa Libel Research Project study, which found that "[t]he actual truth or falsity of that which was published is rarely addressed." Bezanson, "Libel Law and the Realities of Litigation: Setting the Record Straight," 71 *Iowa L. Rev.* 266, 230 (1985).

31. *See* Larry Worrall, head of the Media/Professional Ins. Co. quoted in Franklin, *A Critique, supra* note 5, at 6 n.27 (characterizing 50 percent of libel actions as nuisance suits); Eberhard, "There's Got To Be A Better Way: Alternatives To The High Cost of Libel," 38 *Mercer L. Rev.* 819, 820 (1987) (citing results of a survey of newspaper editors

indicating that one-third of the cost of defending libel suits was spent defending nuisance suits). These figures, coming as they do from the targets of libel suits, are hardly unbiased. Nonetheless, the exceptionally low success rates of plaintiffs in defamation actions clearly demonstrates that many persons are bringing suits that they must know have little chance of success.

32. This was one of the major findings of the ILRP study on why libel plaintiffs bring suit. This study found that money is rarely a motive. Instead, plaintiffs bring suit "to correct the record and to get even." Interestingly, plaintiffs claimed that a favorable decision was not necessary for them to consider the suit a success: "Instead, plaintiffs see the act of initiating suit, independent of its result, as an effective and public form of reply or response. By invoking the formal judicial system, the plaintiffs legitimate their claim of falsity. Reputational repair follows without the assistance of—indeed in spite of—the judicial system." Bezanson, *supra* note 30 at 228.

33. One group that has been accused of using harassment suits is the Church of Scientology. In a famous internal memo, L. Ron Hubbard, the founder of the Church, wrote: "[W]e do not want Scientology to be reported in the press, anywhere else than on the religious page of newspapers. It is destructive word of mouth to permit the public presses to express their biased and badly reported sensationalism. Therefore, we should be very alert to sue for slander at the slightest chance so as to discourage the public presses from mentioning scientology." Shaffer, "Church of Scientology Attacks Investigator and Critics," *Wash. Post,* August 16, 1978 at A14.

In another part of the memo Hubbard wrote: "The purpose of a suit is to harass and discourage rather than to win." In the course of one defamation suit that the Church of Scientology had brought, the judge noted that the Church was "litigious" and that a Lexis search showed that it had been a party to over 30 other reported cases (not all necessarily involving defamation). Church of Scientology v. Siegelman 475 F. Supp. 960 (S.B.N. 1979). Another organization that has been accused of similar tactics is Synanon, which as of 1982 had brought defamation suits seeking a total of $400 million in damages. See *N.Y. Times,* June 4, 1982, at A21. In addition, between 1978 and 1979, Synanon sent 960 form letters to various members of the media demanding corrections and retractions. See LDRC Bulletin, No. 3 at 27 (1982). Other organizations that may be making extensive use of defamation litigation include police associations, Franklin, *A Litigation Study,* supra note 29 at 807, LDRC Bulletin No. 7 at 66, 67 (1983).

34. "A fair estimate would place the total of million-dollar defamation awards at somewhere between 25 and 30 in an over-20-year period. However, most of these awards have been imposed in the past three years, with half or more of these coming within the past year." LDRC Bulletin No. 9 at 27 (1984).

35. Three studies attest to the relative unprofitability of libel suits. The study by Franklin, which included 291 cases spanning a period of four years, showed that only 37 cases went to trial of which 23 resulted in awards for plaintiffs. Thirteen of those awards were reversed upon appeal, and five of the remaining awards were reduced. Franklin, *A Litigation Study, supra* note 28 at 804–5 & n.21. These data were collated in a study conducted by the Libel Defense Resource Center, which found that of 47 trials in which damages were awarded, only seven were affirmed on appeal, 18 others were set aside entirely and one was reduced. Two others were settled and 19 others were still on appeal at the conclusion of the study. LDRC Bulletin No. 4 (Part 1) at 7 (1982). And, as previously noted, the ILRP Study found that damage awards were sustained in only 10 percent of defamation suits.

36. Bezanson, *The Libel Suit in Retrospect: What Plaintiffs Want And What Plaintiffs Get,* 74 Cal. L. Rev. 789, 791 n.4. [hereinafter *The Libel Suit in Retrospect*].

37. Barrett, *Declaratory Judgments For Libel: A Better Alternative*, 74 *Cal. L. Rev.* 847, 859 (1986). On the other hand, the ILRP Study found that the cost to plaintiffs of bringing the defamation suits was quite low. Eighty percent of the plaintiffs in that study had engaged their lawyers on a contingency fee basis, as had virtually all of the public figure plaintiffs. The ILRP Study concluded that low cost was a major incentive for plaintiffs to bring suit. Bezanson, *Setting the Record Straight, supra* note 30, at 228.

38. *See* R. Smolla, *supra* note 24 at 75.

39. For instance, of the $7 to $9 million spent on the *Westmoreland* case, approximately $3.25 million was spent by the plaintiff's side. *N.Y. Times,* Feb. 18, 1985, at A1. Similarly, the plaintiff in Tavoulareas v. Washington Post testified that he had spent $1.8 million on lawyer's fees in the case. Lewis, "New York Times v. Sullivan Reconsidered," 83 *Colum. L. Rev.* 603, 613 (1983). Legal fees in Rancho La Costa v. Penthouse Int'l reportedly reached $4 million for each side. R. Smolla, *supra* note 32 at 175.

40. Soloksi, *supra* note 17 at 220.

41. Bezanson, *supra* note 30 at 228.

42. D. Trubek, J. Grossman, W. Felstiner, H. Kritzer & A. Sarat, 1 Civil Litigation Research Project Final Report S23 (1983). *See also* Bezanson, *The Libel Suit in Retrospect, supra* note 36, at 790 n.3: "Information from a variety of sources, including the case history of over 1300 insurance claims, suggest that the overall incidence of settlement activity in libel cases is much lower than for civil litigation in general. Perhaps 25% of libel claims involve some source of negotiated resolution, although only a small proportion— perhaps—10%—involve financial settlement."

43. *See* Priest & Klein, *supra* note 28, at 2 & n.1, n.2: "It is well known, however, that only a very small fraction of disputes come to trial and an even smaller fraction is appealed."

44. *See, e.g.,* LDRC Bulletin No. 4 (Part 1) at 7 (1982) (finding that out of 47 cases in which damages were awarded, defendants appealed 46); Bezanson, *Setting The Record Straight, supra* note 30, at 231.

45. This model of the process by which disputes are selected for litigation is explained and elaborated on in Priest & Klein, *supra* note 28.

46. Indeed, it is difficult to justify constitutional privilege except as an attempt to correct market failure. Where the market is working properly, we generally rely on it to determine how scarce resources should be allocated. For this process to work, consumers must pay a price for goods that reflects their true social cost. Shielding producers from a portion of their costs distorts this process and could lead to suboptimal resource allocations. The gain to consumers from the additional production of information would be more than offset by the loss of the resources required to produce it.

The common assertion that constitutional privilege is justified because free speech is "more important," or "socially desirable" than ordinary (e.g., tangible) goods is unpersuasive. If consumers agree that free speech is valuable, they are free to obtain whatever quantity of information they desire as long as they are willing to pay the costs. Strict liability for defamation does not, after all, prohibit any speech from taking place. It only makes it more expensive. The media will produce whatever quantity of information that consumers are willing to pay for. Intervention is justified only because consumers are unable to transmit their true demand through market channels.

47. The main exception are the adherents to the marketplace of ideas metaphor, who maintain that even falsehood is a valuable contribution to public debate. Mill, for example, believed that falsehood resulted in the "clearer perception and livelier impression of truth, produced by its collision with error." As noted in part I, however, the market place model

is unsatisfactory. Falsehood is far more likely to detract from public debate and lead to mistakes by the people who rely on such information.

48. Hunsaker, "Adequate Breathing Space in a Poisonous Atmosphere: Balancing Freedom and Responsibility in the Open Society." *Duquesne L. Rev.* 9, 15–16 (1977–78).

49. These awards, if sustained, would pose an enormous threat to the media. For example, Mr. Sullivan was awarded $500,000 in his suit against the *New York Times*. Four other suits had been filed against the *Times* based on the same advertisement. In one, a $500,000 verdict had been entered against the *Times*, and in the others, a total of $2 million in damages was sought. Awards of this magnitude constituted a significant threat to the continued existence of the *Times* and bankruptcy remains a possibility for other media defendants hit with large verdicts. The *Times*, *See* e.g., Guccione V. Hustler Magazine, Inc. *7 Media L. Rptr.* 2077 (Ohio Ct. App. 1981) ($40,300,000 awarded at trial; case reversed and remanded); Pring v. Penthouse International, Ltd., *7 Media L. Rptr* 1101 (D.Wyo. 1981) 695 F.2d 438 (10th Cir. 1982) *cert. denied,* 462 U.S. 1132 (1983). In one case involving a $9.2 Million award, the defendant, Alton Telegraph, was forced to declare bankruptcy. Kupferberg, "Libel Fever," 20 *Colum. Journalism Rev.* No. 3 at 36 (1981).

50. *See* New York Times v. Sullivan, 376 U., 254, 279 (without the protections of the fault requirement, "would be critics of official conduct may be deterred from voicing their criticism, even though it is believed to be true. . . . because of doubt whether it can be proved in court of fear of the expense of having to do so.") *See also* Washington Post v. Keogh, 365 F.2d 965, 968 (D.C. Cir. 1966), *cert. denied,* 385 U.S. 1011 (1967) ("[t]he threat of being put to the defense of a lawsuit brought by a popular public official may be as chilling to the exercise of First Amendment freedoms as fear of the outcome of the lawsuit itself").

51. Some lower courts had taken the position that, because of the First Amendment interests involved in libel suits, defendants should be according greater access to summary judgment. *See,* e.g., Southard v. Forbes, Inc., 588 F.2d 140, 145 (5th Cir.) *cert. denied,* 444 U.S. 832 (1979); Vandenburg v. Newsweek, Inc. 441 F.2d 378, 379 (5th Cir.), *cert. denied,* 404 U.S. 864 (1971); Karp v. Miami Herald Pub. Co., 359 So.2d 580, 581 (1978) ("summary judgment is especially appropriate in libel cases where the facts are not essentially in dispute because of the chilling effect of libel suits upon First Amendment freedoms"). *But see* Greenberg v. CBS, 419 N.Y.S.2d 988, 9912 (N.Y. App. Div. 1979) ("solicitude for first amendment freedoms was not intended to abrogate the fundamental rules governing the administration of summary judgment").

The Supreme Court indicated its disfavor of expansive use of summary judgment in Hutchinson v. Proxmire, 443 U.S. 111 (1978). The trial court in this case, after reviewing the case law on actual malice, concluded that summary judgment "may well be the rule rather than the exception." Hutchinson v. Proxmire, 431 F. Supp. 1311, 1330 (W.D. Wis. 1977). The Supreme Court criticized this practice, stating that "[t]he proof of 'actual malice' calls a defendant's state of mind into question and does not readily lend itself to summary disposition." 443 U.S. 111, at 120 n.9. *Hutchinson* seems to have had little effect, though, on the success rate of summary judgment petitions, which has remained around 75%. LDRC Bulletin No. 4. (Part 2) at 2 (1982).

The Court has recently retreated somewhat from its position in *Hutchinson.* In Anderson v. Liberty Lobby, 106 S.Ct. 2505 (1986), the court held that cases brought by public figures must be dismissed before trial unless the plaintiff can produce clear and convincing evidence on the issue of actual malice.

52. Bezanson, *supra* note 30 at 231. Bezanson goes on to note that "the fault requirement also leaves invitingly open the possibility of winning even when the publication was

true or not probably false. In these respects, the constitutional privileges not only fail to deter or discourage unwarranted suits, they may encourage them." *Id.* at 232. One wonders how many of the plaintiffs in the ILRP study who claimed to have sued to set the record straight were truly interested in a judicial pronouncement on the accuracy of the publication.

53. *See* Franklin, *A Litigation Study supra* note 29 at 39 n. 172.

54. *See also* Anderson. "Reputation, Compensation, and Proof," 25 *Wm. & Mary L. rev.* 747 (1984). Anderson would limit recovery to the amount of "actual injury" suffered by the plaintiff. This would include nonpecuniary reputational losses, but not mental anguish.

55. *See* Ashdown, Gertz & Firestone, "A Study in Constitutional Policy-Making," 61 *Minn. L. Rev.* 645, 670 (1977). Ingber, *supra* note 20 at 852–56. In Ingber's proposal, pecuniary damages would be recoverable without the need to prove fault. A plaintiff proving scienter would also be entitled to recover actual, nonpecuniary damages.

56. Brill, "Redoing Libel Law," *The American Lawyer*, at 1, 14 (Sept. 1984). In Brill's proposal, a successful plaintiff would be entitled to actual pecuniary loss plus a limit of three times the cost of a full-page ad in the defendant's newspaper or magazine, or two minutes of advertising on the show the offending story was broadcast on.

57. *See* Time, Inc. v. Firestone, 424 U.S. 448 (1976). As a result of the expansive interpretation of the "actual damage" limitation, it is nearly impossible to demonstrate that an award should be reduced because of inadequate evidence to support it. *See* Franklin, "Winners and Losers and Why: A Study of Defamation Litigation," 1980 *Am. B. Found. Res. J.* 455, 493 n.83 (finding only one case, out of 3.5 years of litigation studied, in which the award was held to be insufficiently supported by the evidence).

58. The Franklin study found that juries are significantly more likely than judges to find for the plaintiff. *See* Franklin, *A Litigation Study, supra* note 28 at 804 & n.20. Moreover, more than half of the jury verdicts for the plaintiff were reversed on appeal, suggesting that jurors are either misunderstanding or ignoring their instructions. *Id.* at 806. The tremendous size of some jury verdicts itself raises the possibility that jurors' animosity toward the defendant, rather than error by the defendant, may be to blame. Guccione v. Hustler Magazine, Inc. seems to be an example of this.

59. A number of commentators have proposed the use of some form of fee shifting in defamation cases. *See*, e.g., Brill, *supra* note 56.

Franklin, *A Critique supra* note 5; Hulme, "Vindicating Reputation: An Alternative to Damages as a Remedy for Defamation," 30 *Am. U.L. Rev.* 375 (1981); Ingber, *supra* note 12. In Brill's proposal, the loser would pay the winner's reasonable legal costs in all cases. Franklin would require free shifting in all cases except those in which the plaintiff suffered special damages and had a reasonable chance for success. Hulme would make the award discretionary with the judge. Ingber would authorize awards of attorneys' fees to the plaintiff only, and only if the plaintiff proved negligence or scienter.

61. An extensive list of articles on fee shifting is given in Christie, "Attorney Fee Shifting: A Bibliography," 47 *Law & Contemp. Probs.* 347 (1984).

62. A Theoretical analysis of the effect of awarding attorneys' fees to the prevailing party can be found in Shavell, "Suit, Settlement and Trial: A Theoretical Analysis Under Alternative Methods for the Allocation of Legal Costs," *11 J. Legal Stud.* 55, 62 (1982).

63. Shavell's analysis supports the conclusion that, under most circumstances, nuisance suits will be less likely under the British system, while meritorious suits will be more likely. The reason is that, "when the plaintiff is relatively optimistic about prevailing, his expected legal costs will be relatively low under the British system—he will be thinking about the possibility of not having to pay any such costs—whereas under the American

system he must bear his own costs with certainty. Thus, he will be likely to find suit a more attractive prospect under the British system. But when the plaintiff is not optimistic, converse reason explains why he would be expected to sue more often under the American system." *Id.* at 59–60. *But see* Braeutigan, Owne, &, Panzar, "An Economic Analysis of Alternative Fee Shifting Systems," 47 *Law and Contemp Probs.* 139, 153 (1984).

64. It is quite difficult to determine this without empirical research. Rowe, *id.* at 149.

65. *See,* e.g., Anderson *supra* note 2 at 437 n.76: "Another method of attacking the problem of defense costs in libel suits might be to require unsuccessful plaintiffs to pay defendant's attorney's fees. This is not an attractive solution because it could impose a severe—possibly disastrous—penalty on the plaintiff who miscalculates the merit of his claim. If the law is to retain a remedy for defamation, it should not put a plaintiff to such great peril for seeking to avail himself of that remedy."

66. *See* Franklin, *A Critique supra* note 5.

67. Rowe, *supra* note 64 at 153.

INDEX